$1695

D1239796

Social Effects of Computer Use and Misuse

What is man that a machine is not?

The computing metaphor is as yet available to only an extremely small set of people. Its acquisition and internalization, hopefully as only one of many ways to see the world, seems to require experience in program composition, a kind of computing literacy. Perhaps such literacy will become very widespread in the advanced societal sectors of the advanced countries. But, should it become a dominant mode of thinking and be restricted to certain social classes, it will prove not merely repressive in the ordinary sense, but an enormously divisive societal force. For then classes which do and do not have access to the metaphor will, in an important sense, lose their ability to communicate with one another.

Joseph Weizenbaum
On the Impact of the Computer on Society

Social Effects of Computer Use and Misuse

J. MACK ADAMS
DOUGLAS H. HADEN

Department of Computer Science
New Mexico State University

JOHN WILEY & SONS

New York • Santa Barbara • London • Sydney • Toronto

Copyright © 1976, by John Wiley & Sons, Inc.

All rights reserved. Published simultaneously in Canada.

No part of this book may be reproduced by any means, nor transmitted, nor translated into a machine language without the written permission of the publisher.

Library of Congress Cataloging in Publication Data:

Adams, J Mack, 1933-
    Social effects of computer use and misuse.

    Published in 1973 under title: Computers: appreciation, applications, implications.
    Includes bibliographies and index.
    1.   Electronic digital computers.   2.   Computers and civilization. I. Haden, Douglas H, 1942-   joint author. II. Title.
QA76.5.A334   1976   001.6   76-10698
ISBN 0-471-00463-4

Printed in the United States of America

10 9 8 7 6 5 4 3

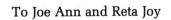

To Joe Ann and Reta Joy

Preface

This book is both an abridgment and an extension of our previous book entitled *Computers: Appreciation, Applications, Implications—An Introduction*. Here, as in that book, we want to cultivate in the reader an appreciation of computers, their uses, and their limitations and, in this way, to help reduce the divisive communication gap between the technological and humanistic aspects of our society. But where the previous text was shaded toward the technical reader at a fairly elementary level, this text is directed toward nontechnical readers at a somewhat higher level. There are no technical details on programming computers, but the sections on social, economic, and philosophical implications and the readings in the Appendix have more depth than the previous text. We still believe that a general understanding of how computers work is necessary to adequately appreciate the implications of their usage, but we realize that many people have neither the time nor interest to study programming and others already have the necessary background. As a result, we have limited our technical discussion to a short introductory chapter and a chapter on the fundamental concept of algorithm and its distinguishing characteristics. However, we hope that the nontechnical person may be motivated to learn more about computer programming after reading this book in order to grasp more firmly the capabilities and limitations of computers.

Each chapter is followed by an annotated bibliography that serves as a guide to further study. In addition, footnotes in the latter chapters contain valuable references and indicate our substantial dependence on other works. In this regard, we especially recognize the influence of *The Computerized Society* by J. Martin and A. R. D. Norman, *The Automated State* by R. McBride, *Privacy and Freedom* and "Civil Liberties and Computerized Data Systems" by A. F. Westin, *An Introduction to Computer Science and Algorithmic Processes* by T. M. Walker and W. W. Cotterman, and *Cybernation: The Silent Conquest* by D. M. Michael. We also recognize the influence of two of the finest papers ever written in the field of computer science: "Computing Machinery and Intelligence" by Alan Turing and "On the Impact of the Computer on Society" by Joseph Weizenbaum. We are extremely pleased to have been able to include these in the readings in the Appendix.

Many business concerns devoted time to correspond with us. We are indebted to them for their comments and suggestions. We especially thank the following companies whose photographs were used as illustrations in the text:

Applied Dynamics, Applied Information Industries, BASF Systems, Beehive Medical Electronics, Inc., Bell Laboratories, Burroughs Corporation, Cal-Comp, Chancellor Industries, Comware, Continental Bank, Hughes Aircraft Co., International Business Machines, National Aeronautics and Space Administration, NCR Corporation, Philips-Electrologica, Quotron Systems, Sperry Rand Corporation (*Sperry Technology*), Univac Division of Sperry Rand Corporation, University of Southern California School of Medicine, U. S. Army, Varian Data Machines, and Volkswagen of America, Inc.

The sources of the readings in the Appendix are credited in the various articles. We greatly appreciate the permission of both the original publishers and the authors to include these. We feel that such readings are essential in adequately presenting material in the social implications area.

Finally, special thanks to Mary Fleming, who did much of the library research for Chapter 7, handled the early correspondence effort, and typed the first drafts, and to our students, who provided the discussion environment in which we formed our thoughts about the social implications of computers and for whom this book is written. Of course, any errors or omissions are ours.

Las Cruces, New Mexico
1976

J. MACK ADAMS

DOUGLAS H. HADEN

Contents

1. Computers: What are they?

What is this machine we call a computer? What are the characteristics of this machine that make it so extremely valuable to mankind, while at the same time its use creates so many unique and difficult social and economic problems? These are the questions that are our main concern. Unfortunately, we cannot leap immediately to the more significant social and economic considerations without first learning something about how a computer works and how a person commands it to perform desired tasks.

A computer seems to be different in kind from most other machines. For the most part it does not move itself or other objects. Indeed, computers are not primarily concerned with physical objects, but with information. Where a bulldozer manipulates dirt and rocks, a computer manipulates symbols that represent information such as number, name, and so on. As a result, our initial, very general, view of a computer will be as a **symbol manipulation device (SMD).**

An SMD takes symbols in, manipulates them in a quite specific manner, and sends the manipulated symbols back out:

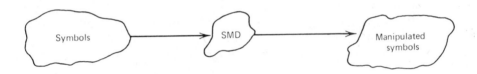

Since the SMD can do esseitially anything to the input symbols, we must tell it what we want done each time we use it. Thus, a better picture of the SMD is the following:

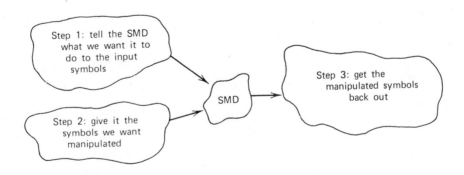

Now, this view of a computer is a little too broad, since it encompasses many real-life situations involving humans rather than machines. The SMD could be a translator at the United Nations:

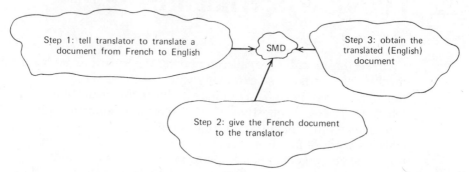

Let's make some observations. (a) If the SMD already knew the requested task (e.g., how to translate from French to English), step 1 could be quite simple, but if the SMD did not know how to do the task, step 1 could be quite complex. (b) The SMD we have considered requires considerable preparation to perform the specified task.

With these observations and the SMD model in mind, let's take a look at the particular SMD we wish to consider here. In this book we are concerned with SMD machines that we call **computers.** We will call step 1, telling the SMD (or computer) what we want done this time, **programming** the SMD (or programming the computer). In fact, we call the instructions we give the computer a **program.** The input symbols of step 2 are called many different things. Some of these are just simply **input, input information, input data,** and **raw data.** We call the manipulated symbols of step 3 several different names too: **results, output, output information, processed data,** and so on. For example,

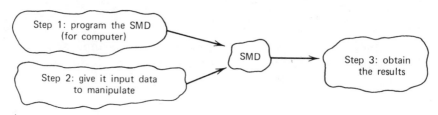

becomes

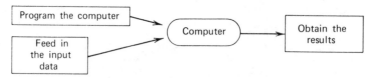

That is what the computer thing is all about: program the computer to do some specific task, feed it some input information to manipulate, and obtain the results. Why there is so much ado about computers is pretty simple: for tedious detail computers are fast, accurate, and can be given (programmed for) a virtually endless number of tasks. People, on the other hand, are often (at least by comparison) not very fast, not very accurate, and balk at being given more than a very restricted number of different tedious tasks. Thus, for many applications, computers make better SMDs than people do. This has many implications—social, economic, scientific, psychological, and philosophical, among others. Once we know more about computers we will consider these implications.

A Modern Data Processing System: An IBM System 370 Model 165 computer can execute an instruction every 80 *billionths* of a second. The basic machine has one-half million bytes of memory. A one-million byte 370 /165 costs about $50,000 per month for the central processing unit only. A typical system would cost about $100,000 per month. This price would include maintenance. (Courtesy of IBM Corporation.)

TYPES OF COMPUTERS

Present-day computers can be divided into two major classes: analog and digital. **Analog computers** represent information in continuous form (e.g., inches, volts). A thermometer represents information in analog form as does a gas gauge. **Digital computers** represent information in discrete form (e.g., beads, gear teeth). A touch-tone telephone accepts dialing information in digital form. By this distinction, a slide rule is an example of an analog calculator (because it represents information in continuous form: distance); an abacus is an example of a digital calculator (because it represents information in discrete form: one bead means 1, two beads mean 2, and so on).

In this book we concern ourselves with digital computers. The reasons for this are (a) things that can be done on analog computers can also be done on digital computers, while the reverse is, in general, not true; (b) to understand the analog computer, an understanding of calculus is almost necessary, while the digital computer can be utilized and understood without any special mathematical background; and (c) the digital computer has had the most social impact.

Digital computers can be further divided into two classes: special purpose and general purpose. A general-purpose digital computer is really quite like the SMD: it can do about any type of symbol manipulation you can specify. The **general-purpose digital computer,** then, is just an SMD: a very flexible symbol manipulator. A **special-purpose digital computer** is a digital computer that is always used to perform the same manipulations or class of manipulations (i.e., a special-purpose digital computer is a digital computer with the program built in or with at least most of the program built in). An example of a special-purpose digital computer is a missile-guidance computer: it has a very specific task for which it is designed and it is not expected to be able to run a payroll program, for example, in addition to its designed task. We graphically depict the computer world as follows:

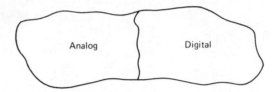

A more detailed picture might be

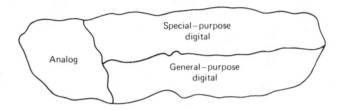

There is an important class of computers called **hybrid computers** that lies in the digital-and-analog area. These computers are used for special applications such as chemical process control. In general, the digital part of the computer is used for control and some computation, and the analog part is used for special computations. The hybrid computer is simply a digital and an analog computer combined with a "black box" between them that permits them to talk* to each other. Thus we have an even more detailed picture:

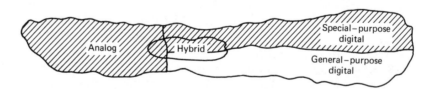

In the remainder of this book the term "computer" will mean a general-purpose digital computer.

FIRST LOOK AT THE INSIDE OF THE COMPUTER

The internal makeup of the computer will not be examined in detail in this book but some terminology is necessary. The term **hardware** refers to the mechanical and electronic components that comprise the computer itself. It is

*With increasing frequency we will begin to speak of a computer in an anthropomorphic manner. Calling a computer a giant brain is an example though we will try to avoid such gross anthropomorphisms here.

distinguished from **software,** the term applied to the computer's programs.

A computer's hardware can be broken down into five functional groups: **input devices, memory, control unit, arithmetic-logic unit,** and **output devices.** Thus, the diagram in Figure 1.1 can be expanded into the diagram shown in Figure 1.2.

As indicated by Figure 1.2, input devices transfer information into the memory (or storage) unit of the computer. Information in memory can be transferred to the arithmetic-logic unit, where it can be manipulated, and the manipulated data can then be stored back into the memory unit. Finally, results in memory can be transformed into some external form by means of output devices. All these actions (transfers and manipulations of data) must be specified by a program that also resides in memory. Thus, both the instructions that specify manipulations to be performed on data and the data itself may reside in the memory unit. This rather interesting state of affairs is called the **stored program concept** and is the basis for current computer architecture. The control unit interprets the instructions of the program and directs the actions of the other units, thereby ensuring that the right thing is done at the right time. Thus, the control unit guides the actions of the other units much as our nervous system guides the actions of our bodies.

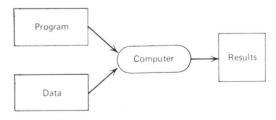

Figure 1.1

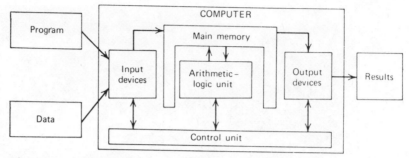

Figure 1.2   Block diagram of a general-purpose digital computer.

Input/output devices

The range of input/output devices (or **I/O devices**) is large. Some typical input devices are punched card readers, punched-paper tape readers, and optical character recognition devices, while typical output devices are printers, card punch units, and plotting devices. Some of these devices transfer information at quite a rapid rate; for example, card reader speeds of 1000 cards per minute are fairly typical. Incidentally, a standard punched card contains up to 80 characters of information, and typical print lines contain either 120 or 132 characters. A sample page of output from a computer printer is shown in Figure 1.3 and a punched card showing some of the allowable symbols on the IBM 360 computer is illustrated in Figure 1.4.

```
REPORT NO: XSA117-7                    UNIVERSITY DATA PROCESSING SCHEDULE

              PAYROLL                        SUMMER 1-2

      REPORT                              NO.       PUNCHED     DEADLINE
    SCHEDULED      PROGRAM  REPORT NAME   COPIES    CARDS       DATE
*****************************************************************************************************

  MONDAY   MAY    22
***********************
             APR250A   NORMAL UPDATE-EDIT    1                  MAY 23
  TUESDAY  MAY    23
***********************
             APR250A   NORMAL UPDATE-EDIT    1                  MAY 24
             APR252A   HOURLY REQUISITION    0                  MAY 24
             APR254A   SALARY REQUISITION    4                  MAY 24
  WEDNESDAY MAY   24
***********************
             APR253A   NORMAL UPDATE-EDIT    1                  MAY 25
             APR252A   HOURLY REQUISITION    4                  MAY 25
             APR254A   SALARY REQUISITION    4                  MAY 25
  THURSDAY MAY    25
***********************
             APR255A   COMPUTATIONS          3                  MAY 25
             APR263A   CHECKWRITER           1                  MAY 25
             APR284A   BANK RECONCILIATION   1                  MAY 25
             APR295A   CREDIT UNION-UNITED FUND 3               MAY 25
             APR296A   STATE-UNEMPLOYMENT-TRIBAL 3              MAY 25
  THURSDAY JUNE   1
***********************
             APR244A   CUMULATIVE UPDATE     1                  JUN 2
  FRIDAY   JUNE   2
***********************
             APR261A   FUND/REPORT           2                  JUN 5
             APR266A   TRIAL BALANCE         1                  JUN 5
             APR267A   STAFF COUNT           1                  JUN 5
             APR268A   SOCIAL SECURITY LIST  2                  JUN 5
```

Figure 1.3   A sample page of computer output: a page of an actual computer report showing the data processing schedule for a university payroll department.

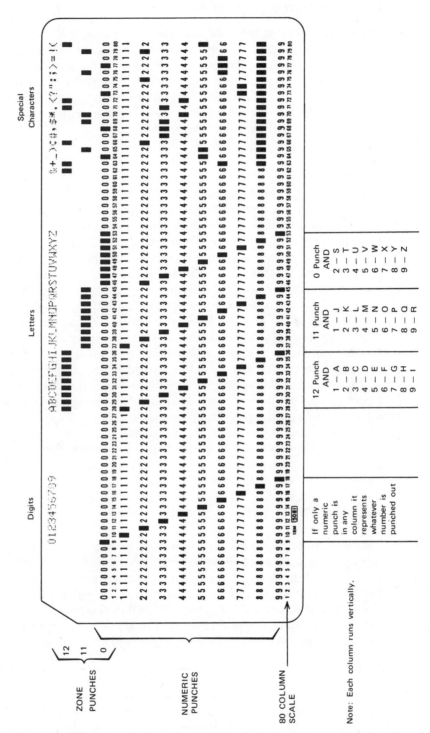

Figure 1.4 Punched card: typical punched card showing some of the allowable symbols on the IBM 360 computer. IBM's third-generation computers use the extended binary coded decimal interchange code (EBCDIC) shown. EBCDIC is an extension of Hollerith's original code.

Some devices can serve as both input and output devices. For example, teletypes and electric typewriters may be connected to a computer, allowing data to be input to the computer from a keyboard and data to be received in printed form from the computer. Naturally, this type of input /output is rather slow, but it may serve very well for humans communicating directly with the computer. Devices used in this way are called **terminals,** and computer usage through a terminal is called **teleprocessing.**

Memory

The memory, arithmetic-logic, and control units of a computer are composed primarily of electronic devices. The memory unit of a computer consists of some number (usually quite large, even into the millions) of units of storage called a **bit.** A bit is similar to an ordinary light switch in that it can be either on or off. In other words, a bit may contain one binary digit (i.e., 0 or 1); in fact, the word bit is a contraction of the two words "binary digit". A bit is about the smallest amount of information you can imagine and you may well wonder how computers can manipulate such things as decimal numbers, names, addresses, and the like, when only bits can be represented. The explanation is that groups of bits can be used to represent more complex units of information. For example, each symbol shown on the card in Figure 1.4 can be represented in the memory unit of an IBM 360 computer as a certain pattern of eight bits. For this reason, a collection of eight bits is often called a **byte.** Larger groups of bits may be used to represent a complete decimal number or an instruction in the program (remember, programs are stored in memory also). These larger groups of bits are sometimes called **words** or **cells.** The actual number of bits in a byte, word, or cell may vary from one computer to the next, but the basic idea of representing complex units of information with collections of bits is the same.

COMMUNICATING WITH THE COMPUTER

Man-machine communication is, at best, quite awkward. A large number of mechanisms and systems have been designed to simplify the effort. One of the most effective approaches is to communicate with the computer in a limited, Englishlike language, and then translate this somewhat stilted language into the computer's "natural" language. We call the computer's natural language **machine language.** Programmers do not often write programs in machine language because of its awkwardness for humans.

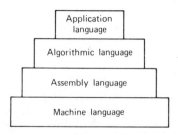

Once a program is written in any of the **higher-level languages** (meaning above the machine-language level), it can be translated into the particular computer's machine language. In fact, the translation can be performed by the computer itself by programs called **compilers** (for application and algorithmic* languages) and **assemblers** (for assembly languages).

We distinguish between languages such as French or English and languages used to communicate with a computer by calling the former **natural languages** and the latter **programming languages.** There are many programming languages and a few of the most important are given below, classified according to their primary usage:

Languages for Numerical Scientific Problems
  FORTRAN (FORmula TRANslating system)
  ALGOL 60 (ALGOrithmic Language)

Languages for Business Data Processing Problems
  COBOL (COmmon Business Oriented Language)
  RPG (Report Program Generator)

Languages for Nonnumeric Probelsm
  LISP (a language for manipulating nonnumeric data structured as lists)
  SNOBOL (a language for manipulating strings of characters)

Languages for Interactive Terminal Usage
  BASIC (Beginners All purpose Symbolic Instruction Code)
  APL (an array processing language par excellence)

Languages for Simulation
  GPSS (General Purpose Systems Simulation language)
  DYNAMO (a language used in the controversial World Model†)

Multipurpose Languages
  ALGOL 68
  PL /1

To give you some notion of the flavor of two of the most widely used languages, portions of WATFOR (a version of FORTRAN) and COBOL programs are given in Figures 1.5 and 1.6, respectively.

```
              DIMENSION X(50)
    C         N REPRESENTS THE NUMBER OF NUMBERS
              READ,N
              DO 12 I=1,N
          12  READ,X(I)
              S=0.
              DO 24 I=1,N
          24  S=S+X(I)
              A=S/N
    C         NOW COMPUTE THE STD. DEV.
              P=0.
              DO 42 I=1,N
          42  P=P+(X(I)-A)**2
              D=(P/N)**0.5
    C         PRINT THE RESULTS
              PRINT, 'THE SUM IS ',S,'THE AVERAGE IS ',A
              PRINT, 'THE STANDARD DEVIATION IS ',D
              STOP
              END
```

Figure 1.5   A WATFOR /FORTRAN program to compute the average and standard deviation of a list of numbers.

*An **algorithm** is a way of doing things. It is like a recipe except that the steps in an algorithm are very carefully defined. We will discuss this in detail in Chapter 2.

†J. W. Forrester, *World Dynamics*, Cambridge, Mass.: Wright-Allen Press, 1971.

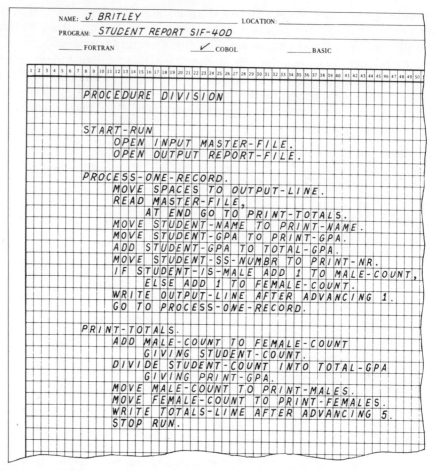

NAME: *J. BRITLEY*   LOCATION: _____

PROGRAM: *STUDENT REPORT SIF-40D*

___ FORTRAN   ✓ COBOL   ___ BASIC

```
PROCEDURE DIVISION

START-RUN
    OPEN INPUT MASTER-FILE.
    OPEN OUTPUT REPORT-FILE.

PROCESS-ONE-RECORD.
    MOVE SPACES TO OUTPUT-LINE.
    READ MASTER-FILE,
        AT END GO TO PRINT-TOTALS.
    MOVE STUDENT-NAME TO PRINT-NAME.
    MOVE STUDENT-GPA TO PRINT-GPA.
    ADD STUDENT-GPA TO TOTAL-GPA.
    MOVE STUDENT-SS-NUMBR TO PRINT-NR.
    IF STUDENT-IS-MALE ADD 1 TO MALE-COUNT,
        ELSE ADD 1 TO FEMALE-COUNT.
    WRITE OUTPUT-LINE AFTER ADVANCING 1.
    GO TO PROCESS-ONE-RECORD.

PRINT-TOTALS.
    ADD MALE-COUNT TO FEMALE-COUNT
        GIVING STUDENT-COUNT.
    DIVIDE STUDENT-COUNT INTO TOTAL-GPA
        GIVING PRINT-GPA.
    MOVE MALE-COUNT TO PRINT-MALES.
    MOVE FEMALE-COUNT TO PRINT-FEMALES.
    WRITE TOTALS-LINE AFTER ADVANCING 5.
    STOP RUN.
```

Figure 1.6 COBOL program example: the readability of the COBOL procedure division is illustrated in this sample program. A person totally unfamiliar with COBOL could probably figure out in a few minutes what the program does. Consider the assignment: "add average gradepoint by sex to the program". You could probably perform this program modification to this program with no real knowledge of COBOL.

EXERCISES

1. Name and describe the two general methods of representing information. Give examples of each method from everyday life.
2. What are the five functional components of a digital computer? List parts of the body that perform the analogous functions for a human and, for each example, indicate whether or not you think the machines' capability exceeds that of the human.
3. In your own words describe what is meant by a program for a general purpose digital computer. Can you think of things other than computers that are programmed?
4. Do you think humans are programmed? If so, how and to what extent?
5. What do you think are the most significant differences between natural languages and programming languages?

BIBLIOGRAPHY*

Adams, J. M., and R. Moon. *An Introduction to Computer Science*. Glenview, Ill.: Scott, Foresman, 1970. 356 pp.

> An introduction to computers, computer programming, and applications (both numerical and nonnumerical) using a hypothetical machine language and FORTRAN.

Awad, E. M. *Business Data Processing*, 4th ed. Englewood Cliffs, N.J.: Prentice-Hall, 1975. 722 pp.

> A business-oriented introduction to computers that includes chapters on COBOL, FORTRAN IV, BASIC, RPG (for System 3).

Blatt, J. M. *Introduction to FORTRAN IV Programming Using the WATFOR/WATFIV Compilers*. Pacific Palisades, Ca.: Goodyear, 1971. 325 pp.

> A revision of an earlier work covering only the WATFOR compiler. Descriptions of special capabilities of WATFIV are included plus more problems, many of which are related to business applications.

Brown, C. *Questions and Answers on Computers*. New York: Drake, 1969. 96 pp.

> This is an introduction to computer logic and devices, hardware, programming, data processing, industrial and scientific applications, microelectronics, and future trends in the field.

Clifford, J. R., and M. Clifford. *Computer Mathematics Handbook*. Boston: Allyn and Bacon, 1974. 338 pp.

> This book is intended for teachers and students of computer programming. It covers the decimal and binary number systems, plus number systems with other bases. Other topics covered include error correcting codes, algebra, symbolic logic, and flow charting.

Cooper, R. H. et al., *File Processing with COBOL/WATBOL: A Structured Programming Approach*. Waterloo, Ontario, Canada: WATFAC, 1974. 336 pp.

> An excellent introduction to COBOL emphasizing structured programming and using the University of Waterloo's WATBOL compiler.

Cress, P., P. Dirksen, and J. W. Graham. *FORTRAN IV with WATFOR and WATFIV*. Englewood Cliffs, N.J.: Prentice-Hall, 1970. 447 pp.

> A revision of a previous text, *FORTRAN IV with WATFOR*, which examines the features of FORTRAN IV with the language extensions implemented at the University of Waterloo, Ontario, Canada. A good text.

Davenport, W. P. *Modern Data Communication: Concepts, Language and Media*. New York: Hayden, 1971. 208 pp.

> Reviews the basic concepts of communications such as coding, channel capacity, modulation, and multiplexing, *without complex mathematics*; designed to serve as both an in-depth introduction and reference guide.

Didday, R. L., and R. L. Page, *FORTRAN for Humans*. St. Paul: West Publishing Co., 1974. 430 pp.

> A delightful, very human introduction to FORTRAN.

---

*References in footnotes are not necessarily included in the Bibliography.

Farina, M. V. *Elementary BASIC with Applications*. Englewood Cliffs, N.J.: Prentice-Hall, 1971. 309 pp.

> Based primarily on the General Electric time-sharing service, this book provides a good introduction to the language with good coverage of basic data processing functions such as sorting and file handling.

Forsythe, A. I., T. A. Keenan, E. I. Organick, and W. Stenberg. *Computer Science: A First Course*. 2nd ed. New York: Wiley, 1975. 842 pp.

> An excellent introduction to computer science emphasizing the development of algorithms. The text relies heavily on developing algorithms by means of flowcharts, but supplementary texts on FORTRAN, BASIC, and PL/I are available.

Foy, N. *The Sun Never Sets on IBM: The Culture and Folklore of IBM World Trade*. New York: William Morrow and Co., 1975. 218 pp.

> The story of IBM, both the domestic and world views are represented. The background, growth, and problems of the company, as well as the influence of the Watsons are examined.

Gilman, L., and A. J. Rose. *APL: An Interactive Approach* 2nd ed. New York: Wiley, 1974. 400 pp.

> The features of APL are explained in a tutorial fashion on the assumption that the reader has access to an APL terminal. The text includes many examples of terminal printouts.

Gross, J. L., and W. S. Brainerd. *Fundamental Programming Concepts*. New York: Harper & Row, 1972. 304 pp.

> An introduction to programming using BASIC, with a discussion of a wide variety of applications including simulation and artificial intelligence.

Hare, V. C. *Introduction to Programming: A BASIC Approach*. New York: Harcourt, Brace, Jovanovich, 1970. 436 pp.

> A text for an introductory course in programming that begins with BASIC and progresses to FORTRAN in later chapters. Some comparative programs are included.

Hughes, J. K. *PL/I Programming*. New York: Wiley, 1973. 751 pp.

> A very complete treatment of PL/I. This book contains several very good reference appendices (e.g., an excellent glossary and a very good treatment of data formats and number systems).

Hull, T. E., and D. D. F. Day. *Computers and Problem Solving*. Don Mills, Ontario: Addison-Wesley (Canada), 1970. 276 pp.

> An introduction to computing using FORTRAN. A fairly wide range of scientific applications are discussed, and there is a brief discussion of business data processing.

Jones, R. L. *Fundamental COBOL for IBM System/360*. Englewood Cliffs. N.J.: Prentice-Hall, 1969. 245 pp.

> A beginning text in the use of COBOL with specific examples relating to the IBM 360.

Katzan, H., Jr. *APL Programming and Computer Techniques*. New York: Van Nostrand Reinhold, 1970. 335 pp.

> Presents the APL language and terminal system as an effective pair for small or large problems, and serves as an introduction to computer techniques. Many examples and summaries are included.

Katzan, H., Jr. *APL Users Guide*. New York: Van Nostrand Reinhold, 1971. 126 pp.

> The language is presented in such a way that the student can use the text as his guide at the terminal while learning the language; includes many examples and test problems.

Katzan, H., Jr. *Introduction to Computer Science*. New York: Petrocelli, 1975. 512 pp.

> The book is organized in four parts: part one, "Fundamental Concepts", introduces computer science, programming, number systems, and basic data structures; part two, "Computer System", covers hardware and architecture; part three, "Computer Software", presents programming languages and operating systems technology; and part four, "Topics in Computer Science", covers structured programming, data structures, numeric computing, automata, and computers and society.

Maniotes, J., and J. S. Quasney. *Computer Careers*. Rochelle Park, N. J.: Hayden Book, 1974. 192 pp.

> Provides a broad overview of the computing field as a career. Includes information on schools and job-hunting procedures.

Martin, H. *Telecommunications and the Computer*. Englewood Cliffs, N.J.: Prentice-Hall, 1969. 470 pp.

> This book concentrates on common-carrier equipment as opposed to the computer manufacturer's equipment, and covers the technical and design aspects of communications hardware and systems.

Maurer, W. D. *Programming: An Introduction to Computer Techniques*. San Francisco: Holden-Day, 1972. 335 pp.

> Provides instruction in the general principles and techniques common to programmers.

McCracken, D. D. *A Guide to ALGOL Programming*. New York: Wiley, 1962. 106 pp.

> An introduction to programming in ALGOL with the emphasis on scientic and engineering applications.

McCracken, D. D., and U. Garbassi. *A Guide to COBOL Programming*. New York: Wiley, 1970. 209 pp.

> Serves as an introduction to COBOL programming and the situations in which it is used. The book includes many examples and problems, and three case studies.

Murach, M. *Standard COBOL*, 2nd ed. Palo Alto, Ca.: 1975. 433 pp.

> A very good introduction to COBOL. The book is in modular form and, after reading the first 5 chapters, you can read and understand any of the remaining 11 chapters.

Murphy, J. S. *Basics of Digital Computers*. New York: Hayden, 1970. 391 pp.

If the reader has some background in computers and programming, this book provides an introduction to basic computer arithmetic: the CPU and programming in the first volume, circuitry and basic units in the second volume, and I/O in the third volume. (This edition is a single volume.)

Polivka, P., and S. Pakin. APL: *The Language and its Usage.* Englewood Cliffs, N. J.: Prentice-Hall, 1975. 496 pp.

A presentation of the APL language organized so that the reader will be able to solve real problems while being introduced to APL concepts.

Roper, J. S. *PL/I In Easy Stages.* Encino. Ca.: Dickenson Publishing Co., 1975. 239 pp.

An introduction to PL/I using programmed instruction.

Rosen, S. (ed.). *Programming Systems and Languages.* New York: McGraw-Hill, 1971. 734 pp.

Five parts include a historical survey, an introduction to FORTRAN, ALGOL, COBOL, and NPL, an introduction to compiling and translating, list processing languages, and operating systems.

Rubin, M. L. (ed.) *Handbook of Data Processing Management, vol. IV, Advanced Technology—Input and Output.* Philadelphia: Auerbach, 1970. 361 pp.

Chapters cover source data automation, key tape devices, OCR, voice response, digital plotters, and display devices. Case studies are used throughout to demonstrate the application of each type of I/O device.

Rummer, D. I. *Introduction to Analog Computer Programming.* New York: Holt, Rinehart and Winston, 1969. 198 pp.

An introductory text on analog programming, for students who have not studied differential equations.

Sammet, J. E. *Programming Languages: History and Fundamentals.* Englewood Cliffs, N.J.: Prentice-Hall, 1969. 785 pp.

A survey and reference guide to computer programming languages. Includes an extensive bibliography.

Sanders, D. H. *Computers in Business,* 3rd ed. New York: McGraw-Hill, 1975. 656 pp.

A business-oriented introduction to computers. This is a very readable text.

Sanderson, P. C. *Computer Languages: A Practical Guide to the Chief Programming Languages.* New York: Philosophical Library. 1970. 200 pp.

Serves as an introduction to computers and describes ALGOL 60, FORTRAN, COBOL, and PL/I. Emphasizes features common to many computers. Includes problems and solutions.

Saxon, J. A. *COBOL: A Self-Instructional Manual,* 2nd ed. Englewood Cliffs, N.J.: Prentice-Hall, 1971. 240 pp.

This introductory COBOL text uses nine complete programs to aid in the teaching of COBOL. Problems include such areas as inventory control, real-estate amortization, file processing, and time-card handling.

Siegel, P. *Understanding Digital Computers.* New York: Wiley, 1971. 462 pp.

Describes the computer and its functions, and has three major sections that move from a theoretical discussion of arithmetic and logic to an exposition of techniques for putting these ideas into practice.

Stuart, F. *FORTRAN Programming*. New York: Wiley, 1969. 353 pp.

> Discusses how to program in FORTRAN, the applications best fitted by FORTRAN programming, and different programming techniques.

Weinberg, G. M. *PL/I Programming: A Manual of Style*. New York: McGraw-Hill, 1970. 441 pp.

> Covers the most commonly used features of PL/L as well as the general topic of programming style. While intended as a second text in PL/I, the book includes a Chapter 0 for the beginning student.

Wessel, R. *Freedom's Edge: The Computer's Threat to Society*. Reading, Mass.: Addison Wesley, 1974. 160 pp.

> The implications of computer technology on society and the rules necessary to govern the use of computers. Coverage includes information banks, privacy, history, and legal issues.

The following periodicals are available in most large libraries and often contain computer related articles. Those marked with an asterisk are very computer oriented.

Accounting Review
*ACM Nat'l Conference Proceedings
Administrative Management
*ADP Newsletter
Advanced Management Journal
*Automation
Magazine of Bank Administration
Bank Systems & Equipment
Banking
Business Horizons
Business Week
*Communications of the ACM
*Computer Bulletin
*Computer Decisions
*Computer Design
*Computer Journal
*Computer Magazine
*Computers & People
*Computer Personnel
*Computing Reviews
*Computing Surveys
*IEEE Computer Society Conf. Proceedings
*Computing Europe
*Computer World
Control Engineering
*Data Base
*Data Communications
*The Data Communications User
*Data Management
*Datamation
Dun's Review
*EDP Analyzer
*EDP Audit, Control & Security Newsletter
EDUCOM Bulletin

Electronic Design
Electronic News
Electronics
Financial Executive
Forbes
Fortune
*Government Systems
Harvard Business Review
*IBM Systems Journal
Ideas for Management
*Information Processing
IE-Industrial Engineering
Industrial Research
Industry Week
*Infosystems
The Internal Auditor
Journal of Accountancy
Journal of Bank Research
Journal of Business
*Journal of Educational Data Processing
Journal of Library Automation
Journal of Marketing
Journal of Marketing Research
Journal of Purchasing
Journal of Retailing
*Journal of Systems Management
Management Accounting
Management Control
Management Review
Management Science
*Modern Data
Modern Office Procedures
*National Computer Conference Proceedings
*Network
The Office
Operations Research
Personnel
Personnel Journal
Purchasing
Scientific American
Sloan Management Review
*IEEE Trans. on Software Engineering
*Software-Practice & Experience
*System/3 World
*Telecommunications

2. The concept of algorithm

The concept of algorithm is probably the most important concept in the field of computer science—it really forms the basis for the field. As a result, we will try to develop the concept carefully in this chapter. Our development will be quite intuitive, and every attempt will be made to relate the idea to our everyday experiences. This intuitive approach can be rigorously formalized into a theory that is fundamental in the still-developing theory of the new field of computer science. We will not give the formal approach here, but appealing treatments are given in texts by Minsky and Korfhage.*

INTUITIVE DEVELOPMENT

A fairly satisfactory definition of the term algorithm is:

A set of well-defined rules for the solution of a problem in a finite number of steps.

There are many similar definitions of the term, such as:

. . . a list of instructions for carrying out some process step by step.†

. . . a step-by-step problem-solving procedure that can be carried out by a machine.‡

. . . a process the execution of which is clearly specified to the smallest details.§

All of these definitions are intuitively suggestive and appealing, but they may still leave the basic concept somewhat vague in your mind.

Perhaps the simplest way to grasp the concept of algorithm is through consideration of the following very common question:

How do you do that?

You are probably asked this question, in one form or another several times every day, and depending on whatever "that" refers to, you may or may not be able to answer the question successfully. Let's take various forms of the question and see how well we can answer them.

Consider first the question:

How do you prepare a cup of hot chocolate?

The following answer is hopefully as satisfying as the resulting chocolate:

Place two or three level teaspoons of cocoa powder in a cup. Add hot milk and stir.

However, this might be criticized by some as being a little vague, so it might be sharpened up by using a diagramatic representation called a **flowchart.** Simple flowcharts are made of rectangles containing descriptions of actions to be taken and diamond-shaped figures containing descriptions of decisions to be made. These figures are connected with directed lines indicating the

---

*M. L. Minsky, *Computation Finite and Infinite Machines.* Englewood Cliffs, N.J.: Prentice-Hall, 1967 and R.R. Korfhage, *Logic and Algorithms.* New York: Wiley, 1966.

†A.I. Forsythe, T.A. Keenan, E.I. Organick, and W. Stenberg, *Computer Science: A Primer.* New York: Wiley, 1969, p. 3.

‡T.E. Hull and D.D.F. Day, *Computers and Problem Solving.* Reading, Mass.: Addison-Wesley, 1968, p.3.

§H. Hermes, *Enumerability, Decidability, Computability.* Berlin: Springer-Verlag, 1965, p.1.

flow of control through the algorithm. A flowchart describing the preparation of cocoa is shown in Figure 2.1. This description should satisfy all but the most peevish, who might want to know the exact temperature of the milk to be added and who might need assurance that the cup was of standard size. At any rate, you would probably agree that this answer could be sharpened to the point where there would be no room for misinterpretation, and we would say that we had an algorithm for performing this task.

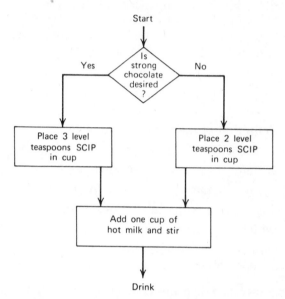

Figure 2.1

Equally precise answers (algorithms) could be provided for similar questions such as "How do you make snickerdoodle cookies?" or slightly different questions such as "How do you fix a flat tire?" but other questions may pose some problems. Consider the important question:

How do you get a date?

You might be able to give some general rules that would be helpful but it is very doubtful that you could ever give an effective answer that was so precise that it would apply to every situation without interpretation. There are many things that we do without being able to explain how we do them; in such cases, we would say we are utilizing **heuristic** methods rather than algorithmic methods. Other examples of heuristic methods are the answers to the questions "How do you translate from Spanish to English?" or "How do you play the stock market successfully?" or "How do you play a good game of chess?". As mankind develops, we seem to be able to explain our environment better and also our actions with respect to our environment, and thus some things appear to move from the heuristic to the algorithmic realm. Fortunately, it is doubtful that life could ever become completely algorithmic.

CHARACTERISTICS OF ALGORITHMS

From our development thus far, we see that the concept of algorithm is something like the idea of a recipe, a process, a method, or a procedure. In fact, we will commonly use **effective procedure** as a synonym for algorithm. Our development should also have indicated that there is a bit more preciseness involved in the concept of algorithm than our intuitive use of the terms recipe, process, and the like. In order to pin this difference down, we discuss two essential characteristics of any algorithm.

Finiteness

An algorithm must always terminate after a finite number of steps. Thus, for example, the following procedure does *not* represent an algorithm:

Step 1   Initialize S to 0.

Step 2   Initialize I to 1.

Step 3   Add I to S.

Step 4   Increment I by 1.

Step 5   Return to Step 3.

This is a procedure to compute the sum of all positive integers and, of course, it would never terminate, since there are an infinite number of positive integers. (Recall the childhood game of two children trying to surpass each other in naming large numbers. Since one child can always add one to the other child's number, the game is only limited by the endurance of the participants.)

A procedure that has all the characteristics of an algorithm except finiteness is sometimes called a **computational method.** Thus, the above procedure would be called a computational method for summing the positive integers but would be of no value, since its execution cannot be completely realized.

In practical problem-solving situations, even the finiteness requirement is not sufficiently restrictive. For example, as Knuth* points out, there is an algorithm that determines whether or not the game of chess is a forced victory for the white pieces. However, even with the help of our fastest computers, executing the algorithm would take considerably longer than a lifetime. Algorithms of such a nature do not constitute effective ways of solving our problems.

Definiteness

Each step of an algorithm must be definite; that is, each operation called for must be precisely and unambiguously defined. This requirement makes the language in which the algorithm is expressed quite important. For example, the use of a natural language such as English to specify algorithms is fraught with danger, because of the possibility of vagueness or ambuigity. As an illustration of this, consider such vague phrases as

a pinch of salt

a dash of tabasco

about a mile past the stop sign

and ambiguous phrases such as

*D.E. Knuth, *Fundamental Algorithms*, vol. 1 of *The Art of Computer Programming*. Reading, Mass.: Addison-Wesley, 1968.

The robbery was committed by three armed bandits.

The couple greatly enjoyed the wild game feast.

In avoiding difficulties of this nature, we find ourselves using a natural language in a more and more restrictive way. In fact, we see that in moving toward a language free of vagueness and ambiguity, we are developing an artificial language for expressing algorithms. Machines require definite unambiguous direction and thus programming languages were developed, although they were not developed by successively restricting natural languages.

In addition to the two essential characteristics of finiteness and definiteness, there are several other important features possessed by most algorithms.

Generality

Most useful algorithms are general enough to be used to solve an entire class of problems rather than just one specific problem. For example, a program to compute the wage of one individual with a fixed hourly pay rate is not nearly as useful as a program that will perform the computation for any individual by accepting his pay rate as input data.

Input

Most algorithms accept input data on which to base the manipulations to be performed. As indicated above, this feature usually allows the algorithm to be more general and hence more useful.

Output

Most algorithms yield output data that provide the desired results. You might think that output would be a feature of all algorithms, but there is at least one useful algorithm that has no specific output. In process-control applications, the computer must often delay a certain amount of time until an operation is to be performed; this is accomplished by a program that merely does nothing at all until the preset amount of time has elapsed. Of course, even in this case, you could say that the output of the algorithm is a measured amount of time.

PHILOSOPHICAL CONSIDERATIONS

The most basic philosophical issue concerning algorithms deals with the extent to which processes can be formulated as algorithms. We have already observed that our lives seem to be moving in the algorithmic direction as we are better able to quantify and explain our environment. What limits are there for this movement from the heuristic to the algorithmic realm? As you probably expect, we can give no definitive answer to this question, but we can state that limits do exist. For example, certain problems have been shown to be unsolvable using algorithmic methods. One such problem is called the "halting problem".

To describe the halting problem we need to consider all syntactically valid computer programs that can be written in a given language. It would be useful to know which of these programs are nonterminating (semantically invalid), since then we could avoid using large amounts of computer time trying to run these programs. This would be particularly useful information in a university environment where students are learning to write computer programs and sometimes inadvertently write nonterminating ones. Thus what we would like is an algorithm for determining whether or not these programs halt, or in other words a solution for the halting problem. It has been proven that for sufficiently powerful languages, we cannot write a program in that language to solve its halting problem.* Many similar unsolvability results have been obtained and there is a great deal of investigation in this area.

Thus we know there exist limits to the extent of solving problems algorithmically, but we do not know to what extent these limits coincide or diverge from limits on solving problems heuristically. In particular, a great debate rages around the question of whether or not all of our actions are amenable to formulation as algorithms. We have more to say on this in Chapter 5 "Artificial Intelligence".

EXERCISES

1. Think of a process with which you are quite familiar and which you believe to be algorithmic. Describe the process as precisely as possible in a manner of your own choosing.
2. Repeat Exercise 1 for a heuristic process. In your description of the process identify the steps that are not algorithmic and indicate why they are not.
3. Must an algorithm possess the characteristic of generality? Justify your answer by giving arguments why it must or an example of an algorithm that is not general.
4. Attempt to formalize the intuitive idea of an algorithm given in this chapter. One possibility is to specify a class of machines and claim that anything that is really an algorithm can be put in the form of one of these machines. Try to think of very, very simple machines.
5. Would you describe your thought process as usually algorithmic or usually heuristic. Give examples to justify your answer.

BIBLIOGRAPHY†

Boillot, M. H., G. M. Gleason, and L. W. Horn. *Essentials of Flowcharting*. Dubuque, Iowa: William Brown, 1975. 114 pp.

An introduction to flowcharting with definitions, illustrations, and examples, including sample COBOL, BASIC, and FORTRAN programs.

* References in footnotes are not necessarily included in the Bibliography. See Chapter 1's Bibliography for a list of computing periodicals.

†C.A.R. Hoare and D.C.S. Allison, "Incomputability", *Computing Surveys*, Vol. 4, No. 3, 1972.

Hermes, H. *Enumerability, Decidability, Computability.* Berlin: Springer-Verlag, 1965. 245 pp.

> An advanced text on the theory of algorithms requiring considerable mathematical background.

Knuth, D. E. *The Art of Computer Programming: Vol. 1, Fundamental Algorithms; Vol. II, Seminumerical Algorithms; Vol. III, Sorting and Searching.* Reading, Mass.: Addison-Wesley, 1968. 634 pp. 1969. 624 pp. 1973. 722 pp.

> The first three volumes in a planned seven-volume series designed to provide a unified, readable, and theoretically sound summary of present knowledge concerning programming techniques and their historical development.

Korfhage, R. R. *Logic and Algorithms: With Applications to the Computer and Information Sciences.* New York: Wiley, 1966. 194 pp.

> Courses in logic are generally offered by departments of mathematics, computer science, philosophy, or electrical engineering. This book draws together material from each of these approaches to the subject and casts the whole setting appropriate to the study of computer and information sciences. In addition, the book provides an elementary discussion of algorithmic problem-solving, including Markov algorithms, Turing machines, and computer languages.

Minsky, M. L. *Computation: Finite and Infinite Machines.* Englewood Cliffs, N.J.: Prentice-Hall, 1967. 317 pp.

> Dependent on only a basic knowledge of algebra for comprehension, this book develops its own mathematics where necessary and covers the range of its subject, from basic principles to current research problems. The prime goal of this study is to introduce the concept of *effective procedure*—a vital intellectual tool employed in the development of theories about complex systems. Another theme of this book is the concept of the *universal computer*—a theoretical and practical device through which a great complexity of behavior can arise from the interactions of simple devices.

Trakhtenbrot, B. A. *Algorithms and Automatic Computing Machines.* Boston: Heath, 1963. 101 pp.

> An excellent informal introduction to the theory of algorithms, requiring minimal mathematical background.

3. History of computation

If, unwarned by my example, any man shall undertake and succeed in really constructing an engine embodying in itself the whole of the executive department of mathematical analysis upon different principles or by simpler mechanical means—I have no fear of leaving my reputation in his charge, for he alone will be fully able to appreciate the nature of my efforts and the value of their results.

Charles Babbage
The Life of a Philosopher

In this chapter we take an unhurried overview of machine-aided manipulation of information. First, we consider the history of computation from 1500 B.C. to the present century, emphasizing the contribution of Charles Babbage. Then, we look at the developments during this century, emphasizing the contribution of John von Neumann. The majority of computation's history is a history of computing devices (i.e., it is a history of hardware); in the concluding part of the chapter we look at the history of sortware development.

This history of computation is, in itself, an important topic. It is necessary in order to obtain the proper perspective required to study the social implications of computrrs. Furthermore, there are some interesting sidelights and personalities in the history.

You need to remember that the "history" of modern computers covers somewhat less than 35 years. The first commercial use of computers was in 1954. The first stored-program computer started operating in 1949. On the other hand, history of computation covers *at least* three millenia.

COMPUTATION FROM 1500 B.C.

For as long as man has been *Homo sapiens* he has used things as tools. One of the early needs he encounted was the ability to count his material possessions. The most available tool consisted of his fingers, and they have served him as a counting tool to this day. Our word "digit" and the decimal number system historically stem from the use of fingers for counting. Eventually, man's number of possessions exceeded his number of fingers. Then he used sticks, stones, scratches, or any units that could be grouped and tallied. The abacus was probably a natural extension of these counting techniques and although its origin seems lost in antiquity, it is still widely used in oriental countries. In the tenth century, Pope Sylvester II was credited with magical powers of divination, possibly because he mastered the abacus that the Saracens were then using.

Even more sophisticated counting devices can be attributed to prehistoric man. Hawkins in *Stonehenge Decoded* has presented a very convincing argument that the awesome arrangement of stones on Salisbury Plain in southern England was a computer constructed by ancient astronomers. For example, a circle of holes called the Aubrey Circle seems to have been used as a digital counting device by moving stones around the circle. This theory on Stonehenge is doubly fascinating to the computer scientist, since Hawkins used an IBM 650 computer to perform the calculations required to support his thesis.

The early use of calculating devices seems to have been fairly widespread. The ancient Chinese used small "counting rods" and calculating devices have been found in ancient Greek ruins. Even the origin of the word "calculus" dates back to a Roman tabulating system using little pebbles, or "calculi".

In the seventeenth century the art of mechanical computing began to become a science. In 1617, Lord Napier performed calculations with "certain pieces of wood or ivory with numbers on them". While still in his teens, the great French mathematician Blaise Pascal designed a device in 1645 "for the execution of all sorts of arithmetical processes in a manner no less novel than convenient". This device, using gears, was the forerunner of the desk calculator and was used, appropriately enough, for the computation of taxes. Another great mathematician, Gottfried Leibniz, improved on Pascal's design a few years later by producing a device that could do all four of the basic arithmetic operations.

Stonehenge: On the Salisbury Plain in England stands an awesome arrangement of stones. The stones have been the subject of countless studies, poems, and legends dating back to the days of King Arthur. The stones have been thought to be a city of the dead, a Druid altar of sacrifice, and a temple to the sun. It took a twentieth-century astronomer and a computer to help unravel the ancient mystery: Stonehenge itself was an astronomical computer.

Another class of mechanisms that contributed greatly to the development of modern computing devices were the early simulacra (devices that simulate) and automata (devices that move by themselves). The history of the urge to develop such devices undoubtedly begins with the rock paintings in prehistoric caves and the "idols" found in burials. One of the first actual examples seems to be the talking statue of the Egyptian god Re-Harmakhis, and Derek de Solla Price* observes that "by the beginning of Greek culture the process of natural exaggeration in mythology and legend had produced at least the concept of simulacra able to do more than merely talk and move their arms". This is evidenced by the stories of the walking statues of Daedalus and the

*Derek J. de Solla Price, "Automata and the Origins of Mechanism and Mechanistic Philosophy", *Technology and Culture*. Vol. 1 No. 1, Winter 1964.

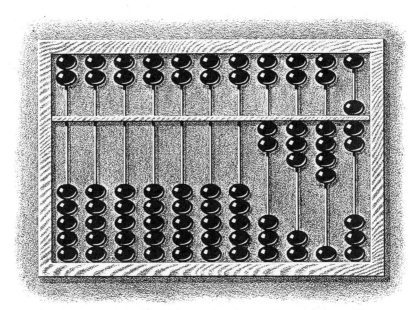

Abacus: The abacus is still used in the Orient and by some in the Western world. It is really just an extension of computing on one's fingers. There are several different versions of what we generically call the abacus. The one above is the Chinese *suan pan*.

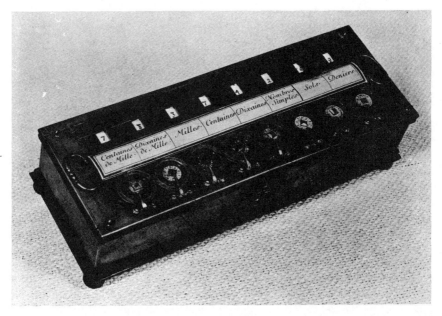

Pascal's adding machine: Pascal started to develop his calculator when he was 19 years old. It was completed in 1642–1643. He built the calculator because he wanted to aid his father, who, at that time, was superintendent of taxes in Rouen, France. It was the first of the numerical wheel calculators.

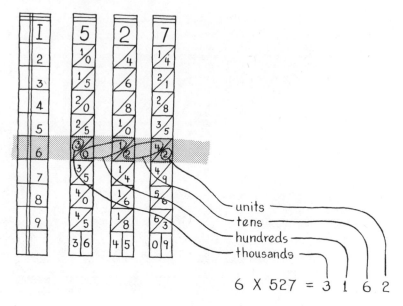

Computing with Napier's bones. The human calculator placed the "bones" of the number he wanted to multiply adjacent to each other on the left side of the Napier device. The computation of the product 6 × 527 is illustrated here. The units position is determined first, a 2. Then the tens digit is determined, 2 + 4 = 6 The hundreds digit, 0 + 1 = 1 and the thousands digit 3, are determined similarly.

Napier's "bones". Adapting the "grating" method of Arab, Hindu, and European human calculators, John Napier, of Merchiston, Scotland, attempted to reduce tedious calculations involving large numbers. His "bones," or rods, made a great impression on the Europeans and Chinese. Each rod was divided into nine squares, each of which was divided diagonally. The top square held a digit, 1–9. The remaining eight squares in the rod held the product of multiplying that number by 2, 3, 4, 5, 6, 7, 8, and 9. Once set up, the products of any numbers could easily be obtained. Note that each square holds the tens and units digits with the tens digit above the diagonal and the units digit below it (e.g., look at 7 × 6, the square is 4 /2, or 42).

flying mechanical dove of Archytas of Tarentum (fourth century B.C.). In addition to biological simulacra, there exist examples of very early cosmological simulacra in the form of water clocks dating back to 300-270 B.C. and a geometrical model of planetary motion circa 370 B.C. Since that time there have been many examples of sophisticated automata, but some of the more interesting ones were the automatons constructed by Jacques Vaucanson.

In 1737 Vaucanson completed a life-sized figure of a musician that played 11 melodies on its flute, "moving the levers realistically by its fingers and blowing into the instrument with its mouth".* A short time later Vaucanson completed another musician that played the flute with one hand and a drum with the other. The most famous of Vaucanson's automatons was "an artificial duck of gilt brass which drinks, eats, flounders in water, digests and excretes like a live duck". Subsequently Vaucanson applied his genius to the development of automatic machine tools, and, according to Silvio Bedini, he "invented and perfected an apparatus for automatic weaving of brocades which has been erroneously attributed to Jacquard". If you are interested in more detail on the history of automata, read Desmonde's article "From Idol to Computer" in the readings at the end of the book. Meanwhile, we will discuss the "Jacquard" loom and its sociological effects.

In 1801, Joseph Marie Jacquard received a bronze medal at the industrial Exposition in Paris for his model of a weaving loom. In 1806, his perfected loom was bought by the state and declared public property. Jacquard was granted an annuity of 3000 francs and a royalty on all looms sold. The Jacquard loom was the first machine to weave in patterns and has had almost countless adaptations in the modern textile industry. Jacquard's loom wove its brocade silks by using punched cards with patterns of holes in them. The different patterns permitted wire hooks to fall through the holes grasping the threads and thus controlling the operations required to reproduce the artists' designs. Within a decade, 11,000 of the machines were at work in French textile plants. Since this step had formerly been done by hand, there was mass technological unemployment; displaced workers took the law into their own hands and smashed a number of looms. Jacquard wrote, "The iron was sold for iron, the wood for wood, and I its inventor was delivered up to public ignominy."† As we will see, it was from Jacquard that Babbage got his idea for using cards in communicating with the analytical engine.

Except for the work of Charles Babbage, the development of mechanized aids to computation for the next 75 years was mostly restricted to a succession of developments that would culminate in the modern desk calculator, and its electronic counterpart—the electronic desk calculator. In 1820, Thomas de Colmar built the prototype of all calculating machines built prior to 1875. The de Colmar machine could perform the four basic arithmetic operations. Subsequently Baldwin invented a key-driven device that did not need to be reset after each operation.

At about the same time as Baldwin's work, Herman Hollerith began experimenting with punched cards as a medium for storing and analyzing demographic data.

In the 1880s the tabulation was moving so slowly on the 1880 census data

---

*Silvio A. Bedini, "The Role of Automata in the History of Technology", *Technology and Culture.* Vol. 1, No. 1, Winter 1964.

†J. Pfeiffer, *The Thinking Machine.* Philadelphia: Lippincott, 1962.

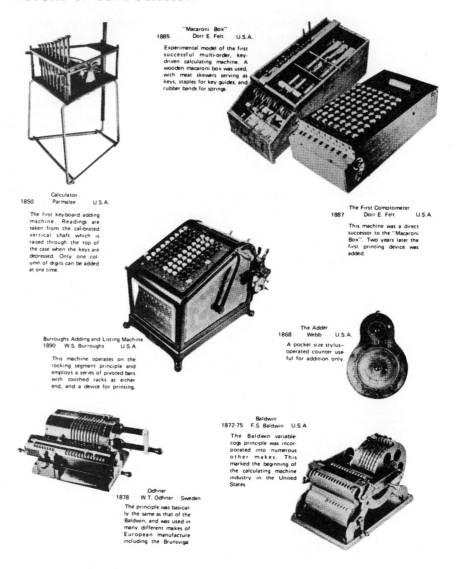

"Macaroni Box"
1885   Dorr E. Felt   U.S.A.

Experimental model of the first successful multi-order, key-driven calculating machine. A wooden macaroni box was used, with meat skewers serving as keys, staples for key guides, and rubber bands for springs.

Calculator
1850   Parmalee   U.S.A.

The first keyboard adding machine. Readings are taken from the calibrated vertical shaft which is raised through the top of the case when the keys are depressed. Only one column of digits can be added at one time.

The First Comptometer
1887   Dorr E. Felt   U.S.A.

This machine was a direct successor to the "Macaroni Box". Two years later the first printing device was added.

Burroughs Adding and Listing Machine
1890   W.S. Burroughs   U.S.A.

This machine operates on the rocking segment principle and employs a series of pivoted bars with toothed racks at either end, and a device for printing.

The Adder
1868   Webb   U.S.A.

A pocket size stylus-operated counter useful for addition only.

Baldwin
1872-75   F.S. Baldwin   U.S.A.

The Baldwin variable-cogs principle was incorporated into numerous other makes. This marked the beginning of the calculating machine industry in the United States.

Odhner
1878   W.T. Odhner   Sweden

The principle was basically the same as that of the Baldwin, and was used in many different makes of European manufacture including the Brunsviga.

Early Calculating devices. (Courtesy of IBM Corporation.)

that the Census Bureau began seeking mechanical aids for use with the 1890 census. In response to this need, Hollerith developed a tabulating device he called a census machine. The 1890 census was performed in one-third the time of the previous census, with increased accuracy. The approach worked so well that Hollerith left the Census Bureau in 1896 to form the Tabulating Machine Company to manufacture and sell his equipment. Through mergers, this company became part of International Business Machines.

AUTOMATIC COMPUTERS: GENESIS

Charles Babbage wrote the following words over 100 years ago:

At a period when the progress of physical science is obstructed by that exhausting intellectual and mental labor indispensable for its advancement . . . I think the applica-

Hollerith's census tabulator: the 1880 census took 7½ years to finish. Hollerith developed his machines to reduce the time required for the census. His machines handled cards at the rate of 50 to 80 per minute. The 1890 census was completed in 2½ years. (Courtesy of IBM Corporation.)

tion of machinery in aid of the most complicated and abstruse calculations can no longer be deemed unworthy of the attention of the country. In fact there is no reason why mental as well as bodily labor should not be economized by the aid of machinery.

Babbage was an English mathematician and inventor and is the first great pioneer in the history of the automatic computer. He not only saw the need for such a machine at a time when few people did, he saw quite clearly how it would have to operate. Furthermore, he spent a major portion of his life and personal fortune figuring out a way to build it.

Babbage never had a chance to complete his "analytical engine". People were interested—the British government gave Babbage 1500 pounds for a simpler "difference engine" which was never fully completed because of the lack of precision machining of mechanical parts.

Babbage's computer, if it had been completed, would have ranked as one of the mechanical marvels of all time: it would have been a miniature universe of wheels within wheels, a supermechanism of 50,000 wheels and gears—plus quantities, large quantities, of clutches, escapements, cams, axles, and cranks.

There is no doubt that Babbage was on the right track. When the inventor died in 1871 he left 400-500 pages of special schematic symbols, five volumes of engineering sketches, and over 400 detailed drawings. Some of this material is so complex that it still baffles curious investigators.

The engine was to include two parts: a "store" and a "mill". The store included an ingenious mechanical memory and contained the constants to be used in solving particular equations. The mill was intended to do the computational work. According to the design plans, it would receive numbers from the store, perform computations on them, and put intermediate results back into the store for future reference. Babbage also worked out a remarkably farsighted way of feeding information into the machine and furnishing a predetermined sequence of orders to be followed automatically. He did this by something that is still a familiar item in the world of twentieth-century paper work: the punched card. Punched cards evolved from an ancestor that appeared during the early violent days of the Industrial Revolution, the Jacquard loom.

Babbage does not go without public honor, however. He can claim dozens of inventions, including flat-rate postage, skeleton keys, the first text in what might be called industrial engineering (reproduced in five languages), and cow catchers for locomotives.

PRE STORED-PROGRAM YEARS

Babbage had designed his machines for the preparation of tables, a time-consuming and error-prone process. Howard Aiken of Harvard designed a machine called an Automatic Sequence-Controlled Calculator—the Mark I—for the preparation of mathematical tables by automatically performing a set sequence of arithmetic operations. The Mark I was more mechanical than electronic. The program of instructions consisted of switch settings, wired control boards, and punched paper tape. Data was represented by patterns of open and closed mechanical relays. Completed in 1944 by IBM and Harvard scientists, it was an electromechanical system using telephone-type relay switches as counters.

For many years the Mark I was thought to be the first automatic computer and only in the early 1970s did it become widely known that it was preceded by a computer that was not only automatic but electronic as well. The ABC (Atanasoff-Berry Computer) was constructed by John V. Atanasoff, a professor at Iowa State University, and Clifford Berry, a graduate student at the university. It was completed in the spring of 1942, thus predating its more widely known predecessor the ENIAC (Electronic Numerical Integrator and Calculator) by almost four years. Since more information is available about the ENIAC, we will discuss it in detail rather than its little-known but extremely significant predecessor.

The ENIAC was designed by John W. Mauchly and J. Presper Eckert of the

Babbage's difference engine: in 1812, while in the Analytical Society quarters looking at a table of logarithms full of mistakes, Babbage began to think in terms of the use of a machine capable of computing mathematical tables. After seeing a model demonstrated, the Royal Society promised to subsidize Babbage's idea for developing a full-sized machine. The British Government built a workshop for him, complete with a fireproof vault for his blueprints. However, Babbage became interested in extending his ideas. This delayed the work on his project until, in 1842, official withdrawal of government support brought the end of Babbage's project. A model of the difference engine was built for the Registrar General in 1859. It was adopted four years later by life insurance companies and was used for several years to compute actuarial tables. (Courtesy of IBM Corporation.)

Moore School of Engineering of the University of Pennsylvania. It was constructed to help break the information bottleneck produced by the need for ballistic-weapons tables during World War II. Military scientists and engineers were producing new shooting weapons—new howitzers, antiaircraft guns, and antitank guns—in all shapes and sizes. These weapons required ballistic tables indicating trajectories for many different conditions (e.g., different types of shells, wind directions, and elevations). To compute a single trajectory for one given set of conditions required about seven man-

Howard Aiken's automatic sequence-controlled calculator, the Mark I: the Mark I was electromechanical. The program consisted of switch settings, wired control boards, and punched paper tape. The Mark I was the first machine to do a long series of arithmetic and logical operations.

Selective sequence electronic calculator: the IBM SSEC was placed into operation at IBM's New York headquarters in 1948. It contained 13,000 tubes and 23,000 relays. (Courtesy of IBM Corporation.)

ENIAC: The first large-scale electronic computer was ENIAC, the electronic numerical integrator and calculator, built by Eckert and Mauchly at the University of Pennsylvania for the Ballistic Research Laboratories of the U.S. Army Ordnance Corps. The really radical aspect of ENIAC was the proposal to build a machine containing 18,000 vacuum tubes. Nothing comparable had ever been attempted. Stories are told about how all the lights in West Philadelphia would dim when ENIAC was turned on, and how the starting transient would always burn out at least three or more tubes. Yet, ENIAC was quite successful. It was dedicated at the Ballistic Research Laboratories in Aberdeen, Maryland on February 15, 1946, and was used as a productive computer until it was turned off for the last time on October 2, 1955, almost 10 years later. (Courtesy Univac Division of Sperry Rand Corporation.)

hours of work at a desk calculator. Hundreds of adding-machine operators were working day and night, grinding out calculations for ballistic tables. Even at that, human calculators could not keep up with the pace of warfare, arid weapons often went to the battlefield without tables.

ENIAC was constructed to produce the needed ballistic tables on a much faster and more accurate basis. A memorandum dated August, 1942, suggesting such a project, had been gathering dust for nearly a year when it was unearthed by a mathematician in uniform, Lt. Herman Goldstine of the Army's Ballistic Research Laboratory in Maryland. He was in Philadelphia trying to recruit more girls to operate adding machines, happened to visit friends at the Moore School, saw the memorandum, and got the project approved within two weeks. ENIAC never did become involved in war work however (it was completed about two months after Japan surrendered).

It seems desirable to bring in some of the details of the ENIAC hardware at this point. ENIAC was very bulky: it occupied 1500 square feet of floor space, weighed more than 30 tons, included miles of wire, had half a million soldered connections, and contained over 18,000 vacuum tubes. ENIAC gives us a modern fable. While it was being built, people who saw problems far more clearly than possibilities had argued that the machine would never work. They had a valid point; according to manufacturers' guarantees, vacuum tubes would last for 2500 hours. Given this figure, there was no getting around the conclusion that, in a machine with 20,000 tubes, a tube would fail every 7.5 minutes. The barrier seemed insurmountable, and if designers had taken it at its face value, we might have no computers today. In fact, by careful design and considerable quality control, Mauchly and Eckert managed to run one to two days between failures. ENIAC could perform about 5000 additions or subtractions per second. Its storage capacity was 20 10-digit numbers. (A typical computer installation in the early 1970s might have a high-speed memory capacity of a million digits.) It was not, however, a stored-program computer: it was programmed by means of switches and plug-in connections.

After ENIAC, many research laboratories, most of them connected with universities, began to construct computers. Eckert and Mauchly designed EDVAC (electronic discrete variable automatic calculator), which differed from ENIAC in two ways: the use of the binary number system and the internal storage of instructions in digital form. Because the completion of EDVAC was delayed until 1952, another computer, the EDSAC, built at Cambridge University in England, was the *first stored-program computer** (it was completed in 1949).

VON NEUMANN AND THE STORED-PROGRAM CONCEPT

Von Neuman (pronounced noi' man) was born in 1903 in Hungary. He received his Ph.D. from the University of Budapest in 1926. Von Neumann came to the United States in 1930 and was naturalized in 1937. He taught (1930-1933) at Princeton, and after 1933 was associated with the Institute for Advanced Study. In 1954, he was appointed a member of the Atomic Energy Commission. He was a founder of the mathematical theory of games, and he also made fundamental contributions to mathematical logic, quantum theory, and to the development of the atomic bomb. His development of the Mathematical Analyzer, Numerical Integrator, and Computer (MANIAC) enabled the United States to produce and test the world's first hydrogen bomb (in 1952). Von Neumann died in 1958.

One frequently hears, in the computing industry, "There's been nothing really new in machine organization since von Neumann!" It is difficult to put any subsequent improvements in the organization of computer hardware on quite as high a level as the development of the **stored-program concept.**

We do not know to whom the honor of inventing the stored-program concept belongs. It will surely stand as one of the great milestones in technological advances. It could be one of those things like the calculus that emerged simultaneously from several minds when the need and the technology met. The leading contenders for the honor are Arthur Burks, Herman Goldstine, and John von Neumann and the Mauchly and Eckert group at the University of Pennsylvania's Moore School of Engineering. Von Neumann is, regardless of the stored-program honor, definitely one of the authors of the first definitive

*See Chapter 1.

paper* on computers. The paper not only specifies the design of a stored-program computer in detail, but it correctly anticipates many of the problems that were to be encountered (as well as ingenious solutions to these problems).

The computer described in the paper was constructed and copied many times. It was variously known as the IAS, Princeton, or von Neumann machine. One version of it, built by RAND, was affectionately called JHONNIAC (over von Neumann's objections). The IAS machine now has its place in history at the Smithsonian Institution.

At the time the paper was written, the principle of automatic calculations was already established as was the great advance gained by electronics. The jump from that state of the art to the detail of the paper has been compared, by Paul Armer of RAND†, to someone jumping from constructing the system of transmitting pictures by means of a rotating scanning disk to writing a description of compatible color televison. For this reason, von Neumann is often accorded the title "father of the stored-program concept"

A reasonable definition of a **stored-program computer** would be the following:

A computer with a storage component that may contain both data to be manipulated and instructions to manipulate the data.

THE UNIVAC I

The Univac I (UNIVersal Automatic Computer) was the first commercially available computer. Until Univac I, computers were each one of a kind. The Univac I was built by the Eckert and Mauchly Computer Company, founded in 1946. The company was purchased by Remington Rand in 1949 and subsequently became the Univac division of Sperry Rand.

The first Univac computer was installed at the U.S. Bureau of the Census in 1951. The speed of technological change for computers can be appreciated by noting that only 13 years later this first Univac I was given to the Smithsonian Institution for its historical value. The first business use of a computer was in 1954 at the General Electric Appliance Park in Kentucky.

POST-UNIVAC I COMPUTERS

Computers built during the period between the Univac I and the later 1950s used vacuum tubes and are identified as **first-generation computers.** IBM, which had not been particularly active in the development of computers, entered the computer business with the IBM 701 in 1953. Late in 1954, IBM installed the first of the IBM 650 computers. This was the most popular computer during the next five years. In this period, IBM gained a dominant position in the computer field, with over two-thirds of the market. It has never lost this dominant position.

*"Preliminary Discussion of the Logical Design of an Electronic Computing Instrument". Report prepared for the Research and Development Service, Ordinance Department, U.S. Army, by the Institute for Advanced Study, Princeton University, 1946.

†*Datamation*, September 1962, p. 25. This is the first of a two-part article discussing the paper. The paper is reproduced in the two issues. The second part is in the October 1962 issue.

(a)

(b)

Univac: the first Univac I computer, part (a), was delivered on June 14, 1951. For almost five years after that it was probably the best large-scale computer available, especially for data processing applications (as opposed to scientific applications). One of its most impressive achievements was its magnetic tape system. Univac I introduced the concept of direct recording onto magnetic tape from a typewriter keyboard. The Univac I was the only computer with a mercury delay line for its memory that achieved the status of a commercial product. By 1953 it was apparent that computers could be produced that would make Univac I obsolete. In 1954 IBM announced its 705 computer. About a year later Remington Rand responded to IBM's announcement with the Univac II, part (b). Production problems forced repeated delays, and orders dwindled as customers switched to IBM's 650 and 705 computers. IBM delivered 650's in 1954 and 705's in 1955. The first Univac II was not delivered until two years later. These two years were sufficient to give IBM a lead in the large-scale commercial computer field that no manufacturer has since been able to challenge. (Photographs by permission of the Univac Division of Sperry Rand Corporation.)

Second-generation computers are characterized by the use of transistors in place of vacuum tubes. The transistor requires less power, is smaller and less expensive, and generates very little heat. Second-generation computers were smaller, required less (even no) air conditioning, and were more reliable than the first-generation machines. The most popular second-generation machines by far were IBM's small-to-medium-scale business-oriented IBM 1401 com-

First-generation computer—the IBM 650: in 1953, IBM announced a magnetic drum computer, the 650. Its drum memory could hold 2000 10-digit words of storage, IBM planned to make only fifty 650's to be sold mainly to scientific users. Instead, it produced and sold over 1000. (Courtesy of IBM Corporation.)

Second-generation computer—the IBM 1401 System: around 1960, IBM came out with the 1400 and 1600 series computers. The 1620 was a very popular small scale scientific computer until the end of the 1960s. Through the 1400 series, in particular the 1401, IBM discovered that some models of computers could be marketed by the thousands. Typical 1401 memory size was 20,000 characters. The 1401 was a decimal, character-oriented, variable-word-length computer. Memory was just a string of characters of storage, each of which was individually addressable. (Courtesy of IBM Corporation.)

puter and their scientific-oriented IBM 1620 computer. IBM's 7090-7094 dominated the large-scale computer market.

Third-generation computers are identified by integrated circuits, their orientation to data communication, and their ability to handle more than one operation simultaneously. The major transition to third-generation computers was in 1965, when IBM began deliveries of its third-generation System /360. During this same time period, Control Data Corporation (CDC) was introducing very fast scientific computers. Most of CDC's effort was

Third-generation computer—IBM 370.

Three generations of electronics: first-generation tube assemblies, such as those shown in the background, were less reliable, consumed more power and generated more heat, and were logically less powerful than the second generation transistor logic card, such as that shown in the left foreground. The integrated circuits of the third generation, shown in the right foreground, provided reliability and compactness not even dreamed of 20 years earlier. The associated reduction in power and cooling requirements has permitted the manufacture of very small computers that can be plugged in almost anywhere. (Also see the "CPU on a card" on page 103.) (Courtesy of the IBM Corporation.)

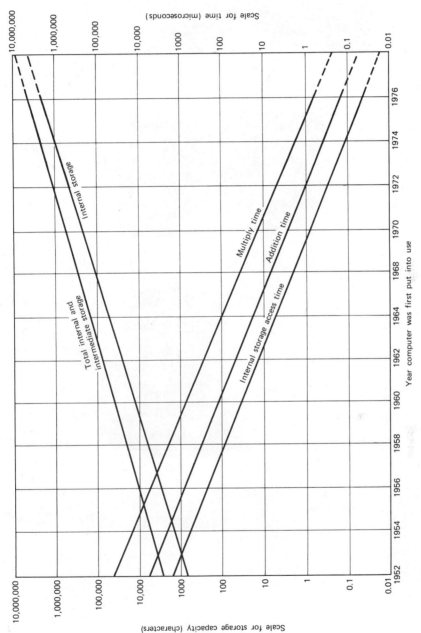

Storage capacity and speed of computers 1952–1976: note that the scale is logarithmic: that 1–100 takes the same distance as 100–1000 or 1000–10,000. It is interesting to note that the three generations do not show up in the shape of the lines. The lines shown in this figure are based on the characteristics of typical computers, and the variation for any specific time period may be substantial.

39

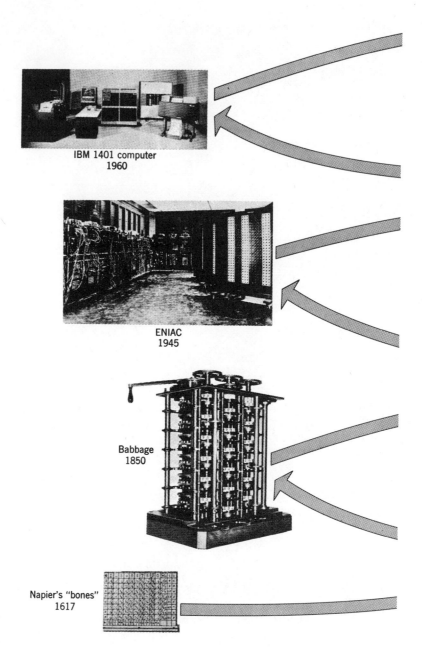

IBM 1401 computer
1960

ENIAC
1945

Babbage
1850

Napier's "bones"
1617

Computation from 1600 to the Present

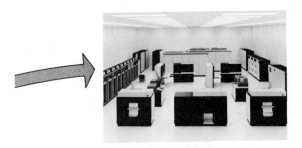

IBM 370/165
1970

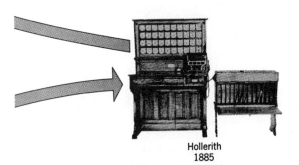

Univac I
1950

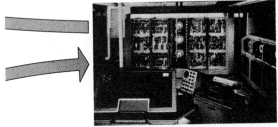

Hollerith
1885

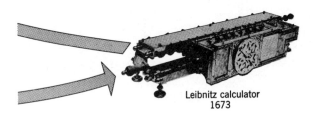

Leibnitz calculator
1673

directed at the large-scale, scientific computer market. Their CDC 3600, CDC 6400, CDC 6600, and CDC 7600 computers broke IBM's hold on that market.

The term "fourth-generation computers" has, as yet, no well-defined meaning.

The price of computers relative to performance has decreased steadily since the days of Univac I. The early market forecasts for computers stated that the United States "might" have need for as many as nine such devices. Sometime in 1970 the eighty thousandth computer was placed in operation in the United States. Almost all of these have orders of magnitude more power than the original ENIAC.

Even minicomputers priced as low or lower than most new automobiles have capabilities far exceeding the early computers. Such computers are being used extensively for special purpose applications and many computer experts view networks of minicomputers as reasonable alternatives to centralized installations with a single large computer. Such a change in the nature of computing systems could have a profound effect on the computing industry, perhaps finally altering the dominant position of IBM in the industry.

AN ASIDE ON IBM

Except for the early Univac I days, IBM has been the dominant manufacturer of computing equipment. Under the direction of T.J. Watson, Sr. and, subsequently, T.J. Watson, Jr., IBM developed a hold on the computer market that has at times seemed monopolistic. Although hardware developments contributed greatly to the success of IBM, the development of a very effective sales force and solid technical groups were also important factors. The Watson's exercised a remarkable motivating force on their personnel and most people have become aware of some of the techniques employed. The "THINK" signs that abounded within the corporation were probably the most well known of these techniques and have been the subject of many parodies. One of the most humorous is a conversation from Michael Frayn's The Tin Men* in which R. V., the chairman of the board of a British television company, is speaking to an underling called Sir Prestwick Wining:

Once he had said to Sir Prestwick, "If I were asked to put my advice to a young man in one word, Prestwick, do you know what that word would be?"
"No?" Sir Prestwick had said.
" 'Think,' Prestwick, 'Think.' "
"I don't know, R. V. 'Detail'?"
"No, Prestwick, 'Think'."
"Er. 'Courage'?"
"No. 'Think.' "
"I give up, R. V. 'Boldness'?"
"For heaven's sake, Prestwick, what is the matter with you? 'Think'!"
" 'Integrity'? 'Loyalty'? 'Leadership?'
" 'Think,' Prestwick! 'Think,' 'Think,' 'Think,' 'Think'!"

*The Tin Men, Boston, Mass.: Little Brown & Co. Copyright 1965 by Michael Frayn.

A short review of the history of hardware

Prehistoric man
Counts on fingers and toes (frequent use of base 10 and 20 as well as subbase 5), hence the origin of the word "digit" referring to number. One-to-one correspondence between strokes in the sand or pebbles in a heap; introduced when number of material possessions exceeded number of fingers and toes.

ca. 1500 B.C.
Greece—a box or sand tray used to hold pebbles for counting.
Orient—beads strung for counting—origin of abacus.
England—Stonehenge: a giant astronomical computer.

1617—John Napier
Napier's rods or Napier's bones—used for mechanically multiplying, dividing, and taking square roots. Published *A Description of the Wonderful World of Logarithms in 1641.*

1642—Blaise Pascal
Invented a device with 10 numbered wheels and a series of gears similar to today's adding machines—used to add and subtract by turning crank.

1673—Gottfried Liebniz
Modified Pascal's ideas into a gear-driven machine that added, subtracted, multiplied, divided, and extracted roots.

1804—Joseph Marie Jacquard
Introduced the automatic loom, the forerunner of modern day automation.

1812—Charles Babbage
Started work on the first of his two machines, the difference engine and the analytical engine. All twentieth-century computers incorporate parts of Babbage's design.

1875—Frank Stephen Baldwin
Granted first U.S. patent for a practical calculating machine that could perform the four fundamental arithmetic operations.

1885—Herman Hollerith
Developed tabulating equipment for use with punched cards to facilitate the 1890 U.S. Census.

1933—Dr. Vannevar Bush
Developed analog machine that was electromechanical (used gears but powered by electricity), as distinguished from today's electronic (no moving parts) machines,

1940-1942—Dr. John V. Atanasoff and Clifford Berry
Built the ABC (Atanasoff-Berry Computer), the first automatic electronic computer.

1939-1944—Dr. Howard Aiken
Built the Mark I or automatic sequence-controlled calculator that was used in the Manhattan Project. Programming was controlled by hand-operated switches, instructions were fed in by a paper tape similar to a player piano roll, and there was a storage unit for numerical data. The console measured 51 × 8 × 6 feet and weighed five tons.

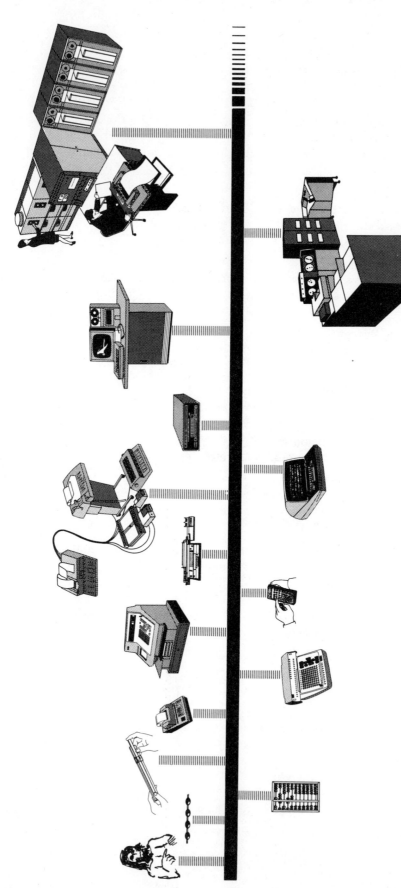

Computational continuum: product announcements now fall onto almost every part of a line drawn from simple calculating devices through our most sophisticated computers. Recent availability of electronic calculators of increasing capabilities and of mini-and midicomputers has filled in the center part of the continuum. In general, the cost of purchasing the device goes up as one goes from left to right, but the cost of a single computation goes down as you go that same direction. This evidences **Grosch's law** (law power of a computer is proportional to the square of the cost). Thus, if one machine costs wtice as much as another, you could expect it to be roughly four times as powerful.

44

1945—Dr. John Mauchley and Dr. J. Presper Eckert
Built ENIAC (Electronic Numerical Integrator and Calculator). It had 18,000 vacuum tubes and was programmed by wiring a board that was then plugged into the machine.

1946—John von Neumann
Coauthor of a definitive paper on the stored-program concept.

1949
EDSAC, the first stored-program computer, built at Cambridge University in England.

1946-1950
Sixty computers built; no two alike.

1950
Univac I, the first assembly-line produced computer (45 built).

1966
Fifteen thousand computers in operation.

1970
Eighty thousand computers in operation.

SOFTWARE: A SHORT HISTORY

The "history" of software must remain brief; it is, at most, a history of a 25-year period. The development of software was a very important advance in computation. Without the often large, bulky, and inefficient compilers and problem-oriented systems, computers would be available only to the high priests of the profession. Software systems brought the computer to almost anyone that was interested.

The first software systems were probably packages of machine language subroutines, since, as Rosen* observes, subroutines were even in use on the preelectronic Mark I. Such subroutine packages made programming more convenient by providing a source of "canned" programs for input/output and common numerical calculations such as the evalution of trigonometric functions.

Subsequent software developments were more and more concerned with the development of more convenient programming languages. In order to facilitate software developments of this nature, programming groups were developed. The first group of this kind associated with a commercial computer effort was directed by Dr. Grace Hopper and was concerned with software development for the Univac machines. In the early 1950s this group and others began to push forward on the development of algorithmic languages.

The development of algorithmic languages and operating systems became intense in the late 1950s and, although there have been occasional fears that such software separates the user too greatly from the machine, the overall effect has been quite beneficial. That is, software has enhanced and magnified the value of the hardware. Today, the importance of software can be gauged by observing that the cost of software development can equal or surpass the cost of developing hardware of a machine.

*S. Rosen, "Programming Systems and Languages—A Historical Survey." *Programming Systems and Languages.* New York: McGraw-Hill, 1967.

Three programming languages have been particularly important, so we will review their development in some detail. The details about FORTRAN and ALGOL development were taken from an article by Saul Rosen*, and the details of the COBOL development were obtained from Rosen and a text by Jean Sammett†.

FORTRAN

IBM, in parallel with its development of the 704 computer's hardware, set up a project headed by John Backus to develop a compiler for the new computer. After the expenditure of about 25 man-years of effort, they produced the first version of FORTRAN. FORTRAN stands for FORmula TRANslating system. It is, in many ways, the most important and most impressive development in the early history of automatic programming.

Like most of the early hardware and software systems, FORTRAN was late in delivery, and didn't really work when it was delivered to the users. At first, many people thought it would never be completed. Then, when it was in field test, with many bugs, many thought it would never work. It gradually got to the point where a FORTRAN program had a reasonable chance of working correctly. Most languages went through this gradual change of status from an experiment to a working system. It is stressed here only because FORTRAN and other standard languages are now almost taken for granted.

It was the development of FORTRAN II that made possible the use of FORTRAN for large problems. FORTRAN II permitted a program to be broken down into subprograms that could be treated and debugged separately. With FORTRAN II in full operation, the use of FORTRAN spread very rapidly.

In May 1962, the ASA FORTRAN Committee to develop an American Standard FORTRAN was formed and eventually produced two standards, known officially as FORTRAN and BASIC FORTRAN, which correspond roughly to FORTRAN IV and FORTRAN II, respectively.

ALGOL

Until the 1960s, large-scale computers were mainly an American phenomenon. However, smaller computers were in use in other parts of the world right from the beginning. An active computer organization, GAMM‡, had been set up in Europe, and in 1957 a number of members of this organization were actively interested in the design of algorithmic languages. They decided to try to reach agreement on a common language for their various computers, and made considerable progress toward the design of such a language. There are many obvious advantages to having generally accepted computer-independent problem-oriented languages. The president of GAMM wrote a letter to the Association for Computing Machinery, suggesting that represen-

*S. Rosen, "Programming Systems and Languages—A Historical Survey". *Programming Systems and Languages*. New York: McGraw-Hill, 1967.

†J.E. Sammett, *Programming Languages: History & Fundamentals*. Englewood Cliffs, N.J.: Prentice-Hall, 1969.

‡Gesellschaft Für Augewandte Mathematik und Mechanik.

tatives of ACM and of GAMM meet together to specify an international language for the description of computing procedures. The meeting of the ACM and GAMM subcommittees was held in 1958, and the result was a preliminary report on an International Algebraic Language, which has since become popularly known as ALGOL; ALGOL stands for ALGOrithmic Language.

ALGOL compilers have been written for many different computers, but, with the exception of Burroughs, no computer manufacturer has pushed ALGOL strongly. It is, however, popular among university and mathematically oriented computer people, especially in Europe. In the United States it is mainly used for pedagogical purposes and the communication of algorithms.

It should be noted that ALGOL was the first language to have a precisely defined syntax. This and other significant features of ALGOL have had a substantial effect on programming language development.

COBOL

The largest user of data processing equipment is the U. S. government. The government must, of course, avoid giving preferential treatment to any one computer manufacturer. More than any other computer user, the government has been plagued by the problems caused by the lack of compatibility among different kinds of computing equipment.

In 1959, a meeting was called in the Pentagon by the Department of Defense. About 40 representatives from users, government installations, computer manufacturers, and other interested parties were present. There was almost unanimous agreement that it was both desirable and feasible to establish a common language for business data processing. Further, they established committees that produced a report giving a framework on which a common business language could be built. The name COBOL, which suggests a COmmon Business-Oriented Language, was adopted.

In January 1960, the report was accepted and approved. The report was published by the Government Printing Office in April 1960.

Perhaps the most significant aspect of this effort is that it was the first attempt to have a group of competitors work together with the objective of developing a language that would be usable on computers from each of the manufacturers. This was particularly significant because many manufacturers had already begun work on developing their own business-oriented languages, and these developments had to be eliminated or subordinated to the results of the joint effort.

The deluge

Somewhere between 150 and 300 fairly major computer languages are in use. ALGOL, PL /I, FORTRAN, and COBOL are the most popular, probably in the reverse order. Jean Sammet describes 120 of them in her *Programming Languages.** She also quotes *Genesis XI,* 6–9:

*J.E. Sammet, *Programming Languages: History & Fundamentals.* Englewood Cliffs, N.J.: Prentice-Hall, 1969.

And the LORD said, Behold, the people is one, and they have all one language; and this they begin to do:and now nothing will be restrained from them, which they have imagined to do.

Go to, let us go down, and there confound their language, that they may not understand one another's speech.

So the LORD scattered them abroad from thence upon the face of all the earth: and they left off to build the city.

Therefore is the name of it called Babel; because the LORD did there confound the language of all the earth: and from thence did the LORD scatter them abroad upon the face of all the earth.

EXERCISES

1. Look into the history of counting. There are many books that consider the history of number theory. Chapter 1 of Ore's *Number Theory and Its History** gives a good brief account of counting and the recording of numbers whereas a deeper treatment can be found in Menninger's *Number Words and Number Symbols: A Cultural History of Numbers.* †Report on an aspect of the history of counting that interests you.

2. Look up "Industrial Revolution" in an encyclopedia and determine the impact of the automatic loom. Was Jacquard's loom part of England's Industrial Revolution? Why not?

3. Look at Jean Sammet's *Programming Languages: History and Fundamentals*‡ for the development of at least one language such as COBOL, ALGOL, or FORTRAN. Give a summary of the development.

4. One of the most recent hardware advances is microprogramming. What is it? Trade journals (e.g., *Datamation, Computers and Automation*) or the *Communications of the Association for Computing Machinery* can be used to obtain an answer. (See the Bibliography in Chapter 1 for a list of periodicals.)

5. One area not treated in this text is the history of corporations in the computing industry. Using references such as those suggested in Chapter 1's Bibliography, report on the history of one of the more prominent computer manufacturers.

6. Using the references given in the first part of the chapter, report on the history of automatons. Include comments on the development of automatons vis-à-vis mechanistic philosophy.

BIBLIOGRAPHY

Bernstein, J. *The Analytical Engine: Computers—Past, Present, and Future.* New York: Random House, 1963. 113 pp.

A pleasant survey of the history of computers including a philosophical discussion on the future of computers and computing.

*O. Ore, *Number Theory and Its History.* New York: McGraw-Hill, 1948

†Menninger, *Number Words and Number Symbols: A Cultural History of Numbers.* Cambridge, Mass.: M.I.T. Press, 1969.

‡J. Sammet, *Programming Languages: History and Fundamentals,* Englewood Cliffs, N.J., Prentice-Hall, 1969.

Goldstine, H. H. *The Computer: from Pascal to von Neuman.* Princeton, N.J.: Princeton University Press, 1972. 378 pp.

> Written by a co-worker of von Neumann, this book combines history and scientific autobiography in an account of the development of the computer from early efforts in the seventeenth century to the postwar developments at the Institute for Advanced Study.

Harmon, M. *Stretching Man's Mind: A History of Data Processing.* New York: Petrocelli, 1975. 239 pp.

> The history of data processing from the earliest inventors through Babbage and modern technical developments. The philosophical aspects of computers, program processing, binary coding, memory, symbolic languages, and the future of computer technology are also discussed.

Hawkins, G. *Stonehenge Decoded.* Garden City, N.Y.: Doubleday, 1965, 202 pp.

> An intriguing account of the development of evidence that "Stonehenge was a sophisticated and brilliantly conceived astronomical observatory, used by three different groups of people over a 400-year period beginning around 1900 B.C.".

Menninger, K. *Number Words and Number Symbols: A Cultural Hstory of Numbers.* Cambridge, Mass.: M.I.T. Press, 1969. 480 pp.

> A scholarly, extensive, and very interesting work on the history of number systems and "how they reflect the cultural 'style' of their makers and users". It includes an excellent discussion of different counting devices, including the abacus, and an interesting section on finger counting.

Ore, O. *Number Theory and Its History.* New York: McGraw-Hill, 1948. 370 pp.

> This text is primarily an introduction to the theory of numbers, but contains a history of counting and recording of numbers in the first chapter.

Rosen, S. *A Quarter Century View.* New York: Association for Computing Machinery, 1971. 64 pp.

> A special edition originally presented to guests at the dinner commemorating the twenty-fifth anniversary of computing at ACM 71. Covers history from 1946 and includes over 100 illustrations. This is a very informative and attractive publication.

Rosen, S. (ed.). *Programming Systems and Languages.* New York: McGraw-Hill, 1967. 734 pp.

> Five parts include a historical survey, an introduction to FORTRAN, ALGOL, COBOL, and NPL, an introduction to compiling and translating, list processing languages, and operating systems.

Rosenberg, J. M. *Computer Prophets.* New York: Macmillan, 1969. 192 pp.

> Brief biographies of 14 key individuals who contributed to the development of the computer, beginning with Blaise Pascal in the seventeenth century.

Sammet, J. E. *Programming Languages: History and Fundamentals.* Englewood Cliffs, N.J.: Prentice-Hall, 1969. 785 pp.

> A survey and reference guide to computer programming languages. Includes extensive bibliography.

Schultz, C. (ed.). *H. P. Luhn: Pioneer of Information Science/Selected Works.* New York: Spartan, 1968. 320 pp.

> Contains four biographical notes, and 30 publications of H. P. Luhn, emphasizing his work as an information scientist from 1948 to 1964.

Shorter, E. *The Historian and the Computer.* Englewood Cliffs, N.J.: Prentice-Hall, 1971. 149 pp.

> Describes the role of the computer in the study of history and presents historical data on computing.

4. Computer applications

Historically computer applications have been divided into two areas: scientific and business applications. Only by historical accident did the scientific uses of computers get ahead of business and other nonnumerical applications. The modern computer, as we saw in Chapter 3, came into being during war times. It was first used for mathematical applications in connection with the war effort. This historical accident has left the quite false impression with some people that computers are just mathematical devices. While the computer is especially adapted to numerical computations, its nonnumeric capabilities are the most promising for future applications of computers.

The present state of the art of computers is such that many varied applications exist, and more are appearing every day. We have reached a point where the old classification scheme appears to be somewhat antiquated: it is just not possible to classify all military, industrial, educational, health related, and decision-making uses of computers as scientific or business applications. The old distinction is important, however, because it is still used by many people and has considerable validity under certain circumstances.

We will discuss a few typical applications beginning with those of more scientific nature and drifting toward those which are more business-oriented. Then the breadth of computer applications will be indicated by a fairly extensive listing of application areas.

SIMPLE DATA EDITING

Let us consider an application where we require a computer to accept temperature readings from a remote thermometer and record the temperature on the printer (this could be a remote sensing of, say, ground temperature in an agricultural application). Because of the possibility of information-transmission errors, false measurements, and other possible failures, we will have the computer examine its input data and reject any obviously erroneous data. Our system might look like Figure 4.1

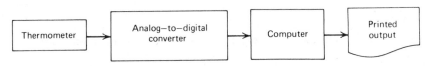

Figure 4.1 Temperature-recording system.

The **analog-to-digital converter** in the figure is a piece of hardware that can convert the analog output of the thermometer to digital form that is acceptable to the computer. Typical analog-to-digital converters cost from $400 to $2500 and are accurate to about three or four decimal places.

How do we program the computer to reject the obviously bad data items? First we have to formulate a solution—we have to design an algorithm to enable us to detect the bad data items. This is often one of the first steps in formulating an algorithm: define all relevant terms. After we have formulated an algorithm, we formalize the solution by flowcharting it. Certainly, one test we can use is reasonableness of adjacent data items. If the reported temperature changes from the previous reading by more than some predefined amount we could reject the new reading as invalid. Another test is reasonableness on an absolute scale: to see if the reported temperature is within expected bounds (e.g., −20 to +130°F). Values that do not pass these tests can be rejected as invalid. (We will consider the more general case of data editing later.) This is a fairly crude algorithm, but it should meet our needs, and it has the advantage of simplicity. The algorithm can be formalized by flowcharting it as shown in Figure 4.2.

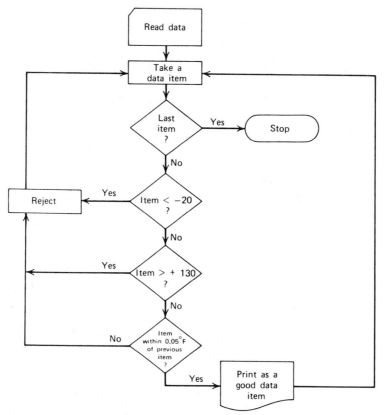

Figure 4.2   An algorithm to reject bad temperature data items.

DATA SMOOTHING

Let us consider a problem that is typical of a large class of scientific applications. In Figure 4.3 the radar is a distance-measuring unit capable of tracking the flight of a missile. It sends the coordinates of the missile to the computer several times each second. The **communication link** could be telephone lines, radio, or any of several other information-transmission mechanisms.

Note that Figure 4.3 is a system flowchart. Flowcharts of programs are quite similar (though different symbols are often used for each). The idea in a system flowchart is to give the viewer a high-level view of system operation (highlighting data flow rather than data manipulation processes). The com-

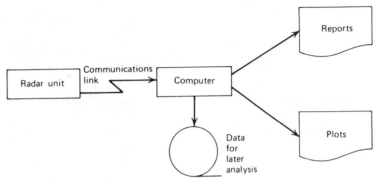

Figure 4.3   Simple missile-tracking system.

puter receives the information from the radar and stores it on one or more reels

of magnetic tape (the symbol ◯ is the specialized flowchart symbol for

magnetic tape just as the symbol ▭ is the specialized flowchart symbol

for card input /output). Either at the same time or at a later time, the computer produces various reports showing the missile's position in space at each instant of time and its speed and acceleration. The computer may also be used to plot graphs of the missile's course, performance, or other relevant items.

We are going to discuss and see examples of both plots and magnetic tape later. For now, let's consider a problem that plagues scientists in almost all fields: bad and missing data. In any communication system, such as our radar-to-computer link in Figure 4.3, signals transmitted at one end can become garbled by the time they are received at the other end (since we often get "trouble on the cable" messages on television, this should be a familiar problem). The cause can be from any of a number of sources: component failure in the communication link, noise from nearby equipment, atmospheric noise (e.g., lightning, or, especially with radio links, noise from the sun), and the like. This can cause data to be transmitted incorrectly or not at all. Furthermore, the radar may not keep perfect track of the missile, and data may be lost for up to several seconds.

Let us assume that a particular missile had a course as shown in Figure 4.4. This is the data received from the radar unit. It is often called **raw data,** or **unprocessed data.** Especially in applications involving graphic data representation, raw data is frequently called **unsmoothed data.** The data points numbered 1, 3, and 5 look quite suspicious and we seem to have lost the missile from time 6 to time 7. Obviously bad data points can be removed and approximations made for missing data points. These techniques are called **data smoothing** and are usually rather mathematically sophisticated. However, we can look at a fairly simple technique that would work in many cases and to a certain degree in most cases. Note that we have two problems: (a) detecting bad data points and approximating the correct value, and (b) replacing missing data with reasonable approximations. A simple means of detecting bad data would be to have missile specialists specify a maximum number of feet the missile should climb or fall in one unit of time. We could then subtract each altitude value from the adjacent ones and see if any of the resulting differences exceeded our maximum-altitude-change parameter. If it did, we would discard it.

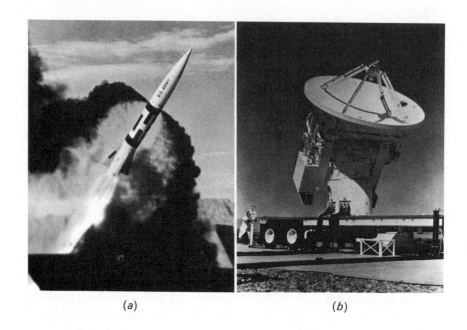

(a)   (b)

(c)

(a) Lance missile: computers are used both in the design and testing of missiles and in navigating missiles. (U.S. Army photograph.)

(b) Missile-tracking radar: this mobile instrumentation radar's data is "piped" into the missile range's real-time computer operations for continuous surveillance of missiles in flight and for later data analysis required by missile designers. (U.S. Army photograph.)

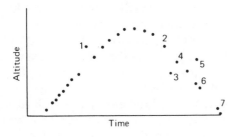

Figure 4.4 Unsmoothed data.

We can replace deleted data points or missing data points by the average value of the adjacent data points that are present. This particular solution is quite crude when compared with the techniques actually used in data smoothing. It consists, essentially, of drawing a straight line between two good points and **interpolating** a value midway between them. This is called **first-degree interpolation.** There are corresponding higher orders of interpolation that produce better values for missing data points. For example, a fifth-degree interpolation produces quite usable data points for missile flights. Details on such techniques can be obtained from texts on numerical analysis such as are listed in the Bibliography.

DATA FILES AND FILE SECURITY

Let us now look at some less scientific applications. One feature that characterizes most nonscientific applications is large to very large data collections. Before we can discuss applications such as these, we need to develop some familiarity with the techniques used to store and manage these massive collections of information. As you can imagine, attempting to store large amounts of data on cards is quite awkward. There are several disadvantages. Cards are bulky and need a special temperature and humidity controlled environment to prevent them from warping. Cards can be read at the fastest at about 2000 cards per minute. (This is quite slow by comparison to other media.) Finally, data stored on a punched card cannot be modified without repunching the card.

To get around these problems, we can store large amounts of data in the computer's secondary storage. **Secondary storage** is a magnetic tape or magnetic disk (or other bulk storage device such as a cell or drum). Blocks of

---

(c) Mission control: the control room in the Range Control Center at the White Sands Missile Range in New Mexico is the nerve center of the national missile range. It is here that data is received from the various instrumentations throughout the range. Here, technicians monitor the missile flight for safety, the missile's flight path is charted, and its inflight behavior is recorded. Scientific data on each test is channeled into the center, recorded, processed, and compiled into a complete report for use in evaluating the individual tests. The three panels in the background on the left are computer-controlled plotters. The range safety officer can observe the missile's predicted impact point from the beginning to the end of the mission. Destruct requests generated by the computer when the missile's projected impact is in a populated area can be approved or vetoed by the safety officer. (U.S. Army photograph.)

data stored in secondary storage are called **data files** and have **data file names.** For example, we could store data containing names of employees, salary information, number of deductions, and so on, as a data file named PAYROLL.

Once a data file is stored in secondary storage, several questions arise: What security does the file have? What protection does the file have from either intentional or accidental damage? Files can be created on most computers so that certain **passwords** known only to the file creator will permit access to the file. There are several things one might want to do to a file: read it, write more information into it, rewrite some old information, or delete the entire file from the computer's secondary storage. It is possible that each level of file action might have a different password. Thus, an entire class could be permitted to read a grade file but only the grader could be permitted to modify the file and only the course instructor could be permitted to delete the file. Passwords are used to gain access to **secure files** and this topic is often referred to as **file security** or **data security.**

File protection refers to the means used to prevent secure or nonsecure files from being damaged intentionally or by accident. One of the simplest and most effective means of providing the file protection is to make a **backup** copy of the file each time it is changed and to keep the backup copies in a safe place. (Backup techniques are discussed in more detail later in this chapter in the section Master Files.) There are quite a few mechanisms that are used to provide file protection. When file protection is defined as above, it is a very loose definition. In fact, there are both **hardware-protection** and **software-protection** devices and systems in use. Hardware protection refers to something such as a switch that must be manually activated before a file can be accessed or a tape "write ring", a plastic plug that must be inserted into a reel of magnetic tape before it can be written on. It is difficult to separate software protection from file security, since most file security is software based. An example of software file protection is a file with an **expiration date.** Expiration dates specify the date after which a file may be modified or deleted. Attempts to change or erase such a software-protected file prior to that date will result in an error, and the file will remain unaltered.

CODING, DATA EDITING, AND THE DATA-BASE CONCEPT

Earlier in this chapter we discussed computer smoothing of raw data. This is a similar application: we want to consider "screening" other than scientific data. The effort of ensuring that all data values in a nonscientific data file are reasonable is called **data editing.**

In general, information is represented by a code rather than by the actual information whenever a substantial savings in storage space can be effected without too much of a loss in convenience. For example, sex might be coded as M or F rather than as "male" or "female". For several technical reasons (e.g., they consume less space and may be used directly to address data structures) codes are often numeric. Thus, sex could be coded as 1 and 2 for male and female, respectively (or, to show lack of male chauvinism, 1 for female, and 2 for male).

Whatever coding scheme you finally use, the codes as well as other information items, should be edited for reasonableness. Figure 4.5 shows part of an algorithm for editing a name.

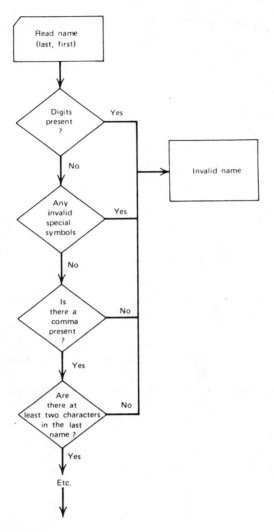

Figure 4.5

There are obviously degrees of data editing. Names could be rather exhaustively tested. For example, you could check for suspicious letter pairs, such as xj. This might require some research to determine which letter pairs occur infrequently or not at all. Names containing such pairs could then be noted as suspicious spellings and require some human verification before acceptance.

This brings us to the topic of systems design for the first time. **Systems design** is a discipline concerned with proper design of a program or system of programs. For example, if a program had room for only two digits to print age, it is possible that a system design flaw might exist: there are quite a few people that have three-digit ages. Similarly, if a payroll system designer allowed for only up to $9999.99 to be paid at any one time, it would become impossible to pay someone his annual salary or a large bonus or commission with the payroll program, though it could probably handle all monthly paychecks (though not even that for a man making over $120,000 per year).

Since it is very important, we will cover design topics as we go through the examples. *Poor systems design is the major cause of man-computer conflicts.*

Once a raw data file has been edited and corrections have been introduced, the file can be used to build a reliable data file. This introduces the symbol

which is used to represent a disk data file. Once we have very few errors in a data file, we can begin to talk of having a data base. A **data base** is a relatively error-free set of data, usually stored in secondary storage. An **adequate** data base is a data base containing all the information necessary for some particular application. For example, to omit date of employment from a payroll file could prevent that file from being an adequate data base for general personnel applications. The system designer is expected to specify data file contents so that the data file will serve as an adequate data base for all anticipated use. Failure to do an adequate system design can be very costly: it is a lot easier to add one inch to the width of a car while it is on the designer's drawing board than after it comes off the assembly line. The same is true of the collection of information, its editing, and its insertion into the data base (Figure 4.6). Not only can the collection of information be expensive, but the conversion of that information into machine-readable form is often the most expensive step in a data processing effort.

Data editing can play a role in helping to ensure that invalid data and human errors do not have the chance to harm people. For example, before entering a "bad risk" indication in an individual's loan file in a bank's data base, a check could be made to see if the person originating the request is one of, say, the bank's four loan officers or the credit-and-collections officer. It could be a keypunch error in a name-and-address change for the same individual.

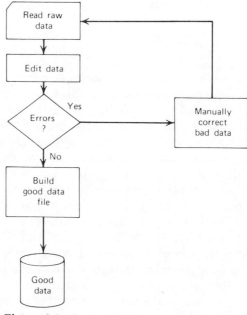

Figure 4.6

DATA COLLECTION

There are many ways to collect information. We saw one of these at the beginning of this chapter. The data was collected **directly** (from the thermometer). This is called **on-line data collection** or **real-time data collection**. An example of a still-direct but now **off-line data collection** would be a cash register that punched paper tape that was later read by a computer (Figure 4.7). Whether it is **on line** (connected to a computer) or **off line** (not connected to a computer), direct data collection usually eliminates the expensive conversion process required to get the raw data in machine-readable form.

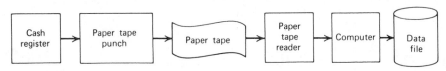

Figure 4.7

Another frequently encountered approach to direct, off-line data collection is to use an optical scanner. **Optical scanners** cover a wide range of capabilities—from being able to detect the presence or absence of a mark (called **mark sensing**) through being able to read standard type fonts to being able to read hand-printed characters (called **optical character recognition** or **OCR**).

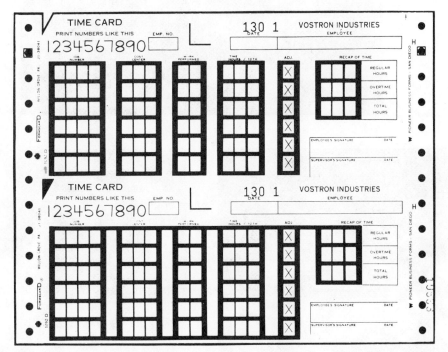

OCR employee time cards: the cards can be preprinted and prepunched with employee identification and date. Employees fill out the card with handwritten characters. The cards can then be read by an OCR input device without being keypunched.

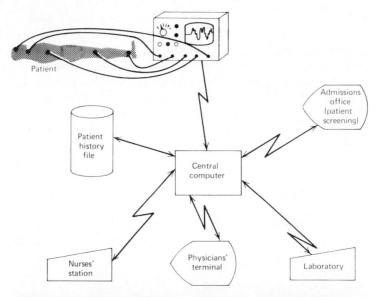

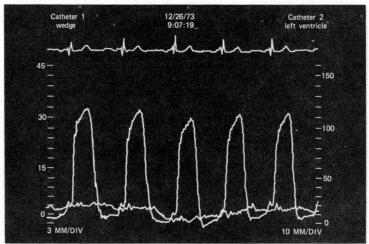

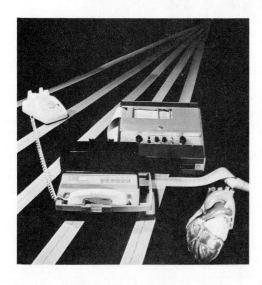

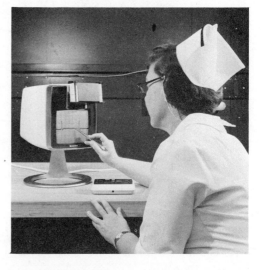

In contrast to direct data collection we will call the remaining techniques "indirect". The term "indirect" is not used very often; in general the remaining techniques are seldom discussed collectively—each just being discussed by its own name. The indirect data collection techniques differ only in conversion method used to get the collected information from some source document (e.g., sales slip, traffic ticket, inventory sheet) into machine-readable form (e.g., punched cards, magnetic tape). Available conversion methods include punching the data onto cards (the most common) or paper tape, keying it onto a magnetic surface such as a reel of magnetic tape or a disk, and keying it directly into a computer. The first two methods are off line and the third is on line.

Let us look at these approaches to getting raw data into a computer-readable form and assess some of their strengths and weaknesses (see Figure 4.8). In general, we would like to use direct, on-line data collection all the time, it certainly has fewer problems and more desirable features than any of the other three methods. However, it is often prohibitively expensive and sometimes the process from which data is being collected does not lend itself well to such

---

The primary features of a computer, speed and accuracy (and, increasingly, reliability), make it well suited for intensive-care patient monitoring and routine diagnosis. It is only logical that, once in the hospital, the computer be used for other applications for which it is well suited (e.g., patient history). The system in the upper-left diagram is found in increasing numbers of hospitals. For example, Beehive Medical's system can perform intensive care monitoring, patient screening, electrocardiogram (ECG) interpretation, pulmonary analysis, patient history, and blood gas analysis functions. The intensive care monitoring system calculates various physiological parameters, allows keyboard entry of other parameters and of physicians and nurses comments, all of which are retained in the patients' disk files. All the data gathered on a patient can be recalled via terminals, so the physician can easily review the patient's progress over time and evaluate treatments. The ECG monitoring section examines every heartbeat for each patient around the clock. Special alarms are given for life-threatening arrhythmias, such as ventricular tachycardia. Respiratory parameters such as respiration rate, airway resistance, tidal volume, pulmonary compliance, and respiratory quotient can be monitored. The keyboard entry parameters include the vital signs not monitored automatccally and other items commonly found on nurses' reports. All data, whether automatically monitored or entered by doctors or nurses via the terminal keyboard, is retained in the patient's file. Data can be retrieved to display the latest measurement of each parameter, for trend displays and for printed reports. The trend displays of a selected parameter are bar graphs for a seven-hour period. The most recent seven hours are displayed first, earlier data is trended with each button depression. Treatment indicators are displayed with the trends so the physician can easily observe the correlation between the treatments and change in the patients condition. The area of ECG analysis by computer is receiving a lot of attention by computer scientists (especially the artificial intelligence people—the accurate recognition of ECG pathologies is a very complex algorithmic task). The Beehive Medical system recognizes normal and 32 abnormal conditions. The bottom two photographs show some of Bell Laboratories' contributions to patient monitoring. Distance need no longer be a factor in the diagnosis of electrocardiograms. If the local physician is not adequately trained in the interpretation of a specific ECG, he can dial a specialist, in a distant city if necessary, and transmit the electrocardiogram while it is being taken in the patient's home or the physician's office. The specialist's analysis can be augmented by computer analyses. (Photographs courtesy Bell Laboratories. Description of Beehive Medical computer system courtesy Beehive Medical Electronics, Inc.)

	Direct	"Indirect"	Comments
On–line	Point–of–sales "magic wand" cash register	Airlines reservation terminal	Can provide immediate error indication to operator, expensive
Off–line	Paper tape punch connected to a cash register	Sales slip which is keypunched onto cards	Low cost, doesn't tie up computer or com— munication lines
Comments	Low error rate, greatly simplified control procedures, expensive	Low cost, substantial error rate and concurrent **control problems, employs** people instead of machines	

Figure 4.8 Data collection techniques—examples and characteristics.

collection methods (e.g., until we can process speech well, an author using a computer for text editing is forced to use an indirect means of getting his material into computer-readable form).

Rather than have each program edit input data, most data processing systems are designed to have one editing program to find all errors and build the data base. Other programs can then assume error-free input. Figure 4.9 represents the steps, following its design, required in constructing a typical data base and using it. As you can see from the double-headed arrows on Program 2, some programs may modify the main data base, generate new files, reference other new or old files, and so on.

MASTER FILES

The main data file in a data processing system is often called the **master file.** When one master file is read, updated, and a new master file written, we call it **father-son processing.** Similarly in **grandfather processing** we always have three files to fall back on—the father and son files from an update run and the master file from which the father file was made. This is a common means of obtaining file backup. The system diagrammed in Figure 4.10 is as good as or superior to grandfather processing, since any number of back up files may be retained. It should be noted that the update information (typically called **transactions**) must also be retained, or the backup would be out of date should it have to be used. Storage of disks is substantially more expensive than storage of tapes and, for this reason, the backup of the master file would probably be placed on magnetic tape.

MANAGEMENT INFORMATION SYSTEMS

Decision making, to be useful, has to be supported by an information base. In a competitive business environment, an information data base is often quite difficult to build and to maintain. Some of the problems encountered are:

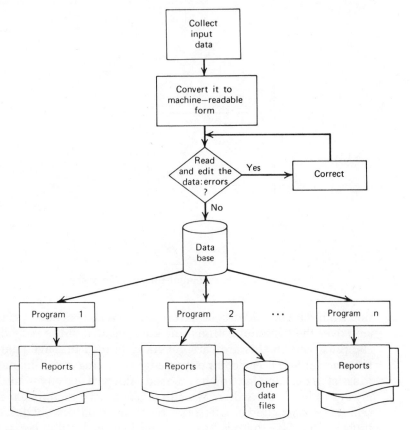

Figure 4.9

difficulty in obtaining information, the rate of change of information, and the confidentiality of information stored in the data base.

A diagram of such a decision-supporting data base is given in Figure 4.11. In order to make the system usable, several additions would be necessary. For example, in order to make sure only your own sources are entering informa-

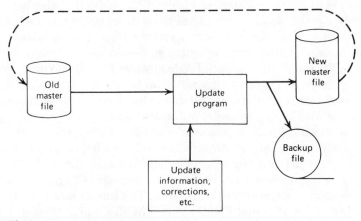

Figure 4.10

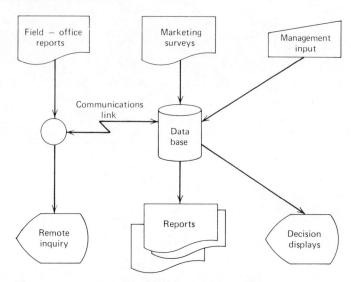

Figure 4.11   Management information system.

tion from remote field offices, information can be encoded prior to transmission over the communications link and decoded at the receiving end.

Applications in this area are generally termed **management information systems** (or **MIS**). The competitive edge of having a well-managed data base to assist in decision making has caused a flurry of activity in the MIS area, not always to the good, either. More than a few corporations have nonworking MIS skeletons in their closets, often resulting in millions of dollars of loss. It is probably the case that we have just reached the level of computer expertise where large-scale MIS is possible. We are beginning to discuss "total MIS", meaning the availability of all corporate data in some meaningfully usable form. While there are certainly only a handful of large corporations that currently have anything approximating total MIS, it does seem to be destined to be here to stay. As systems become more and more complex, correspondingly more information is required to be able to manage them. As the consequences of poor management of complex systems (e.g., ecological systems) become apparent, we see that we can afford to invest a lot in MIS if it will improve our management judgement.

Let us consider a specific application of MIS that also lets us see some of the new point-of-sale approaches to retail marketing. Unprecedented growth in the retail industry has been matched with an even greater increase in information and control requirements and data-collection costs. To aid management in the retail store, **point-of-sale systems** have been devised that collect management and control information at the sales-transaction point. For example, food-store systems are available to handle such problems as voids, merchandise and bottle refunds, automatic sorting and recording of taxable and nontaxable items, customer change dispensing, check authorization, productivity reports, automatic checker and store balance reports, and government-sponsored food programs. One such system is the NCR 255 Food Store system shown in Figure 4.12. This system consists of terminals designed to operate around a powerful minicomputer. The minicomputer provides central control of the terminal system and provides memory for storage of all system totals and program instructions. The system is controlled by an application

A corporation with a computerized management information system (one that is well designed and actually works) has a substantial competitive edge over corporations still relying on manual systems. The computer terminal is becoming an increasingly common item on the decision-maker's desk. The photograph on the upper left shows a stock market analyst using a computer terminal to assist him in recommending stock activity to a client. The right-hand figures illustrate Tektronix's 4610 hard-copy unit and companion computer graphic terminal. The 4610 produces 4″ × 11″ copies that can be presented to management for analysis. The lower-left photograph is of Bunker-Ramo's Market Decision System 7. Using this system the decision maker may view displays such as tickers and newswires, stock watch, most activities, most advanced, most declined, electronic futures board, market trends, and the like. (Courtesy Bunker-Ramo Information Services Division, Quotron Systems, and Tektronix.)

software package written specifically for the food store industry. Program loading and information storage can be accomplished via a magnetic tape cassette. The cassettes can then be forwarded to a large-scale computer for further processing of store orders, direct deliveries, payroll, inventory, and similar data. The terminal itself performs the arithmetic functions required for addition, subtraction, computation of sales tax, discounts, and various extensions (an **extension** is the multiplication of a price by the number of items purchased). The terminal has stand-alone capabilities as a normal cash

Shareholders, a Los Angeles-based financial services company that manages seven mutual funds, pension funds, an executive search firm, and a real-estate subsidiary, is using a computer to manage its vast amount of paperwork and to provide investors with timely and accurate information.

In the late 1960s, several of Shareholders' funds were out-performing the stock market averages by a wide margin. Investors were buying shares faster than the existing services could keep up with the resulting paperwork. This accelerated rate of growth took its toll. One of Shareholders' subsidiaries, Enterprise Fund, was forced to stop selling shares for nine months because of the tremendous paperwork backlog.

Each week some 1200 inquiries are routed to account representatives, who first make sure the person calling has the right to the information, then summon the account history from the computer. According to a Shareholders executive, "A few years ago we couldn't keep pace with our own growth. Now we are current every midnight on all transactions for all funds through the close of business that day. We keep track of about 400,000 individual accounts." (Courtesy of IBM and *Data Processor* magazine.)

register. The printing stations located in the terminal itself provide both the customer and the checker with complete information regarding transactions.

Management information systems are demanding input data from the checkout counter in increasingly greater volume, with more accuracy, and at a faster speed than noncomputerized food store systems can provide. Systems such as NCR's 255 supermarket system overcome most of the problems encountered with manual systems. Even greater improvement in meeting management's needs for information can be obtained when the basic NCR 255 point-of-sale terminal is expanded to include several different types of optional peripheral equipment. For instance, a scanning system equipped with a laser light source can be attached to the system. As the checker moves items across the checkout counter, the **Universal Product Code (UPC)** printed on each item is optically read by the built-in scanner. Omnidirectional scanning capabilities eliminate any need for precise alignment of the UPC symbol with the scanning slot. Items can be moved across the scanner as rapidly as they can be handled by the checker. Rejected UPC's can be reread or their data manually entered through the keyboard. One user, Publix Super Markets, Inc., a Florida based food chain, is using 900 terminals with scanners and coin and stamp dispensers and 180 miniprocessors in 90 of their 180 supermarkets.

The point-of-sale terminal has also found its way into retail department and clothing store use with only slight modifications. NCR's store system consists of point-of-sale recording devices located at selling stations throughout a

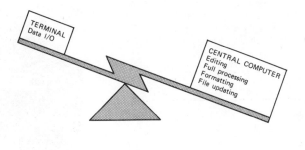

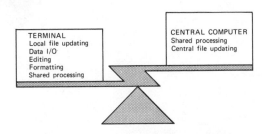

Burroughs TC 500 terminal computer: The TC 500 has a 20,480 digit disk memory, is programmable in COBOL, and is microprogrammable. It prints 20 characters per second, positions the typing element at 200 characters per second, and, especially with the forms-handler option, is able to handle a substantial volume of printed output from the central computer. Terminal /computer combinations such as TC 500 permit a better balance between terminal functions and central computer functions than conventional "dumb terminal" systems. It is not uncommon to put a full-sized computer system into terminal usage. IBM's 1130 is a common **satellite computer** to a System 360 or 370. Similarly, an NCR Century 100, Burroughs 2500, or CDC Cyber 70 would make logical satellite computers to larger machines in their respective families or even to computers of other manufacturers. **CPU-to-CPU communication** is becoming more standardized and interfacing quite different computers is not the task it once was. (Courtesy of Burroughs Corporation.)

store and a data collector that writes complete transaction information on standard magnetic tape for subsequent processing by a central computer. The merchandise is tagged with color-coded tags. The tag contains information on vendor, style, color, size, department, stockkeeping unit, season, price, unit price, multiple price unit, and so on. Tag codes are check digited to detect misread information. J. C. Penney Company, Inc. is using 17,000 point-of-sale

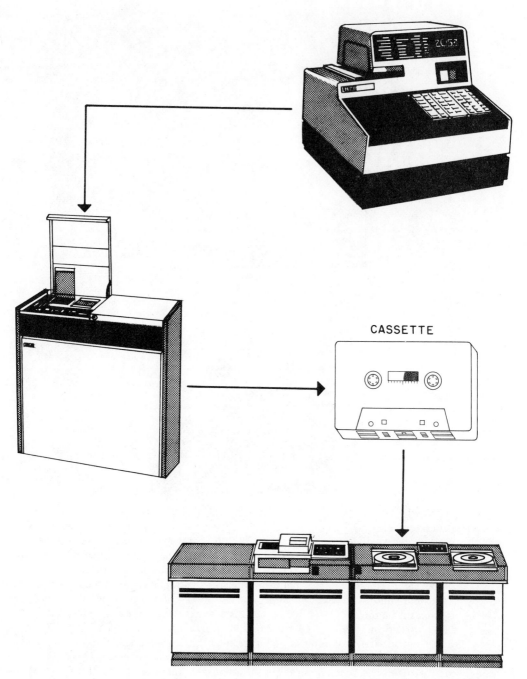

CASSETTE

Figure 4.12a

68

Figure 4.12b

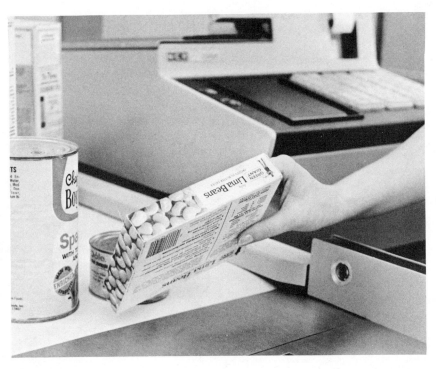

Figure 4.12c

terminals and 300 in-store computers and associated peripheral equipment.

The final major step in improving our meeting management's information needs is to make the retail point-of-sale system operate on line with a central computer (called, in retail systems, a **host processor**) that might be serving several different retail stores. Figure 4.13 shows an on-line retail-store system. The benefits of an on-line system include extended automatic credit and check authorization and more up-to-date management information.

The output of a retail management information system would include reports to improve cash control, equipment and employee utilization, inventory control, new-item tracking, data validity, the number of returned checks, and so on. Figure 4.14 shows some sample management reports from a regular retail system. In addition to reports such as these, IBM's retail point-of-sale system includes the following:

1. Credit-management reports focusing on on-line authorization of credit sales and on-line processing of store credit transactions.
2. Inventory-control reports to help provide faster turnover of merchandise, tracking of flash-sale items, and reduction of out-of-stock and over-stock situations.
3. Manpower-management reports to help management have the right number of people at the right points of sale at each hour of the business day to meet the demand for customer service.

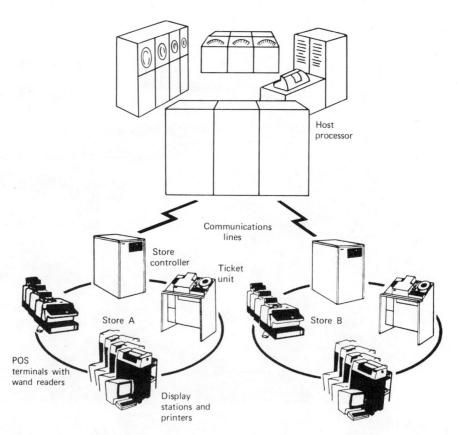

Figure 4.13   An on-line, retail-store system.

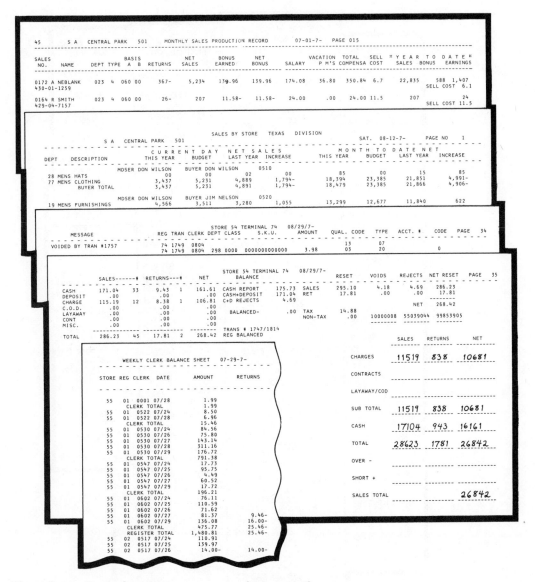

Figure 4.14 Typical management reports from a retail system.

Some typical supermarket management-information reports are shown in Figure 4.15.

A list of some of the benefits of (especially on-line) point-of-sale retail terminals is given below. It is just a partial list. Even with all this benefit however, the cost of such a facility must be justified and adequate backup facilities must be preplanned if the system is to be successful. The benefits include:

1. Improved checkout operations.
2. Significantly reduced price marking and re-marking of merchandise.
3. Obtaining of item-movement information.
4. Assistance in bookkeeping.

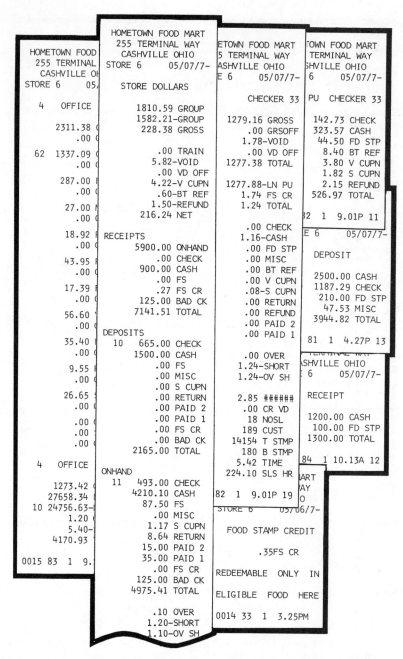

Figure 4.15 Management and administrative reports that can be generated without a host processor.

5. Reduction in checkout effort (through price look-up, automatic calculation of tax, stamps, discounts, and so on).

6. Tracking and verifying checks prior to tendering.

7. Recording of productivity data.

8. Logging file/audit data.

9. Inventory replenishment.

10. Out-of-stock reduction.
11. Promotional analysis.
12. Sales performance monitoring.
13. Labor scheduling.
14. General accounting.
15. Cash control.
16. Demographic analysis.
17. Stock-Shrinkage monitoring.
18. New-item tracking.
19. Automatic order generation.
20. Coupon control.

DATA COMMUNICATION SYSTEMS

The benefits of on-line data processing are enough to make it attractive to many people. On-line processing requires a communications link between remote terminals and the central computer. Today, over half the information sent over the country's telephone lines is machine-to-machine communication, what American Telephone and Telegraph calls **machine talk.** The increasing use of on-line, real-time systems is causing the demand for machine-to-machine communication facilities to increase. In this section we will see how communication systems work, what commercial facilities are available, and what equipment is available to enable management to obtain low-cost, reliable communication between a remote terminal and a central computer or between computers.

The communication system

Let us look at the important parts of a simple communication system then expand it to include the features of a real-world communication system.

Figure 4.16 shows the minimum components of a communication system: a message sender, a message medium, and a message receiver. When one person talks to another, the person talking is the message source, the air between the two is the message medium, and the person listening is the message receiver. Any given medium is limited in its capacity to carry messages. For example, there is a maximum number of message characters that can be placed on a page of this book. In a similar manner, an electrical wire or a radio or television frequency has a maximum message capacity. The message medium, as limited by its message capacity, is called the **message channel** or just **channel.** The purpose of communicating is to convey information from the message source to the message receiver. The message sent is that

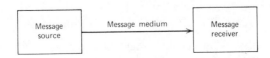

Figure 4.16   The simple communication system.

information. The rate of information transmission is measured in baud. One **baud** is one bit of information per second.*

The most frequently encountered communication channel is the standard telephone line which has some properties not covered in our model of a simple communication system. A telephone line:

1. Is an *analog* information channel.
2. Has a very limited information capacity.
3. Has a considerable amount of **noise** (any signal that interferes with the message being sent).

All three of these provide us with problems when we try to transmit digital information rapidly and reliably. Our information is, of course, digital and so we find ourselves in need of a digital-to-analog converter on the sending end and an analog-to-digital converter on the receiving end. The digital-to-analog converter converts the digital information to a series of audible tones and is called a **modulator.** The analog-to-digital converter converts tthe tones back into the digital information and is called a **demodulator.** If information can be sent either direction through a converter it is called a modulator /demodulator or, more commonly, a **modem** or **data set.** Figure 4.17 shows two typical modems.

The information capacity of a channel is called the channel's **bandwidth** and it is related to the amount of channel noise: the more noise the smaller a channel's bandwidth. Effort has to be exerted to keep the noise level as low as is economically possible. This is done by doing things such as shielding the channel from unwanted electrical disturbances. Nevertheless, all real-world channels are beset with random noise caused by natural events (such as lightning) and by other signals interacting with the signals of the channel. Thus, the bits of information we transmit usually have additional bits with them that permit noise-caused errors to be detected. With some of the more elegant codes, errors are not only detectable but are also correctable.

Communication channels are classified into **channel grades** by bandwidth. The bandwidth of a regular telephone line is adequate to carry normal speech. For this reason, telephone lines are called **voice-grade** channels. Channels that carry even less information are called **subvoice** channels. Since the physical media that are used in data channels have bandwidths much larger than needed for a single voice-grade channel, one data channel is normally made to carry as many voice grade channels as noise conditions and maximum permissible error rates will allow. A channel with capacity greater than voice grade is called a **wideband** channel.

In addition to grade, data channels are classed by the number of directions data can be transmitted and whether or not both directions can be used at once. **Simplex** channels communicate information in one direction only. **Half-duplex** channels can communicate in either direction but only in one direction at a time. **Full-duplex** channels can transmit information in both directions at the same time.

A modem is normally wired directly to the digital device (computer or remote terminal) and to the channel. This is a cumbersome arrangement for

---

*Actually, baud is the number of signal elements per second, in an equal-length code. Since codes in use today represent one bit of information with each signal element, the simpler definition used above is valid and is the generally accepted definition for computer communication systems.

Figure 4.17 Modems. (a) RFL 3952—up to 2400 baud. (Courtesy RFL Industries.) (b) Bell System's 103A data set—300 baud connected to an IBM 1050 terminal at Ohio State University's College of Medicine. (Courtesy Mountain States Telephone Company.)

digital devices that need to be moved frequently. A rather low-cost and convenient solution is to convey audible tones between the channel and the modem through an **acoustic coupler** (see Figure 4.18).

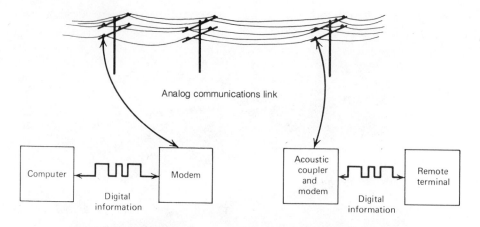

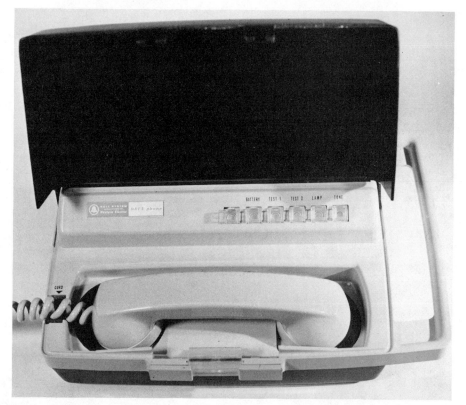

Figure 4.18 The acoustic coupler.

Commercial facilities

Improper selection of data communication channels can be a very costly error. You can probably guess most of the parameters used in a cost analysis: number of hours of channel time needed per month, channel grade, and the pricing schedule of the company providing the channel. A voice-grade channel can reliably carry up to 2400 baud of data. There are three types of voice-grade service available: the public switched network, WATS, and private lines. At the present time, the **public switched network** (the regular dial-up telephone system including Direct Distance Dialing) is the most commonly used means of transmitting data. Using the public switched network offers the advantage of nationwide access: all you need is a telephone line and an acoustic coupler or a wired-in modem. For data volumes that can be accommodated by voice-grade lines and relatively low levels of channel usage (e.g., 50–80 hours per month), regular dial-up lines are usually more economical than other types of channels. Either higher transmission speeds or higher levels of channel usage make long-distance dial-up lines very costly.

Wide Area Telephone Service (WATS) is a packaged voice-and-data-communications service available from the Bell System. A special access line is provided for unrestricted calls for up to a specified number of hours per month. There are two basic WATS plans to choose from:

1. WATS 240—up to 240 hours per month of unrestricted use and an overtime rate charged for each tenth of an hour used beyond 240 hours.
2. WATS 10—same as WATS 240 except the limit is 10 hours.

Rates for WATS lines depend on what geographical area you want to reach. The states immediately adjacent to your state are in the first price range. Other price ranges extend further out with the fifth price range taking in the entire United States except Alaska and Hawaii.

Private lines (now called **tie lines** by the Bell System) are connected 24 hours a day, every day. Since private lines are not switched, as are regular dial-up and WATS channels, they can be **conditioned** (electrical adjustments made to a privately leased line to improve its communications capability). Due to this conditioning, private line users can often attain data rates up to 9600 baud.

In 1969 the Federal Communications Commission (FCC) granted permission for Microwave Communications, Inc. to function as a communications common carrier for special communication services. (A **common carrier** carries goods for all persons indiscriminately and is regulated by some government agency—a communications common carrier's "goods" are the various forms of information carried.) This decision by the FCC opened the door to an entire new industry: nationwide non-Bell System communication facilities. Because these systems have been *designed* to carry digital information, costs are lower than corresponding-grade analog channels. AT&T has countered this move by constructing their own digital data systems.

While land-based digital data facilities have been superior to the analog systems we have been using, more and more data is being conveyed over satellite channels. The commercial use of communication satellites began in 1965 and has blossomed since then. There is hardly any part of the earth not covered by satellite communications. The cost of satellite channels are already lower than the cost of comparable AT&T channels. For example, a New York-to-Los Angeles simplex satellite channel costs less than half the cost of a comparable AT&T simplex channel.

The system that will almost certainly become the largest business data communication facility in the United States is already rather complete: the cable television system (denoted **CATV**, for community-antenna television). The FCC requires that cable television facilities be able to carry information not only from the cable television station (called the **head end**) to the subscriber but from the subscriber back to the head end as well. There are already over a dozen pilot cities testing the wired-city concept. The idea is to place a subscriber response system in each home and to provide services such as the following (which are all currently available in the various test sites):

1. Police and fire notification—the subscriber's response unit can relay fire and burglary alarms to a security agency or the fire department or the police.
2. Armchair shopping—the subscriber can shop from home, selecting items based on the information displayed on the television screen at the subscriber's request.
3. Voter information—public issues can be publicly debated with viewer participation, or local government can sample public opinion on current issues before taking action.
4. Reservations—the subscriber can order and receive conformations for all kinds of reservations (theater, airlines, sports events, hotel accommodations).
5. Two-way messages—both group and individual two-way interactive communications can be accomplished.
6. Medical and health services—health care and emergency treatment information can be requested by the subscriber or a physician can monitor a patient at home easing the high cost of long-term hospitalization.

This is just a partial list: retrieval from a computerized library, game playing, and a computerized recipe file are some other applications. It is quite likely that, by the middle 1980s, subscriber response units, connected through CATV lines to centralized computers, will be as common place as telephones are today.

Front ends

Whatever the means used to connect remote devices to a central computer, the fewer separate data channels we need, the lower the cost of the system. We use various **front-end** processors to consolidate several remote data channels into a single channel. These processors not only consolidate data channels but perform various housekeeping operations, error testing, data editing, and the like. While differing in the technique used to accomplish their task, **multiplexers** and **concentrators** permit connection of more peripherals to the central processor while using fewer channels. For example, a multiplexer might be used to combine many voice-grade channels into a single wideband channel. Figure 4.19 shows the improvement in number of channels through the use of multiplexers. Even though the multiplexer system requires a higher-grade channel, the channel tariff structure makes it economically attractive to group many lower speed channels into a single higher-speed channel.

When there are not very many remote terminals to be serviced by a central computer, the overall performance of the system will generally be quite adequate. However, as the number of terminals increases, system performance degrades. The central computer spends more and more of its time performing such operations as the following:

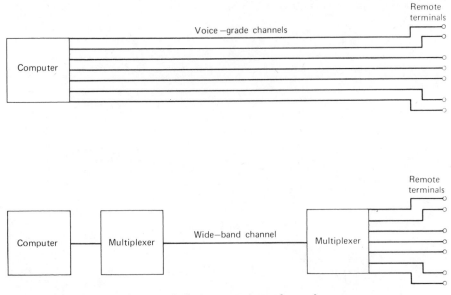

Figure 4.19   Using a front-end device to reduce channel costs.

1. Error detection and retransmission processing.
2. Message routing among the various programs in the central computer.
3. Code translation into the internal code of the central computer.
4. Other housekeeping—stacking messages by priority until they can be processed, verifying security authorizations, generating control reports, and so on.

One solution to the problem is the **programmable communications processor,** which is usually a complete minicomputer system.

Computer networks

Information networks have been around a lot longer than electronic computers: pneumatic tube systems, messenger services, and the telephone system are just a few examples. Since many of the goals of modern computing systems are the same as the goals of these older information networks (e.g., sending information from one specific place to another specific place, sharing expensive resources, and convenience), it is natural that we should interconnect our computers to form **computer networks.** Two of the general classes of computer networks are the star and ring networks (see Figure 4.20). A **star network** has a single central computer that services the remote users and a **ring network** has computers in different locations with two or more communications paths uniting each computer with the rest of the network.

Star networks are simpler in structure and much easier to organize than ring networks. The star configuration permits the sharing of costly and unique resources (such as programs and data bases) where the ring configuration provides this and the possibility of additional reliability. Many real-world computer networks are some combination of the star and ring classes.

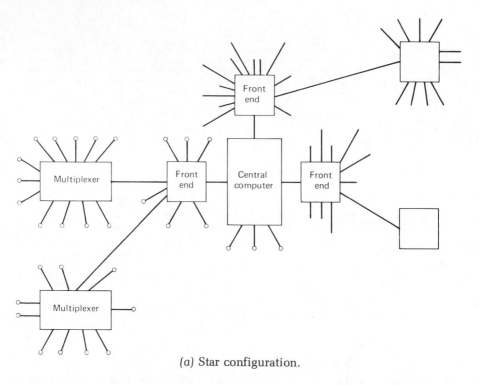

(a) Star configuration.

Figure 4.20   Computer networks—users might have only a terminal or might have a complete computer system.

While there are a lot of problems to be overcome in constructing any network, the increased ability and convenience and the decreased cost when compared with alternative approaches make them attractive (even with their attendant problems). Computer networks offer a compromise between the extremes of centralization (all computers in a single location) and decentralization (computers distributed among the users with no central facility). Furthermore, data communications are becoming more reliable and we are coming to know more about network behavior as we gain experience with them. The cost of tying into a star service network (there are several dozen companies offering such services) already is less than $200 per month and is becoming cheaper. The U. S. government has been investing substantial sums in network development over the past decade as have several other parties. It will probably be a rare business that is not connected to one or more computer networks by the middle 1980s, even if the business has its own computer. A nationwide electronic funds transfer system will probably make that claim true by itself.

SIMULATION

The role computers and simulation are playing in the design of our future world is hard to overstate. Space researchers use simulation to test a missile's design before building the first mock-up. It is a lot safer and a lot less expensive to have a missile "crash" in a computer's memory than on a real launch. There are several approaches to simulation, and many involve substantial mathematics. The idea is to get the computer to *internalize some*

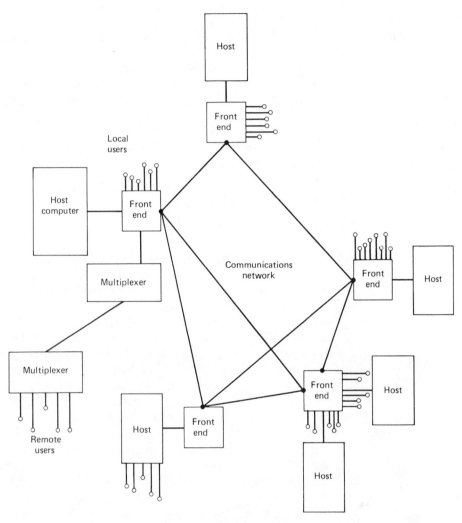

(b) Ring configuration.

Figure 4.20   (continued)

model of reality. For example a computer program whose variables behave enough like the similar variables in the real-world to be useful.

The uses of simulation are quite varied. Probably the most frequently encountered use, and also one of the most interesting, is to aid decision makers. This covers a very wide spectrum, from permitting an aircraft designer to try alternative wing designs through assisting a corporate executive in predicting the effect of increasing the amount of available warehouse space to giving a city commission a means of evaluating the total, citywide impact of a proposed low-cost housing development. In general, **decision-making simulation applications** consist of a model of some real or proposed system, two or more alternative paths of action, and one or more human decision makers. The scenario calls for the decision maker to "run" the model under each of the proposed alternatives and compare overall simulated system performances. As we will discuss momentarily, some rather impressive uses have been made of this type of simulation. A second class of simulation uses is training. In **training simulation applications** the people being trained interact with a model of a system they are going to manage once trained. For example, pilots are trained in computer-controlled simulators. They can receive almost the same experience as flying an actual plane but can "crash" their flight simulator without harm to anyone. It also permits more severe situations to be thrust on the pilot trainee than could be attempted in a real-world plane. Another example would be stock market analyst trainees playing a stock market game where the game is a model of the real stock market. Games such as this are used extensively in training farmers, stock market analysts, corporate executives, municipal leaders, ecosystem managers, and the like.

Let us consider some specific applications of simulation then we will look at the simulation process itself.

Applications of simulation

The breadth of simulation applications is really quite outstanding. We are going to consider a selected few in some detail in this section. (Several texts give good treatment of simulation applications. Especially recommended are the three by Starbuck and Dutton, Hausrath, and Guetzkow, Kotter, and Schultz listed in the Bibliography at the end of this chapter.) The first application we are going to consider is in the field of medical education. The University of Southern California School of Medicine has developed a computer model of certain portions of the human body and uses the model and a human manikin to train clinical anesthesiologists. The manikin, called Sim One, is lifelike in appearance, having a plastic skin that resembles its human counterpart in color and texture. Sim One is in the position of a patient lying on an operating table with his left arm extended, ready for intravenous injection. The right arm is fitted with a blood-pressure cuff, and a stethoscope is taped in place over the approximate location of the heart. Sim One breathes, has a heartbeat with temporal and carotid pulses, and a measurable blood pressure. He opens and closes his mouth, blinks his eyes, and "responds" to four intravenously administered drugs and two gases administered through mask or tube. Responses to the agents and method of treatment occur in real time, detected, controlled, and enacted under the control of the computer's program.

To illustrate this sequence of events, we may describe a typical case as follows. Oxygen is administered through a mask to Sim One for a period of five minutes in order to raise the oxygen level in the tissues (to provide an extra margin of safety during the time in which a real patient might go without oxygen during the operation). Sodium pentothol is administered intravenously, which renders the Sim One "unconscious". Succinylcholine is injected which produces paralysis of skeletal muscles and indeed causes Sim One to stop breathing. The anesthesiologist then quickly slips off the mask and inserts the airway tube into the trachea, sealing it inside the walls of the trachea by inflating the baloon-like rubber cuff of the tube. Through this tube, connected to the anesthesia machine, the anesthesiologist then administers oxygen and nitrous oxide by squeezing the inflated reservoir bag. During all of this activity, Sim One's computer registers all of the anesthesiologist's actions and the agents administered and dictates the appropriate physiologic responses to the manikin. At any time, the instructor has the option of "overrid-

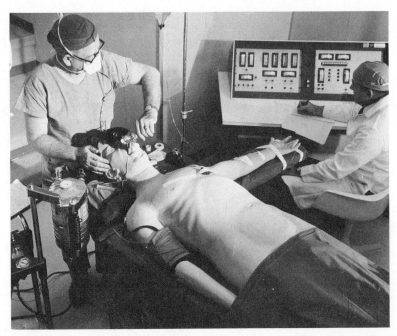

Sim One in use at the University of California School of Medicine. Sim One was conceived by USC School of Medicine and designed by the Electronics Division of Aerojet-General Corporation. (Courtesy of USC School of Medicine.)

ing" the physiologic program in order to produce such problem situations as cardiac arrest, abnormally increased or decreased blood pressure, left or right block of the bronchus, increased or decreased breathing rate, cardiac arrhythmia, venticular fibrillation, increased jaw tension, and even vomiting.

The second application of simulation we are going to look at has more obvious overtones of social implications. It illustrates how simulation can be used to assist the decision maker. In 1970, under the direction of Professor Dennis Meadows, the Club of Rome (an informal international association) initiated the first phase of what they call the Project of the Prediceament of Mankind. The intent of the overall project is to "examine the complex of problems troubling men of all nations."* In particular they are concerned with such things as poverty, degradation to the environment, loss of faith in institutions, urban spread, insecurity of employment, and the like. Their Phase One study, with financial support from the Volkswagen Foundation, examined the five basic factors that determine, and thereby limit, growth on our planet—population, agricultural production, natural resources, industrial production, and pollution. In order to study the very complex interactions among these factors the study team adopted J. W. Forrester's World Model† and modified it to meet their needs. This model is a computer simulation of the interaction of the variables that determine our "five basic factors" mentioned above. The results of the study were published in popular form in the highly controversial book *The Limits to Growth*.‡ A year later the

*D. Meadows, et al., *The Limits to Growth*. New York: Universe Books, 1972, p. 10.
†J. Forrester, *World Dynamics*. Cambridge, Mass.: Wright-Allen Press, 1971.
‡D. Meadows, et al., *The Limits to Growth*. New York: Universe Books, 1972.

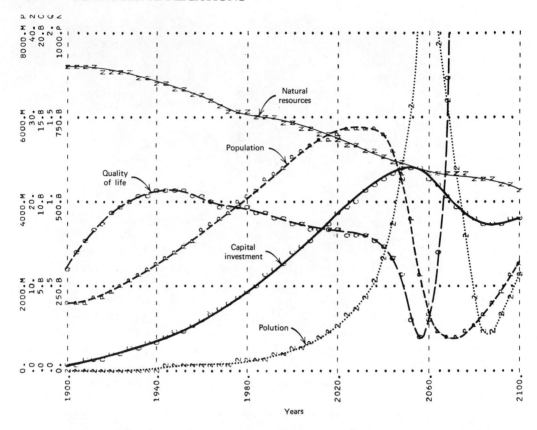

Forrester's world model: J. W. Forrester of MIT has created a world model to be used in testing suggested world management policies. The model has been used rather extensively by the international team headed by Dennis Meadows under the auspices of The Club of Rome, a private group of some 75 members who have joined together to understand better the changes now occurring in the world. This diagram shows the world model's prediction of variable interactions given that we could reduce our consumption of natural resources to 25 percent of the present rate. There has been a strong reaction to the use of the model's predictions. Many questions have to be answered before world leaders will accept the model as valid. It is not hard to believe, however, that the model can eventually be made valid enough that it can predict the effect of a suggested policy better than can any men.

technical papers were published.* A simplistic summary of their report might be "The earth's interacting resources probably cannot support present rates of economic and population growth beyond the year 2100, if that long, even after allowing for advances in technology". The basic approach to using the model is to select a set of parameters (e.g., known reserves of resources, death-rate-from-crowding multiplier, available land area, capital investment ratio in agriculture, . . .) and run the model on a computer. Then as undesirable consequences are predicted by the model, alter your parameters and run the model again to see what is required to obtain a more desirable prediction. Through this process the Meadows team searched for optimum parameters. (We will not attempt a presentation of their results here, interested readers are

*Dennis Meadows and Donalla Meadows, *Toward Global Equilibrium: Collected Papers.* Cambridge, Mass.: Wright-Allen Press, 1973.

referred to the Meadowses' books already mentioned.) The model has received a lot of criticism. One of the best retorts comes from Paul Ehrlich, noted
professor of biology at Stanford University, "The Meadowses and the M.I.T.
team have done a great service in constructing a preliminary model of the
world in which all the assumptions and parameters are explicit and thus open
to criticism and modification. Those who object to the characteristics of the
model are challenged to help improve it . . .". Unless one takes the stand that
the natural processes of the world cannot, for some mystical reason, be
simulated, we seem to be left with the realization that whatever degree of
adequacy the current model does or does not have we will someday evolve a
model that is adequate to predict the outcome of world policy matters. We will
discuss the implications of the Meadowses' model in further detail in Chapter
9.

It is worth noting that the above two examples of computerized simulation
applications typify the two major reasons that computers are so often used in
the simulation arts: (1) computers can respond very rapidly and accurately to
many interacting real-time stimuli, and (2) computers can carry out vast
numbers of repetitive steps accurately and economically. Sim One had need
for the first set of reasons and the world model the second set.

(See figures on pages 86 and 87.)

The computer, performing an analytical simulation of a thermal (heat flow) model, is
able to provide solutions for complex thermal systems. However, before the computer
can perform the computations and manipulative iterations, thermal information must
be in a form the computer can act on.

Not surprisingly, the job of creating a thermal representation of an object is still more
art than science. Almost like a sculptor or artist, beginning with mechanical part
drawings, the engineer must size up the rough shape of the equipment to be thermally
simulated and dissect it into familiar geometric shapes of known heat flow characteristics. From these shapes, a mathematical model representing the thermal parameters of
a physical unit is constructed.

For example, after considering the various shapes and thicknesses of the Zeus-Nike X
inertial platform (see photos on page 86) the engineer determines their relationship to similarly shaped geometric thermal building blocks: cubes, rectangles, cyclin-
ders or other suitable forms. He must decide how accurately or coarsely to subdivide
the platform giving particular attention to heat generation and areas where high
temperature gradients are suspected. Geometric representations must then be converted into mathematical expressions.

To prepare input data for computer analysis, each geometric element is represented
by a node point at its center. The node points are then interconnected by thermal
conductances representing the ease of heat flow between elements (top photo on page
87). Input data necessary to calculate conductance values include: element width,
height, distance between nodes, material conductivity, density, specific heat, and heat
generation and its location. All this data is punched on data cards.

The transient analysis modeling technique used for this problem, solving a typical
200-node transient model (bottom photo on page 87), requires the computer to perform 60 million mathematical operations plus considerable other operations and data
manipulations. This takes the Sperry Univac 1108 at Sperry's Great Neck facility
aproximately five minutes.

Without the computer it would be impossible to obtain analytical solutions of
complex multipath thermal systems. (Photographs courtesy of *Sperry Technology* by
permission of Sperry Rand Corporation, New York.)

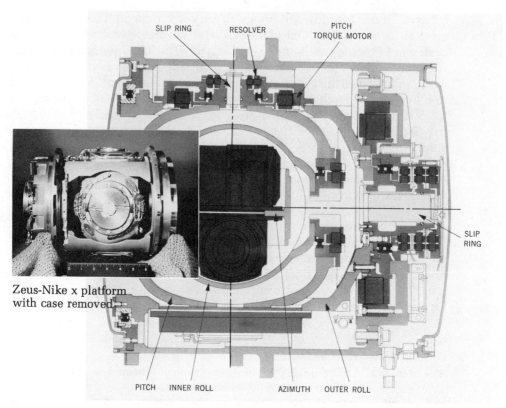

SLIP RING   RESOLVER   PITCH TORQUE MOTOR

SLIP RING

Zeus-Nike x platform
with case removed

PITCH   INNER ROLL   AZIMUTH   OUTER ROLL

Cutaway drawing of the Zeus-Nike X platform illustrating the type of areas that relate to thermal building blocks

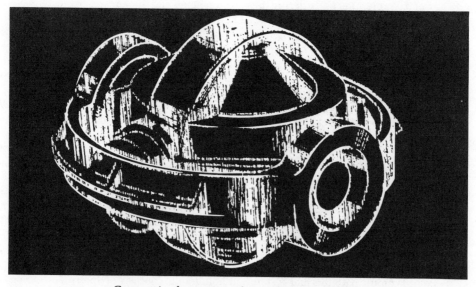

Geometric abstraction of Zeus-Nike X platform

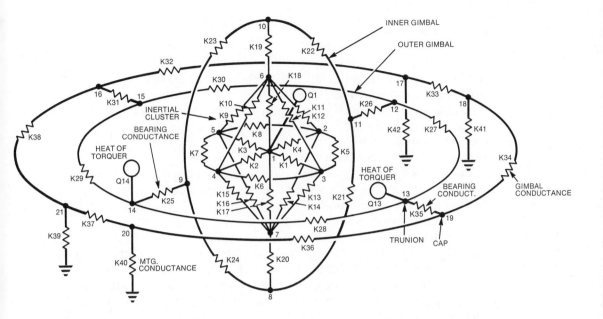

CORRESPONDING MATHEMATICAL THERMAL MODEL

Corresponding mathematical thermal model

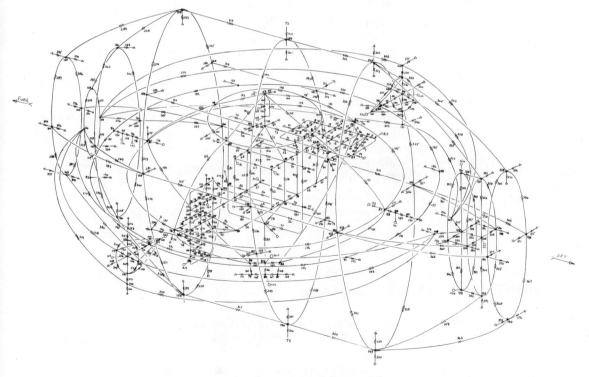

A 200-node version of the model

The techniques of simulation

Though the actual techniques used vary quite a bit most computerized models can be classified as either *discrete* or *continuous*. In a **discrete model** each separate **transaction** (e.g., customer, inventory part, unit of money) is moved through the model on a step-by-step basis. To make the model as true to life as possible the action at each step is typically **probabilistic** (i.e., while the behavior of each individual transaction is randomly determined the behavior of all transactions is statistically regular).

Continuous models* typically look at the aggregate effect of large quantities of transactions at each unit of simulated time. Since large numbers of transactions are viewed at each unit of time the random effects of individual transactions usually "wash out" of the model. Consequently continuous models are usually **deterministic** (i.e., contain no probabilistic elements). An example of a continuous deterministic system is the simulation of the three-body problem. Seamen of the fifteenth century began to become involved in world trade for the first time and a need arose for a better system of navigation. The relative positions of the sun, earth, and moon at any given instant could give them this system if the positions could only be predicted by an accurate method. The mathematicians and physicists of the time had a knowledge of the inertial and gravitational laws governing the motions of bodies, but knew of no analytical method to express the movements of the celestial bodies together with the effect they had on each other. The scientists of today still lack the knowledge to solve this three-body celestial mechanics problem analytically, but a solution was obtained hundreds of years ago by a relatively simple technique. A simulation of the three-body problem was developed in which the known laws of force and motion were applied to only one of the bodies at a time. The change in position of one of the bodies was computed for a future time, assuming that only a small amount of time was to elapse and all other bodies would remain stationary. The changes for the other two bodies were calculated in the same manner and then time was incremented and the process repeated again and again. Some men spent their lifetimes calculating the step-by-step solution to this problem. Each calculation depended on the last, making the possibility of error significant, but valid navigational tables were nevertheless produced in this fashion. The only significant differences in the solution of the same problem today are the time required to obtain the answers and the accuracy obtainable, both due to modern computational devices.

OTHER COMPUTER APPLICATIONS

There are full texts devoted solely to brief descriptions of some of the areas in which computers have been applied. Here is a partial listing of some major applications:

Continuous models could be taken to mean truly continuous models (i.e., a physical mock-up of a system or an analog computer model). The term is, unfortunately, used to designate both types of modeling. Of course, any simulation done by means of a digital computer is, by the very nature of the computer, discrete. Thus, the continuous models we refer to in this text are really discrete models wherin the time step is small enough to be considered to have a negligible effect on the model.

(a)

(b)

(c)

Flexible computer-controlled laser system revolutionizes garment industry: a space-age material cutter—heralded by the garment industry as the most significant development since the sewing machine—is causing far-reaching changes in the clothing business. The equipment was made possible by combining a computer with a precision laser into one rapid fabric cutting system called a **lasercutter.** It was developed by Hughes Aircraft Co.

I. General business

    1. Payroll

    2. Personnel

    3. Accounting and bookkeeping

    4. Control and auditing

    5. Billing

    6. Inventory

Grand Central has 18 stores in Utah, Idaho, and Wyoming. To plan new stores, the company's management felt they needed more up-to-date information on inventory movement. They also wanted more detailed reports.

In the past, store personnel wrote quantities and prices of merchandise, varying from apparel, yardage, and notions to toys and garden items, on preprinted inventory sheets. This system of recording inventory for each of the stores' 17 different departments—over 100,000 items—required manually extending quantities and prices before data was keypunched for computer process.

Because of this time lag, Grand Central was delayed in closing its books for a six-month period. The company did not have up-to-date information on merchandise. And, because its accounting staff was not large enough to handle the job of extending out prices, as many as 50 accounting clerks had to be hired twice a year.

Now when store personnel take inventory they simply place pencil marks in the target areas of an 8½″ × 11″ sheet.

As inventory sheets are processed through an optical mark reader at a speed of about one per second, data is stored on magnetic tape. The optical mark reader helps to eliminate input errors by reading documents on a field by field basis. It diverts any sheets with marking errors into a separate output for further review by the staff. Information on tape is read directly to the computer where it undergoes an additional edit check. Corrections are made on an edit printout and a final inventory report is produced.

In generating the inventory report, the computer automatically extends all quantities and prices and develops cost as well as retail figures through a standard markup application. The inventory printout indicates both the retail and cost value of merchandise at every store by department and status and gives the overall store totals as well as a total for the entire chain. (Courtesy of IBM and *Data Processor* magazine.)

     7.   Simulation*

     8.   Marketing

     9.   Information storage and retrieval

II. Science

     1.   Mathematical analyses

     2.   Simulation

     3.   Pure mathematics

     4.   Real-time experiments

III. Professions

     1.   Medical

        (a)   Research

        (b)   Billing

        (c)   Diagnosis

        (d)   On-line patient monitoring

     2.   Legal

     3.   Library science

     4.   Pharmaceutical

IV. Process control

     1.   Steel mills

     2.   Chemical plants.

     3.   Automotive checkout

V. Space applications

     1.   Missile guidance

     2.   Navigation

     3.   Space-vehicle control

     4.   Monitoring of astronauts' body functions

     5.   Research and analyses

     6.   Simulation

     7.   Tracking space vehicles

VI. Military

     1.   Logistics

     2.   Personnel applications

     3.   Weapons control

     4.   Design

     5.   Simulation and tactics

*The applications may overlap—there are inventory and marketing applications of simulation, for example.

Three million abstracts. When a biologist in Australia wants to know what research has been done in viral hepatitis, he turns to the BioSciences Information Service. Soon, he may even have his own terminal to tap into the organization's files of more than three million abstracts.

These abstracts sum up virtually all published findings on research in biology since 1926 when the organization was founded.

To help record and retrieve the information, BioSciences Information Service uses a computer and a rather large data base. Approximately 60 million index references including a half-million biological terms are contained in the data base, which can be

Dr. Katherine Costello, M.I.T., analyses a blood sample for drug content. Data is relayed from a gas chromatograph to a computer. The computer compares the data with reference data to determine what drug is in the sample being examined. (Courtesy National Aeronautics and Space Administration.)

VII. Government

1. Data banks
2. Record keeping
3. Research in national statistics
4. Simulation

VIII. Law enforcement

1. National Crime Information Center (NCIC)
2. Research and simulation

---

accessed via remote terminals. The file indexes *Biological Abstracts*, the firms twice-monthly publication.

Input for *Biological Abstracts* comes from some 10,000 scientific journals printed in over 100 countries. As journals arrive, their contents are indexed by biological editors. A citation sheet is prepared for each paper in the journal and a copy is passed along to typists who prepare it for publication (top photo on page 92). Another copy is entered into the computerized data base by operators using remote terminals (bottom photo on page 92).

The firm currently offers search services through staff scientists who use the computer's retrieval powers, but work out adaptations of requests before developing search profiles. In addition to supporting these search services, the system produces substantial index content for all biological periodicals.

Two machine-readable data bases support a new monthly journal, *Abstracts on Health Effects of Environmental Pollutants*. These are the data bases of *Biological Abstracts* and of MEDLARS, the computer system linking large medical school libraries.

Further degrees of common compatability between large scientific data base systems are being developed by the service in current joint efforts with the Chemical Abstracts Service of the American Chemical Society. (Courtesy of IBM Corporation and *Data Processor.*)

Terminal systems are being used by Bell Laboratories for control of inventory stock. Inventory records retrieved from a computer's memory via terminal contain information such as when and where inventory items were sent out, how long they will be gone, and if a particular item is available from the central stock. (Courtesy of Bell Laboratories.)

A device that extends the applications of computers into new areas easily accessed by many people is the voice-response unit which uses the ordinary telephone for a terminal. Units such as the Applied Information Industries VSC-8000 can put full spoken sentences together to answer an inquiry. These systems typically have such human-voice characteristics as variable word and pause length and the ability to make

new words from the existing vocabulary (e.g., having phrases "pay", "install", and "—ment", words such as "payment" and "installment" can be formed). To use the system the caller dials it and a "ready" tone or spoken salutation is generated by the system. The user then keys in his inquiry using a Touch-Tone telephone and the voice response unit transmits the inquiry to a host computer that performs the actual search or computation. The voice-response unit then receives commands from the computer in the form of data track addresses which are used to locate specific words, phrases, or sentences on the vocabulary storage device in the response unit. The stored words are converted to audio and the caller hears the message. One can imagine a typical "conversation" between human caller and computer being as follows:

CALLER: Dials computer on a Touch-Tone telephone.
SYSTEM: "Key in access code".
CALLER: Keys in 60682531
SYSTEM: "You entered 60682531". System performs authorization checks. "Access approved, enter request code".
CALLER: Keys 196, for driver's licence check.
SYSTEM: "Driver's license check requested. Enter license number and state code".
CALLER: Keys AEK349 for license number and 42 for state code.
SYSTEM: Performs search of its files (e.g., requires seven seconds). "License holder is John M. Miles. Only want is seven-month old traffic violation—nonmoving, New York City P.D. Miles does have an emergency telephone call pending from area code 215 telephone number 564-5170. Press number 1 button for replay of telephone number. Press number 2 button for replay of want. Do you have any more requests? If so enter request code.
CALLER: Hangs up.

The application could be a surgeon calling his now-computerized answering service to request information on the blood count for a patient in a given room of a given hospital. Or it could be a stockbroker inquiring about the current cost of a certain stock, or a bank teller obtaining a customer's balance, or a salesman inquiring to see if an adequate quantity of a particular part is on hand for him to guarantee deliver to his customer. The photographs above show some of the variety already available in terminals for Touch-Tone/voice response use. (Photographs courtesy of Applied Information Industries, page 94, Comware, above left, and Chancellor Industries, above right.)

IX. The arts

    1. Extensions of the artist

    2. Music composition

    3. Poetry writing

    4. Script writing for TV plays

X. Miscellaneous

    1. Air traffic control

    2. Scheduling (almost anything)

    3. Project control

    4. Typesetting

    5. Banking

    6. Subscription

    7. Airline reservations

    8. Designing of other computers

    9. Education

EXERCISES

1. Describe the new developments in data base technology being fostered by CODASYL. These developments are described in many different sources including *Information Systems: Theory and Practice* (Hamilton Publishing Co.), National Bureau of Standards Handbook 113, *CODASYL Data Description Language,* and the October 1974 *Honeywell Computer Journal* article "The Data Base Concept" by Sven Eriksen.

2. From a text on data base management systems (e.g., *Data Management Systems,* Melville Publishing Co. or *Data Base Management Systems,* American Elsevier) describe one of the major data base management systems such as IBM's IMS or GIS, Informatics' MARK IV, and Univac's UNIMS.

3. From trade journals such as *Datamation* and *Computer World* obtain descriptions of two or three cases where lack of adequate master file backup cost a concern over $100,000.

4. From sources such as Meadows, et al., *Limits to Growth* (Universe Books) and Forresters' *World Dynamics* (Wright-Allen Press) obtain a description of the World Model and criticize its use.

5. From sources such as *Datamation, Computer World,* and the *FBI Law Enforcement Bulletin* obtain a detailed description of the National Crime Information Center's operation, successes and failures, and transaction volume.

6. Make a list of tasks that were once heuristic and are now algorithmic.

7. Make a list of present-day heuristic tasks where it would be desirable to have them become algorithmic (e.g., medical diagnosis).

8. Differentiate among data file and data base.

9. What is often the most expensive step in a data processing system?

10. Give a flowchart description of an editing test of the following items, all of

which are in a driver's license data base: age, sex, glasses required?, eye color, hair color, height in inches, weight in pounds, and type of license (of four types).

11. Specify a reasonable storage medium (disk, tape, main memory) for each of the following applications:
(a) Archive file of three million characters.
(b) On-line 4 million character registrar's data file.
(c) Backup file of (a).
(d) Back file of (b).
(e) File of 20 eight-character account codes referenced every time a job is run on the computer

12. In most data processing systems, why is there a program that has editing as its sole function? Why are codes used in place of actual information? What does coding information cost us?

13. Distinguish between on line and off line.

14. What does on-line data collection usually buy us?

15. Differentiate between file security and file protection.

16. Write up a simulation application from one of the texts in the Bibliography for this chapter.

17. Differentiate among stochastic (probabilistic), deterministic, continuous, and discrete with regard to simulation.

18. Using the Bibliography at the end of Chapter 1, find 5 to 10 articles on Electronic Funds Transfer Systems. Using these, estimate the long-term impact of such a system on our society.

19. List 10 more advantages of on-line, point-of-sale systems than were listed in this chapter.

BIBLIOGRAPHY

Albrecht, B. et al. *What To Do After You Hit Return*. Menlo Park, Ca.: People's Computer Co., 1975. 158 pp.

> Subtitled "PCC's first book of computer games," this catalog covers games written in BASIC ranging from simple word and number games to simulations.

Collen, M. F. (ed.). *Hospital Computer Systems*. New York: Wiley, 1974. 768 pp.

> A collection of papers on applications of computers to hospital patient care.

Davenport, W. P. *Modern Data Communication: Concepts, Language and Media*. New York: Hayden, 1971. 208 pp.

> Reviews the basic concepts of communications such as coding, channel capacity, modulation, and multiplexing *without complex mathematics;* designed to serve as both an in-depth introduction and reference guide.

Dutton, J. M., and W. H. Starbuck. *Computer Simulation of Human Behavior*. New York: Wiley, 1971. 708 pp.

> This book is concerned with the description of human behavior and the use of simulation in making descriptive statements about human behavior. The book contains an extensive bibliography.

Gordon, G. *System Simulation*. Englewood Cliffs, N.J.: Prentice-Hall, 1969, 303 pp.

> Describes and defines the simulation of one computer system by another and discusses techniques and methods used in modeling.

Hamming, R. W. *Computers and Society*. New York: McGraw-Hill, 1972. 284 pp.

> Introduction to the computer. Stresses *types* of applications. Not really a social implications text as much as a general introduction to computers.

King, P. F. *A Computer Program for Positional Games*. Springfield, Va.: National Technical Information Service, July 1971. 96 pp. AD-726 622.

> The theory of operation of computer programs constructed to play "positional" games is discussed.

Lyon, J. K. *An Introduction to Data Base Design*. New York: Wiley-Interscience, 1971. 96 pp.

> After a basic introduction to the data base, this book covers logical organization, graphical notation, modeling, physical organization, implementation, and efficiency. A number of examples of data base design are given.

Maisel, H., and G. Gnugnoli. *Simulation of Discrete Stochastic Systems*. Chicago: Science Research Associates, 1972. 465 pp.

> Though the title might not indicate such, this book is an introductory text. The book gives excellent treatment to basic simulation concepts, validity of models, and the GPSS simulation language. FORTRAN, PL/1, and SIMSCRIPT are also briefly covered as possible simulation tools.

Martin, J., and A. R. D. Norman. *The Computerized Society*. Englewood Cliffs, N.J.: Prentice-Hall, 1970, 560 pp.

> The authors see a sudden and massive spread of computer usage in the years ahead and attempt to explain to the "man in the street" what the real impact will be on society by examining a number of application areas.

Martin, J. *Computer Data-Base Organization*. Englewood Cliffs, N.J.: Prentice-Hall, 1975. 558 pp.

> As many of Martin's books are, this is a readable introduction to a fairly technical topic. Covers the technical aspects of data-base design and structure. Could be read by someone that had first read an introduction-to-computers book.

Martin, J. *Telecommunications and the Computer*. Englewood Cliffs, N.J.: Prentice-Hall, 1969, 470 pp.

> This book concentrates on common carrier equipment as opposed to the computer manufacturer's equipment, and covers the technical and design aspects of communications hardware and systems.

Murdick, R. G., and J. E. Ross. *Information Systems for Modern Management* (2nd ed.). Englewood Cliffs, N.J.: Prentice-Hall, 1975. 671 pp.

> Describes how management is improved through the design and utilization of management information systems. Covers information and decision making processes, management science, and the implementation and future of management information systems.

Myers, C. A. *Computers in Knowledge-Based Fields.* Cambridge, Mass.: M.I.T. Press, 1970. 126 pp.

> Surveys the role of the computer now and future prospects in such fields as education, library systems, law, medicine, and national data banks.

Nolan, R. L. *Managing the Data Resource Function.* St. Paul, Minn.: West Publishing Co., 1974. 394 pp.

> A book of readings covering the development of the data resource function, management of the computer, assessment of the data resource function, administrative issues, system design, and future considerations.

Reichardt, J. *The Computer in Art.* New York: Van Nostrand Reinhold. 96 pp.

> How computers can be used to produce drawings, sculptures, and animated films.

Reitman, J. *Computer Simulation Applications.* New York: Wiley, 1971. 265 pp.

> Shows how to apply system simulation to a variety of problems, including such applications as scheduling, resource allocation, traffic analysis, computer systems, and weapon systems.

Sackman, H., and N. Nie (eds.) *The Information Utility and Social Choice.* Montvale, N.J.: AFIPS, 1970. 299 pp.

> Selected papers from a conference cosponsored by the University of Chicago Encyclopedia Britannica, and AFIPS covering such topics as what direction an information utility should take, how it will be regulated in the public interest, and the impact of evolving information utilities on politics.

Schriber, T. J. *FORTRAN Case Studies for Business Applications.* New York: Wiley, 1969. 100 pp.

> A workbook consisting of 11 FORTRAN case studies of business data processing problems. For each, there is a problem analysis, a flowchart, the FORTRAN program, and sample output. Problems include inventory control, rate of return, depreciation, amortization, and the like.

Spencer, D. D. *Game Playing with Computers.* New York: Spartan, 1968. 441 pp.

> Discuss how computers may be programmed to play various games such as chess, tic-tac-toe, and monopoly, among others.

Teague, R., and C. Erickson. *Computers and Society.* St. Paul: West Publishing Co., 1974. 374 pp.

> An interesting collection of readings on the role of computers in society.

Thierauf, R. J. *Systems Analysis and Design of Real-Time Management Information Systems.* Englewood Cliffs, N.J.: Prentice-Hall, 1975. 624 pp.

> Centers on the actual procedures involved in the analysis and design of a real-time MIS from feasibility study through implementation. Topics include systems analysis and design and the future of the MIS.

Weiss, E. (ed.). *Computer Usage/Applications.* New York: McGraw-Hill, 1970. 313 pp.

> Covers a wide variety of computer applications and provides a brief description of how each application is implemented on the computer. Seventeen

applications are described including block diagrams and principle computer functions.

Weiss, B. (ed.). *Digital Computers in the Behavioral Laboratory*. Englewood Cliffs, N.J.: Prentice-Hall, 1973. 460 pp.

Covers a wide range of applications of computers to the behavioral sciences. Explores the laboratory use of computers in the psychological sciences.

Wilson, A. *The Bomb and the Computer*, New York: Delacorte, 1968. 218 pp.

A history of war gaming from the earliest known attempts to the present day with many references to specific games and their uses in particular situations.

5. Artificial intelligence

There is only one condition in which we can imagine managers not needing subordinates, and masters not needing slaves. This condition would be that each (inanimate) instrument could do its own work, at the word of command or by intelligent anticipation, like the statues of Daedalus or the tripods made by Hephaestus, of which Homer relates that "Of their own motion they entered the conclave of Gods of Olympus" as if a shuttle should weave of itself, and a piectrum should do its own harp playing.

Aristotle
The Politics, ca.350B.C.

Regardless of how artificial you may think some human intelligence is, by artificial intelligence we shall mean intelligent, manlike behavior in a machine. As a result, we start our discussion with the obvious question:

What constitutes intelligent behavior?

At least some notion of an answer must be formulated if we are to attempt to say whether or not a machine is exhibiting intelligent behavior. It would be desirable to jot down your own ideas on an answer to this question before proceeding to the next paragraph. In that way you may subsequently be able to separate out and objectively compare your own feelings on the matter with the views presented here.

Many first attempts at describing intelligent behavior might involve requiring a reasonable performance at some nontrivial task. We might ask, for example, that a machine play a good game of chess or carry on a passable conversation in written form. Depending on your viewpoint, you might require only the performance of one or a few such tasks, or you might require an entire range of capabilities. At any rate, this is an approach that is not unreasonable and that is similar to the approach taken by Alan Turing in an attempt to answer the question "Can machines think?". **Turing's test,** as it has come to be called, is in the form of an imitation game:

The new form of the problem can be described in terms of a game which we call the "imitation game". It is played with three people, a man (A), a woman (B), and an interrogator (C) who may be of either sex. The interrogator stays in a room apart from the other two. The object of the game for the interrogator is to determine which of the other two is the man and which is the woman. He knows them by labels X and Y, and at the end of the game he says either "X is A and Y is B" or "X is B and Y is A". The interrogator is allowed to put questions to A and B thus:

C: "Will X please tell me the length of his or her hair?"

Now suppose X is actually A, then A must answer. It is A's object in the game to try to cause C to make the wrong identification. His answer might therefore be:

"My hair is shingled, and the longest strands are about nine inches long."

In order that tones of voice may not help the interrogator the answers should be written, or better still, typewritten. The ideal arrangement is to have a teleprinter communicating between the two rooms. Alternatively, the questions and answers can be repeated by an intermediary. The object of the game for the third player (B) is to help the interrogator. The best strategy for her is probably to give truthful answers. She can add such things as "I am the woman, don't listen to him!" to her answers, but it will avail nothing as the man can make similar remarks.

We now ask the question, "What will happen when the machine takes the part of A in this game?" Will the interrogator decide wrongly as often when the game is played like this as he does when the game is played between a man and a woman? These questions replace our original, "Can machines think?"

Further discussion of the imitation game and the general topic of artificial intelligence are given in Turing's paper, which is reproduced in the Appendix. We highly recommend that the paper be read in its entirety since it is one of the most thoughtful approaches to the possibility of artificial intelligence.

The imitation game would require a machine to be able to simulate a wide range of human behavior and thus constitutes a fairly stringent test. Even though Turing's test might not be accepted by everyone, it provides a reasonable operational definition, at least for our purposes.

Having pondered briefly the question of what constitutes intelligent behavior, we now move to a discussion of the research efforts in artificial intelligence. One researcher has broken the approaches to artificial intelligence into the categories of artificial networks, artificial evolution, and heuristic programming.* **Artificial networks** consist of many relatively simple logical elements with many interconnections in a manner roughly analogous to some models of the brain. The **artificial evolution** approach involves allowing computer-simulated systems to evolve in a manner similar to natural selection by introducing many mutations. The initial system is endowed with some basic primitive capability and hopefully enhances this capability through the simulated evolutionary process.

The third approach, **heuristic programming,** is considered the most promising by many and is currently receiving the greatest attention. This approach involves attempting to write programs that will emulate the general problem-solving techniques that humans seem to use. These techniques are not guaranteed to be successful, since we are not always successful; hence they are called nonalgorithmic or heuristic. Even though they are not always successful, sometimes they allow one to cut through great masses of possibilities to arrive at solutions that would be physically impossible by exhaustive enumeration of all cases. For example, chess masters seem to employ very powerful heuristic techniques to cut the myriads of possibilities down to a tractable number that can be examined in detail.

We will give a quick outline of the state of affairs in a few specific research areas. For the most part, the workers in these areas have used the heuristic programming approach.

GAME PLAYING

The playing of nontrivial games involves substantial problem-solving ability and thus provides researchers with a means of studying problem-solving techniques in a relatively controlled and structured environment. Computer programs have been written that play checkers, chess, GO, and other games.

Most of the work on checkers has been done by Arthur Samuel. Samuel

*J. R. Slagle, *Artificial Intelligence: The Heuristic Programming Approach*. New York: McGraw-Hill, 1971.

The single-circuit board in the photograph is a complete computer central processing unit. We are already to the time where a complete "CPU on a card" costs less than $100 and probably less than five years from such a device being available in less than one cubic inch of space and selling for $1. Caxton Foster in the *Communications of the ACM*, Vol. 15, No. 7, pages 557–565, has explored some uses that might be made of such a device. Imagine, for example, how an alarm clock could be improved. Instead of having to reset it for holidays and weekends and remember to turn the alarm on each evening (and not too early or it will go off at 7:30 P.M. instead of 7:30 A.M.!) we could add our tiny computer and program the alarm for all foreseeable circumstances including leap year and movable holidays. He suggests adding a tiny computer to a watch so, for example, it could flash the message on the face of the watch that "you have a dentist appointment in 47.3 minutes".

The tiny computer could be added to locks so each lock could remember who was allowed to open it. Thus, we would each need only one key card instead of a ring of keys. By adding our tiny computer to a typewriter we could compose and edit a letter with a final clean, errorless copy. Our typewriter could even remember addresses and frequently misspelled words for us. By adding our tiny computer to television sets we could, per the computations of Foster, having better quality pictures and fit all the TV channels presently allocated into the space now reserved for Channel 2. This would be done by sending an initial full picture and then sending only the changes between successive frames.

Well, the list goes on and on. The games Space War, Nim, Kalah, Chess, and GO have been computerized already. Your computerized watch, TV set, or typewriter could also become your fourth for bridge. (Photograph courtesy Philips-Electrologica, Netherlands.)

wrote his first checker-playing program in 1947, and his current program plays an excellent game. For example, the current program won a game with the champion of Connecticut. This successful state of affairs was only realized after long and substantial effort, however.

Many people have been involved in the efforts on chess, even Turing proposed a procedure. Turing's procedure was never programmed, but in 1957 a program was developed by Alex Bernstein that played two "passable amateur games". More recent programs have been entered in tournament play at the Class C and Class D levels. The winner of the Second Annual Computer Chess Championship at the 1971 National Meeting of the Association for Computing Machinery was a program called Chess 3.5, developed at Northwestern University, and it is classified as a Class C player. It should be noted, however, that early optimism about chess-playing programs has not been well founded. In 1957 a very prominent researcher predicted that "within ten years a digital computer will be the world's chess champion". The current state of affairs is discussed in an article by Michie,[*] which gives a U.S. Chess Federation rating of 1500 for the best chess program as compared to 1600-1900 for strong amateurs. The highest rating was 2824, assigned to Bobby Fischer.

Work on programs for the ancient oriental game of GO has been much more limited but illustrates an almost classic pattern in artificial intelligence research. In a sense, GO seems to be a much more complex game than either chess or checkers, since the size of its game tree has been estimated at 10^{761} as opposed to 10^{120} for chess and 10^{40} for checkers. Nevertheless, a program has been written by Albert Zobrist[†] which plays reasonably well at the beginners level by using some clever pattern recognition techniques. However, little progress seems to have been made beyond this level. This sequence of relatively easily won initial success followed by inordinate difficulties has been quite common in artificial intelligence research; another classic example being natural language translation. This pattern has produced some very pessimistic views that we will discuss later.

THEOREM PROVING

Theorem proving is also intellectually challenging, involving as it does a logical reasoning process and apparently the use of heuristic techniques to choose promising lines of attack. One of the earliest programs in this area was the Logic Theorist developed by Newell, Shaw, and Simon in 1957. This program was able to prove standard theorems in logic by using techniques that modeled the methods used by college sophomores in logic classes. Later programs have been based on a powerful rule of inference called the resolution principle, which is discussed quite clearly in a text by Nilsson.[‡] It now appears that the best approach might be the use of the resolution principle combined with time-saving heuristics, since the number of possible lines of reasoning for substantial proofs is staggering.

QUESTION ANSWERING AND CONVERSATION

Many question-answering programs have been written; most of them require that facts be stated in a restricted form of English. Two of the major problems in this area are the syntactical and semantical analyses of English sentences, and the determination of a correct line of deduction to generate a meaningful answer. The ultimate goal in this area would be a general conversational program, and approximations to this goal have been made.

A program called ELIZA has been developed by Joseph Wiezenbaum; it carries on a relatively successful conversation in which the computer re-

[*]D. Michie, "The Path to Championship Chess by Computer". *Computers and Automation and People*, **22**, 1, January 1973.

[†]Albert Zobrist, "A Model of Visual Organization for the Game of GO"., *AFIPS Conference Proceedings*, **34**, May 1969.

[‡]N.J. Nilsson, *Problem Solving Methods in Artificial Intelligence*. New York: McGraw-Hill, 1971.

Bell Laboratories scientists have devised a system with which a computer can produce nearly natural sounding synthetic speech directly from ordinary English text fed in by a teletypewriter. From a clearer understanding of how people really use language and tailor it to match their intended meaning, the researchers succeeded in programming a computer with a group of complex rules relating to timing, pitch, and stress. These rules plus some mathematical approximations of the shapes and motions that the human vocal tract assumes when uttering common sounds and sound sequences, together with basic word categories and definitions, comprise the information written into the computer memory that is used to produce the speech sounds. (Courtesy of Bell Laboratories.)

sponds roughly in the fashion of a psychotherapist. A conversation of this type is given below, where the lines printed in capital letters represent the computer responses.

Men are all alike.

IN WHAT WAY

They're always bugging us about something or other.

CAN YOU THINK OF A SPECIFIC EXAMPLE

Well, my boyfriend made me come here.

YOUR BOYFRIEND MADE YOU COME HERE

He says I'm depressed much of the time.

I AM SORRY TO HEAR YOU ARE DEPRESSED

It's true, I am unhappy.

DO YOU THINK COMING HERE WILL HELP YOU NOT TO BE UNHAPPY
I need some help, that much seems certain.
WHAT WOULD IT MEAN TO YOU IF YOU GOT SOME HELP
Perhaps I could learn to get along with my mother.
TELL ME MORE ABOUT YOUR FAMILY
My mother takes care of me.
WHO ELSE IN YOUR FAMILY TAKES CARE OF YOU
My father.
YOUR FATHER
You are like my father in some ways.
WHAT RESEMBLANCE DO YOU SEE
You are not very aggressive but I think you don't want me to notice that.
WHAT MAKES YOU THINK I AM NOT VERY AGGRESSIVE
You don't argue with me.
WHY DO YOU THINK I DON'T ARGUE WITH YOU
You are afraid of me.
DOES IT PLEASE YOU TO BELIEVE I AM AFRAID OF YOU
My father is afraid of everybody.
WHAT ELSE COMES TO MIND WHEN YOU THINK OF YOUR FATHER
Bullies.
DOES THAT HAVE ANYTHING TO DO WITH THE FACT THAT YOUR
BOYFRIEND MADE YOU COME HERE

Evidently, some subjects who have conversed with ELIZA have been hard to convince that ELIZA is not human, and thus for these people ELIZA has passed a form of Turing's test.

The general procedure used in the ELIZA program to generate responses is relatively simple. The sentence typed in by the human is scanned for the occurrence of a **keyword** (one of a group of words previously stored in the computer). If the input sentence contains a keyword, a computer response is generated by means of a rule associated with the keyword. If a keyword is not found, a rather arbitrary (content-free) response is made, or, under certain conditions, an earlier response is used to generate a new response. For more information on this subject, read Weizenbaum's article entitled "Contextual Understanding by Computers", reproduced in the Appendix.

Although results from ELIZA and similar programs have been encouraging, many problems exist in developing a general conversational program, and some computer scientists believe that the problem may be unsolvable.

FINE ARTS

Some interesting computer programs have been written to generate graphic art forms and to produce musical compositions. Purely mechanical approaches produce rather unsophisticated works, but man and machine working in a complementary fashion produce some very interesting results. Perhaps the most striking examples of this is the work of John Whitney, which involves sophisticated and colorful moving patterns. A film entitled "Graphic Motion" provides an appealing example of Whitney's work. Work on dynamic graphic art forms requires considerable resources and thus is not

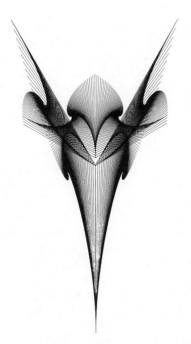 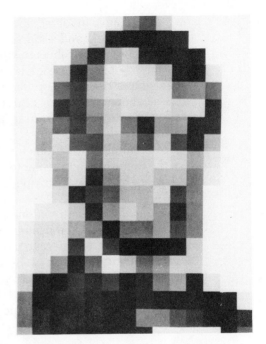

While a few attempts have been made to automate the artist, most computer art efforts try to **extend the artist,** to give him a new medium in which to express himself. Shown here on the left is an example of computer art entitled "Hummingbird". The artist used computerized plotting equipment to produce the picture. This method allowed him to express himself in a mode of art that would have been too time consuming to explore manually. At right is a portrait depicting a famous face composed entirely of cubes in different intensities of gray. (If you don't recognize the picture try looking at it from 15 feet or more, or while you're squinting, or with your eyeglasses removed.) Such a picture is part of an experiment to learn the least amount of information a picture may contain and still be recognized. (Courtesy of CalComp and Bell Laboratories.)

widely pursued. On the other hand, many people are using the computer to produce static graphic art forms.

The use of computers to produce literary work has been the subject of some speculation, but much of the speculation has been in a humerous vein. An amusing commentary on this subject is given in "Artificial Intelligence and Intelligent Artifice", from *The Digital Villain* by Robert M. Baer. This article has been reproduced in the Appendix.

ROBOTS

Considerable research is being done on the development of computer programs to control the actions of robots. For example, in 1962 a computer was connected to a mechanical manipulator (hand) at M.I.T.* The hand contained "sense elements" and the computer was programmed to accept data from these elements and direct the stacking of blocks. Subsequent projects at M.I.T.

*J. R. Slagle, *Artificial Intelligence: The Heuristic Programming Approach.* New York: McGraw-Hill, 1971.

and Stanford have involved directing and controlling the interaction between a mechanical hand and a mechanical eye. Still other projects seek to control the actions of mobile robots to guide them over paths or allow them to search for specified objects. One such battery-powered robot, called The Beast, was built at Johns Hopkins University to simply roam the halls of the Applied Physics Laboratory and to "search" for an electric outlet whenever its battery became run-down. On finding an outlet, The Beast recharged itself and continued to roam.*

The potential applications for "intelligent" robots is indeed great, ranging from the investigation of remote and hostile environments to overcoming the limitations of the handicapped. One wonders, however, if a more subtle motivation also exists—the same driving force that perhaps motivated the creators of the early automatons discussed in Chapter 4. That is, the desire to explain the universe in mechanistic terms. Derek de Solla Price† suggests this possibility as an alternative to the usual belief that physical mechanism led to the mechanistic philosophy. In all probability the two are inextricably entwined and "From the Lascaux Caves to the Strassbourg Clock to electronic and cybernetic brains, the road of evolution has run straight and steady, oddly bordered by the twin causes and effects of mechanistic philosophy and of high technology".‡

SUMMARY

Although there are many other areas of artificial intelligence research, the ones we have discussed give a fairly representative view of the progress and difficulties in all areas. There has been significant success, but optimistic predictions have often given way to disappointment. The difficulties have been severe enough to justify some reasonably sound arguments for fundamental limitations on artificial intelligence. Dreyfus has given such arguments, and only time will tell whether optimism or skepticism was well-founded. Regardless of the outcome, artificial intelligence research is important and significant, since, as Dreyfus§ states:

Indeed if reasoning can be programmed into a computer, this will confirm an understanding of the nature of man, which Western thinkers have been groping toward for two thousand years but which they only now have the tools to express and implement. The incarnation of this intuition will drastically change our understanding of ourselves. If, on the other hand artificial intelligence should turn out to be impossible, then we will have to distinguish human from artificial reason, and this too will radically change our view of ourselves.

EXERCISES

1. Look up definitions of the word "intelligence" in several dictionaries. Choose the definition that you prefer or create your own definition if none

---

*Ibid.

†Derek J. De Solla Price, "Automata and the Origins of Mechanism and Mechanistic Philosophy". *Technology and Culture*, Vol. 1, No. 1, Winter 1964.

‡*Ibid.*

§H. L. Dreyfus, *What Computers Can't Do: A Critique of Artificial Reason*. New York: Harper & Row. 1972.

of them please you. Use this as a basis for a position paper pro or con the possibility of artificial intelligence.

2. Read Turing's paper that appears in the readings section at the end of the book. Discuss the areas in which his arguments seem weak or unsatisfactory to you.

3. Set up Turing's test with human participants and record the resulting conversations. Indicate the parts of the conversations that would be most difficult for a computer to simulate.

4. Study the ELIZA conversation given in this chapter and try to identify content-free responses. Also, try to identify responses that are the result of fairly obvious transformations. From the remaining responses, if any, choose the one that you feel is most "intelligent".

5. From recent issues of journals or trade magazines, try to determine the present status of chess-playing programs.

BIBLIOGRAPHY

Baer, Robert M. *The Digital Villain*. Reading, Mass.: Addison-Wesley Publishing Co., 1972. 187 pp.

> An imaginative and entertaining introduction to computer science and the social issues of computer usage. Part II of the book contains some very amusing excerpts from literary and dramatic works dealing with computers, robots, and artificial intelligence.

Dreyfus, H. L. *What Computers Can't Do: A Critique of Artificial Reason*. New York: Harper & Row, 1972. 259 pp.

> This text contains a thoughtful and critical review of research in the field of artificial intelligence and presents arguments for the existence of fundamental barriers in this field.

Feigenbaum, E. A., and J. Feldman. *Computers and Thought*. New York: McGraw-Hill, 1963. 535 pp.

> A collection of 20 basic papers on various aspects of artificial intelligence research.

Fogel, L. J., A. J. Owens, and M. J. Walsh. *Artificial Intelligence through Simulated Evolution*. New York: Wiley, 1966. 170 pp.

> Approaches to artificial intelligence via evolving programs. Requires no mathematical background to be able to read all but one chapter.

Frayn, Michael. *The Tin Men*. Boston: Little Brown and Co., 1965. 216 pp.

> This fictional work is an hilarious satire on computers, automation, and the scientists working in these areas.

Jackson, P. C. *Introduction to Artificial Intelligence*. New York: Petrocelli Books, 1974. 453 pp.

> This book is an engaging survey and tutorial of the field of artificial intelligence. The scope of the book is quite broad, ranging from a discussion of natural intelligence to treatments of technical areas such as theorem proving and semantic information processing, minimizing the need for previous, formal exposure to mathematics and computers.

Minsky, M. (ed.). *Semantic Information Processing*. Cambridge, Mass.: M.I.T. Press, 1968. 438 pp.

> Each chapter covers an experiment involving computer programs to solve different kinds of artificial intelligence problems.

Newborn, M. *Computer Chess*. New York: Academic Press, 1975. 200 pp.

> Presents 38 games between computer and computer, or between computer and man, including games from the first U.S. Computer Chess Championship.

Nilsson, N. J. *Problem Solving Methods in Artificial Intelligence*. New York: McGraw-Hill, 1971. 255 pp.

> The first part of this book (five chapters) deals with the principal problem areas that have been attacked by researchers in the field to date and concentrates on methods of heuristic search. The final three chapters deal with automatic theorem proving.

Pylyshyn, Z. W. *Perspectives on the Computer Revolution*. Englewood Cliffs: N. J.: Prentice-Hall, 1970. 540 pp.

> An overview of how computerization has affected present culture and technology, with a discussion of where present trends will bring us in the future.

Slagle, J. R. *Artificial Intelligence: The Heuristic Programming Approach*. New York: McGraw-Hill, 1971, 196 pp.

> This text contains a general discussion of a wide variety of attempts to program machines to exhibit intelligent behavior and thus gives a valuable overview of the field.

Teague, R. and C. Erickson. *Computers and Society*. St. Paul, Minn.: West Publishing Co., 1974. 374 pp.

> An interesting collection of readings on the role of computers in society.

Weizenbaum, J. "ELIZA—A Computer Program for the Study of Natural-Language Communication between Man and Machine". *Communications of the Association for Computing Machinery*, **9**, 1, 1966.

> Contains an interesting man-machine "conversation" and a general description of the methods used to generate the machine responses.

⑥. Misuse of computers

The powerful products of our present-day technology offer many opportunities for abuse: nuclear weapons, chemical and biological warfare, and drugs are a few examples. It is not so easy to visualize the misuse of computers, since computers deal with a more abstract quantity—information. Some abuses, such as invasion of privacy, are fairly apparent but others are more subtle. We will emphasize a broad range of abuses in this chapter and investigate the privacy issue more intensely in the next chapter.

Whether the use of computers in personality analysis, computerized dating, or astrological projections constitutes misuse of computers is less clear than cases of privacy invasion. The problem in the former cases is that computer-printed information has connotations of having a "stamp of the truth" on it. Computers do not make mistakes very often and when they do, they usually catch the error and request human assistance. Thus, one of the major advantages of computers, accuracy, works to engender a feeling that computer-processed data is error free. The fallacy here is illustrated by the systems analyst's expression **GIGO** (for Garbage In, Garbage Out). The results produced by a computer are dependent on both the fidelity of the input data and the algorithm used to process the data. *If you do not have adequate information necessary to produce certain results, the best algorithm and the most reliable of all computers will be of no avail.*

If we do not know how to predict a person's future or select the best compatibility match for some individual, then the most powerful of computers will not assist us to any end other than to provide our advertising agency with a come-on gimmick. In general we must (a) know what information to collect, (b) know what algorithm to use to process the information, and (c) have a reliable computer, before we can say that the results of a data processing effort are valid. Even this statement assumes no mistakes in data collection, no errors in converting the data to machine-readable form, and that the user of the results can, in fact, understand the output.

ACCIDENTAL MISUSE AND MURPHY'S LAW

One of the topics discussed at the 1970 Spring Joint Computer Conference panel session "Lessons of the Sixties" was Murphy's law. The contention is that many of the problems encountered in using computers arise because systems analysts and systems designers ignore Murphy's law.

One statement of **Murphy's Law** is, simply, if it can go wrong, it will. This has been restated by some experienced systems analysts as: if it can't go wrong, it still will. This is not meant to be a flippant comment. Systems designers repeatedly have to make assumptions about the particular environment in which a computer is to be used. When the assumptions prove to be untrue—that is, when Murphy's law is not properly taken into consideration—the computer will not be able to perform as expected. The complications resulting from the reduced performance may vary widely: from a lost-parts order to a $1 million-accounting mistake. Let's consider two such circumstances:

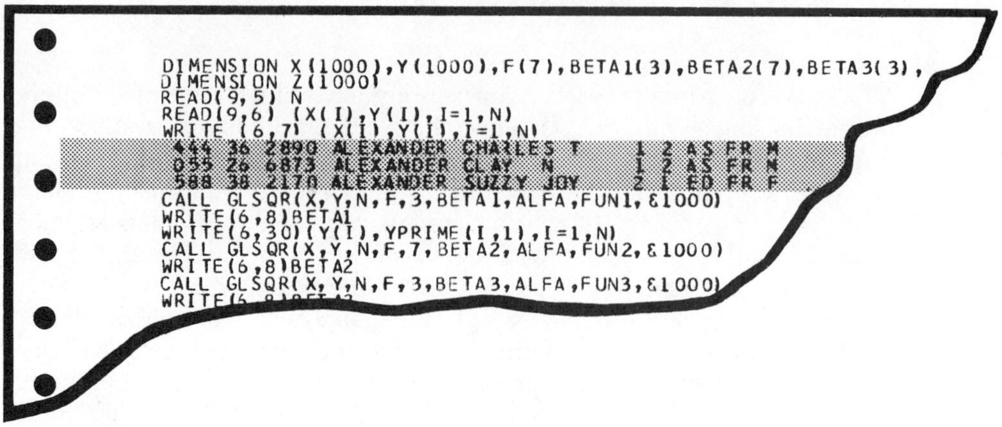

```
DIMENSION X(1000),Y(1000),F(7),BETA1(3),BETA2(7),BETA3(3),
DIMENSION Z(1000)
READ(9,5) N
READ(9,6) (X(I),Y(I),I=1,N)
WRITE (6,7) (X(I),Y(I),I=1,N)
444 36 2890 ALEXANDER CHARLES T      1 2 AS FR M
055 26 6873 ALEXANDER CLAY  N        1 2 AS FR M
588 38 2170 ALEXANDER SUZZY JOY      2 1 ED FR F
CALL GLSQR(X,Y,N,F,3,BETA1,ALFA,FUN1,&1000)
WRITE(6,8)BETA1
WRITE(6,30)(Y(I),YPRIME(I,1),I=1,N)
CALL GLSQR(X,Y,N,F,7,BETA2,ALFA,FUN2,&1000)
WRITE(6,8)BETA2
CALL GLSQR(X,Y,N,F,3,BETA3,ALFA,FUN3,&1000)
WRITE(6,8)BETA3
```

Figure 6.1

1. Notice the accompanying listing (Figure 6.1). It is a copy of part of the standard first page of a program that was run at a university during the spring semester of 1970. The "interspersed records" (shaded in the listing) are from a listing of the university's student information file. The security attached to the file should prevent unauthorized access to the information in the file. In fact, what you see listed simply should not have been possible. Even a very skilled programmer would have to be quite persistent (and quite lucky) to get a listing such as the one shown. In doing an after-the-fact analysis, the actual cause of the problem is easy to understand (to anyone that is knowledgeable about how a computer functions). What happened is that, from a security point of view, an assumption was made (else the item was never considered) that a certain human error would never be made. True to Murphy's law, it was made. Here the harm was small. In a defense security environment or even a credit-reporting environment, the harm might be greater.

2. This case deals with a parallel lack of forethought. In a payroll program, tax tables are different for married and single taxpayers. Thus, it is quite meaningful to read in a marital-status code (e.g., one of the digits 1 or 2) and use this status code to subscript a two-part tax table. The problem arises when, true to Murphy's law, someone punches an A, *, # sign, or 6, or something similar, instead of one of the valid codes, 1 or 2. It will happen. When it happened the first 6 or 10 times at a certain installation, it caused the processing of the payroll to be delayed—something that can be very bad if the delay becomes substantial. One solution is to add an edit program ahead of the payroll program. Thus, bad input data can be rejected instead of letting it disable the payroll program.

The examples could go on for a long time. Some people make quite an effort to collect computerized *faux pas*. One man's solution to this class of problems is given in Withington's "Cosmetic Programming" in the Appendix. This is one of the best and most useful articles written in this area; it gives sage advice to the practicing systems analyst.

Why is this topic being introduced here? Well, from the system's *user's* point of view, problems such as the above are examples of computer failures.

It is most likely that the failures were either in the design of the application of the computer or in a simple human error. It is very unlikely that either a "computer error" or "computer malfunction" was involved. *When a computerized process breaks down due to an error in systems design, we certainly have a case where a computer has been misused.*

A very large portion of the anticomputer sentiment in existence today is due solely to computers being misused in this fashion. Systems are often automated before we have the ability to adequately handle the processes to be automated. This certainly happened with the mass automation of the accounts receivables of oil companies and of book clubs. Sluggish, nonresponsive computerized systems seemed impersonal and cold compared with the hand-maintained books. In fact, we have come to praise errors because they are so human. The euphemisms "cold and calculating", "depersonalized", and the like, reflect the impact of poor systems design on computer users.

We have two kinds of **misuse** of computers: **intentional** and **accidental.** The latter category is quite threatening. The intentional "do badder" is not filled with the zeal of the "priests of automation". These men, also called "priests of the new technology", like most converts to any new order, are fired with the fervor of the True Believer.* This malady of zealousness is all too common among technologists as our current struggles with pollution attest. However, computer science seems particularly susceptible due to its relative newness and its dynamic nature. These have combined to bring an extraordinarily large number of relatively young scientists to decision making positions of considerable power. In many cases these scientists have not realized that, "Good science is a strange mixture of passionate conviction that one's own approach is correct—to get the sense of personal involvement that makes hard work a pleasure—and an openness to the virtue of other approaches."† While passionate conviction has been abundantly present, openness to other approaches and objective appraisals of the effects of computer usage has often been lacking. This has been particularly true in the use of computers for automation. We will discuss this important area much more in a later chapter, but we should observe here that automation for automation's sake is one of the greatest misuse sources. Even where automation is warranted from a technical standpoint a complete analysis of the effects (social, economic, psychological, and philosophical) should be made before implementing the automated system. A curiously appropriate example is related by Gerald Weinberg in his book entitled *The Psychology of Computer Programming*‡:

As a simple example, consider the establishment which replaced its ancient elevators with spanking new automatic ones. This was most unfortunate for the programmers, for the old elevator operator had run an informal pickup and delivery service for them between the programming floor—the eighth—and the machine room—the basement. Of course, nobody could justify hiring a messenger just for going from the eighth floor to the basement, so the programmers lost a lot of productive time. Another function this operator served was locator of missing persons. With the machine room on one floor, keypunch room on another and programmers' offices on a third, chances of finding a missing programmer in the first place you looked were less than fifty-fifty.

*The True Believer makes an interesting study. See Eric Hoffer's *The True Believer*, New York: Harper & Row, 1966.

†M. Arbib, *The Metaphorical Brain*. New York: Wiley-Interscience, 1972.

‡G. M. Weinberg, *The Psychology of Computer Programming*. New York: Van Nostrand Reinhold, 1971, p. 51.

The elevator operator, however, could be relied upon to know immediately on which floor a given person could be found. With these two losses—plus the loss of other services such as rerouting of misdelivered mail and relaying of important messages —the new automatic elevators proved to be a net loss, even though the elevator service itself seemed a bit faster.

THE ALMOST-PERFECT-MACHINE PROBLEM

Some of the ways in which a computer can be misused are presently just vague images lurking on the horizon. One of the more threatening of these could be called the "almost-perfect-machine problem". Anything that is prone to frequent malfunctions is so distrusted by man that it does not pose much of a threat. Things that have total reliability (if such exist) are also not much of a threat. But, consider the machines that will function reliably for a long time and then malfunction. Nicholas Charney's comments below* show how such machines could pose a very real threat. They lead you into trusting them and then:

People are afraid of machines—and rightly so—and the machine that tops the blacklist—and rightly so—is the computer.

The computer is often seen as an invisible, superhuman force that permeates our lives, robbing us of our identity and humanity. Names are replaced by numbers, the numbers are fed into computers, and our lives are controlled by this outside accountant *extraordinaire* who sends home our school grades, tells us how much we owe Carte Blanche, computes our bank balance, and keeps track of our phone calls.

Given the fact that a computer is really not more than a giant adding machine, performing faithfully and quickly, why is it that people become upset by a timesaving machine which makes their lives so much easier and pleasanter? (Even the complaining Berkeley student might want his IBM number back if he found how long he would have to wait in lines without it.)

I think the reasons why people are afraid of machines are quite clear—and they are not the most important reasons. First, people are often afraid of machines because they feel inferior to them—machines can do so many things faster and more accurately. Second, people are insecure about their own human warmth and feelings and worry that in many ways they are like a machine—no soul, no compassion, no free-will. And third, people blame machines for ills that really result from other sources —impersonalization results when large numbers of people are thrown together; yet machines, in trying to create order out of potential chaos, become scapegoats for those who are unsure of their own identities.†

And so, ironically enough, as the world gets smaller and the number of people gets larger, human contact increases and human security decreases. Is the computer at fault? I doubt it.

Why, then should people be afraid of computers?

Given their astonishing capacity for doing numerical calculations, computers can become quite powerful—even in the role of servant to man. As time goes on and computers are used more and more to solve complex mathematical equations which pertain to the regulation of our economy, our defense system, and our political system—only then does the fear of computers become legitimate.

For example, what happens if one of these mathematical equations or models is inaccurate or incomplete? What happens when there is poor judgement in deciding

*Reprinted from *Psychology Today* magazine, January 1968. Copyright © Ziff-Davis Publishing Company.

†Editorial note: This is often called the **blame-the-machine fallacy.**

One of the most humorous explorations of the possible consequences of computer error has been BASF's popular "Recurring Computer Nightmare" series. The ad copy states the problem well:

"It could have been the programmer, or maybe it was Twinkie crumbs on the drive rollers. The fact remains, just one little computer error could bend your . . . operation way out of shape".

(From Nightmare #11) The consequence of hardware (or software) malfunction might not be very humorous in the real-world situation. Through experience we have found that such malfunction can be, at the least, very expensive to repair in terms of harm done to people and may not even be repairable. We can afford to spend quite a bit of money to pay for reliable hardware and software and for adequate system design (Ads courtesy BASF Systems.)

"You mene I've bin spending this whol term with a defektiv reeding machin?"

Reprinted with permission of *Datamation* ® copyright C Technical Publishing Co.

From *Saturday Review/World*, September 21, 1974 by Sidney Harris. Drawing by Sidney Harris, copyright © 1974, Saturday Review, Inc.)

what data to give the computer? What happens if—Machine forbid—the electronic wizard makes an error? Probably nothing would happen. The miscalculation would be caught, corrected, and everything would proceed without a hitch.

But as computers become even better, mathematical models more accurate, and mistakes fewer, people might begin to rely on the Machine's answers more and more. Eventually the computer would be making calculations of such a complex and detailed nature that the quantitative transformations would result in qualitative differences between the input and the output. Then errors would be difficult, if not impossible, to recognize.

The ultimate danger might come if the output of the computer were tied directly into regulating and modifying the system—just the way computers are used today to make instantaneous decisions in guiding a rocket to safe landing. Thus, a futuristic society guided by a self-generative, self-regulatory computer could compound an even minor miscalculation into something grotesque—long before the consequences could be recognized or averted.

INTENTIONAL MISUSE

So far we have considered mostly the accidental misuse of computers. The intentional misuse is, both because of the "less potential harm" argument already given and because of the already established means for detecting such, of less concern to us. Yet, there are some pretty big problem areas even here. Auditors have to be trained to search for a new breed of techniques for misappropriating monies. For example, consider a computer that handled stock transactions. A program that was supposed to make stock and corresponding fund transfers could, rather than transfer, for example, $100,000 directly from account X to account Y, let the $100,000 rest in account Z for several minutes in the process of being transferred. If the volume of transactions were high enough, there would always be another $100,000 ready to "rest" in account Z on its way from one account to another account. Thus, by borrowing the $100,000 from many different people for at most several minutes per person, one could manage to borrow the $100,000 (or whatever amount the transaction volume would permit) indefinitely.

Another example is the so-called "salami payroll". In the salami payroll, the culprit takes a very small slice of each payee's money. For example, some computations inherently cause fractions of a cent to arise as the result (e.g., the FICA computation for a particular individual might be $43.682914). A programmer could deposit all round-off amounts to his own account. Given a payroll of many thousands the total slice becomes quite a nice little sum of money. In a typical payroll, a clever culprit could get away with one to two cents per person and still have the payroll "balance".

A few real-life examples of intentional misuse selected from Gellman's "Using the Computer to Steal"* are given below.

1. Between 1959 and 1963, the manager of data processing for a stockbroker embezzled over $80,000 from the company by having checks made payable to fictitious payees. Only the inadvertent return of a check revealed the thefts.

2. A group of individuals in an investment firm embezzled customer funds and then told the customers that a service agency has processed their accounts incorrectly. Because the public was ready to believe the cry of "computer error", considerable time elapsed before the crime was discovered.

3. A manager of claims in a government-sponsored medical aid scheme introduced false doctor claims and directed the payment checks to an office he had rented under a fictitious name.

4. Programmers have stolen information from a payroll system for use in union bargaining.

5. Programmers have stolen information from a payroll system and sold it to a life insurance company agent.

6. Programmers and operators have stolen and sold name and address files.

7. At a large Canadian department store, a systems analyst placed orders for expensive appliances and coded them as "special pricing orders". Using his knowledge of the system information flow and procedures, he intercepted the documents as they reached the "special pricing orders" desk. He then changed the list price to a price of six or seven dollars and then put the forged documents back into the regular stream. The appliances were delivered to him and he paid his account promptly. The practice was

*Harvey S. Gellman, "Using the Computer to Steal", *Computers and Automation*, April 1971. Reprinted with permission from *Computers and Automation*, April 1971 copyright © 1971 by and published by Berkeley Enterprises, Inc., 815 Washington Street, Newtonville, Massachusetts, 02160.

discovered by outside systems consultants called in to review the adequacy of the system's internal control procedures.

8. An executive of a stockbrokerage firm embezzled about $250,000 by personally creating punched cards to transfer credits to his own account from the company's interest revenue account.

9. In 1970 five men, including a bank vice-president, were charged with defrauding two banks of more than $1 million by using a computer. Deposit slips for cash deposits were made out when they were actually depositing checks. Since cash deposits are recorded for immediate credit, checks subsequently drawn appeared to be covered by the false cash deposits. If the deposits had been correctly made as check deposits, the computer would not have credited the money to the account immediately, so that when withdrawals were made the computer would have indicated insufficient funds available, with an uncollectable check on deposit. Ordinarily, a teller or branch manager would notice checks deposited as cash and refuse to accept them. In this case an assistant branch manager (one of the thieves) accepted the checks. The scheme was uncovered by accident when a bank messenger failed to deliver a bundle of deposits to the clearing house, leaving $440,000 worth of check withdrawals uncovered.

Still more examples of computer abuse have been compiled by the Stanford Research Institute for the National Science Foundation.* A few of the more bizarre cases are given below.

1. A programmer was accused of bigotry because he programmed a computer to eliminate black people in screening and selecting new employees.

2. A computer dating bureau was charged by the California State Attorney with making flase claims that a computer was being used to evaluate data and match clients.

3. The California State Personnel Board disciplined two psychiatrist case workers for refusing to submit welfare data because they claimed the computer system lacked security and confidentiality.

4. An employee in an insurance company changed several deceased insured person's account numbers to his own to collect their pensions. He was caught when a staple in a punch card forced manual handling which revealed several cards with the same number.

5. Equity Funding Life Insurance Company created 56,000 fake insurance policies and sold them to re-insurers. The loss was estimated at $2 billion. According to one investigator, "The computer was an integral part of the whole scheme. Without it they probably could not have carried it off because it enabled them to bury the phony business".

MISUSE SOLUTIONS

Although one might shoot or bomb a computer, as has happened in several recorded instances, effective solutions to computer misuse undoubtedly lie through somewhat more sophisticated means. One of the most frequently

*D. B. Parker, S. Nycum, and O. S. Oüra, *Computer Abuse*, National Technical Information Service, Accession No. PB 231–320, November 1973.

proposed solutions would be equally effective in both the intentional and accidental misuse areas. It calls for a high degree of professionalism among practicing computer specialists. Almost certainly the computer specialists of the future will have to be certified or licensed. One major facet of professionalism is the ability of the given profession to police itself. Independent of your own views about the American Medical Association, the AMA has been relatively successful in policing the medical profession.

While the computer professsion has its professional associations, notably the Association for Computing Machinery (ACM) and the Data Processing Management Association (DPMA), they have not been heavily involved in the relevant social and political issues affecting the profession (e.g., neither has greatly helped the government to establish standards in politically sensitive areas*).

Some steps have been taken, however. The ACM has established an Ombudsman Project (in 1971) to perform such services as helping a person that is being badgered by computerized billing, evaluating questionable computerized dating services, and serving as expert witnesses in court cases. In each case the ACM ombudsman will get involved only when requested (typically requests come from the Better Business Bureau, Chamber of Commerce, concerned individuals, and the like). Reaction to this program has, in general, been quite favorable.†

The ACM has been concerned for many years with ethics in computing. In 1966 the ACM adopted a set of guidelines for conduct in information processing and in the April 1973 issue of the *Communications of the ACM,* a "Proposed ACM Code of Professional Conduct" and a "Proposed ACM Policy Regarding Procedure in Professional Conduct Cases" were published. The Code of Professional Conduct was adopted a few months later.

Certification and licensing have often been proposed as methods for regulating computer professions and thereby reducing computer misuse. Both of these possibilities would presumably require practitioners of the computer professions to demonstrate an acceptable level of technical competence and adhere to high ethical standards. But licensing implies mandatory control as exemplified by the medical profession, and thus would require legislative action. Such action can only be the result of considerable social pressure and in view of the arguments against licensing, such pressure is unlikely to occur. The arguments in opposition to licensing are:

1. Licensing may lessen competition.
2. Licensing may increase costs to an unreasonable level by effectively reducing the supply of "acceptable professionals".
3. The computing field is so dynamic that testing technical competence would be difficult and controversial.
4. The task of implementation would be substantial since there were 250,000 computer programmers in 1970 and estimates for 1975 exceed 500,000.
5. The Labor Department has declared computer programmers to be nonprofessionals and thus nonexempt (i.e., they have to keep track of hours worked and be paid overtime as required by law).

*See, for example, the editorial report in the April 1970 issue of *Datamation* (pp. 188–190).
†However, see Alan Taylor's "ACM Offers Goodwill (Little Else) to Customers" in the December 1972 issue of *Computerworld.*

On the other hand, certification implies a recommended but voluntary procedure and thus receives wider support than licensing. Indeed, a certification effort is well underway. The DPMA proposed the idea of an international certification program in 1959 and subsequently developed a certification examination. The examination was first conducted in 1962 and has been offered annually since then. The concept was officially embraced by a much broader spectrum of professional organizations in 1973 with the formation of the Institute for Certification of Computer Professionals (ICCP). In 1974, the ICCP acquired the testing and certification programs of the DPMA, and it now administers the examination for the Certificate in Data Processing (CDP)*. Eight professional societies—including the Data Processing Management Association, the Association for Computing Machinery, and the Institute of Electrical and Electronic Engineers—are members of the ICCP, giving it a broad base of support. With this support, it is very likely that certification of computer professionals will be increasingly important in the next few years.

Another hope for improvement in the accidental misuse of computers is that, during the rest of this century, we will develop a new professional. This new scientist /technician could be called a **general systems analyst.** Such analysts certainly cannot be produced by our current educational system. They must be specialists, to be sure, but will need three or maybe even five specialty areas. One of the major problems today is that practicing analysts have so little formal breadth that they are unable to grasp the whole system being studied. **Total systems** is a term being applied to this problem area; today's analysts must be able to see far beyond the obvious bounds of their designated system. The economic importance of the total system view is clear from a simple example. Suppose an analyst is assigned to redesign a payroll system (see Figure 6.2). If the view is restricted to just that—a payroll system—the analyst will quite possibly elect a very expensive path for the company. Far better if one takes a total system view and identifies all the parts in the payroll system. Looking at the payroll as a **subsystem,** one will be able to see that it interfaces into several other areas (other subsystems). This larger view will permit a much more adequate (both in the sense of desirable system features and in the sense of cost /benefit) system to be designed.

Our current educational system has a very hard time turning out a researcher or technician with enough formal breadth to consider total systems at all. The new total system analyst or general system analyst or cyberneticist or whatever must be knowledgeable in such areas as:

Mathematical modeling

Accounting

Environmental science

Management systems analysis

Psychology

Professional responsibility and professional ethics

Economics

Computer science

---

*Information about the CDP Examination may be obtained from ICCP, Certification and Testing Section, P. O. Box 195, Park Ridge, Ill. 60068.

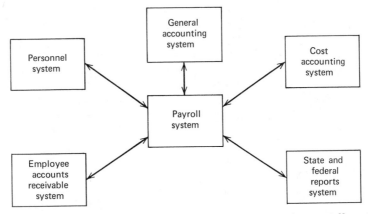

Figure 6.2   Part of the total-system environment of a payroll system.

Knowledge of the humanistic aspects of systems is of particular importance since, as Drucker* observes: "The scientifically trained man again is expected to become a humanist; otherwise he will lack the knowledge and perception needed to make his science effective."

Proposed solutions in the intentional misuse area call for management to recognize the power of control in combating fraud. Management, at the top, should initiate the following:

1. A study of the data security needs of the organization, measurement of risks, and costs of disruptions or losses.
2. A determination of how well the existing security systems meet these needs.
3. The development and implementation of a data security system that covers security of computer programs and data.

Competent outside experts should be used, since the organization's own people will probably not be rigorous in checking their own work. Furthermore, it is protection from inside people that is most frequently overlooked. All executives in the organization need to be sensitized to questions such as the following:

1. Do we maintain computer files that, if lost, could stall our day-to-day operations or involve a loss of a substantial amount of money?
2. Could someone alter one of our computer programs without detection? Could someone alter our financial records or any other data files without detection?
4. Could someone enter our computer room and physically damage the system?
5. Do we know the estimated cost of recreating our current computer data files if they were destroyed?
6. Do we have a periodic independent review of our data security function by computer experts?

---

*P. F. Drucker, *Rise of the Knowledge Worker*, Encyclopedia Britannica Book of the Year, 1973.

SUMMARY

In this chapter we have attempted to organize computer abuses into two broad areas, accidental and intentional, and we have given examples of a wide range of abuses. The most widely advocated solutions to computer misuse have also been discussed, with the emphasis on certification and licensing. In the subsequent chapters we will deal in greater depth with more specific problem areas and possible solutions to the problems.

Exercises

1. Do you think the potential danger from misuse of computers exceeds that of other technological development? Give arguments to support your position.
2. Describe an example of Murphy's law from your own experience. It need not involve computers.
3. Describe an example of the "almost-perfect-machine problem" from your own experience. It need not involve computers.
4. If you have access to the employees of a computer center, try to obtain from them a specific example of intentional computer misuse which occurred at their installation.
5. Obtain up-to-date information on the CDP exam and report on your findings. In particular, decide for yourself whether certification of this nature will significantly reduce misuse of computers.
6. Read and summarize the "Proposed ACM Code of Professional Conduct" published in the April 1973 issue of the *Communications of the ACM*. Do you think such codes serve a useful purpose?
7. Try to obtain an appointment with a manager in a computer installation in order to obtain his answers to the questions immediately preceding the summary of this chapter. Report your findings.

BIBLIOGRAPHY

Bemer, R. W. (ed.) *Computers and Crisis.* New York: Association for Computing Machinery. 1971. 400 pp.

The condensed proceedings of the 1970 ACM conference at which no formal papers were given. This book is a highly edited account of seminar discussions focusing on the use of computers and their influence on society.

Brooks, Frederick P. *The Mythical Man-Month.* Reading, Mass.: Addison-Wesley, 1975. 195 pp.

A very interesting and thoughtful discussion of the problems involved in large software projects. The author is eminently qualified to give such a discussion, having served as project manager for the development of the IBM System /360 and later as manager of the Operating System /360 software project during its design phase.

Hoffer, E. *The True Believer,* New York: Harper & Row, 1951. 160 pp.

A highly provocative analysis of the fanatic and a study of mass movements from early Christianity to modern nationalism and communism.

Parker, D. B., S. Nycum and O. S. Oüra. *Computer Abuse.* Springfield, Va.: National Technical Information Service, 1973.

> This is a very interesting collection of case histories of computer abuse and conclusions as to what the problems are and what needs to be done. It is the result of a Stanford Research Institute study and is well worth reading. It can be understood by the nontechnical reader.

Porter, W. T. *EDP Controls and Auditing.* Belmont, Ca.: Wadsworth Publishing, 1974. 240 pp.

> A brief introduction to the impact of computers on auditing. Several chapters are devoted to computer controls, their review, and evaluation. Audit trails and computer auditing are covered.

Pylyshyn, Z. W. *Perspectives on the Computer Revolution.* Englewood Cliffs, N.J.: Prentice-Hall, 1970, 540 pp.

> An overview of how computerization has affected present culture and technology, with a discussion of where present trends will bring us in the future.

Rothman, S., and C. Mossman. *Computers and Society.* Second Edition, Chicago: Science Research Associates, 1976. 423 pp.

> General introduction to computers with no programming. Several chapters are related to social implications, and the future of computing is discussed.

Teague, R. and C. Erickson. *Computers and Society.* St. Paul: West Publishing Co., 1974. 374 pp.

> An interesting collection of readings on the role of computers in society.

Weinberg, G. M. *The Psychology of Computer Programming.* New York: Van Nostrand Reinhold, 1971. 288 pp.

> A very readable book that inaugurates a radically new point of view by depicting the human element in computer programming. It investigates the thought processes of programmers as they carry out their daily activities. The book demonstrates how programming is not just hardware and software but a human activity full of psychological ramifications that need to be more fully understood.

7. Privileged information and privacy

The makers of our Constitution undertook to secure conditions favorable to the pursuit of happiness. They recognized the significance of man's spiritual nature, of his feelings and of his intellect. They knew that only a part of the pain, pleasure and satisfactions of life are to be found in material things. They sought to protect Americans in their beliefs, their thoughts, their emotions and their sensations. They conferred, as against the Government, the right to be let alone. . . .

Judge Louis Brandeis*

I give the fight up: let there be an end,
A privacy, an obscure nook for me.
I want to be forgotten even by God.

Robert Browning†

About 45 years ago Judge Louis Brandeis stated that individual privacy was "the most comprehensive of rights and the right most valued by civilized men".‡ Is it possible then that an open society dictates a right to privacy among its members? Futurist Ursula K. Le Guin explored the need for privacy in *The Dispossessed*:§

Aside from sexual pairing there was no reason for not sleeping in a dormitory. You could choose a small one or a large one, and if you didn't like your roommates, you could move to another dormitory. Everybody had the workshop, laboratory, studio, barn, or office that he needed for his work; one could be as private or as public as one chose in the baths; sexual privacy was freely available and socially expected; and beyond that privacy was not functional. It was excess, waste. The economy of Anarres would not support the building, maintenance, heating, lighting of individual houses and apartments . . . for those who accepted the privilege and obligation of human solidarity, privacy was a value only where it served a function.

Le Guin is telling of the physicist Shevek's formative years. She continues:

Shevek's first reaction to being put in a private room, then, was half disapproval and half shame. Why had they stuck him in here? He soon found out why. It was the right kind of place for his kind of work. If ideas arrived at midnight, he could turn on the light and write them down; if they came at dawn, they weren't jostled out of his head by the conversation and commotion of four or five roommates getting up; if they didn't come at all and he had to spend whole days sitting at his desk staring out the window, there was nobody behind his back to wonder why he was slacking. Privacy, in fact, was almost as desirable for physics as it was for sex.

*Olmstead v. United States, 277 U.S.C. 438, 478.
†Paracelsus, pt. V.
‡Olmstead v. United States, 277 U.S.C. 438, 478.
§Ursula K. Le Guin, The Dispossessed. New York: Harper & Row, 1974, p. 97.

Well, then, what is this privacy that some feel is so vital? Judge Brandeis called privacy "the right to be let alone".* Alan F. Westin, a noted privacy authority, has defined privacy as the right to decide what information about oneself one wants to share with others.† Westin goes on to define four areas of privacy for the individual:‡

1. Personal autonomy.
2. Emotional release.
3. Self-evaluation.
4. Limited and protected communication.

He argues that privacy in these areas is crucial to a free society because:§

1. It nurtures the development of self-reliance and self-realization in the citizen.
2. It protects the innovative and critical role of private organizations.
3. It shields valuable areas of social and political life from supervision and authority, thus working against the rise of totalitarianism.

HISTORY OF RECORDS

Record keeping is not new. Ancient civilizations shifted from old traditions to written records as commerce and intellectual development required them. From the time written records began to emerge, until the nineteenth century, records about individuals were collected and kept mostly by local authorities. The few central records that were compiled were **administrative surveys** developed for the purpose of collecting taxes, conscripting soldiers, etc. A second type of information collection developed from antiquity to the nineteenth century was the **intelligence system.** As the name implies, this was usually a bundle of letters and reports on an individual by informers and paid agents. About 1750, the notion of a national census was revived for the first time since the Roman era. Public opposition was strong at first, many people suspecting a scheme to raise taxes. The clergy, for whom the Biblical injunction against the taking of a census still held,** also were opposed. Resistance gradually subsided; first in Scandinavia and the German states, then generally throughout the Continent and North America. In the American democracy, where a State's Congressional representation constitutionally depends in part on the size of its population, a national census, at least to the extent of a simple head count, was an obvious political necessity. Probing by census takers for information about income, family life, living habits, and other personal matters turned citizens obstinate and made the census more difficult to take. The problems in gathering information from an antagonistic public led to the

*Olmstead v. United States, 277 U.S.C. 438, 478.
†A. F. Westin, Privacy and Freedom. New York: Antheneum, 1967, p. 7.
‡A. F. Westin, Privacy and Freedom. New York: Antheneum, 1967, pp. 33–39.
§A. F. Westin, "Civil Liberties and Computerized Data Systems", in M. Greenberger (ed.), Computers, Communications, and the Public Interest. Baltimore: The Johns Hopkins Press, 1971, p. 152.
**II Samuel 24 and I Chronicles, 21, 23, 27.

creation of the third class of records, the so-called **statistical* file,** a file where facts about individuals cannot be discerned.

ENTER THE COMPUTER

During the years 1955–1970, computerized data systems came into existence. During the late 1950s and early 1960s, many agencies and departments of the government as well as many businesses made their files machine readable. This occurred at the local, state, and federal levels. During the early and middle 1960s, certain public agencies put machine-readable data from various sources into common computer systems. Finally, from the middle 1960s to 1970, centralized computer services with data banks became a reality. These, then, are considered by Westin to be the first three stages of information integration in government records in modern times.†

1. Computerization of files (1950s–1960s).
2. The data bank (early and middle 1960s).
3. The centralized computer service with data bank (middle 1960s–1970).

During the 1970s and to 1985, Westin sees greater integration and greater risks. He continues his stage numbering:

4. Integrated (or total) management information systems.
5. Regional federated information systems (here, federated means to link diverse data banks).
6. National information systems.

Somewhere between steps 1 and 3 above computerized information systems began to attract public concern.

INCREASING PUBLIC CONCERN

Actually, public awareness of governmental information systems is a good deal older than the 1950s. George Orwell's famous book, *1984*, published a generation ago, focused public attention on the fictional fishbowl existence of human life in the "big brother" era and the potential threats to a free system posed by some political, technical, and social innovations.

During the "Cold War" period of the late 1940s and 1950s, widespread abuses engulfed various governmental and private efforts to ferret out alleged "subversives". Intellectual dissent was driven somewhat into hiding. Terms such as "security risk", "loyalty oaths", "pinko", and "guilt by association" came into common usage during what later became known as the "McCarthy era" of the early half of the 1950s. Many Americans were required to defend publicly their loyalty, often despite years of service to this country. Indis-

---

*The word statistics came into use in the eighteenth century to denote information on the condition of a state. See "Statistics", *Oxford English Dictionary*, **X**, 864, 1933.

†A. F. Westin, "Civil Liberties and Computerized Data Systems", in M. Greenberger (ed.), *Computers, Communications, and the Public Interest*. Baltimore: The John Hopkins Press, 1971, pp. 158–163.

criminate use of dubious informers, wiretapping, surveillance, neighborhood snooping, and other flagrant invasions of personal privacy were encountered with increasing frequency.

In the 1960s the former Special Subcommittee on Government Information of the Committee on Government Operations launched extensive investigations into the practice of telephone monitoring and the use of lie detectors by federal agencies. Hearings, studies and reports based on these investigations revealed numerous examples of privacy invasion affecting federal employees and the public in their dealings with federal agencies.*

In 1964, the chairman of the Government Operations Committee created a Special Subcommittee on Invasion of Privacy, which began inquiries into federal investigative activities, the proposed establishment of a national data bank by the government, computerized personal record keeping, and related privacy matters. Hearings were held during 1965 and 1966 into such issues and a report, concentrating on the national-data-bank concept was issued by the Committee in 1968†

The subcommittee also held hearings in 1968 on the privacy abuses inherent in the operation of private commercial credit reporting organizations‡. Increasing concern over invasion of privacy during the 1960s resulted in congressional efforts to deal with aspects of the problem on a piecemeal basis. The enactment of the Fair Credit Reporting Act of 1970 was directed at many of the privacy abuses uncovered by the subcommittee on the invasion of privacy two years earlier. (We will return to the Fiar Credit Reporting Act later.) The investigation of military surveillance over American political dissidents by the Senate Subcommittee on Constitutional Rights headed by Senator Ervin revealed yet another dimension of abuses during the late 1960s involving intelligence gathering activities that violated basic privacy rights. Such surveillance actions were prompted by the rash of civil disturbances and racial and political unrest on college campuses. During this same period, legislation was first considered to protect the constitutional rights to privacy of federal employees. The Ervin bill has been passed by the Senate during several recent Congresses, but it has never been acted upon in the House.§

A study by the National Academy of Sciences Project on computer databanks was published in 1972. Entitled *Databanks in a Free Society***, this study outlined what the use of computers is actually doing to record-keeping processes in the United States, and what the growth of large-scale data banks—both manual and automated—implies for the individuals' constitutional right to privacy and due process.

---

*Two fairly recent publications in the same area are *Telephone Monitoring Practices by Federal Agencies*. Washington: Government Printing Office, 1974 and *The Use of Polygraphs and Similar Devices by Federal Agencies*. Washington: Government Printing Office, 1974.

†*Special Inquiry on Invasion of Privacy*. Washington: Government Printing Office, part 1—1965, part 2—1966; *The Computer and Invasion of Privacy*. Washington: Government Printing Office, 1966; and *Privacy and the National Data Bank Concept*. Washington: Government Printing Office, 1968. For a thorough treatment of this proposal, see A. R. Miller's *The Assault on Privacy*. Ann Arbor: University of Michigan Press, 1971, pp. 54–67.

‡*Commercial Credit Bureaus*. Washington: Government Printing Office, 1968.

§See R. M. Foley and P. Coxson, "S.782—A Bill to Protect the Constitutional Right to Privacy of Federal Employees", *American University Law Review*, June-August, 1970, pp. 532–549.

**Alan F. Westin and Michael A. Baker, *Databnnaks in a Free Society*, report of the Project on Computer Databanks, Computer Science and Engineering Board, National Academy of Sciences, New York: Quadrangle Books, 1972.

During this same period, Elliott Richardson, then Secretary of Health, Education and Welfare, named an Advisory Committee on Automated Personal Data Systems to make an intensive study of the impact of computer data banks on individual privacy. Its detailed report, *Records, Computers, and the Rights of Citizens** was published in 1973 and recommended the enactment of federal legislation guaranteeing to all Americans a "code of fair information practices".

Late in 1972, meanwhile, the Foreign Operations and Government Information Subcommittee began an investigation of a comprehensive report of the President's Domestic Council proposing a nationwide system of computer and communications technology to create "wired cities" and a "wired nation". The report, entitled *Communications for Social Needs; Technological Opportunities*, was prepared in 1971. Although the report was formally rejected, according to a White House spokesman the "big brother" implications were another ominous indication of the possible threats to individual privacy in America. This investigation led to broad investigative hearings by the subcommittee into advanced information technology and the use of information systems by the federal government. These hearings began in April 1973, and concluded early in 1974.†

Another related investigation affecting individual privacy was also conducted by the subcommittee during this same period. It involved the issuance of a presidential executive order in January 1973 to permit the Agriculture Department to inspect some three million income tax returns of persons having farming operations, for the purpose of compiling special mailing lists to make statistical surveys. Hearings were held in May and August 1973. The order aroused widespread public concern and opposition and was strongly criticized in the subsequent unanimous report issued by the committee in October 1973.‡ In the interim, the Internal Revenue Service had postponed implementation of the order and it was finally rescinded in the spring of 1974.

The growing concern of Americans of all walks of life to the threat of a "big brother" society has been reflected in the Congress. Recently hundreds of members of Congress of both parties and of all shades of political ideology have introduced or cosponsored legislation to impose effective safeguards on both government and business in their collection and use of personal data.

Former President Nixon's State of the Union Message to Congress on January 30, 1974, also took note of the need to protect individual privacy. He said:§

One of the basic rights we cherish most in America is the right of privacy. With the advance of technology, that right has been increasingly threatened. The problem is not simply one of setting effective curbs on invasions of privacy, but even more fundamentally one of limiting the uses to which essentially private information is put, and of recognizing the basic proprietary rights each individual has in information concerning himself.

**Records, Computers, and the Rights of Citizens*. Washington: Government Printing Office, 1973.

†*Federal Information Systems and Plans—Federal Use and Development of Advanced Information Technology*. Washington: Government Printing Office, 1973, and *Federal Information Systems and Plans—Implications and Issues*. Washington: Government Printing Office, 1974.

‡*Executive Orders 11697 and 11709 Permitting Inspection by the Department of Agriculture of Farmers' Income Tax Returns*. Washington: Government Printing Office, 1973.

§*Congressional Record*, January 30, 1974 (daily edition), p. H372.

Privacy, of course, is not absolute; it may conflict, for example, with the need to pursue justice. But where conflicts occur, an intelligent balance must be struck.

One part of the current problem is that as technology has increased the ability of government and private organizations to gather and disseminate information about individuals, the safeguards needed to protect the privacy of individuals and communications have not kept pace. Another part of the problem is that clear definitions and standards concerning the right of privacy have not been developed and agreed upon.

To carry forward these efforts he established, early in 1974, a cabinet-level "Committee on the Right of Privacy" within the White House's Domestic Council headed by then-Vice-President Gerald R. Ford. At its July meeting, that committee urged the enactment of privacy legislation. Additional impetus in Congress to enact privacy safeguards into law has resulted from recent revelations connected with Watergate-related investigations. They included such activities as the break-in at the Democratic National Committee's headquarters in June 1972, the slowly emerging series of revelations of the "White House enemies' lists", the break-in of the office of Daniel Ellsberg's psychiatrist, the misuse of CIA-produced "personality profiles" on Ellsberg, the wiretapping of the phones of government employees and news reporters, and surreptitious taping of personal conversations within the Oval Office of the White House as well as political surveillance, spying, and "mail covers".

Other pressure for action to preserve the individual's right to privacy from further erosion came from individual computer companies and trade associations representing the American computer industry. These experts presented testimony stressing the importance of privacy and the safeguarding of the integrity of stored data on individuals during the Foreign Operations and Government Information Subcommittee's hearings on information technology early in 1974. A nationwide IBM institutional advertisement, entitled "Four Principles of Privacy", endorsed these basic purposes as "sound public policy" cornerstones:*

1. Individuals should have access to information about themselves in record-keeping systems. And there should be some procedure for individuals to find out how this information is being used.
2. There should be some way for an individual to correct or amend an inaccurate record.
3. An individual should be able to prevent information from being improperly disclosed or used for other than authorized purposes without his or her consent, unless required by law.
4. The custodian of data files containing sensitive information should take reasonable precautions to be sure that the data are reliable and not misused.

The broad principles involved in what is conveniently called "the individual right of privacy" are deeply rooted in our history and derived from the Bill of Rights of the U. S. Constitution.

The fourth amendment to the Constitution was written as the result of the American colonial experience with warrants and writs issued under King George III of England that often gave his officers an excuse to search anyone,

---

*See "IBM Reports—Four Principles of Privacy", full page advertisement, Newsweek, July 8, 1974, p. 48.

anywhere, any time. In their famous 1890 *Harvard Law Review* article "The Right to Privacy", Samuel Warren and Louis D. Brandeis concluded:*

It would doubtless be desirable that the privacy of the individual should receive the added protection of the criminal law, but for this, legislation would be required. ... The common law has always recognized a man's house as his castle, impregnable, often, even to its own officers engaged in the execution of its commands. Shall the courts thus close the front entrance to constituted authority, and open wide the back door to idle or prurient curiosity?

On August 12, 1974, President Ford pledged his personal and official dedication to the individual right of privacy. He declared, "There will be hot pursuit of tough laws to prevent illegal invasion of privacy in both government and private activities". The result of that "hot pursuit" was the Privacy Act of 1974 which we will consider in detail shortly.

DEFINING THE PROBLEM

We have seen that the role of computerized information systems in the invasion of privacy is a topic that is receiving growing public and political attention. The prospect of a national computerized data center is not the sole source of concern for privacy in the twentieth century. In fact, as we have just seen, the problems certainly do not seem to be solely a product of computers. In 1927 Judge Brandeis observed†

Legislation, both statutory and constitutional, is enacted, it is true, from an experience of evils, but its general language should not, therefore, be necessarily confined to the form that evil had theretofore taken. Time works changes, brings into existence new conditions and purposes.
When the Fourth and Fifth Amendments were adopted, "the form that evil had theretofore taken," had been necessarily simple. Force and violence were then the only means known to many by which a Government could directly effect self-incrimination. It could compel the individual to testify—a compulsion effected, if need be, by torture. It could secure possession of his papers and other articles incident to his private life—a seizure effected, if need be, by breaking and entry. Protection against such invasion of "the sanctities of a man's home and the privacies of life" was provided in the Fourth and Fifth Amendments by specific language. ... But "time works changes, brings into existence new conditions and purposes." Subtler and more far-reaching means of invading privacy have become available to the Government. *Discovery and invention have made it possible for the Government, by means far more effective than stretching upon the rack, to obtain disclosure in court of what is whispered in the closet.*

It is important to keep perspective. The *basic* problems, we have said, are not new. Furthermore, much of the "computers and privacy" issue is probably a subtopic of the more general topic, "government surveillance of citizens". Senator Sam J. Ervin, a long-time champion of the right to privacy, headed the Senate Subcommittee on Constitutional Rights probing of alleged Pentagon spy activities. It was not until these hearings that many Americans became aware of the extent to which the government has gone and might go in its task of keeping tabs on us. Ervin said that the reason the hearings had been called was because Americans from all walks of life were complaining "about the

*4 *Harvard Law Review*, **193** 1890.
†*Olmstead* v. *United States*, 277 U.S.C. 438, 472 (italics added).

growing collection of information about them . . . that they are pressured into revealing to the wrong *people* [not computers or computer systems], for the wrong purpose at the wrong time".* Where then *does* the computer fit in? *Why so much furor about computers and privacy? The computer has been the catalyst to speed the previously slow erosion of individual privacy that seems to be the by-product of large centralized governments. Much of today's individual privacy is ironically a function of government and social inefficiency and complexity.* Information that would substantially threaten this privacy is already on file, in many cases it is already in machine-readable form. To search for such information has been financially impractical. It has been possessed by hundreds of different public and private agencies. With the advent of centralized data centers the cost of such a search is reduced substantially. The computer can cut through the complexity and inefficiency of government agencies and reduce the cost of obtaining information to the point that it is now practical (i.e., economical and fast) to pursue a full search of an individual's or group's information files—for good or malign intent. Instead of concentrating law enforcement resources in investigating suspected offenders, society can invest in watching all citizens, just waiting for someone to step off the defined proper path for the good citizen. (See Auden's poem "The Unknown Citizen" in the Appendix.)

Davis has suggested that the increasing emphasis on the availability of information is a natural process: that the United States, in the 1950s, transitioned from an industrial nation to a postindustrial nation. "It meant, in practical terms, that success for organizations was dependent on the proper use of information as the basis for control. ..."† She feels the key to success in preindustrial societies is based on the proper management of energy and production processes, and in postindustrial societies on proper management of information. Maybe, then, modern governments *must* invade individual privacy to obtain enough information to be able to govern? A system that has attracted substantial concern‡ in the area of the gathering of information about citizens is the FBI's National Crime Information Center (**NCIC**) and especially NCIC's Computerized Criminal History (**CCH**) file.§ Let us briefly consider this system as an example of an information-gathering system our government feels it needs. Then we will discuss the regulation of NCIC and other government and private information systems.

NCIC

The original network of 15 law enforcement control terminals and one FBI field office has expanded to 90 law enforcement control terminals, terminals in all FBI offices, NCIC service to all 50 states, the District of Columbia,

---

*The U.S. Senate's Committee on the Judiciary's Subcommittee on Constitutional Rights has published a series on *Federal Data Banks, Computers, and the Bill of Rights*, which is available from the Government Printing Office, Washington, D.C. At this time there are six volumes in the series.

†R. M. Davis, "Privacy and Security in Data Systems", *Computers and People*, Vol. 23, No. 3, p. 22.

‡Read "The National Crime Information Center (NCIC) of the FBI: Do We Want It?" in the Appendix.

§The CCH file was once proposed as a separate system, the National Criminal History System (NCHS).

Canada, 25 metropolitan areas, and 9 federal agencies. (A **control terminal** is defined as "a State agency or large core city operating a metropolitan area system that shares with the FBI the responsibility for overall system discipline as well as for the accuracy and validity of records entered in the system".)

The first computer-to-computer interface was with the California Highway Patrol in April 1967. The tie in of the St. Louis, Mo., Police Department's computerized system soon followed. These events marked the first use of computer communication technology to link together local, state, and federal governments in an operational system for a common purpose.

In the beginning, there were five computerized files: wanted persons; stolen vehicles, license plates, and guns; and stolen identifiable articles. In 1968, a securities file was added, and the vehicle file was expanded to include aircraft and snowmobiles. In the following year, a boat file was added. The most recent addition was in November 1971, when the Computerized Criminal History file was added.

The City of Little Rock Police Department now operates an on-line criminal information system. The multiprocessing system in use is the Varian V 73 System. This system includes two Varian 73 central processing units, four disk-storage drives, two magnetic tape drives, two data communications controllers, five video display keyboard units, and two teletypes. The system operates four functional areas within the Department—field requests, investigations, record keeping, and management controls. Rapid response to police officers checking wants, warrants, vehicles, and missing persons allows access to information in seconds that manually took minutes to obtain. Investigators are aided by the quick access and correlation of facts from one source that includes information on previous burglaries and known criminals. The parking-and-traffic-ticket division maintains a system using a mark sense card reader for identifying returned tickets. The management controls included in the system are able to analyze data for frequency of crimes in a given neighborhood to establish the personnel assignments required and measure the resulting effectiveness of possible reallocations of manpower and equipment. The system can also provide access to local, state, and national criminal date bases. (Courtesy of Varian Data Machines.)

As of July 1, 1975, there were 5,503,390 active records in NCIC, with the breakdown showing 154,768 wanted persons, 859,197 vehicles, 316,456 license plates, 1,051,862 articles, 889,767 guns, 1,612,372 securities, 11,901 boats, and 607,067 criminal history records. In June, 1975, NCIC network transactions totaled 5,145,390, averaging 171,513 daily. NCIC's average search success rate is 885 "hits" per day. The peak hour of system utilization is from 12 midnight to 1 A.M. EDT.*

Fully aware that such a system could be misused (by the government or by individuals) the question of NCIC and similar systems' regulation was turned over to **Project SEARCH** (System for Electronic Analysis and Retrieval of Criminal Histories) by the Law Enforcement Assistance Administration. Project SEARCH's recommendations cover a wide range of areas, from physical system security through a Code of Ethics to model state legislation for criminal-offender record information. The recommendations of Project SEARCH's Committee on Security and Privacy will be considered in detail in the next section.

PRIVACY SAFEGUARDS: SOME SUGGESTED SOLUTIONS

The solution to potential privacy invasion can seldom be as trivial as avoiding data bank aggregations. Robert McBride, in *The Automated State,*† has pointed out that to argue against an information system on the grounds that we cannot guarantee that no individual will ever be threatened by the system is like arguing against banks on the grounds that no one can guarantee that they will never be robbed or embezzled.   In fact, *we find the problem not to be whether or not the right to privacy is legitimate but how to resolve the conflict of that right with the right of society to have certain kinds of information that contributes to the general good.*‡ Safeguard recommendations, coming typically from privacy advocates, have tended to ignore this "conflicting right" of society. Such recommendations often portray *any* aggragation of information as clandestine.

A plethora of recommendations

Intelligence systems, on the other hand, do pose a very real threat to the individual's privacy. This is probably more true of their legal use than it is of their illegal use. Given the increasing need for information for decision making as our culture accelerates, the integration of many special-purpose intelligence systems (such as criminal-history, security, medical-history, employment, and marketing-profile systems) to produce a comprehensive

---

*NCIC Newsletter, Federal Bureau of Investigation, U. S. Department of Justice. Washington: Government Printing Office, July, 1975. The hit rate is from correspondence with the Chief of the NCIC Section of the Bureau (dated October 1975).

†R. McBride, *The Automated State.* New York: Chilton, 1967, p. 190.

‡A very brief but interesting consideration of the relations among computers, privacy, and public policy is given in "A Problem-List of Issues Concerning Computers and Public Policy" in the *Communications of the Association for Computing Machinery,* Vol. 17, No. 9, pp. 495–503. This is the report of the ACM Committee on Computers and Public Policy.

dossier is almost an inevietable development. Terry M. Walker and William W. Cotterman, in *An Introduction to Computer Science and Algorithmic Processes*, argue that the decision to create such a dossier must*

... emphatically not be left to administrators or technicians no matter how highly placed. The impact of a system including such a dossier on the individual would be massive. The proverbial clean slate would be a forgotten concept, because mistakes, though forgiven, would never be forgotten.

While there have been some efforts to stem the haphazard growth of computer information system applications, these systems, especially in government, have tended to evolve rather than be designed. Controls and intents present at the inception of an information system are too easily forgotten once the system is available to its users. The principal threat comes from seemingly harmless systems that, when interconnected and correlated, form a complete basis for producing the comprehensive dossiers mentioned earlier.

Westin has defined some general things we must do to provide safeguards against legal misuses of information systems:†

1. We must define the core elements of individual privacy and due process that deserve protection in computerized information systems.
2. We need new regulatory institutions. He suggests a telecommunications agency, interagency and intergovernment coordinating committees, regulatory mechanisms for particular fields, and special offices to supervise long-range plans for state information systems.
3. We badly need national studies of where computerization of personal records stand right now.
4. We need to guard ourselves against computer information banks becoming powerful tools for maintenance of an intolerable status quo.

At a lower, more technical, level some government leaders and computer science experts have suggested a computer bill of rights. Some items suggested are:

1. An individual has the right to read his own file, to challenge certain kinds of entries in his file, and to impose certain restrictions on access to his file.
2. If an organization or individual obtains access to certain information in a file by deceit, this is a civil wrong and a crime. The injured party has the right to sue for damages.
3. Every access of an individual's file is to be recorded, together with the authorization for the access and identification of the person or organization requesting the access. The individual has a right to see all such access records.
4. Adequate auditing procedures must be demonstrated and independent information auditors employed periodically to testify to the adequacy of system technical safeguards and management compliance with laws and regulations governing computerized information systems.

*T. M. Walker and W. W. Cotterman, *An Introduction to Computer Science and Algorithmic Processes*. Boston: Allyn and Bacon, 1970, p. 526.

†A. F. Westin, "Civil Liberties and Computerized Data Systems" in M. Greenberger (ed.), *Computers, Communications and the Public Interest*. Baltimore: The Johns Hopkins Press, 1971, pp. 165–167.

Implementing proposals such as these calls for definitions by experts as to what steps in technical areas will provide adequate file security in an information system environment. These technical safeguards are going to increase the cost of the computerized information system.* But, as Paul Baran of Sperry Rand Corporation has said, " . . . here is an example of the trade-off between dollars and the type of society we want". Baran's own specific technical safeguards include the following:†

1. Provisions for minimal cryptographic type protection to all communications lines that carry potentially embarrassing data—not superduper unbreakable cryptography—just some minimally reversible, logical operations upon the data stream to make the eavesdropper's job so difficult that it isn't worth his time.
2. Never store file data in the complete clear. Perform some simple (but key-controllable) operation on the data so that a simple access to storage will not dump stored data out into the clear.
3. Make random external auditing of file operating programs a standard practice to insure that no programmer has intentionally or inadvertently slipped in a secret door to permit a remote point access to information to which he is not entitled.
4. Provide mechanisms to detect abnormal informational requests. That is, if a particular file is receiving an excessive number of crossfile inquiries coming from one source, flag the request to a human system manager.
5. Build on provisions to record the source of requests for information interrogations.
6. Audit information requests and inform authorities of suspected misuse of the system.

There are many facets to even the technical safeguards problems. One of these has been thought of by the FBI. New FBI security regulations require any computer processing of criminal histories to be restricted to law-enforcement use under the control of law enforcement officials. Without such a regulation non-law-enforcement users of a multiprogramming system would possibly be able to obtain otherwise secure information. There are software safeguards to prevent such unauthorized file access, but they have been shown to be singularly unsuccessful.

A lot of experts have recommended solutions to portions of the "privacy problem" as have many laymen and lawmakers. In 1974 there were 102 privacy bills, spawned by 207 sponsors, floating around the House. In the Senate, 62 lawmakers were sponsoring similar legislation. In 1975, even after the passage of the Privacy Act of 1974, there were still over 100 privacy bills in process in Congress. And that's not counting the activity at the state and local levels. Speaking on this, John L. Kirkley‡ feels that

On the surface, all this concern sounds very healthy. But once the bandwagon moves on and a new, burning issue claims the attention of our lawmakers . . . who cleans up the litter that's left behind?

---

*See R. M. Davis, "Privacy and Security in Data Systems", *Computers and People*, Vol. 23, No. 3. See pp. 23–25 for an analysis of the costs of privacy and security. Also see R. C. Goldstein, "The Costs of Privacy", *Datamation*, October 1975, pp. 65–69.

†P. Baran, "Communications, Computers and People" in *Computers: Their Impact on Society*. Washington, D.C.: Thompson, 1967, pp. 48–49.

‡J. L. Kirkley, "A Plea for Privacy", *Datamation*, May 1974, p. 49.

Obviously the lawyers and the courts—a time consuming and expensive process. And while they're untangling the many laws, the data banks will continue to grow and interconnect, and many of the clever protective techniques signed into law will have been circumvented by new and even more clever techniques.

The conclusion reached by Kirkley is that no static legislation, no matter how well thought out, is going to be able to keep up with the rapid evolution of information systems. Increasing numbers of computer experts and lawmakers are calling for the establishment of new federal regulatory agencies. We are beginning to talk of "information auditors" that would audit information systems as regular auditors do financial systems.

Synthesizing recommendations

Let us now look at the recommendations of two groups concerned with computers and privacy. While aimed primarily at criminal-history systems, the recommendations (contained in abbreviated form in the Appendix) of the Project SEARCH Committee on Security and Privacy contain the elements common to privacy preservation in many kinds of information systems. Note how many of the recommendations we have seen above are reflected in the Project SEARCH recommendations. Recall that Project SEARCH was given the task of determining means of preventing the misuse of computerized law enforcement records systems. The Committee on Security and Privacy has produced, among other documents, model legislation for a state Criminal Offender Record Information Act and model regulations for administering a criminal record information system. Their recommendations (see the Appendix for specific details) call for the establishment of a Records Control Committee and a Security and Privacy Council to oversee the administration of the system and resolve complaints about its use. They provide the individual with rights of access and challenge and make misuse of the system a crime. Information in the system is "aged" and, depending on the seriousness of the crime, eventually purged from the system.

The second group's proposed privacy guidelines, the "Summary and Recommendations" of the Advisory Committee on Automated Personal Data Systems, to the Secretary of the Department of Health, Education, and Welfare is also contained in the Appendix. This is from *Records, Computers, and the Rights of Citizens*,* a report believed by many to to be the most thoughtful and comprehensive study available to date of the "computers and privacy" issue. Read the complete Summary in the Appendix; be sure to note how many of the recommendations we have already seen are included in the Summary and to pay special attention to the Social Security Number recommendations. The justification of these recommendations is given in detail in the report.† Briefly, the authors state eight criteria a standard universal identifier (**SUI**) must pass and weigh the Social Security Number (**SSN**) against them.‡

UNIQUENESS.   The SSN is not a unique label. More than 4.2 million people, by the Social Security Administration's own estimates, have two or more

Records, Computers, and the Rights of Citizens, Report of the Secretary's Advisory Committee on Automated Personal Data Systems, U.S. Department of Health, Education, and Welfare. Washington: Government Printing Office, 1973.
†Ibid., pp. 108–122.
‡Ibid., pp. 112–113.

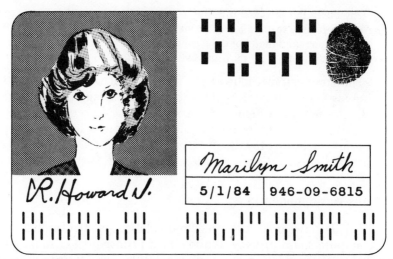

The birth card: The benefits are probably too great to forestall, for any length of time, a **universal identification card.** The card could serve as a driver's license, military or company ID, and universal banking ID and credit card. The card itself would need to contain very little information. If a traffic policeman needed to know whether your card carried driving privileges or whether or not you were required to wear glasses he could insert your card in his car terminal and obtain the information in a few seconds. The returned information would also let him know if you were wanted by the police or, for that matter, if you had an urgent telephone call pending. The card bearer could buy anything anywhere if he was permitted the purchase and had enough credit in his account. For example, he could obtain medication from a pharmacy simply by presenting his card. The pharmacist's terminal would let him know if the card bearer was authorized the drug and if he had enough credit to pay for it. Such a system could change our way of life at all levels. Its implications could transcend those of the automobile, airplane, telephone, and television. Its potential is great and it is probably inevitable. What would a man that had lived most of his life in the nineteenth century think of Master Charge or BankAmericard? To that man we would already have a universal identification card.

SSNs. More serious, although much less prevalent, are the instances in which more than one person has been issued or uses the same SSN.*

PERMANENCE.   The SSN is, in almost all cases, permanent for an individual throughout his life.

UBIQUITY.   The SSN is nearly universal for adult Americans, much less so for those of high-school age and below.

AVAILABILITY.   The SSN of an individual is readily verifiable by the Social Security Administration for some users, and not at all for others. It is regainable from the Social Security Administration by persons who have lost their

---

*"Account number 078-05-1120 was the first of many numbers now referred to as 'pocketbook' numbers. It first appeared on a sample account number card contained in wallets sold . . . nationwide in 1938. Many people who purchased the wallets assumed the number to be their own personal account number. It was reported thousands of times on employers' quarterly reports; 1943 was the high year, with 5,755 wage earners listed as owning the famous number. More recently, the IRS requirement that the Social Security Account Number be shown on all tax returns resulted in 39 taxpayers showing 078-05-1120 as their number. The number continues to be reported at least 10 times each quarter. There are now over 20 different 'pocketbook' numbers. . . . ." *Account Number and Employee Contact Manual* (Baltimore, Maryland: Social Security Administration), Section 121.

cards and forgotten their numbers, but not immediately. An individual's SSN, however, is increasingly ascertainable from many sources other than the Social Security Administration.

INDISPENSABILITY.   The incentives and requirements to report one's SSN correctly are growing, though in some contexts there are incentives to omit or falsify the number.

ARBITRARINESS.   The SSN is not entirely arbitrary; the State of issuance is coded into the number.

BREVITY.   The SSN with its nine digits is three places longer than an alpha-numeric label capable of numbering 500 million people without duplication, and two places longer than one that can accommodate 17 billion people. The SSN could therefore be shorter if it were alpha-numeric.

RELIABILITY.   The SSN has no check-feature, and most randomly chosen nine-digit numbers cannot be distinguished from valid SSNs. It is thus particularly prone to undetectable errors of transcription and oral reporting.

Thus, by their criteria, the SSN cannot fully qualify as an SUI; it only approximates one.

The report also lists some reasons why we may not want an SUI at all, whatever its advantages:*

*Ibid., pp. 111–112.

1. The bureaucratic apparatus needed to assign and administer an SUI would represent another imposition of government control on an already heavily burdened citizenry.
2. To realize all the supposed benefits of an SUI, mandatory personal identity cards would have to be presented whenever called for. Loss or theft of an SUI card would cause serious inconvenience, and the mere threat of official confiscation would be a powerful weapon of intimidation.
3. The national population register that an SUI implies could serve as the skeleton for a national dossier system to maintain information on every citizen from cradle to grave.
4. An unchangeable SUI used everywhere would make it much easier for an individual to be traced, and his behavior monitored and controlled, through the records maintained about him by a wide range of different institutions.
5. A permanent SUI issued at birth could create an incentive for institutions to pool or link their records, thereby making it possible to bring a lifetime of information to bear on any decision about a given individual. American culture is rich in the belief that an individual can pull up stakes and make a fresh start, but a universally identified man might become a prisoner of his recorded past.

They conclude their analysis:*

If use of the SSN as an identifier continues to expand, the incentives to link records and to broaden access to them are likely to increase. Until safeguards such as we have recommended in this report have been implemented, and demonstrated to be effective, there can be no assurance that the consequences for individuals of such linking and accessibility will be benign. At best, individuals may be frustrated and annoyed by unwarranted exchanges of information about them. At worst, they may be threatened with denial of status and benefits without due process, since at the present time record linking and access are, in the main, accomplished without any provision for the data subject to protest, interfere, correct, comment, and, in most instances, even to know what linking of which records is taking place for what purpose.

THE STATUTES: A BEGINNING

Let us now look at the statutes that have been enacted as a result of :

1. The public and political pressures we traced in the section "History of Records".
2. The coalescing of privacy safeguard suggestions we saw in the last section.

There are three primary federal statutes and several lesser ones that deserve our attention. Some of these "lesser" statutes are mentioned in the Exercises at the end of this chapter and some are covered in a little more detail in the Bibliography for this chapter. (A word is needed about this chapter's Bibliography. It is annotated with the intent of extending the chapter as well as providing supportive and follow-up materials for the consideration of privacy issues. As such, it would be worth a few minutes of your time to scan it now and become familiar with its content.) The three primary statutes are:

*Ibid., p. 121.

1. The Freedom of Information Act enacted in 1966 and 1967.
2. The Fair Credit Reporting Act enacted in 1970.
3. The Privacy Act of 1974.

The **Freedom of Information Act* (FOIA)** is significant not because of its original purpose but because it forms the statutory base for the Privacy Act of 1974—that act being an amendment of the FOIA. The FOIA is an outgrowth of the 1946 Administrative Procedures Act. It was enacted in 1966 and amended rather heavily in 1967. The FOIA regulates mostly federal agencies with but a few regulations for state and local governments and private organizations. The act requires federal agencies to make known to the public their operations. Federal agencies must make available for public inspection the agencies' structures, purpose, policies, rules and regulations, and the like. It establishes a recourse through the courts for individuals seeking information from any federal agency that refuses to comply. On the surface, especially with original intent in mind, the FOIA is not much of a privacy act. In fact, it was not, in 1967, a *privacy* act at all.

The **Fair Credit Reporting Act† (FCRA),** which we saw in our discussion of the history of records, was passed in 1970. Its stated purpose is

to require that consumer reporting agencies adopt reasonable procedures for meeting the needs of commerce for consumer credit, personnel, insurance, and other information in a manner which is fair and equitable to the consumer, with regard to the confidentiality, accuracy, relevancy, and proper utilization of such information. . . .

The FCRA is possibly the first privacy-related law that has any teeth. It is real, relatively well tested by the courts, and sort of adequate (though in need of some attention). It provides that‡

A consumer reporting agency may furnish a consumer report under the following circumstances and no other:
   (1) In response to the order of a court . . .
   (2) In accordance with the written instructions of the consumer to whom it relates.
   (3) To a person which it has reason to believe—
      (A) intends to use the information in connection with a credit transaction involving the consumer on whom the information is to be furnished . . . ; or
      (B) intends to use the information for employment purposes; or
      (C) intends to use the information in connection with the underwriting of insurance involving the consumer; or
      (D) intends to use the information in connection with a determination of the consumer's eligibility for a license or other benefit granted by a governmental instrumentality required by law to consider an applicant's financial responsibility or status; or
      (E) otherwise has a legitimate business need for the information in connection with a business transaction involving the consumer.

Reporting of obsolete information is prohibited§

*5 U.S.C. 522.
†15 U.S.C. 1681.
‡Ibid., Section 1681b.
§Ibid., Section 1681c.

(a) Except as authorized under subsection (b) [see below] of this section, no consumer reporting agency may make any consumer report containing any of the following items of information:

(1) Bankruptcies which . . . antedate the report by more than fourteen years.

(2) Suits and judgments which . . . antedate the report by more than seven years or until the governing statute of limitations has expired, whichever is the longer period.

(3) Paid tax liens which . . . antedate the report by more than seven years.

(4) Accounts placed for collection or charged to profit and loss which antedate the report by more than seven years.

(5) Records of arrest, indictment, or conviction of crime which . . . antedate the report by more than seven years.

(6) Any other adverse item of information which antedates the report by more than seven years.

(b) The provisions of subsection (a) [the above section] of this section are not applicable in the case of any consumer credit report to be used in connection with—

(1) a credit transaction involving . . . a principal amount of $50,000 or more;

(2) the underwriting of life insurance involving . . . a face amount of $50,000 or more; or

(3) the employment of any individual at an annual salary which equals . . . $20,000 or more.

The act also provides some protection against erroneous information and disclosure to the wrong person. Upon appearance of the consumer in person with proper identification or by telephone with prior written request and proper identification*

(a) Every consumer reporting agency shall . . . clearly and accurately disclose to the consumer:

(1) The nature and substance of all information (except medical information) in its files on the consumer at the time of the request.

(2) The sources of the information; except that the sources of information acquired solely for use in preparing an investigative consumer report and actually used for no other purpose need not be disclosed. . . .

(3) The recipients of any consumer report on the consumer which it has furnished—

(A) for employment purposes within the two-year period preceding the request, and

(B) for any other purpose within the six-month period preceding the request.

Finally, the act provides recourse to the courts in cases where consumers' rights under the act are violated.

The FCRA has several loopholes but is a major step in the right general direction. Hearings have been held and proposals have been made to amend the act but so far no action has been taken.

The **Privacy Act of 1974†** **(PA74)** is the end product of the sequence of events we saw in our discussion of the section, "History of Records". As a recap of that section, the following are substantial contributions to the final form of the act (the tabulation of the legislative history of PA74 is given in the Bibliography for this chapter: recall that PA74 is just an amendement of FOIA):

1. Legislation proposed by many members of Congress (especially

---

*Ibid., Section g.

†5 U.S.C. 552.

influencial was that proposed by Representative Edward Koch and Senator Sam Ervin).

2. *Records, Computers, and the Rights of Citizens.*

3. *Federal Information Systems and Plans—Federal Use and Development of Advanced Information Technology.*

4. *Federal Information Systems and Plans—Implications and Issues.*

5. IBM's "Four Principles of Privacy".

In the Privacy Act of 1974, the Congress finds that*

(1) the privacy of an individual is directly affected by the collection, maintenance, use, and dissemination of personal information by federal agencies;

(2) the increasing use of computers and sophisticated information technology, while essential to the efficient operations of the government, has greatly magnified the harm to individual privacy that can occur from any collection, maintenance, use, or dissemination of personal information;

(3) the opportunities for an individual to secure employment, insurance, and credit, and his right to due process, and other legal protections are endangered by the misuse of certain information systems;

(4) the right to privacy is a personal and fundamental right protected by the Constitution of the United States; and

(5) in order to protect the privacy of individuals identified in information systems maintained by federal agencies, it is necessary and proper for the Congress to regulate the collection, maintenance, use, and dissemination of information by such agencies.

The stated purpose of the act is†

to provide certain safeguards for an individual against an invasion of personal privacy by requiring federal agencies, except as otherwise provided by law, to—

(1) permit an individual to determine what records pertaining to him are collected, maintained, used, or disseminated by such agencies;

(2) permit an individual to prevent records pertaining to him obtained by such agencies for a particular purpose from being used or made available for another purpose without his consent;

(3) permit an individual to gain access to information pertaining to him in federal agency records, to have a copy made of all or any portion thereof, and to correct or amend such records;

(4) collect, maintain, use, or disseminate any record of identifiable personal information in a manner that assures that such action is for a necessary and lawful purpose, that the information is current and accurate for its intended use, and that adequate safeguards are provided to prevent misuse of such information;

(5) permit exemptions from the requirements with respect to records provided in this Act only in those cases where there is an important public policy need for such exemption as has been determined by specific statutory authority; and

(6) be subject to civil suit for any damages which occur as a result of willfull or intentional action which violates any individual's rights under this Act.

Of substantial interest and concern is item (5) above. The general exemptions from the control imposed by PA74 are federal agencies whose system of records is‡

---

*Ibid., Section 2. (a).

†Ibid., Section 2. (b).

‡Ibid., Section j.

(1) maintained by the Central Intelligence Agency; or

(2) maintained by an agency or component thereof which performs as its principal function any activity pertaining to the enforcement of criminal laws, including police efforts to prevent, control, or reduce crime or to apprehend criminals, and the activities of prosecutors, courts, correctional, probation, pardon, or parole authorities, and which consists of (A) information compiled for the purpose of identifying individual criminal offenders and alleged offenders and consisting only of identifying data and notations of arrests, the nature and disposition of criminal charges, sentencing, confinement, release, and parole and probation status; (B) information compiled for the purpose of a criminal investigation, including reports of informants and investigators, and associated with an identifiable individual; or (C) reports identifiable to an individual compiled at any stage of the process of enforcement of the criminal laws from arrest or indictment through release from supervision.

The specific exemptions includes systems of records that are*

(1) specifically required by executive order to be kept secret in the interest of the national defense or foreign policy;

(2) related solely to the internal personnel rules and practices of an agency;

(3) specifically exempted from disclosure by statute;

(4) trade secrets and commercial or financial information obtained from a person and privileged or confidential;

(5) inter-agency or intra-agency memorandums or letters which would not be available by law to a party other than an agency in litigation with the agency;

(6) personnel and medical files and similar files the disclosure of which would constitute a clearly unwarranted invasion of personal privacy;

(7) investigatory files compiled for law enforcement purposes except to the extent available by law to a party other than an agency;

(8) contained in or related to examination, operating, or condition reports prepared by or for the use of an agency responsible for the regulation or supervision of financial institutions; or

(9) geological and geophysical information and data, including maps, concerning wells.

or are†

(1) maintained in connection with providing protective services to the President of the United States . . . ;

(2) required by statute to be maintained and used solely as statistical records;

(3) investigatory material compiled solely for the purpose of determining suitability, eligibility, or qualifications for federal civilian employment, military service, federal contracts, or access to classified information . . . ;

(4) testing or examination material used solely to determine individual qualifications for appointment or promotion in the federal service . . . ;

(5) evaluation material used to determine potential for promotion in the armed services.

Justification of exemption under the "in the interest of national defense or foreign policy" clause of Section b (1) is made in a very interesting publication *Executive Classification of Information—Security Classification Problems Involving Exemption (b) (1) of the Freedom of Information Act* which is described in the Bibliography for this chapter.

Other major provisions of PA74 include establishment of a Privacy Protec-

*Ibid., Section b.
†Ibid., Section k.

tion Study Commission to monitor enforcement of the act and to study privacy issues that will have to be dealt with in the future, the requirement that all federal agencies publish annual reports on the nature of their personal information systems, tight regulation of interagency transfer of information, control over the sale of an individual's name and address as part of a mailing list, and restrictions on the spread of the use of the Social Security number as a standard universal identifier. Specifically, in the case of the Social Security number,*

(a) (1) It shall be unlawful for any federal, *state* or *local* government agency to deny to any individual any right, benefit, or privilege provided by law because of such individual's refusal to disclose his social security account number.
     (2) the provisions of [the above] paragraph . . . of this subsection shall not apply with respect to—
         (A) any disclosure which is required by federal statute, or
         (B) the disclosure of a social security number to any federal, *state* or *local* agency maintaining a system of records in existence and operating before January 1, 1975, if such disclosure was required under statute or regulation adopted prior to such date to verify the identity of an individual.
(b) Any federal, *state*, or *local* government agency which requests an individual to disclose his social security account number shall inform that individual whether that disclosure is mandatory or voluntary, by what statutory or other authority such number is solicited, and what uses will be made of it.

Note the extension of PA74 to state and local governments.

By the standards of most privacy advocates, PA74 is too weak and has too many exclusions and loopholes. For example, within the very week that PA74 became effective there was congressional concern over a tactic adopted by the Department of Health, Education and Welfare (HEW) to avoid keeping records on information its own agencies share with one another. By defining its 11 separate agencies as one agency for the purposes of PA74, HEW has sidestepped the need to keep a set of records showing when one HEW agency accesses the personal information of individuals kept by another HEW agency.† It is true that the Act is vague. The Office of Management and Budget (OMB) has published a set of guidelines for implementing PA74.‡ It has been suggested that the vagueness might be due to the act being "more of a preventative or anticipatory measure than one to curtail specific abuses. It is easy to collect horror stories involving misuse of private information—but the most persuasive abuses are more subtle, more difficult to track down, and often perpetrated by agencies whose intentions are of the best."§

At this time there is almost no regulation of law-enforcement and criminal-records systems, several bills are now before Congress. Passage of some measure in this area is expected within a year or two and is expected to be in a form similar to the recommendations of Project SEARCH that we have discussed** No legislation governing data banks kept for national defense and

*Ibid., Section 7 (italics added).

†"HEW Privacy Act Tactic Sparks Concern", *Computerworld*, October 1, 1974, pp. 1, 5.

‡*Privacy Act Implementation: Guidelines and Responsibilities.* Washington: Government Printing Office, 1975

§C. Holden, "Privacy: Congressional Efforts Are Coming to Fruition", *Science*, May 16, 1975, pp. 714–715.

**J. Poage, "Federal Law Protecting Your Right to Privacy", *Computers and Society* (a publication of the ACM), Summer 1975, p. 7.

foreign policy has been seriously proposed.* Many states have enacted a variety of privacy laws in the past year or two. We will have to wait for the courts to decide the fate of those laws. (A set of laws that was similar, but more generally applicable, to PA74 lasted only three days in Oregon. The privacy law was killed by a special session of the Oregon legislature because of the tight clamp it placed on police and court records.†

SUMMARY AND SOME COMMENTS

We have seen that privacy appears to be a fundamental need of the human. There seems to be little evidence that this need is waning as our technology advances.‡ The computer, while not creating any new privacy problems, magnifies the old ones. This is primarily because of the substantial reduction in time and cost to retrieve correlated information via computerized data banks. Through a plethora of privacy safeguard recommendations we have found several that keep reappearing. Some of these are:

1. Making it a crime to keep the existence of a data bank secret.
2. Giving individuals the legal right to examine any information about them recorded in a data bank and legal recourse should they not agree with what is recorded.
3. Aging information and mandatory discarding of information after a certain period of time.
4. Making it a crime to obtain information from a data bank by fraudulent means.
5. Providing regulations and procedures for auditing the data base to detect violations of laws.
6. Establishing a board, apart from the regular management of an agency, to review complaints, investigate abnormalities, and administer regulations.

Yet, even with a commonly agreed-on set of privacy guidelines it is hard to imagine any mechanism that would prevent the more insidious of the two types of computer misuse discussed in Chapter 6—accidental misuse. Speaking directly to the privacy issue Judge Brandeis said:§

Experience should teach us to be most on our guard to protect liberty when the Government's purposes are beneficent. Men born to freedom are naturally alert to repel invasion of their liberty by evil-minded rulers. The greatest dangers to liberty lurk in insidious encroachment by men of zeal, well-meaning but without understanding.

Part of his solution was to prohibit the admission of evidence gained from the new technology (he was dealing with the telephone and wire-tapping) into a

---

*Ibid.

†"Oregon Privacy Law Too Tough, Meets Death After Three Days", *Computerworld*, October 1, 1975, pp. 1, 2.

‡For an excellent treatment of the history of privacy, see M. Ernst and A. Schwartz, *The Right to Be Let Alone*, New York: Macmillan, 1962. There have also been several best-selling exposés. For example: V. Packard, *The Naked Society*. New York: David McKay, 1964; M. Benton, *The Privacy Invaders*, New York: Coward-McCann, 1964; M. Gross, *The Brain Watchers*, New York: Random House, 1962; and H. Block, *Buy Now, Pay Later*, New York: Morrow, 1961.

§*Olmstead* v. *United States* 277 U.S.C. 438, 479.

court of law. Perhaps we should add a corresponding provision that information obtained from a data bank of any kind without a court order must be held inadmissable in a court of law. Discussing this and some very similar problems in a multistate information system for psychiatric patient records, William Curran and his colleagues have provided a clever means, if it stands the test of time and courts, to completely make all records in an information system unavailable for inspection "by any agency or individual other than the

The "on-line" city. Garland, Texas officials have learned from experience that explosive expansion puts stress on the city's financial, physical, and personnel resources. Garland's population has doubled in 10 years and is expected to more than double again by 1990. Late in 1971, Garland commissioned IBM to develop a five-year data processing plan for its 23 city departments. Two years later they began operations with several computers. Their primary computer receives input from two smaller computers, IBM System /7s—one that monitors pumping operations for the city-owned water system and another that controls circulation of 130,000 volumes in the city's library. Another computer, an IBM Data Acquisition and Control System, optimizes traffic flow by controlling traffic lights at 23 downtown intersections. It will eventually manage a total of 85 intersections. The above photograph shows Garland City Manager Charles E. Duckworth, left, and Assistant City Manager G. Chris Hartung in the computer traffic control center.

In addition to tax, police, and library records, Garland's information system includes data on all power, water, sewer, and sanitation utility accounts; general ledger, budgetary, and work order control systems maintained by the accounting department; personnel records and records for CARE (Citizens Attitude and Response Evaluation)—a complaint and request tracking system.

In the utility operation, involving monthly reading of 65,000 meters, preparing 31,000 bills, and posting payments to an equal number of accounts, three customer service clerks are using computer terminals to process an average of 13,000 inquiries each month.

For the police department, the on-line system has both improved day-to-day operations and solved a physical storage problem by eliminating a file of 30,000 criminal record folders—each involving as many as 25 pieces of paper.

"With our old system, if a patrolman called his dispatcher seeking identification of the driver of a car bearing a certain license number", says Police Chief Youngeblood, "there wasn't much we could provide other than name and address. The patrolman has to make his decision to apprehend or not, without information that might be important to his safety or that of the suspect".

Now a brief summary of each criminal record, stored on magnetic disk, is available via three terminals and one printer located in the police department. The summary also contains microfilm cassette and frame index numbers indicating location of the entire criminal record in a microfilm file.

"We find that 95 percent of our incoming radio inquiries can be answered in seconds", Chief Youngeblood says. "If that data is not adequate, we go into the microfilm record and still get an answer in a minute." The police system interfaces with area, state, and federal crime information systems.

For the future, Garland is developing an expanded police system to cover traffic, courts, and criminal investigation; a city-wide microfilm indexing system; and a housing inventory and geographic data base system to generate maps displaying police, utilities, and activity related to assessed property values. With the geographic system, partially funded by federal monies, the city will be able to analyze, for example, the relationship between crime and street lighting and "what if" questions involving sanitation pickup routing, police dispatch, and overall community planning. (Courtesy of IBM and *Data Processor* magazine.)

---

agency or facility submitting them and . . . not subject to subpoena in any court, tribunal, or administrative agency".* They are discussing bill 8971a, which was passed by the New York General Assembly and made part of the Civil Rights Law in that state. This was accomplished by a rather inspired approach:†

The prohibition of any subpoena was justified to the legislature on the grounds that all of these records are secondary sources of the information contained therein. The best evidence is in the records maintained by the facility in the original jurisdiction. Therefore, any subpoena should be addressed, not to MSIS, but to the facility at which the records originated.

It is our opinion, then, that the rights to privacy are not outmoded in the cybernetic age; that the basic problems of human nature will not be swept away by any new technology. Political power will probably always corrupt unless limited. *We must redefine guarantees of civil liberties to make them relevant in a cybernetic age just as our forefathers redefined those guarantees when industrialization and urbanization altered the agricultural society in which these rights were first defined in the American Constitution.* Finally, we feel that the greatest threat from computer abuse in the privacy area comes not so much from the direct "police state" picture that first comes to mind when one speaks of computerized privacy invasion but rather from the indirect effects of living in a culture where computerized information systems deny citizens the type of privacy Westin means when he speaks of privacy for emotional release and self-evaluation or the type of privacy that Le Guin might call "creative loneliness" or what William James meant when he called religion the "experiences of individual men in their solitude". Or what Emerson meant when he described solitude as "the safeguard of mediocrity"

---

*William J. Curran, Eugene M. Laska, Honora Kaplan, and Reta Bank, "Protection of Privacy and Confidentiality", *Science*, **182**, November 1973, p. 799.
†Ibid.

and "to genius the stern friend". It is the passing of the secluded retreat that we feel poses the worst threat. We will explore this and other indirect effects in detail in Chapter 9, "Social and Philosophical Implications".

EXERCISES

1. From Ernst and Schwartz's *Privacy: The Right to Be Let Alone* (The Macmillan Co.) or Westin's *Privacy and Freedom* (Atheneum) or any other references you have available, collect 10 different definitions of privacy.
2. Differentiate between privacy and security.
3. Obtain from your local credit bureau (or a local lending institution) the laws relating to credit and privacy in your state. What are your rights?
4. The Family Educational Rights and Privacy Act of 1974 has substantial impact on record keeping practices of school systems. What are they? Do you have the legal right to see any record kept about you? Do your parents have the legal right to see such records? What is the impact of this act on recommendations made in your behalf by faculty and filed by, say, your school's placement office? Why is this act called the Sunshine Law?
5. Obtain a copy of the "Privacy Act of 1974". This is available in most libraries as Public Law 93-579, an amendment to title 5, U.S. Code, Section 552. What are your rights under this Act? Do any private institutions come under its jurisdiction? From *Computerworld* issues of 1974 obtain the history of this Act. Is the final version very similar to the original proposals? What areas were compromised? Why?
6. Some states have publications detailing citizens' rights to privacy in that state. For example, Massachusetts' Governor's Commission on Privacy and Personal Data has a publication *Privacy in Massachusetts: Your Rights Under the Law*. Does your state have such a publication? What are your rights in your state?
7. Can you refuse to give your school system your Social Security number?
8. Associated Credit Bureaus, Inc. publishes several booklets about the FCRA. Obtain some or similar publications from your local credit bureau and report on them.
9. Review your information file with your local credit bureau. This should cost you a nominal amount of money.
10. Look up privacy-related statutes not discussed in this chapter. For example, do you have the right to suppress any evidence in a court of law if it was obtained from a wiretap or surveillance of your communications and was not authorized by an appropriate court? The answer is yes, but exceptions can be made for reasons of national security. [See 18 U.S.C. 2518 (10) (a) (1968).] What if you are talking with someone who was being illegally wiretapped? The evidence so obtained *could be used* to prosecute you. [See 18 U.S.C. 2518 (7) (a) (1968).] What are your rights (federal and state) with regard to mailing lists? (See 39 U.S.C. 3008 and 39 U.S.C. 3010.) Do you wish your name removed from mailing lists? Contact Direct Mail Marketing Association's Mail Preference Service, 6 East 43rd St., New York, NY 10017. If you are a veteran discharged prior to March 22, 1974 you have a three-digit code in box 11-C of your DD-214.

That code gives the detailed circumstances of your discharge and is called a "separation program number" or SPN. Your SPN might have adverse effects on your future employment prospects. The code was supposed to be confidential but it has been published in several national magazines (e.g., *Penthouse*). Codes can indicate such judgments as "apathetic attitude", "marginal producer", or sexual behavior. Since the military has dropped the code it will issue new discharge papers without the code if you request such be done. How would you find about all that if you hadn't read it here? What paths are open to you to obtain information on your privacy rights?

11. Explore the privacy implications of a nationwide EFTS such as described in Chapter 4. This can lead to an interesting discussion of tradeoffs and of threats to individual privacy.

12. Can you be issued a Social Security number against your will? Can a child? (See 42 U.S.C. 405.)

13. What is the estimated cost of enacting PA74? Hint: who would (should) make the estimate?

BIBLIOGRAPHY

Anderson, R. E., and E. Fagerlund. "Privacy and the Computer: An Annotated Bibliography". *Communications of the Association for Computing Machinery* **13,** 11, 1972.

> The bibliography consists of the following: a bibliography of bibliographies; over 60 references representing a general review of "privacy and the computer"; 30 additional references, which focus upon computers and privacy within governmental information systems; and hearings and other reports of the United States Congress.

Approaches to Privacy and Security in Computer Systems. Washington: Government Printing Office, 1974. 72 pp.

> Suggestions for safeguarding the privacy of individuals in computer-based record-keeping systems. Proposals made by legislators, managers, industrialists, and technologists.

Attorney General's Memorandum on the 1974 Amendments to the Freedom of Information Act. Washington: Government Printing Office, 1975. about 68 pp.

> A memorandum for the executive departments and agencies concerning the amendments to the Freedom of Information Act (5 U.S.C. 552) effected by P.L. 93-502, enacted November 21, 1974, and effective February 19, 1975. These amendments are not nearly as concerned with invasion of privacy as is the Privacy Act of 1974 but are still quite relevant to the privacy issue. This publication references the Privacy Act of 1974 as well as many court decisions and other references. The Foreword by the U.S. Attorney General, Edward H. Levi, concludes with [italics added]:

> The President has asked me, in issuing these guidelines, to emphasize on his behalf that it is not only the duty but the mission of every agency to make these Amendments effective in achieving the important purposes for which they were designed. *The Department of Justice will continue to regard the encouragement of sound and effective implementation of the Freedom of Information Act as one of its most important responsibilities.*

Executive Classification of Information—Security Classification Problems Involving Exemption (b) (1) of the Freedom of Information Act. Washington: Government Printing Office, 1973. 113 pp.

> Section (b) (1) of the Freedom of Information Act (5 U.S.C. 552) reads
>
> > (b) This section does not apply to matters that are—
> > > (1) specifically required by Executive order to be kept secret int he interest of national defense or foreign policy;
>
> and this publication is a report by the Committee on Government Operations concerning various issues involving the President's role in limiting the dissemination of information affecting the defense and foreign policy areas. Gives an interesting history of the classification system from 1912 to the present. Concludes with a recommendation that a
>
> > ... statutory system should be established, perhaps as an amendment to the Freedom of Information Act, to make it clear that Congress intends a proper balancing between the safeguarding of information classified under strict guidelines to protect vital defense and foreign policy secrets and the right of the American public to know how the affairs of their government are being conducted. Congress should also take this necessary action to assure maximum credibility of all citizens in our governmental institutions and in our elected and appointed officials.

Fair Credit Reporting Act, 15 U.S.C. 1681. Washington: Government Printing Office, 1970. 7 pp.

> The Fair Credit Reporting Act was enacted in 1970 to curb abusive practices of credit reporting and credit granting agencies. This act is discussed in this chapter.

Family Educational Rights and Privacy Act of 1974

> Originally a 1974 amendment (Public Law 93-380) to the Secondary Education Act of 1965 (20 U.S.C. 821), this act was further modified in response to criticism by school officials that the original act would result in an unmanageable increase in workloads and other problems (Section 2 of S. J. Res. 40, 93rd Congress). As modified, the Family Educational Rights and Privacy Act of 1974 prohibits provision of federal aid to any educational agency or institution that prevents or has a policy of preventing parents of its students or former students from having the right to inspect and review the education records of their children. The act bars federal aid to any educational institution or agency that releases personally identifiable information, other than directory information to which a parent has not objected after reasonable notice, without written consent of the student's parents, to anyone other than: (1) other school officials within the educational institution or a local agency that has been determined by the school to have legitimate educational interests in such records or (2) officials of other schools in which the student intends to enroll.

Freedom of Information Act, 5 U.S.C. 552. Washington: Government Printing Office, 1967. About 2 pp.

> The laws governing general agencies with regard to the recording, storing, and processing of information. An outgrowth of the 1946 Administrative Procedures Act, the law's intent is to require each federal agency to make its operations known to the public. This law and its 1974 amendments are

discussed in this chapter. This law is the foundation statute for the Privacy Act of 1974.

Freedom of Information Act, 1974 Amendments, Public Law 93-502. Washington: Government Printing Office, 1974. 5 pp.

> Amendments to the Freedom of Information Act, 5 U.S.C. 552. Not as directly involved with the invasion-of-privacy issue as the Privacy Act of 1974, this set of Amendments modify the same statute as does that act.

Gotlieb, C. C., and A. Borodin. *Social Issues in Computing.* New York: Academic Press, 1973. 284 pp.

> A comprehensive treatment of the social issues in computing.

Hutton, E. J. *The Constitutional Right of Privacy: Supreme Court Decisions and Congressional Action in Brief.* Washington: Congressional Research Service, Library of Congress, 1974. 32 pp.

> A collection of Supreme Court decisions that interact with the right-of-privacy issue. Well written and quite readable, this booklet considers interactions between privacy and such areas as freedom of the press, search and seizure, and pornography. Traces the origins of the Supreme Court's view of privacy from its roots in the Fourth Amendment, through prohibition (which retarded the development of the Fourth Amendment as a vehicle for the right of privacy) and the historic *Griswold* opinion [381 U.S.C. 479 (1965)], to the period right before the passage of the Privacy Act of 1974.

Miller, A. R. *The Assault on Privacy.* Ann Arbor, Mich.: University of Michigan Press, 1971. 333 pp.

> The author is concerned with a variety of organizational practices in handling information about individuals, and he discusses and documents rather carefully a wide variety of such practices.

Privacy Act of 1974. Washington: Government Printing Office, 1974. 15 pp.

> From the Act:

> To amend title 5, United States Code, by adding a section 552a to safeguard individual privacy from the misuse of Federal records, to provide that individuals be granted access to records concerning them which are maintained by Federal agencies, to establish a Privacy Protection Study Commission, and for other purposes.

> This act has the following legislative history and is discussed in detail in this chapter:
> > *House Report* No. 93-1416 accompanying H. R. 16373 (Comm. on Government Operations).
> > *Senate Report* No. 93-1183 (Comm. on Government Operations).
> > *Congressional Record*, Vol. 120 (1974):
> > > Nov. 21, considered and passed Senate.
> > > Dec. 11, considered and passed House, amended, in lieu of H. R. 16373.
> > > Dec. 17, Senate concurred in House amendment with amendments.
> > > Dec. 18, House concurred in Senate amendments.
> > *Weekly Compilation of Presidential Documents*, Vol. 11, No. 1:
> > > Jan. 1, Presidential statement.

Privacy Act of 1974: Report together with Additional Views. House of Representatives' Report No. 93-1416. Washington: Congressional Research Service, Library of Congress, 1975. 42 pp.

>   Meant to accompany H. R. 16373 (the House bill that merged with S.3418 in the Senate to become the Privacy Act of 1974), this is a readable collection of statutes, reports, noted opinions, definitions, and connecting dialog criticizing the (then) proposed legislation.

Protecting Individual Privacy in Federal Gathering, Use and Disclosure of Information. Senate Report No. 93-1183. Washington: Government Printing Office, 1974.

>   Meant to accompany S.3418 (the Senate bill that became the Privacy Act of 1974), this is a less interesting but more complete report than its parallel in the House (see *Privacy Act of 1974: Report Together with Additional Views* in this Bibliography).

Plyslyshyn, Z. W. *Perspectives on the Computer Revolution.* Englewood Cliffs, N.J.: Prentice-Hall, 1970. 540 pp.

>   An overview of how computerization has affected present culture and technology, with a discussion of where present trends will bring us in the future.

Records, Computers and the Rights of Citizens. Washington: Government Printing Office, 1973. 346 pp.

>   A report to the Secretary of Health, Education and Welfare by an advisory committee set up to examine the potential harmful consequences of the use of computers to maintain files about people, to recommend safeguards and remedies, and to propose policy with respect to the use of Social Security number as a standard universal identifier.

Rothman, S., and C. Mossman. *Computers and Society.* Chicago: Science Research Associates, 1976. 423 pp.

>   General introduction to computers, with no programming. Several chapters are related to social implications and the future of computing is discussed.

Smith, R. E. *Privacy Journal.* Washington: Robert Ellis Smith.

>   This is a monthly publication of a private individual devoted to "privacy in a computer age". Generally interesting and containing many good references. First issue was November 1974.

Teague, R., and C. Erickson. *Computers and Society.* St. Paul: West Publishing Co., 1974. 374 pp.

>   An interesting collection of readings on the role of computers in society.

Westin, A. F. *Information Technology in a Democracy.* Cambridge, Mass.: Harvard University Press, 1971. 499 pp.

>   A collection of papers on information technology in government decision making, covering a wide range of topics from theoretical statements to factual descriptions of information systems.

Westin, A. F. *Privacy and Freedom.* New York: Atheneum, 1967. 487 pp.

>   A complete and authoritative study of privacy in America. This is a four-part discussion on protecting society against the spread of privacy-invading practices and techniques.

⑧₀ Social and economic implications

Both optimists and pessimists often claim that automation is simply the latest stage in the evolution of technological means for removing the burdens of work. The assertion is misleading. There is a very good possibility that automation is so different in degree as to be a profound difference in kind, and that it will pose unique problems for society, changing our basic values and the ways we express and enforce them.

Donald N. Michael,
Cybernation: The Silent Conquest

In order to understand what the problems are and, even more, will be, we have to know something of the nature and use of automation and computers. There are two important classes of devices. One class, usually referred to when one speaks of **automation,** is made up of devices that automatically perform sensing and motor tasks, replacing or improving on human capacities for performing these functions. The second class consists of the now-familiar devices called computers.

As observed by Michael,* one of the most important changes produced is that the use of these machines does not merely involve replacing men by having machines do tasks that men did before. It is, as John Diebold says, a way of "thinking as much as it is a way of doing . . . . It is no longer necessary to think in terms of individual machines, or even in terms of groups of machines; instead, for the first time, it is practical to look at an entire production or information-handling process as an integrated system and not as a series of individual steps." For example, if the building trades were to be automated, it would not mean inventing machines to do the various tasks now done by men. Instead, buildings would be designed so that they could be built by machines. One might build an automatic bricklayer, but it is more likely that housing would be designed so that bricks would not be laid.

The two device classes overlap. At one end are the automatic producers of material objects and, at the other, the sophisticated analyzers and interpreters of complex data. In the middle zone are the mixed systems, in which computers control complicated processes, such as the operations of an oil refinery. Also in the middle zone are those routine, automatic, data processing activities which provide men with the basis for controlling, or at least understanding, what is happening to a particular environment.

In order to eliminate the awkwardness of repeating the words "automation" and "computers" each time we wish to refer to both at the same time, we will adopt Michael's term **cybernation** to refer to both automation and computers. His word derives from **cybernetics,** a term invented by Norbert Wiener to mean the *processes of communication and control in animals and machines.* Wiener derived the term from the Greek word for "steersman". The theory and practice of cybernetics underlie all systematic design and application of automation and computers.

In this chapter, we look at some of the problems engendered by cybernation and some proposed solutions to these problems.

*Cybernation: The Silent Conquest. A report by Donald N. Michael to the Center for the Study of Democratic Institutions, Santa Barbara, Ca., 1962, p. 5.

A car so advanced, it can tell you just about everything that's right or wrong with it.

Remarkable new invention in every 1972 Volkswagen.

We've all been through it.

The agony of an automotive checkup. You sit nervously thumbing through old magazines, praying that somehow you can get out of there for less than $50.

Then, the moment of truth.

A Service Manager telling you that one of his best mechanics thinks you need a new generator.

Those days will be over soon if you own a 1972 Volkswagen.

For instead of a mechanic telling you what he thinks is wrong with your car, now your car can tell you for sure.

Sound amazing?

It is.

A car wired like a space capsule.

When Man went to the Moon, the success of each mission depended a great deal on a highly technical computerized system that told the Astronauts the exact condition of their space vehicle.

A similar system is now built into every 1972 Volkswagen.

The system in the car.

Running throughout the car is a network of sensors, each reporting the condition of various parts of the car.

Most of these sensor points are located in key areas like the engine or the electrical system, but many are found in seemingly insignificant places like the heated rear window.

The information from all areas is channeled to one central socket located in the rear engine compartment.

The socket is about the size of a pack of cigarettes.

We mention the size only because of

what happens next. And that's what this amazing socket can do.

60 vital service checks.

Soon you'll be able to take any 1972 Volkswagen into an authorized VW dealership for the most advanced automotive check-up in the world today.

At that time, your car will actually be plugged into a computer.

And in half the time it takes to perform a conventional check-up, 60 vital service checks will be made and recorded.

AN AMAZING SOCKET, BUILT INTO THE BACK OF EVERY 1972 VOLKSWAGEN, THAT WHEN PLUGGED INTO A COMPUTER, WILL ACTUALLY REPORT THE CONDITION OF YOUR CAR—DIRECTLY TO YOU!

Checks wheel alignment in 10 seconds.

In 10 seconds, you'll know if your front wheels are properly aligned.

In a minute, you'll know the condition of the compression of all engine cylinders.

Without a mechanic so much as taking a

peek, you'll know whether or not your battery needs water.

Ignition, cylinder compression, dwell angle, generator, electrical system—

All checked out without human error.

In effect, your car will be telling you how it feels directly.

And once again, this information is emanating from that one tiny socket built into the back of every 1972 Volkswagen.

Results printed out in plain English.

One half of the system is already here. Built into every new Volkswagen.

The other half, the computer, is on its way.

Imagine.

A computer five feet away from your car is printing out in plain English just about everything that's right or wrong with that car.

When all 60 service checks have been made, the print-out sheet is yours to keep.

What better proof to show that your automobile has finally had a thorough physical check-up?

A new way to look at a VW.

It started with economy, back in 1949, when it wasn't fashionable for an automobile to be economical.

But since when has a VW been fashionable?

Since never.

Obviously, the Volkswagen Beetle hasn't made it on looks alone.

But then, that's always been the plan.

While everyone else has been worrying about how their cars looked, we've been worrying about how ours acted.

And now, after all that time, we've even advanced it to a stage where it can speak.

VW

Volkswagen's Computer Diagnosis: Volkswagen's computerized self-analysis system makes use of a socket built into new VWs to enable the car to "tell" a computer how it "feels." Principal components of the system are the central socket ① and the "umbilical cord" for connecting the car to the computer ②. The thin armored cable leading off the top of the plug is for reading engine oil temperature. Each Volkswagen has its own program card ③. Results of the checks performed on the vehicle are recorded by a printer ④. This printed record tells the mechanic and the customer what work is needed to bring the car to standard specifications. Some of the tests are performed by the mechanic using a hand-held input unit ⑤. Front wheel alignment is inspected using a photoelectric unit ⑥. Headlights are checked for brightness and adjustment using the tester ⑦. Proper setting of the car is ensured by positioning it on four pads ⑧. (Courtesy of Volkswagen of America, Inc.)

If there were a way to monitor every investment decision, you'd get better pension fund performance.

We have a way. Management of pension fund portfolios involves hundreds of decisions. From the analyst's first consideration to the trader's execution, the quality of all these decisions determines how well your fund will perform. At Continental Bank we've developed a system of decision measurement and control that improves investment results. It's a major breakthrough in performance management.

Here's how it works: Every investment decision and decision maker is monitored and evaluated through the use of advanced computer programming. This gives management an immediate, detailed picture of portfolio progress and specific action indicators for any necessary adjustments.

But that isn't all. Continental's newest investment tool is the computerized Investment Planning System. It enables us to analyze a far greater array of financial criteria than we could with human resources alone. Over 1,800 companies are continuously and systematically tracked. This gives Continental's trust investment analysts an up-to-the-minute evaluation and projection of current investment opportunities, with emphasis on detecting undervalued and overvalued securities.

We are prepared to demonstrate the effectiveness of this system. If you administer a pension fund and would like detailed information on how Continental Bank can provide not only the best qualified people but the most sophisticated computer systems to give you superior pension fund performance, call Edward D. Benninghoven, Vice President at 312/828-3500.

CONTINENTAL BANK
Continental Illinois National Bank and Trust Company of Chicago,
231 South La Salle Street, Chicago, Illinois 60693. Member F.D.I.C.

Bank advertisement illustrating use of a remote terminal and acoustic telephone coupler: management information systems have been playing larger and larger roles in many industries, and banking is no exception. As this advertisement illustrates, decision assistance via computer and computer expertise are marketable assets. (Reprinted with permission of Continental Bank.)

ECONOMIC IMPLICATIONS

Much of the debate in the area of the economic implications of cybernation can be divided into two distinct camps. First, there are people such as W. H. (Ping) Ferry of the Center for the Study of Democratic Institutions, who argues that cybernation will have a **revolutionary impact** on Western civilization—that the impact of cybernation on productivity and employment

"En garde, Mr. Benson!"

© DATAMATION®

and on social values, especially the Protestant work ethic, will cause a change that is a change in kind. On the other hand, are government spokesmen arguing that the impact of cybernation will be to produce changes in degree not changes in kind. This is the **evolutionary impact** school. Some have called the revolutionary impact argument the **heavy-impact** position and the evolutionary impact argument the **normal-impact** position.

It is not our purpose here to try to resolve the revolutionary/evolutionary argument. Both sides seem to miss the mark in presenting their evidence. It seems like it is more important to them to win the argument than to think through the evidence. We will attempt to present some arguments from both sides and a concluding comparison.

Revolutionary impact

One of the best statements of the revolutionary impact position has been made by the Ad Hoc Committee on the Triple Revolution. Their report was presented to President Lyndon B. Johnson in 1964. It described three revolutions:

1. Weaponary revolution.
2. Human rights' revolution.
3. Cybernation revolution.

The latter topic was the primary concern of the report. It describes this revolution as follows.*

A new era of production has begun. Its principles of organization are as different from those of the industrial era as those of the industrial era were different from the agricultural. The cybernation revolution has been brought about by the combination of the computer and the automated self-regulating machine. This results in a system of

*R. MacBride, *The Automated State.* New York: Chilton, 1967, p. 192.

almost unlimited productive capacity which requires progressively less human labor. Cybernation is already reorganizing the economic and social system to meet its own needs.

Distribution of titles of consumption (i.e., money) has been via jobs. The report points out that this will have to end.* The continuance of the income-through-jobs link as the only major mechanism for distributing effective demand—for granting the right to consume—now acts as the main brake on the almost unlimited capacity of a cybernated productive system.

Further, up to this time resources have been distributed on the basis of contributions to production, with machines and men competing for employment on somewhat equal terms. In the developing cybernated system, potentially unlimited output can be achieved by systems of machines which will require little cooperation from human beings.

As a consequence, we have the paradox†

. . . that a substantial proportion of the population is subsisting on minimal incomes, often below the poverty line, at a time when sufficient productive potential is available to supply the needs of everyone in the U.S.

In the view of the committee, the traditional link (read "Capitalist Spirit" in the Appendix) between jobs and income must be broken.

The report cites as evidence, the following‡

1. The increased efficiency of machine systems is shown in the more rapid increase in productivity per man-hour since 1960, a year that marks the first visible upsurge of the cybernation revolution. In 1961, 1962, and 1963, productivity per man-hour rose at an average pace above 3.6 percent—a rate well above both the historical average and the postwar rate.
2. A $30 billion annual increase in gross national product is now required to prevent unemployment rates from rising. An additional $40 to $60 billion increase would be required to bring unemployment rates down to an acceptable level.
3. Besides the 5.5 percent of the labor force who are officially designated as unemployed, nearly 4 percent of the labor force sought full-time work in 1962 but could find only part-time jobs. The number of people who have voluntarily removed themselves from the labor force is not constant but increases continuously.
4. Well over half of the new jobs created during 1957–1962 were in the public sector—predominantly in teaching.
5. Of the 4,300,000 jobs created in this period, only about 200,000 were provided by private industry through its own efforts.
6. Some 38,000,000 Americans still live in poverty. The percentage of total income received by the poorest 20 percent of the population was 4.9 percent in 1944 and 4.7 percent in 1963.

The revolutionary impact position is supported by others than the Ad Hoc Committee on the Triple Revolution. The First Annual Conference on the Cybercultural Revolution exhibited substantial evidence in support of the revolutionary impact position. As far back as 1963, at the Fall Joint Computer

*Ibid., p. 195.
†Ibid.
‡Ibid., p. 168.

Conference, a panel of representatives from the public sector and from industry came to the unanimous conclusion that we would be faced with large numbers of idle people in the near future.

A more organized presentation of evidence in support of the position of the Ad Hoc Committee on the Triple Revolution was made by one of the Committee's members, Ben B. Seligman. He came to the conclusion that there are almost 3 million people out of work for reasons other than ordinary adjustment. Furthermore, he concluded that the economy must provide well over 2 million jobs to keep unemployment from rising (above the 1.5 million jobs needed to counter the annual increase in the work force).

Finally, the argument is frequently encountered that cybernation is causing an increase in the level of required skills and that the less skilled end of the population is being displaced out of the job market as a consequence.

Evolutionary impact

Much of the evolutionary impact argument is specific refutation of various aspects of the revolutionary impact position. A large part of that evidence is drawn from specific instances of computer application.

For example,*

... within one year after the installation of the computer, about one-third of the approximately 2,800 employees in units whose work was directly affected had been reassigned to other positions either within the same unit or elsewhere in the office. A majority remained in the same position. Close to one-sixth had quit, retired, died, or had taken leave of absence. Only nine persons had been laid off. Altogether employment in the affected unit had been reduced by about 25 percent at the end of the year.

The National Commission on Technology, Automation, and Economic Progress was formed in 1964 to investigate the impact of technological and economic change in production employment over the next 10 years. Their report was published early in 1966. It concluded that, while productivity growth is substantial, it is not consistent with the revolutionary impact thesis. (Five Commission members did, however, dissent from the report because it "lacks the tone of urgency, which we believe [the report's] subject matter requires and which its recommendations reflect".)

The Commission's conclusions were surprisingly strong, given the generally optimistic anticipation of the majority of the Commission's members. They concluded that there will be some that cannot or should not participate in the job economy. For these, they proposed establishment of an adequate system of income maintenance, guaranteeing a minimum income at an acceptable level.† The Commission recommended the creation of 500,000 full-time public service jobs (with an increase each year for five years).

Comparison

Neither the revolutionary nor evolutionary argument is conclusive. It is worth noting that the Ad Hoc Committee on the Triple Revolution and the

---

*U.S. Department of Labor Bulletin #1276, *Adjustments to the Introduction of Office Automation,* 1960, p. 3.

†The much-publicized negative income tax was originally proposed by an economic advisor to Senator Barry Goldwater (R-Ariz.).

National Commission on Technology, Automation, and Economic Progress, beginning with completely divergent premises, proceed to surprisingly similar recommendations. The provisions (income by right, negative income tax, public works programs) proposed by both groups are quite similar.

Yet, in 1956, E. M. Hugh-Jones, in *The Push-Button World** described a computer able to calculate the wages of an employee in two seconds, predicted a 32-hour work week "in a few years," and quoted John Diebold as anticipating shortly a five-day weekend. Today, with computers thousands of times faster, we do not seem too much closer to fulfilling these predictions.

Similar unemployment predictions have been alarming. Norbert Wiener wrote:†

Let us remember that the automatic machine . . . as the precise economic equivalent of slave labor must accept the economic condition of slave labor. It is perfectly clear that this will produce an unemployment situation, in comparison with which . . . the depression of the thirties will seem a pleasant joke.

Many equally dire prophecies have followed Wiener's prediction; yet, we do not seem to have hit the massive technological unemployment that has been predicted. A fairly recent treatment of this subject is given in a paper entitled "Computers and Employment".‡

Another interesting question revolves around the most appropriate directions for extending the cybernation continuum. The most obvious direction would seem to be the development of completely automated factories, distribution systems, service facilities, and the like. In addition to economic difficulties this route might produce some serious dangers to our autonomy and self-sufficiency, given our current capability or lack thereof, for dealing with highly automated systems. The ultimate danger of this type is intriguingly described by Forster§ in his fictional account of an automated society. The current economic practicality of such an approach is also questionable and in the near future it seems considerably more practical to develop systems of machines supervised, helped, and controlled by a human. A scenario for such development is given in the paper, "Robots, Productivity and Quality".**

Social implications

It may be that the major effects of cybernation will be much more subtle than massive unemployment. For example, the trend in recent years to rigidly enforce retirement regulations and even give incentives for early retirement can be traced in part to the pressure of a larger pool of available workers, which has cybernation as one of its major causes. This policy of compelling or encouraging retirement has obvious humane considerations, but it could also

*E. M. Hugh-Jones, *The Push-Button World*, Norman, Okla.: University of Oklahoma Press, 1956.

†N. Wiener, *The Human Use of Human Beings*. Boston: Houghton Mifflin Co., 1950, p. 220.

‡A. Borodin and C. C. Gotlieb, "Computers and Employment", *Communications of the ACM*, Vol. 15, No. 7, pp. 695–702.

§E. M. Forster, "The Machine Stops", *Fairy Tales for Computers*, New York: The Eakins Press, 1969.

**C. Rosen, "Robots, Productivity and Quality", *Proceedings of the ACM 1972 Annual Conference*, pp. 47–57.

rob us of badly needed maturity in critical areas. This problem was well stated in an advertisement in *Time Magazine*.*

People become obsolete before their time in our assembly line culture. We no longer grow old gracefully. Years of experience are not always valued. Instead of using the wisdom of age to help solve our problems, we have turned the aged themselves into a problem. Our preoccupation with youth has made us forget that, often, people considered "too old" have the youngest ideas of all.

Another subtle effect of cybernation seems to be the effect on the organizational structures of corporations and governments. Since a great deal of power accrues to those people in an organization who control information and its flow, we see that the power structure changes as traditional methods of record keeping give way to systems based on computerized data bases. Departments that kept records in traditional files find their control of the information diminishes as the files are computerized, with a concomitant increase in the importance of computer departments. Also, the usual methods of information flow may be replaced by sophisticated terminal-oriented systems directly tied in to computer systems. Because of this, certain departments may find themselves bypassed and the influence they might have previously exerted on the data may disappear. Such departments may thus lose a considerable amount of their influence on other departments within the organization.

Still another more subtle effect of cybernation may come through increased leisure time. In the nineteenth century the 16-hour workday was defended on the grounds that workers would only use extra leisure time to get drunk. Today we are less worried about such use of leisure time, although the picture of a society of beer-drinking television addicts is still used by some people as an ominous scenario for the future. The problems of a possible over abundance of leisure time are undoubtedly more subtle than this and probably revolve around the psychological impact of identifying leisure with idleness—the absence of work.

In his scholarly book, *Leisure the Basis of Culture*, Josef Pieper predicts† the destructive consequence of the twentieth-century "cult" of work and argues against our puritanical (and pragmatic) conceptions about labor and leisure. To Pieper, leisure is an attitude of the mind and a condition of the soul that fosters a capacity to perceive the real world. He argues that *leisure has been, and always will be, the foundation of any culture.*

The ethic (recall the Protestant ethic as described in the "Capitalist Spirit" in the Appendix) that work is somehow good, idleness evil, and that man must work to eat may no longer be appropriate. Many have drawn an analogy between ancient Rome with her slave and patrician classes and a future Western culture with its machine and human classes.

Education is stressed, by many writers on the topic of leisure and cybernation, as the single hope to maintain a meaningful life and an organized society in a leisureful world. Most are content that, with adequate education for the use of leisure time, man will enter into a utopialike cybernated world. But not all: Jacques Ellul in his penetrating analysis of our technical civilization, *The Technological Society*‡, says:

*From an Atlantic Richfield "The Ideal /The Real" advertisement.
†J. Pieper, *Leisure the Basis of Culture*. New York: Random House, 1963.
‡J. Ellul, *The Technological Society*, New York: Vintage Books, 1967, p. 401.

. . . that leisure, instead of being a vacuum representing a break with society, is literally stuffed with technical mechanisms of compensation and integrations . . . (leisure) is a mechanized time . . . and leaves man no more free than labor itself.

If we carry this line of thought to extremes, we are reminded of the words of Valéry*

THE MACHINE RULES. Human life is rigorously controlled by it, dominated by the terrible precise will of mechanisms. These creatures of man are exacting. They are reacting on their creators, making them like themselves. They want well-trained humans; they are gradually wiping out the differences between men, fitting them into their own orderly functioning, into the uniformity of their own regimes. They are thus shaping humanity for their own use, almost in their own image.

Thus, our apparent leisure may be nothing more than a chimera behind which stands a subtle demon regulator of free time for the ends of a mechanistic society. After a particularly intimate encounter with the frenetic rush of the freeway, who is prepared to totally deny this point of view?

   These more subtle social implications may have profound effects not only on the way we live and work but more importantly on the philosophical aspects of our life: how we view ourselves and our relationship to the world around us. Since such effects could well be the most important of all, we will devote the final chapter to an extended discussion of social and philosophical implications.

SUMMARY

   We have discussed the economic implications of cybernation from the two extremes of revolutionary and evolutionary impact and have noted that our experience over the last few years might incline us toward the evolutionary impact argument. However, our capability for gauging such effects is considerably less than perfect and it may be that the economic implications are somewhat more long-term and subtle than initially thought. In any event, efforts to gauge the economic effects must continue and a great deal of energy should be devoted to planning the appropriate directions for extending cybernation.

EXERCISES

1. Make a list of some systems you use that have been completely or partially automated within the last 10 years. In each case indicate the effects on you, if any. Do you consider the automated systems more or less effective?
2. Try to obtain an interview with the manager of a facility that has automated some of its operations and try to ascertain the current and projected effect on employment in the facility. (Note that this must be done very tactfully.) Report on your findings.
3. Do you feel that your happiness is inextricably linked to the performance of some meaningful work? State your position on this and try to contrast it with the position of someone in a previous generation.

*P. Valéry, "On Intelligence", *Fairy Tales for Computers*. New York: The Eakins Press, 1969.

4. If you were somehow granted 10 additional hours of leisure time each week, how would you utilize that time?
5. Conduct a poll of several organizations to determine the average age of their work force now and 10 years ago. Try to get enough results to make the study meaningful. Determine averages over all the organizations and compare these with statistics such as life expectancy, average age of the population of the United States, and so on, now and 10 years ago.
6. Determine your feelings about retirement (premature as they may be) and then determine the feelings of at least one person in each of the following age groups: 40–50, 50–60, 60–70, greater than 70.

BIBLIOGRAPHY

Diebold, J. *Man and the Computer: Technology as an Agent of Social Change.* New York: Praeger, 1969. 157 pp.

> Based on speeches and other previously published documents, this book explores some examples of change and raises some long-term questions; areas covered include education, international affairs, and management.

Landon, K. C. *Computers and Bureaucratic Reform.* New York: Wiley, 1974. 325 pp.

> Explores the interaction between society and the emerging computer technology. By relegating the technical material to appendices, the book is made readable to the layperson but still remains interesting to the computer professional.

McBride, R. *The Automated State.* New York: Chilton, 1967. 407 pp.

> Focuses on the probable aspects of the computer's impact on people and examines the ways in which the computer is most likely to affect jobs, businesses, and personal decisions. The book explores the evolution of nationwide networks of computers, the invasion-of-privacy issue, and the impact of computers on the federal government. This is an excellent source book for copies of often hard-to-find documents such as the Triple Revolution Memorandum and the report of the National Commission on Technology, Automation, and Economic Progress.

Gotlieb, C. C., and Borodin, A. *Social Issues in Computing.* New York: Academic Press, 1973. 284 pp.

> A comprehensive treatment of the social issues in computing.

Michael, D. N. *Cybernation: The Silent Conquest.* A report by Donald N. Michael to the Center for the Study of Democratic Institutions. Santa Barbara, Ca.: 1962. 48 pp.

> This booklet is an excellent treatment of the social implications of computers and automation. It treats both the advantages and disadvantages of cybernation and has a thought-provoking section on the control of cybernation.

Pieper, J. *Leisure, the Basis of Culture.* New York: Random House, 1963, 127 pp.

> This book is a quite scholarly but still readable essay on the "cult of work". It puts forth the thesis (among others) that leisure is fundamental to the birth of social institutions and that the worship of the machine, of know-how, and of time will cause a drift toward the slave society.

Pylyshyn, Z. W. *Perspectives on the Computer Revolution.* Englewood Cliffs, N.J.: Prentice-Hall, 1970.

> An overview of how computerization has affected present culture and technology, with a discussion of where present trends will bring us in the future.

Ritterbush, R. C. (ed.). *Technology as Institutionally Related to Human Values.* Washington, D.C.: Acropolis Books, 1974. 198 pp.

> Addresses man's tendency to use knowledge to do evil. Presents some solutions to the problems that follow in the wake of technology. An interesting collection of papers.

Rothman, S., and C. Mossman. *Computers and Society.* Second Edition Chicago: Science Research Associates, 1976. 423 pp.

> General introduction to computers, with no programming. Several chapters are related to social implications, and the future of computing is discussed.

Shepard, J. M. *Automation and Alienation.* Cambridge, Mass.: M.I.T. Press, 1971. 163 pp.

> Analyzes the impact of automation, including computers, on office and factory workers, and dispels many of the fears of worker alienation resulting from automation and information technology.

Taviss, I. (ed.). *The Computer Impact.* Englewood Cliffs, N.J.: Prentice-Hall, 1970, 297 pp.

> Examines how computers have changed or helped to change business, technological, and cultural environments, how changes will continue, and in what possible directions.

Teague, R., and C. Erickson. *Computers and Society.* St. Paul: West Publishing Co., 1974. 373 pp.

> An interesting collection of readings on the role of computers in society.

Walker, T. M., and W. W. Cotterman. *An Introduction to Computer Science and Algorithmic Processes.* Boston: Allyn and Bacon, 1970. 563 pp.

> A general introductory text covering PL /I and FORTRAN, this book contains a good section on the social implications of computing with especially good treatment of the economic implications of computing.

Wiener, N. *The Human Use of Human Beings.* Boston: Houghton Mifflin, 1950. 199 pp.

> A nontechnical treatment of the place of cybernetics in society.

⑨. Social and philosophical implications

Men have become the tools of their tools.

Thoreau

In the space of one hundred and seventy-six years the Lower Mississippi has shortened itself two hundred and forty-two miles. That is an average of a trifle over one mile and a third per year. Therefore, any calm person, who is not blind or idiotic, can see that in the old Oolitic Silurian Period, just a million years ago next November, the Lower Mississippi River was upward of one million three hundred thousand miles long, and stuck out over the Gulf of Mexico like a fishing rod. And by the same token any person can see that seven hundred and forty-two years from now the Lower Mississippi will be only a mile and three quarters long, and Cairo and New Orleans will have joined their streets together, and be plodding comfortably along under a single mayor and a mutual board of aldermen. There is something fascinating about science. One gets such wholesale returns of conjecture out of such a trifling investment of fact.

Mark Twain,
Life on the Mississippi

A PERSPECTIVE

We may be in the process of becoming slaves of "quantification" and "accountability". Illich* observes that "People have a native capacity for healing, consoling, moving, learning, building their houses, and burying their dead" Yet, we squander this native talent by allowing minorities of professionals in these areas to regulate and control these activities. People have a great native talent for making heuristic judgments and decisions of great depth about both their private and public affairs. They feel intuitively the worth of an action, the significance of work and the quality of life. If we allow this marvelously accurate ability to be replaced by inferior algorithmic approximations, we may suffer the greatest loss of all. But quantification seems increasingly to be the order of the day, as Alfred North Whitehead observed: "Through and through the world is infested with quantity: to talk sense is to talk quantities. It is no use saying the nation is large—how large? It is no use saying radium is scarce—how scarce?" Thus, it seems to be of no use to say the quality of life is good, instead—how good? Then we may presumably answer with reams of statistics, all with appropriate acronyms (e.g., GNP, CPI) and all made possible by the great quantifier—the computer. Yet, is this what we really wish from the computer? If so, we implicitly relinquish control over important areas of social judgment and depend with blind faith on the cybernated

*I. Illich, *Tools for Conviviality*, New York: Harper & Row, 1973.

systems. As an alternative, could we not insist that the cybernated systems serve every individual rather than attempting to serve society as a whole and succeeding only in controlling every individual? In answering this question we must face rather directly the deeper philosophical question: Is man inherently mechanistic and is machine dominance therefore the inevitable consequence of our evolving society? In his excellent article, "On the Impact of Computers on Society", in the Appendix, Professor Joseph Weizenbaum addresses this fundamental question.

Weizenbaum argues that the computer will soon bring about a major crisis in the mental life of our civilization. Galileo removed man from the center of the universe, Darwin from his place separate from animals, Marx made him question his political free will, and Freud showed his rationality to be an illusion. The possibility that the computer will demonstrate that "the brain is merely a meat machine" is engaging academicians, industrialists, and journalists.*

Weizenbaum feels that "the computer revolution need not and ought not to call man's dignity and autonomy into question", that it is a pathology that moves men to wring from the computer revolution unwarranted, maybe damaging interpretations. He argues that, while the computer is less dangerous than first thought, it still offers many pitfalls. He discusses several of his fears of indirect effects on society:

1. That policy makers will abdicate their decision-making responsibility to a technology they do not even understand.
2. That individuals will respond to the determinism of a cybernated world with the belief that the forces that formulate the large questions of the day, and circumscribe the range of possible answers, are anonymous, hence irresponsible.
3. That computer-based knowledge systems become essentially unmodifiable except in that they can grow. That they will be passed from one generation to another, always growing.

*For an interesting treatment of these considerations, see Bruce Mazlish's "The Fourth Discontinuity" in the Appendix.

"He's charged with expressing contempt for data-processing."

Drawing by Koren; © 1970
The New Yorker Magazine, Inc.

4. That the cybernated world could well replace the ebb and flow of culture with a world without values, a world in which what counts for a fact has long ago been determined and forever fixed.

Weizenbaum expresses quite convincingly the view that societal effects of computers have not yet occurred to any great degree, and that these effects are indirect. He indicates that they may well develop relatively slowly over generations and thus are somewhat longer-term than most experts might anticipate. In fact, the most significant effects may come through a chain of relatively minor but subtle effects that may be long in developing, but may have profound and widespread implications.

Yet, it is quite possible that the increased use of cybernated systems could produce a more human, more personalized, society than man has ever seen. From sheer weight of numbers and complexity the individual in our society is restricted in his freedom of choice. We are literally inundated with complexity and although we may wish for greater simplicity, we must recognize its improbability. It seems rather that we must approach this complexity through abstraction, or more precisely through successive levels of abstraction which allow us to view our society with various levels of detail appropriate to the particular problem at hand. Cybernated systems may be able to help us establish such levels of abstraction and thereby defeat, or at least subdue, the dragon of complexity. If so, this could bring us a more human society rather than a more depersonalized one. Such a serendipitous turn of events could bring about the visions of Norman Cousins*, that the ". . . computer makes

*N. Cousins, "The Computer and the Poet", *Saturday Review*, July 23, 1966.

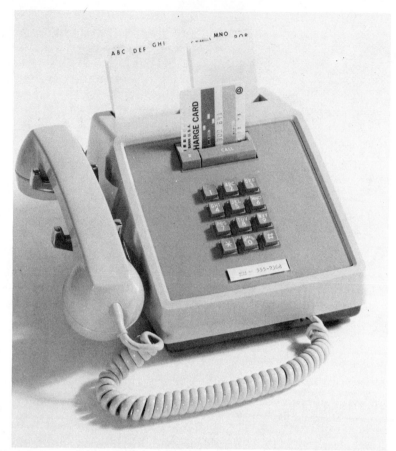

The Touch-Tone credit-card dialer developed by engineers at Bell Labs could speed consumer and business chores such as the payment of bills, credit verification, and inventory control with data transmitted over telephone circuits to a computerized account. The completely automated process could help eliminate much of the vast amount of paper that is now produced by credit slips and checks. (Courtesy Bell Labs.)

possible a phenomenal leap in human proficiency; it demolishes the fences around the practical and even the theoretical intelligence . . . the computer will [possibly] make it easier . . . for human beings to know who they really are, to identify their real problems, to respond more fully to beauty, to place adequate value on life, and to make their world safer than it now is".

The central issue, then, would seem to be whether cybernated systems can and will be used to keep us afloat in a sea of complexity or whether the adverse effects will provide the crowning complexity which finally and completely subjugates man to his tools. For this reason and because of the other adverse effects discussed earlier, we must endeavor to control cybernation to our ends.

CONTROL OF CYBERNATION

Time is crucial in any plan to cope with cybernation. Ways of controlling its adverse effects require thinking farther ahead than we usually do. In a society in the process of becoming cybernated, education and training for work as well as education and training for leisure must begin early in life. Shifts in behavior, attitudes, and aspirations take a long time to mature. It will be extraordinarily difficult to produce appropriate "culture bearers", both parents and teachers, in sufficient numbers, distribution, and quality, in the time available. It is hard to see, for example, how Congress, composed in good part of older men acting from traditional perspectives and operating by seniority, could recognize soon enough and then legislate well enough to produce the fundamental shifts needed to meet the complexities of cybernation. It is hard to see how our style of pragmatic making do and frantic crash programs can radically change in the next few years. The differences expressed in the public statements of business and labor demonstrate that any reconcilliation of interests will be a very long-range effort, indeed. "Drastic" actions to forestall or eliminate the ill effects of cybernation will not be taken in time, unless we change our operating style radically.

Among the many factors contributing to the stability of a social system are two intimately entwined ones: the types of tasks that are performed, and the nature of the relationship between the attitudes of the members of society toward these tasks and their opinions about the proper goals of the individual members of the society and the right ways of reaching them.

The long-range stability of the social system depends on a population of young people properly educated to enter an adult world of tasks and attitudes. Once, the pace of change was slow enough to permit a comfortable margin of compatibility between the adult world and the world children were trained to expect. This compatibility no longer exists. Now we have to ask: "What should be the education of a population more and more enveloped in cybernation? What are the appropriate attitudes toward and training for participation in government, the use of leisure, standards of consumption, particular occupations?" Alvin Toffler has some very pertinent remarks in this regard in his book *Future Shock*.*

Education must cope with the transitional period when the disruption among different socioeconomic and occupational groups will be the greatest and the later, relatively stable period, if it ever comes to exist, when most people would have adequate income and shorter working hours. The problem involves looking ahead 5, 10, or 20 years to see what are likely to be the occupational and social needs and attitudes of those future periods; planning the intellectual and social education of each age group in the numbers needed; motivating young people to seek certain types of jobs and to adopt the desirable necessary attitudes; providing enough suitable teachers; being able to alter all of these as the actualities in society and technology indicate; and directing the pattern of cybernation so that it fits with the expected kinds and distribution of abilities and attitudes produced by home and school.

To what extent education and technology can be coordinated is not at all clear, if only because we do not know, even for today's world, the criteria for judging the consonance or dissonance in our educational, attitudinal, and occupational systems. We think that parts of the social system are badly out of phase with other parts and that as a whole, the system is progressively less capable of coping with the problems it produces. But there is little consensus on the "causes" and even less on what can be done about them. All we have at

*A. Toffler, *Future Shock*. New York: Random House, 1970.

Man–machine continuum: Is it possible, rather, is it meaningful, to extend the computational continuum all the way to man? If so, we must discuss two classical dimensions of man's being: his mind and his body. While both lines have quite a few mechanisms and techniques along them, the machine-to-man's-body line is without doubt more densely filled than is the machine-to-man's-mind line. It is also more evenly filled —almost every part of the line has at least one device associated with it. On the machine end, the line has simple machines such as the lever and the gear. As one moves toward man, the machines increase in capability and come more to resemble man. In many cases, the machines excel over man in speed or capacity. Only quite recently, have entries appeared on the end of the line nearest man. Recent medical advances have married man and machine: artificial corneas, heart valves, larynx, and limbs and heart pacemakers are nearing the commonplace. Artificial organs seem near: there are currently 99 federal research contracts outstanding to produce an artificial heart, and heart–lung machines currently exist as do kidney machines. One of the most promising developments in the area of prosthetic devices is already in the

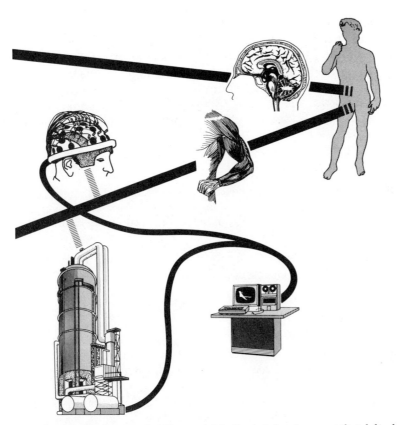

experimental stage at the Harvard Medical School: an artificial limb activated by thought signals. We *can* justly discuss mechanized men and humanized machines in at least the body sphere. The machine to man's-mind continuum is not nearly as densely filled. The entries on this continuum are mostly lumped at the machine end of the line. Pattern recognition and computer game playing are examples of whole areas of research into the machine simulation of human cognition. The rest of the line is mostly empty today. Yet almost daily a new technological advance enters another item onto the line. There is at least one more entry on the line. As we have advanced technologically, we have made machines more manlike. It is also true that man is today much more machinelike than ever before. Would not a fifteenth-century man consider a twentieth-century American almost an automaton? Unlike his remote relative, the modern American has little need for myth. He sees himself not at the center of the universe, upon the throne of God's Chosen, but merely as an evolutionarily advanced animal on a small planet in one arm of one rather average galaxy.

present is the hope that most people can be educated for significant participation in a rapidly increasing world. We have no evidence that it can be done.

If we do not find the answers to these questions fairly soon, we may have a population in the next 10-20 years more and more out of touch with national and international realities. If we fail to find the answers, we can bumble along, very probably heading into disaster, or we can restrict the extension of cybernation, permitting it only where necessary for the national interest.

Perhaps time has already run out. Even if our style somehow should shift to long-range planning, it would not eliminate the inadequate training and values of much of our present adolescent and preadolescent population, as well as of those adults who will be displaced or remain unhired as a result of cybernation in the next decade. Only a partial solution exists in this case: begin now a program of economic and social first aid for these people.

An Office of Technology Assessment has been created to determine for Congress the indirect effects of new technology. It is feared by many as the foundation for a technology-control office. Men such as Joseph Coates, program director for the National Science Foundation, think the fears are unfounded. He warns that we "cannot afford to play the [technology] planning game by ear".

But, for many, planning is not enough. These feelings have been summarized by Harvey Wheeler:*

The days when scientists could be left free to do anything they wanted are finished—or should be. At a time when there is almost instant transferral from theories to facts, even facts as horrendous as the hydrogen bomb, the need for controlling developmental science by law is unavoidable.

In summary, it seems we sorely need a "cybercultural ethos"—read "An Ethos for the Age of Cyberculture" in the Appendix.

A MORATORIUM ON CYBERNATION?

Can we control the effects of cybernation by making it illegal or unprofitable to develop cybernation technology? No, not without virtually stopping the development of almost all new technology and a good part of the general development of scientific knowledge. The accumulation of knowledge in many areas of science depends on computers. To refine computers and make them more versatile requires research in almost every scientific area. It also requires the development of a technology, probably automated, to produce the articles needed to build new computers. As long as we choose to compete with other parts of the world, we shall have to develop new products and new means for producing them better. Cybernation may be the only way to do it on a significant scale. As long as we choose to live in a world guided by science and its technology, we have no choice but to encourage the development of cybernation. If we insist on this framework, the answers to coping with its effects must be found elsewhere than in a moratorium on its development.

He who rides a tiger is afraid to dismount.
Chinese Proverb

*H. Wheeler, "Bringing Science Under Law" in *The Center Magazine*. Santa Barbara, Ca.: The Center for the Study of Democratic Institutions, March 1969, p. 59.

"Monarchy is dying. Long live machines."

© DATAMATION ®

EXERCISES

1. Try to identify aspects of your life that seem dictated by machines or cybernated systems. In each case indicate how the machine or the system could be changed to reduce its controlling influence.
2. Attempt to construct a quantitative measure of the quality of your own life. Identify areas that seem difficult or impossible to quantify.
3. Develop a four-year curriculum that you feel would minimize "future shock". Do not feel limited to traditional subjects or to usual pedagogical methods.
4. Obtain a copy of the film "Future Shock" based on Toffler's book *Future Shock* and write a one-page summary of the impact of future shock in the area of computers and computing.
5. From the Weizenbaum paper, "On the Impact of Computers on Society", in the Appendix, compile a list of its 10 major points (including the 4 listed in this chapter).

BIBLIOGRAPHY

Bemer, R. W. (ed.). *Computers and Crisis*. New York: Association for Computing Machinery, 1971. 400 pp.

> The condensed proceedings of the 1970 ACM conference at which no formal papers were given. This book is a highly edited account of seminar discussions focusing on the use of computers and their influence on society.

Gotlieb, C. C., and Borodin, A. *Social Issues in Computing*. New York: Academic Press, 1973. 284 pp.

> A comprehensive treatment of the social issues in computing.

Greenberger, M. *Computers, Communications, and the Public Interest.* Baltimore, Md.: Johns Hopkins University Press, 1971. 312 pp.

> An edited record of the lectures and discussions in a series of symposia held jointly by Johns Hopkins University and the Brookings Institute between September 1969 and May 1970. Emphasis is primarily on public policy matters.

Landon, K. C. *Computers and Bureaucratic Reform.* New York: Wiley, 1974. 325 pp.

> Explores the interaction between society and the emerging computer technology. By relegating the technical material to appendices, the book is made readable to the layperson but still remains interesting to the computer professional.

Martin, J., and A. R. D. Norman. *The Computerized Society.* Englewood Cliffs, N.J.: Prentice-Hall, 1970. 560 pp.

> The authors see a sudden and massive spread of computer usage in the years ahead and attempt to explain to the "man in the street" what the real impact will be on society by examining a number of application areas.

Negroponte, N. *The Architecture Machine: Toward a More Human Environment.* Cambridge, Mass.: M.I.T. Press, 1970. 153 pp.

> Describes how computers do and will eventually aid in making our living environments more functional and comfortable.

Pylyshyn, Z. W. *Perspectives on the Computer Revolution.* Englewood Cliffs, N.J.: Prentice-Hall, 1970. 540 pp.

> An overview of how computerization has affected present culture and technology, with a discussion of where present trends will bring us in the future.

Ritterbush, P. C. (ed.). *Technology as Institutionally Related to Human Values.* Washington, D.C.: Acropolis Books, 1974. 198 pp.

> Addresses man's tendency to use knowledge to do evil. Presents some solutions to the problems that follow in the wake of technology. An interesting collection of papers.

Rothman, S., and C. Mossman. *Computers and Society.* Second Edition Chicago: Science Research Associates, 1976. 423 pp.

> General introduction to computers, with no programming. Several chapters are related to social implications, and the future of computing is discussed.

Sackman, H., and N. Nie (eds.). *The Information Utility and Social Choice.* Montvale, N.J.: AFIPS, 1970. 299 pp.

> Selected papers from a conference cosponsored by the University of Chicago, Encyclopedia Britannica, and AFIPS cover such topics as what direction an information utility should take, how it will be regulated in the public interest, and the impact of evolving information utilities on politics.

Taviss, I. (ed.). *The Computer Impact.* Englewood Cliffs, N.J.: Prentice-Hall, 1970. 297 pp.

> Examines how computers have changed or helped to change business, technological and cultural environments, how changes will continue, and in what possible directions.

Teague, R., and C. Erickson. *Computers and Society.* St. Paul: West Publishing Co., 1974. 374 pp.

> An interesting collection of readings on the role of computers in society.

Toffler, A. *Future Shock.* New York: Random House, 1970. 561 pp.

> Contains an extensive discussion of the effects of technological change on almost every aspect of our lives; stimulating and thought provoking.

Tomeski, E., and H. Lazarus. *People-Oriented Computer Systems—The Computer in Crisis.* Van Nostrand Reinhold, 1975. 300 pp.

> Emphasizes the human use of computers and a more humanistic approach to solving computer problems. The impact of technology on organizations, key facets of the systems approach, and the relation between computer and human systems.

Turn, R. *Computers in the 1980s.* New York: Columbia University Press, 1974. 257 pp.

> A very readable (though slightly technical) forecast of computer development in the next decade. Computer characteristics such as speed of the main computer, size of memory, and physical characteristics are forecast. Turn is a senior systems analyst for The Rand Corporation.

Computers have figured in many works of fiction. Listed below are some that explore, in one way or another, some of the implications of computers or of men and machines.

> Computers
>> *The Forbin Project* D. F. Jones (Berkley)
>> *When Harlie Was One* David Gerrold *(Ballantine)*
>> *2001: A Space Odessey* A. C. Clarke (Signet)
>> *The Moon is a Harsh Mistress* Robert Heinlein (Berkley)
>> *Humanity Prime* Bruce McAllister (Ace)
>> *The Computer Connection* Alfred Bester (Berkley-Putnam)
>> *Cybernia* Lou Cameron (Fawcett)
>> *Player Piano* Kurt Vonnegut (Avon)
> Robots
>> *Caves of Steel* Isaac Asimov (various) mystery
>> *Naked Sun* Isaac Asimov (various) mystery
>> *I, Robot* Isaac Asimov (various) short stories
>> *Rest of the Robots* Isaac Asimov (various) short stories
>> *Adam Link, Robot* Eondo Binder (Paperback Library)
>> *RUR* Karel Capek (various) orioin of term "robot"; play
>> *City* Clifford Simak (Ace) series of related short stories
>> *The Werewolf Among Us* Dean Koontz (Ballantine)
>> *Space Skimmer* David Gerrold (Ballantine)
>> *Warlock in Spite of Himself* C. Stasheff (Ace)
>> *The Humanoids* Jack Williamson (Lancer)
>> *The Coming of the Robots* S. Moskowitz (ed.) (Collier)
>> *The Pseudo-People* W. Nolan (ed.) (Berkley)
>> *The Robot and the Man* Martin Greenberg (ed.) anthology
>> *Science Fiction Thinking Machines* G. Conklin (ed.) (Vanguard)
>> *Invasion of the Robots* Roger Elwood (ed.) anthology
>> *Cyborg* Martin Caidin (Paperback Library)
>> *Candy Man* Vincent King (Ballantine)

Man /Machine Interface
  Nova Samuel Delaney (Bantam)
  Metropolis Thea Van Harbon (various)
  The Ship Who Sang Anne McCaffery (Ballantine)
  Man and Machines Robert Silverberg (ed.) (Hawthorne)
Man-Made Men
  Frankenstein Mary Shelley (various)
  The Sword of the Golem Abraham Rothberg (Bantam)

From idol to computer

WILLIAM H. DESMONDE*

It is amusing to note that computers are being used extensively today both for landing men on the moon and for the casting of horoscopes. A psychologist might adduce from this curious combination that, even in a highly rational society, part of the human psyche tends to cling to archaic, magical ideas.

Perhaps further light can be shed on this atavism by glancing back into the the origins of man's ideas about automata. Historians of science trace the beginnings of machines to the worship of idols. It will be recalled that the Ten Commandments forbids idolatry. This prohibition is related to the thought that, if man can fashion a god, then in some sense man can control God, or even be God. A human (who is finite, as opposed to God who is assumed to be infinite) caught up in the worship of idols may hence become swollen with self-delusion and accept no boundaries on his wishes. This is one way of defining a psychotic. And a psychotic society tends ultimately to stunt its own growth or to destroy itself. The moral of this sermon, applied to modern technology, is that a computer is basically merely a very useful tool, not a way of attaining megalomaniacal control over the universe.

The fact is that science is rooted in primitive magical and mystical conceptions of man and his environment. Newton, for example, conducted experiments in alchemy, Kepler cast horoscopes, and Copernicus cited the legendary Egyptian priest Hermes Trismegistus to support his heliocentric hypothesis.

The computer, too, has a long and bizarre history. The origins of the automatic data processing machine appear

*William H. Desmonde, "From Idol to Computer", *Datamation*, January 1970. Reprinted with permission of *Datamation*® copyright© 1970 by Technical Publishing company, Greenwich, Conn. 06830.

to be related to early man's desire to imitate the creatory by simulating the universe around him, an urge first appearing in primitive art and persisting into the Turing machine which inspired John von Neumann to develop the stored program calculator. From the earliest times, man has sculptured, carved, or painted images on stone, wood, bone, or on the walls of caves. Primitives are believed to have used many representations of animals for magical purposes; these images were thought to facilitate hunting or to insure the growth of herds. The talisman, fetish, and idol found throughout primitive cultures, were symbols of the gods. Many of the earliest of these images were simply stones or natural objects which were believed to possess marvelous properties because of their shape. Later, with the development of magic, men thought that gods or supernatural beings could be drawn into things by means of appropriate charms and rituals. The fashioning of natural objects into images very likely was a consequence of this belief.

The first objects of worship seem to have been representations of mother goddesses. This form of veneration of creativity stretches far back into the prehistory of our species. Statuettes of nude women with huge breasts and bulging abdomens have been found in Aurignacian deposits dating thirty to forty thousand years ago. These figurines, which represent females in an advanced stage of pregnancy, are generally termed Paleolithic Venuses. Later finds in Mesopotamia and Syria go back to the fifth millenium BC. It is believed that these statuettes magically insured fertility and the safe delivery of children. The goddess was originally a mother image who cast her mysterious and magical qualities upon her devotees. Many of man's oldest conceptions of the nature of the universe start with a primal goddess. Sometimes it was believed that the world was generated from an egg emerging from a great mother goddess. In other primitive cosmologies the universe was born, or was constructed from the body of a primal maternal divinity. These ideas persist in the everyday expression, "Mother Nature."

A variant of the idol is the mask, an artifact found throughout the world by ethnologists. Simulated heads and animal costumes were employed extensively in primitive dramatic presentations, which were in the nature of religious rituals. Masks were also frequently used in dances, puberty ceremonials, and in fertility and funeral rites. In donning a mask, primitive man believed himself magically to be transformed into another being, often of a supernatural nature.

According to authorities, automata originated in the articulated idol or mask. Masks were sometimes constructed so that facial gestures would increase their expressiveness. Moving jaws or ears also enhanced their effectiveness. Figurines with articulated heads, arms, legs, or hands, dating back to early periods of man's history, have been discovered in many corners of the world. In Mexico, for instance, where archeologists have uncovered numerous remains of pre-Columbian cultures, large numbers of such idols have been found. The doll, which today is simply a child's toy, can be traced back to statuettes constructed by primitive man. Similarly the marionette or puppet, found in numerous early societies, was first used in ritual practices. Articulated statuettes have been found in Greece, around the Bosphoros, in Asia Minor, in Cyrenaica, in Italy, and in Gaul. These figurines usually had joints at the shoulders and haunches.

SPEAKING, MOVING STATUES

The ancient Egyptians believed that statues could be brought to life by inducing the spirits of the gods to enter these images through magical ceremonies. These idols possessed powers to do good and evil, and to affect the lives of men. In ancient Thebes statues spoke and made gestures with their heads and arms. Oracles in Rome were delivered by mechanically operated figures called *neuropastes*. On exhibit at the Louvre is a terra cotta Greek idol with articulated legs, as well as a talking statue of the Egyptian god Re-Harmakis. The latter was operated by a speaking tube leading behind the statue to a hidden priest who identified himself with the god and who uttered words in moments of divine inspiration.

The age-old desire to create life probably is related to man's yearning to imitate God or to be godlike. The long history of robots begins with this urge. Numerous myths of animated statues have come down to us from the Graeco-Roman culture. The image of Hera at Sybaris streamed blood and turned on its pedestal in a flash of anger. Roman historians tell of statues which bled or collapsed at critical moments, or which moved when necessary. For example, at the time of the invasions of Rome it was often thought that certain statues came to life and fought the enemy. Homer's Iliad recounts moving statues built by Vulcan. It will be remembered that in Shakespeare's *Julius Caesar* Mark Anthony sought to inflame the mob by relating that Pompeii's statue ran blood when Caesar was assassinated.

It is difficult to say whether many of the early automata were toys or were magical devices used in religious rituals. According to legend, the ancient Greek Daedalus devised flying birds and walking statues. Archytas of Tarentum in the fourth century BC was reputed to have made a mechanical wooden flying dove operated by counterweights and air pressure. But it is from the city of Alexandria, in its time the culture center of the world, that we have the first exact details of how to construct a mechanical automaton. The ancient technician Ctesibus made a moving statue. He also described the workings of a mechanical theater and a water powered pipe organ. Archimedes is well known as the inventor of numerous mechanical devices. Philo the Byzantian constructed numerous gadgets in which water, acting on floats, furnished the motive power for mechanical movement. Heron of Alexandria, who lived about the second century BC, is famous for his numerous steam and water powered automata. He constructed an automatic theater with dancing bacchantes revolving and pivoting on a turntable serving as a stage. Another of his gadgets was what we would now call a coin-operated slot machine. This was designed for use in temples: the coin caused holy water to flow, thereby enabling the worshipper to wash his hands before sacrificing to the god. Heron also constructed a working steam boiler, but this was never put to practical use.

A turning point in the development of the technological skills required for the construction of automata occurred when man began to construct models of the heavens. Ancient man was dominated by astrological ideas. God had created the heavens and set the stars and planets in motion as part of a divine plan. Hence these early celestial models were built for meditational purposes or for controlling earthly events in accordance with God's will. Among the first types of astronomical simulacra were maps of stars on the ceilings of Egyptian tombs. The Babylonians also made simple visual models of the cosmos, and achieved outstanding success in the prediction of heavenly events through arithmetic techniques. The principles of the rationality of astronomical motions and the orderlinesss of number greatly influenced the Greeks. Pythagorean mystical notions that the universe could be explained by number, plus Babylonian theory translated into geometric representation, led to the development of Greek astronomy and mathematics. There are indications that by the time of Plato simple animated cosmological simulacra had been developed. Indeed, this philosopher may have based much of his imagery upon these devices. It is known that by 370 BC there existed a geometric model of planetary motion.

Instruments for telling time were intimately connected with the invention of astronomical simulacra. What is remarkable about the early water clocks, as well as the sundials with which they were associated, is that their prime function was religious, not keeping track of the time. The basic mechanisms of water clocks appear to extend back to the period 300–270 BC. Excavations reveal that as far back as the third century BC there was a water clock edifice in the public square in Athens. These devices were constructed to simulate the glory and magnificence of the gods. Early water clocks developed in Chinese culture appear to have been imbedded in a similar metaphysical conception. Throughout ancient cultures the fundamental purpose of the calendar was to ascertain when holy days were to be celebrated.

AUTOMATIC WATER CLOCKS

A close relationship existed between the clepsydra (water-flowing) principles used in celestial clock-simulators and the numerous automata associated with Heron of Alexandria. Evidence indicates that the technology employed in these devices was at a much higher level than is indicated by literary sources. A recently discovered complex astronomical calculator, built about 65 AD, possessed gear trains which turned indicators at speeds comparable to the motions of the planets.

It would appear that the ancient mechanical craft tradition was preserved in Islamic automatic water clocks. These devices were celestial simulators with associated manikins such as singing birds. (These were the ancestors of the modern cuckoo clock.) Gadgets, operated through the motive power of a clock (such as moving or articulated figurines) are referred to as "jackwork." In the Islamic clocks, dripping water supplied the basic motion. The energy was transmitted either through a block pulled by string or chain, through string wound around a pulley, or by gearing device. This motion was used to trip levers consecutively, thus opening doors, activating statuettes, causing balls to fall on gongs, moving eyes, heads, or bodies of figurines, or turning globes or models of the heavens. Water was also used to force air in such a way as to blow whistles and to sound pipes.

This body of knowledge concerning clockwork and jackwork arrived in Europe in the thirteenth century associated with ideas about perpetual motion machines. By 1320 the water clock was adapted to the working of complex automata simulating the Ptolemaic universe. The famous de Dondi astrarium or planetarium, completed in Padua in 1364, had the primary purpose of depicting the motions of the sun, moon, and the five planets according to the geocentric theory. A series of edifice clocks were constructed at Strasbourg and throughout Europe during the sixteenth to eighteenth centuries. These large showpieces were often a major feature of the great cathedrals. London's Big Ben belongs to this tradition. The association of jackwork with clock continued with mechanical clocks, carillons, and innumerable other figurines serving as part of these monumental automata.

CLOCKS TO COMPUTERS

The clock is the technological ancestor of the modern computer, and is the prototype of the complex scientific instrument. Probably the development of the clock was vital to the rise of experimental physics. But the mechanical clock, like its ancient predecessors, seems not originally to have had the primary purpose of telling time. The early monumental clocks in Europe were showpieces depicting eclipses and the motions of the heavenly bodies, and computing the church calendar. The keeping of time and the ringing of bells at intervals was a byproduct of their main function of enhancing an awareness of the greatness of God in his orderly creation.

Myths and legends of fantastic automata were rampant during the Middle ages. The philosopher Albertus Magnus (1204–1282) was reputed to have constructed a mobile robot. Oracular heads were common: Pope Sylvester II devised a speaking head which made prophesies, and Roger Bacon (1214–1292), who had a reputation as a magician, constructed a similar device. Stories of man-made creatures of flesh and blood made by alchemists and occultists go back at least to the beginnings of the Christian Era. Hebrew mysticism contained formulas for making an artificial man. These cabbalistic procedures had to be carried out during an ecstatic state by combining sacred letters representing the basic attributes of the deity. The famous robot called the *golem* was reputed to have been constructed in 1580 by Rabbi Loew of Prague. Tales of these types survived into modern times in such works of fiction as Goethe's *Faust* and the horror story *Frankenstein*. The latter book, by Mary Shelley, was influenced not only by the golem legend, but also by discussions between the poets Byron and Shelley on the implications of the work of Erasmus, Darwin and Galvani on the chemical and electrical characteristics of protoplasm.

Descartes (1596–1650), the philosopher who invented analytical geometry, extended the idea of the machine to the bodies of living beings. It seems likely that he was influenced by jackwork or other automata which he had seen in Europe. There is a story that Descartes himself long considered the construction of a human automaton. According to one tale, he actually built a gorgeous blond robot named Francine. However, during a sea voyage her packing case was accidentally opened, and the captain of the ship, thinking she was the work of a sorcerer, threw her overboard.

During the Renaissance another line of technological development took the form of devices in grottoes in the fancy gardens of the aristocracy. Elaborate fountains and waterfalls were built, following ancient Greek hydraulic principles, with complex automata which moved and sang. In the royal chateau of Henry IV of France (1698) a number of connected grottoes and fountains depicted famous mythological characters in action. In the largest of these chambers the legendary hero Perseus, fully armed, descended from the ceiling with a sword and killed a dragon rising from the water.

Still another branch in the evolution of machines was the production of musical automata. These gadgets, which survive in our little modern music boxes, were very popular for centuries. Numerous automata called androids were constructed, perhaps as early as the fifteenth century, in which human figures played the piano and other instruments. In 1599 Queen Elizabeth of England made a gift of an organ clock to the Sultan of Turkey. The mechanical organ was first described in the seventeenth century. During the eighteenth century a large variety of androids and other automata, such as singing birds enclosed in snuff boxes, were manufactured and sold all over the world.

The skill of the clockmaker gradually combined with the craft of the jeweler, resulting in the production of numerous fine works of mechanical art. As has been stated, the art of making complex and delicate instruments, a development indispensable to the rise of science, is traceable to the clockmaker. The Pascaline, the digital computer built by Pascal in 1645, made use of the same type of technology as the elaborate musical automata which were built during this period.

EARLY LOGIC

The idea of a calculus to explain all natural phenomena stemmed from the "Art" of Ramon Lull (about 1272). Lull conceived of a device, which can be thought of as an early type of logic machine, embodying a universal algorithm. This Art became one of the major intellectual forces in the Renaissance, and is known to have had an important influence upon both Descartes and Leibnitz.

Lull developed his Art as the result of an ecstatic vision (just as Descartes conceived of analytical geometry in a dream). The conception behind his idea was that the entire universe stemmed from basic archetypes or principles pre-existing in the mind of God. These were the fundamental exemplars of all created material things, and consisted of such divine attributes as Goodness, Greatness, Eternity, Power, Wisdom, Will, Virtue, Truth, and Glory. These principles expanded into all of the levels of the natural world. Thus, Goodness initially emanated into the goodness of angels, next into the goodness of heavenly bodies, then into the goodness of man, etc.

In its simplest form the Art of Ramon Lull consisted of a set of concentric revolving wheels, on each of which was inscribed the names of the archetypes. By turning the wheels, it would be possible to form every possible combination of the basic factors. In this way, the characteristics of any created thing could be calculated. Since Lull thought within a Ptolemaic world view, his technique could be applied to astrology to predict all earthly events.

In a certain sense, it might be stated that Ramon Lull sought to create an idol. For if his Art had really worked, it would have been possible to simulate completely the workings of God in his creation. But Gödel and Turing have proved that Lull's dream cannot be attained, for no axiom system or Turing machine can comprehend all of reality. It could be said that, although Turing helped provide the idea for the modern computer, he also showed that it is idolatry to overestimate its capabilities.

(For further information on Lull the reader is referred to the work of Frances A. Yates. Some of the leading historians of automata are Derek J. de Solla Price, Alfred Chapuis, Silvio Bedini, and Robert Brumbaugh.)

Computing machinery and intelligence

A. M. TURING*

1. THE IMITATION GAME

I propose to consider the question "Can machines think?" This should begin with definitions of the meaning of the terms *machine* and *think*. The definitions might be framed so as to reflect so far as possible the normal use of the words, but this attitude is dangerous. If the meaning of the words *machine* and *think* are to be found by examining how they are commonly used, it is difficult to escape the conclusion that the meaning and the answer to the question "Can machines think?" is to be sought in a statistical survey such as a Gallup poll. But this is absurd. Instead of attempting such a definition I shall replace the question by another, which is closely related to it and is expressed in relatively unambiguous words.

The new form of the problem can be described in terms of a game which we call the "imitation game." It is played with three people, a man (A), a woman (B), and an interrogator (C) who may be of either sex. The interrogator stays in a room apart from the other two. The object of the game for the interrogator is to determine which of the other two is the man and which is the woman. He knows them by labels X and Y, and at the end of the game he says either "X is A and Y is B" or "X is B and Y is A." The interrogator is allowed to put questions to A and B thus:

C: Will X please tell me the length of his or her hair?

Now suppose X is actually A, then A must answer. It is A's object in the game to try and cause C to make the wrong identification. His answer might there-

* A. M. Turing, "Computing Machinery and Intelligence", *Mind*. 59:236, 1950. Reprinted from *Mind: A Quarterly Review of Psychology and Philosophy*, 1950, by permission of *Mind*.

fore be "My hair is shingled, and the longest strands are about nine inches long."

In order that tones of voice may not help the interrogator, the answers should be written or better still, typewritten. The ideal arrangement is to have a teleprinter communicating between the two rooms. Alternatively the question and answers can be repeated by an intermediary. The object of the game for the third player (B) is to help the interrogator. The best strategy for her is probably to give truthful answers. She can add such things as "I am the woman, don't listen to him!" to her answers, but it will avail nothing as the man can make similar remarks.

We now ask the question, "What will happen when a machine takes the part of A in this game?" Will the interrogator decide wrongly as often when the game is played like this as he does when the game is played between a man and a woman? These questions replace our original "Can machines think?"

2. CRITIQUE OF THE NEW PROBLEM

As well as asking "What is the answer to this new form of the question," one may ask "Is this new question a worthy one to investigate?" This latter question we investigate without further ado, there by cutting short an infinite regress.

The new problem has the advantage of drawing a fairly sharp line between the physical and the intellectual capacities of a man. No engineer or chemist claims to be able to produce a material which is indistinguishable from the human skin. It is possible that at some time this might be done, but even supposing this invention available we should feel there was little point in trying to make a "thinking machine" more human by dressing it up in such artificial flesh. The form in which we have set the problem reflects this fact in the condition which prevents the interrogator from seeing or touching the other competitors or hearing their voices. Some other advantages of the proposed criterion may be shown up by specimen questions and answers. Thus:

Q: Please write me a sonnet on the subject of the Fourth Bridge.
A: Count me out on this one. I never could write poetry.
Q: Add 34957 to 70764
A: (pause about 30 seconds and then give as answer): 105621.
Q: Do you play chess?
A: Yes.
Q: I have K at my K1 and no other pieces. You have only K at K6 and R at R1. It is your move. What do you play?
A: (after a pause of 15 seconds): R-R8 mate.

The question and answer method seems to be suitable for introducing almost any one of the fields of human endeavor that we wish to include. We do not wish to penalize the machine for its inability to shine in beauty competitions nor to penalize a man for losing in a race against an airplane. The conditions of our game make these disabilities irrelevant. The "witnesses" can brag, if they consider it advisable, as much as they please about their charms, strength, or heroism, but the interrogator cannot demand practical demonstrations.

The game may perhaps be criticized on the ground that the odds are weighted too heavily against the machine. If the man were to try and pretend to be the machine he would clearly make a very poor showing. He would be given away at once by slowness and inaccuracy in arithmetic. May not machines carry out something which ought to be described as thinking but which is very different from what a man does? This objection is a very strong one, but at least we can say that if, nevertheless, a machine can be constructed to play the imitation game satisfactorily, we need not be troubled by this objection.

It might be urged that when playing the "imitation game" the best strategy for the machine may possibly be something other than imitation of the behavior of a man. This may be, but I think it is unlikely that there is any great effect of this kind. In any case there is no intention to investigate here the theory of the game, and it will be assumed that the best strategy is to try to provide answers that would naturally be given by a man.

3. THE MACHINES CONCERNED IN THE GAME

The question which we put in Sec. 1 will not be quite definite until we have specified what we mean by the word machine. It is natural that we should wish to permit every kind of engineering technique to be used in our machines. We also wish to allow the possibility that an engineer or team of engineers may construct a machine which works but whose manner of operation cannot be satisfactorily described by its constructors because they have applied a method which is largely experimental. Finally, we wish to exclude from the machines men born in the usual manner. It is difficult to frame the definitions so as to satisfy these three conditions. One might for instance insist that the team of engineers should be all of one sex, but this would not really be satisfactory, for it is probably possible to rear a complete individual from a single cell of the skin (say) of a man. To do so would be a feat of biological technique deserving of the very highest praise, but we would not be inclined to regard it as a case of "constructing a thinking machine." This prompts us to abandon the requirement that every kind of technique should be permitted. We are the more ready to do so in view of the fact that the present interest in "thinking machines" has been aroused by a particular kind of machine, usually called an "electronic computer" or "digital computer." Following this suggestion we only permit digital computers to take part in our game.

This restriction appears at first sight to be a very drastic one. I shall attempt to show that it is not so in reality. To do this necessitates a short account of the nature and properties of these computers.

It may also be said that this identification of machines with digital computers, like our criterion for "thinking," will only be unsatisfactory if (contrary to my belief) it turns out that digital computers are unable to give a good showing in the game.

There are already a number of digital computers in working order, and it may be asked, "Why not try the experiment straight away? It would be easy to satisfy the conditions of the game. A number of interrogators could be used and statistics compiled to show how often the right identification was given." The short answer is that we are not asking whether all digital computers would do well in the game nor whether the computers at present available would do well, but whether there are imaginable computers which would do well. But this is only the short answer. We shall see this question in a different light later.

4. DIGITAL COMPUTERS

The idea behind digital computers may be explained by saying that these machines are intended to carry out any operations which could be done by a human computer. The human computer is supposed to be following fixed rules; he has no authority to deviate from them in any detail. We may suppose that these rules are supplied in a book, which is altered whenever he is put on to a new job. He has also an unlimited supply of paper on which he does his calculations. He may also do his multiplications and additions on a "desk machine," but this is not important.

If we use the above explanation as a definition we shall be in danger of circularity of argument. We avoid this by giving an outline of the means by which the desired effect is achieved. A digital com-

puter can usually be regarded as consisting of three parts:

i. Store
ii. Executive unit
iii. Control

The store is a store of information and corresponds to the human computer's paper, whether this is the paper on which he does his calculations or that on which his book of rules is printed. Insofar as the human computer does calculations in his head, a part of the store will correspond to his memory.

The executive unit is the part which carries out the various individual operations involved in a calculation. What these individual operations are will vary from machine to machine. Usually fairly lengthy operations can be done, such as "multiply 3,540,675,445 by 7,076,345,687," but in some machines only very simple ones, such as "write down 0," are possible.

We have mentioned that the "book of rules" supplied to the computer is replaced in the machine by a part of the store. It is then called the "table of instructions." It is the duty of the control to see that these instructions are obeyed correctly and in the right order. The control is so constructed that this necessarily happens.

The information in the store is usually broken up into packets of moderately small size. In one machine, for instance, a packet might consist of ten decimal digits. Numbers are assigned to the parts of the store in which the various packets of information are stored in some systematic manner. A typical instruction might say—"Add the number stored in position 6,809 to that in 4,302 and put the result back into the latter storage position."

Needless to say, it would not occur in the machine expressed in English. It would more likely be coded in a form such as 6809430217. Here 17 says which of various possible operations is to be performed on the two numbers. In this case the operation is that described above, viz., "Add the number. . . . " It will be noticed that the instruction takes up ten digits and so forms one packet of information, very conveniently. The control will normally take the instructions to be obeyed in the order of the positions in which they are stored, but occasionally an instruction such as "Now obey the instruction stored in position 5606, and continue from there" may be encountered, or again "If position 4505 contains 0 obey next the instruction stored in 6707, otherwise continue straight on." Instructions of these latter types are very important because they make it possible for a sequence of operations to be repeated over and over again until some condition is fulfilled but in doing so to obey, not fresh instructions on each repetition, but the same ones over and over again. To take a domestic analogy: Suppose Mother wants Tommy to call at the cobbler's every morning on his way to school to see if her shoes are done. She can ask him afresh every morning. Alternatively she can stick up a notice once and for all in the hall which he will see when he leaves for school and which tells him to call for the shoes and also to destroy the notice when he comes back if he has the shoes with him.

The reader must accept it as a fact that digital computers can be constructed, and indeed have been constructed, according to the principles we have described, and that they can in fact mimic the actions of a human computer very closely.

The book of rules which we have described our human computer as using is of course a convenient fiction. Actual human computers really remember what they have got to do. If one wants to make a machine mimic the behavior of the human computer in some complex operation, one has to ask him how it is done and then translate the answer into the form of an instruction table. Constructing instruction tables is usually described as "programming." To "program a machine to carry out the operation A" means to put the appropriate instruction table into the machine so that it will do A.

An interesting variant on the idea of a digital computer is a "digital computer with a random element." These have instructions involving the throwing of a die or some equivalent electronic process; one such instruction might for instance be "Throw the die and put the resulting number into store 1000." Sometimes such a machine is described as having free will (though I would not use this phrase myself). It is not normally possible to determine from observing a machine whether it has a random element, for a similar effect can be produced by such devices as making the choices depend on the digits of the decimal for π.

Most actual digital computers have only a finite store. There is no theoretical difficulty in the idea of a computer with an unlimited store. Of course only a finite part can have been used at any one time. Likewise only a finite amount can have been constructed, but we can imagine more and more being added as required. Such computers have special theoretical interest and will be called infinitive capacity computers.

The idea of a digital computer is an old one. Charles Babbage, Lucasian Professor of Mathematics at Cambridge from 1828 to 1839, planned such a machine, called the Analytical Engine, but it was never completed. Although Babbage had all the essential ideas, his machine was not at that time such a very attractive prospect. The speed which would have been available would be definitely faster than a human computer but something like one hundred times slower than the Manchester machine, itself one of the slower of the modern machines. The storage was to be purely mechanical, using wheels and cards.

The fact that Babbage's Analytical Engine was to be entirely mechanical will help us to rid outselves of a superstition. Importance is often attached to the fact that modern digital computers are electrical and that the nervous system also is electrical. Since Babbage's machine was not electrical and since all digital computers are in a sense equivalent, we see that this use of electricity cannot be of theoretical importance. Of course, electricity usually comes in where fast signaling is concerned, so that it is not surprising that we find it in both these connections. In the nervous system chemical phenomena are at least as important as electrical. In certain computers the storage system is mainly acoustic. The feature of using electricity is thus seen to be only a very superficial similarity. If we wish to find such similarities we should look rather for mathematical analogies of function.

5. Universality of Digital Computers

The digital computers considered in the last section may be classified amongst the "discrete-state machines." These are the machines which move by sudden jumps or clicks from the one quite definite state to another. These states are sufficiently different for the possibility of confusion between them to be ignored. Strictly speaking there are no such machines. Everything really moves continuously. But there are many kinds of machine which can profitably be *thought of* as being discrete-state machines. For instance, in considering the switches for a lighting system it is a convenient fiction that each switch must be definitely on or definitely off. There must be intermediate positions, but for most purposes we can forget about them. As an example of a discrete-state machine we might consider a wheel which clicks round through 120 degrees once a second but may be stopped by a lever which can be operated from outside; in addition a lamp is to light in one of the positions of the wheel. This machine could be described abstractly as follows. The internal state of the machine (which is described by the position of the wheel) may be q_1, q_2, or q_3. There is an input signal i_0 or i_1 (position of lever). The internal state at any moment is de-

termined by the last state and input signal according to the table

Last State

q_1 q_2 q_3

Input		
i_4	q_2 q_3 q_1	
i_1	q_1 q_2 q_3	

The output signals, the only externally visible indication of the internal state (the light), are described by the table

State	q_1 q_2 q_3
Output	o_0 o_0 o_1

This example is typical of discrete-state machines. They can be described by such tables provided they have only a finite number of possible states.

It will seem that given the initial state of the machine and the input signals it is always possible to predict all future states. This is reminiscent of Laplace's view that from the complete state of the universe at one moment of time, as described by the positions and velocities of all particles, it should be possible to predict all future states. The prediction which we are considering is, however, rather nearer to practicability than that considered by Laplace. The system of the "universe as a whole" is such that quite small errors in the initial conditions can have an overwhelming effect at a later time. The displacement of a single electron by a billionth of a centimeter at one moment might make the difference between a man being killed by an avalanche a year later or escaping. It is an essential property of the mechanical systems which we have called "discrete-state machines" that this phenomenon does not occur. Even when we consider the actual physical machines instead of the idealized machines, reasonably accurate knowledge of the state at one moment yields reasonably accurate knowledge any number of steps later.

As we have mentioned, digital computers fall wtthin the class of discrete-state machines. But the number of states of which such a machine is capable is usually enormously large. For instance, the number for the machine now working at Manchester is about 2^{165000} i.e., about 10^{50000}. Compare this with our example of the clicking wheel described above, which had three states. It is not difficult to see why the number of states should be so immense. The computer includes a store corresponding to the paper used by a human computer. It must be possible to write into the store any one of the combinations of symbols which might have been written on the paper. For simplicity suppose that only digits from 0 to 9 are used as symbols. Variations in handwriting are ignored. Suppose the computer is allowed one hundred sheets of paper each containing fifty lines each with room for thirty digits. Then the number of states is $10^{100\times50\times30}$, i.e., 10^{150000}. This is about the number of states of three Manchester machines put together. The logarithm to the base 2 of the number of states is usually called the "storage capacity" of the machine. Thus the Manchester machine has a storage capacity of about 165,000 and the wheel machine of our example about 1.6. If two machines are put together their capacities must be added to obtain the capacity of the resultant machine. This leads to the possibility of statements such as "The Manchester machine contains sixty-four magnetic tracks each with a capacity of 2,560, eight electronic tubes with a capacity of 1,280. Miscellaneous storage amounts to about 300, making a total of 174,380."

Given the table corresponding to a discrete-state machine, it is possible to predict what it will do. There is no reason why this calculation should not be carried out by means of a digital computer. Provided it could be carried out by means of a digital computer. Provided it could be carried out sufficiently quickly, the digital computer could mimic the behavior of any discrete-state machine. The

imitation game could then be played with the machine in question (as B) and the mimicking digital computer (as A), and the interrogator would be unable to distinguish them. Of course, the digital computer must have an adequate storage capacity as well as working sufficiently fast. Moreover, it must be programmed afresh for each new machine which it is desired to mimic.

This special property of digital computers, that they can mimic any discrete-state machine, is described by saying that they are *universal* machines. The existence of machines with this property has the important consequence that, considerations of speed apart, it is unnecessary to design various new machines to do various computing processes. They can all be done with one digital computer, suitably programmed for each case. It will be seen that as a consequence of this all digital computers are in a sense equivalent.

We may now consider again the point raised at the end of Sec. 3. It was suggested tentatively that the question "Can machines think?" should be replaced by "Are there imaginable digital computers which would do well in the imitation game?" If we wish we can make this superficially more general and ask, "Are there discrete-state machines which would do well?" But in view of the universality property we see that either of these questions is equivalent to this: "Let us fix our attention on one particular digital computer C. Is it true that by modifying this computer to have an adequate storage, suitably increasing its speed of action, and providing it with an appropriate program, C can be made to play satisfactorily the part of A in the imitation game, the part of B being taken by a man?"

6. CONTRARY VIEWS ON THE MAIN QUESTION

We may now consider the ground to have been cleared and we are ready to proceed to the debate on our question "Can machines think?" and the variant of it quoted at the end of the last section. We cannot altogether abandon the original form of the problem, for opinions will differ as to the appropriateness of the substitution, and we must at least listen to what has to be said in this connection.

It will simplify matters for the reader if I explain first my own beliefs in the matter. Consider first the more accurate form of the question. I believe that in about fifty years' time it will be possible to program computers, with a storage capacity of about 10^9, to make them play the imitation game so well that an average interrogator will not have more than 70 per cent chance of making the right identification after 5 minutes of questioning. The original question. "Can machines think?" I believe to be too meaningless to deserve discussion. Nevertheless I believe that at the end of the century the use of words and general educated opinion will have altered so much that one will be able to speak of machines thinking without expecting to be contradicted. I believe further that no useful purpose is served by concealing these beliefs. The popular view that scientists proceed inexorably from well-established fact to well-established fact, never being influenced by any unproved conjecture, is quite mistaken. Provided it is made clear which are proved facts and which are conjectures, no harm can result. Conjectures are of great importance since they suggest useful lines of research.

I now proceed to consider opinions opposed to my own.

1. *The theological objection.* Thinking is a function of man's immortal soul.[1] God has given an immortal soul to every

[1] Possibly this view is heretical. St. Thomas Aquinas (*Summa Theologica.* quoted by Bertrand Russell, p. 480) states that God cannot make a man to have no soul. But this may not be a real restriction on His powers, but only a result of the fact that men's souls are immortal and therefore indestructible.

man and woman, but not to any other animal or to machines. Hence no animal or machine can think.

I am unable to accept any part of this, but will attempt to reply in theological terms. I should find the argument more convincing if animals were classed with men, for there is a greater difference, to my mind, between the typical animate and the inanimate than there is between man and the other animals. The arbitrary character of the orthodox view becomes clearer if we consider how it might appear to a member of some other religious community. How do Christians regard the Moslem view that women have no souls? But let us leave this point aside and return to the main argument. It appears to me that the argument quoted above implies a serious restriction of the omnipotence of the Almighty. It is admitted that there are certain things that He cannot do, such as making one equal to two, but should we not believe that He has freedom to confer a soul on an elephant if He sees fit? We might expect that He would only exercise this power in conjunction with a mutation which provided the elephant with an appropriately improved brain to minister to the needs of this soul. An argument of exactly similar form may be made for the case of machines. It may seem different because it is more difficult to "swallow." But this really only means that we think it would be less likely that He would consider the circumstances suitable for conferring a soul. The circumstances in question are discussed in the rest of this paper. In attempting to construct such machines we should not be irreverently usurping His power of creating souls, any more than we are in the procreation of children: Rather we are, in either case, instruments of His will providing mansions for the souls that He creates.

However, this is mere speculation. I am not very impressed with theological arguments whatever they may be used to support. Such arguments have often been found unsatisfactory in the past. In the time of Galileo it was argued that the texts "And the sun stood still . . . and hasted not to go down about a whole day" (Joshua x. 13) and "He laid the foundations of the earth, that it should not move at any time" (Psalm cv. 5) were an adequate refutation of the Copernican theory. With our present knowledge such an argument appears futile. When that knowledge was not available it made a quite different impression.

2. *The "heads in the sand" objection.* "The consequences of machines thinking would be too dreadful. Let us hope and believe that they cannot do so."

This argument is seldom expressed quite so openly as in the form above. But it affects most of us who think about it at all. We like to believe that man is in some subtle way superior to the rest of creation. It is best if he can be shown to be *necessarily* superior, for then there is no danger of him losing his commanding position. The popularity of the theological argument is clearly connected with this feeling. It is likely to be quite strong in intellectual people, since they value the power of thinking more highly than others, and are more inclined to base their belief in the superiority of man on this power.

I do not think that this argument is sufficiently substantial to require refutation. Consolation would be more appropriate: Perhaps this should be sought in the transmigration of souls.

3. *The mathematical objection.* There are a number of results of mathematical logic which can be used to show that there are limitations to the powers of discrete-state machines. The best known of these results is known as *Gödel's* theorem,[2] and shows that in any sufficiently powerful logical system statements can be formulated which can neither be proved nor disproved within the system, unless possibly the system itself is inconsistent. There are other, in

some respects similar, results due to *Church, Kleene,* . . . and *Turing.* The latter result is the most convenient to consider, since it refers directly to machines, whereas the others can only be used in a comparatively indirect argument: For instance, if Gödel's theorem is to be used we need in addition to have some means of describing logical systems in terms of machines, and machines in terms of logical systems. The result in question refers to a type of machine which is essentially a digital computer with an infinite capacity. It states that there are certain things that such a machine cannot do. If it is rigged up to give answers to questions as in the imitation game, there will be some questions to which it will either give a wrong answer or fail to give an answer at all, however much time is allowed for a reply. There may, of course, be many such questions, and questions which cannot be answered by one machine may be satisfactorily answered by another. We are of course supposing for the present that the questions are of the kind of which an answer "Yes" or "No" is appropriate, rather than questions such as "What do you think of Picasso?" The questions that we know the machines must fail on are of this type: "Consider the machine specified as follows. . . . Will this machine ever answer 'yes' to any question?" The dots are to be replaced by a description of some machine in a standard form, which could be something like that used in Sec. 5. When the machine described bears a certain comparatively simple relation to the machine which is under interrogation, it can be shown that the answer is either wrong or not forthcoming. This is the mathematical result: It is argued that it proves a disability of machines to which the human intellect is not subject.

The short answer to this argument is that, although it is established that there are limitations to the powers of any particular machine, it has only been stated, without any sort of proof, that no such limitations apply to the human intellect.

[2]Author's names in italics refer to the Bibliography.

But I do not think this view can be dismissed quite so lightly. Whenever one of these machines is asked the appropriate critical question, and gives a definite answer, we know that this answer must be wrong, and this gives us a certain feeling of superiority. Is this feeling illusory? It is no doubt quite genuine, but I do not think too much importance should be attached to it. We too often give wrong answers to questions ourselves to be justified in being very pleased at such evidence of fallibility on the part of the machines. Further, our superiority can only be felt on such an occasion in relation to the one machine over which we have scored our petty triumph. There would be no question of triumphing simultaneously over *all* machines. In short, then, there might be men cleverer than any given machine, but then again there might be other machines cleverer again, and so on.

Those who hold to the mathematical argument would, I think, mostly be willing to accept the imitation game as a basis for discussion. Those who believe in the two previous objections would probably not be interested in any criteria.

4. *The argument from consciousness.* This argument is very well expressed in *Professor Jefferson's* Lister Oration for 1949, from which I quote. "Not until a machine can write a sonnet or compose a concerto because of thoughts and emotions felt, and not by the chance fall of symbols, could we agree that machine equals brain—that is, not only write it but know that it had written it. No mechanism could feel (and not merely artificially signal, an easy contrivance) pleasure at its successes, grief when its valves fuse, be warmed by flattery, be made miserable by its mistakes, be charmed by sex, be angry or depressed when it cannot get what it wants."

This argument appears to be a denial of the validity of our test. According to the most extreme form of this view the only way by which one could be sure that a machine thinks is to be the machine and

to feel oneself thinking. One could then describe these feelings to the world, but of course no one would be justified in taking any notice. Likewise according to this view the only way to know that a *man* thinks is to be that particular man. It is in fact the solipsist point of view. It may be the most logical view to hold, but it makes communication of ideas difficult. A is liable to believe "A thinks but B does not," whilst B believes "B thinks but A does not." Instead of arguing continually over this point it is usual to have the polite convention that everyone thinks.

I am sure that Professor Jefferson does not wish to adopt the extreme and solipsist point of view. Probably he would be quite willing to accept the imitation game as a test. The game (with the player B omitted) is frequently used in practice under the name of viva voce to discover whether some one really understands something or has "learnt it parrot fashion." Let us listen in to a part of such a viva voce:

Interrogator: In the first line of your sonnet which reads "Shall I compare thee to a summer's day," would not "a spring day" do as well or better?
Witness: It wouldn't scan.
Interrogator: How about "a winter's day"? That would scan all right.
Witness: Yes, but nobody wants to be compared to a winter's day.
Interrogator: Would you say Mr. Pickwick reminded you of Christmas?
Witness: In a way.
Interrogator: Yet Christmas is a winter's day, and I do not think Mr. Pickwick would mind the comparison.
Witness: I don't think you're serious. By a winter's day one means a typical winter's day, rather than a special one like Christmas.

And so on. What would Professor Jefferson say if the sonnet-writing machine was able to answer like this in the viva voce? I do not know whether he would regard the machine as merely "artificially signaling" these answers, but if the answers were as satisfactory and sustained as in the above passage I do not think he would describe it as "an easy contrivance." This phrase is, I think, intended to cover such devices as the inclusion in the machine of a record of someone reading a sonnet with appropriate switching to turn it on from time to time.

In short then I think that most of those who support the argument from consciousness could be persuaded to abandon it rather than be forced into the solipsist position. They will then probably be willing to accept our test.

I do not wish to give the impression that I think there is no mystery about consciousness. There is, for instance, something of a paradox connected with any attempt to localize it. But I do not think these mysteries necessarily need to be solved before we can answer the question with which we are concerned in this paper.

5. *Arguments from various disabilities.* These arguments take the form "I grant you that you can make machines do all the things you have mentioned, but you will never be able to make one to do X." Numerous features X are suggested in this connection. I offer a selection:

Be kind, resourceful, beautiful, friendly . . . have initiative, have a sense of humor, tell right from wrong, make mistakes . . . fall in love, enjoy strawberries and cream . . . make someone fall in love with it, learn from experience . . . use words properly, be the subject of its own thought . . . have as much diversity of behavior as a man, do something really new. . . .

No support is usually offered for these statements. I believe they are mostly founded on the principle of scientific induction. A man has seen thousands of machines in his lifetime. From what he sees of them he draws a number of general conclusions. They are ugly, each is designed for a very limited purpose, when required for a minutely different purpose they are useless, the variety of behavior of any one of them is very small, etc., etc. Naturally he concludes that these are necessary properties of machines in general. Many of these limitations are associated with the very small storage capacity of most machines. (I am assuming that the idea of storage capacity is extended in some way to cover machines other than discrete-state machines. The exact definition does not matter as no mathematical accuracy is claimed in the present discussion.) A few years ago, when very little had been heard of digital computers, it was possible to elicit much incredulity concerning them if one mentioned their properties without describing their construction. That was presumably due to a similar application of the principle of scientific induction. These applications of the principle are of course largely unconscious. When a burned child fears the fire and shows that he fears it by avoiding it, I should say that he was applying scientific induction. (I could of course also describe his behavior in many other ways.) The works and customs of mankind do not seem to be very suitable material to which to apply scientific induction. A very large part of space time must be investigated if reliable results are to be obtained. Otherwise we may (as most English children do) decide that everybody speaks English, and that it is silly to learn French.

There are, however, special remarks to be made about many of the disabilities that have been mentioned. The inability to enjoy strawberries and cream may have struck the reader as frivolous. Possibly a machine might be made to enjoy this delicious dish, but any attempt to make one do so would be idiotic. What is important about this disability is that it contributes to some of the other disabilities e.g., to the difficulty of the same kind of friendliness occurring between man and machine as between white man and white man or between black man and black man.

The claim that "machines cannot make mistakes" seems a curious one. One is tempted to retort, "Are they any the worse for that?" But let us adopt a more sympathetic attitude and try to see what is really meant. I think this criticism can be explained in terms of the imitation game. It is claimed that the interrogator could distinguish the machine from the man simply by setting them a number of problems in arithmetic. The machine would be unmasked because of its deadly accuracy. The reply to this is simple. The machine (programmed for playing the game) would not attempt to give the *right* answers to the arithmetic problems. It would deliberately introduce mistakes in a manner calculated to confuse the interrogator. A mechanical fault would probably show itself through an unsuitable decision as to what sort of a mistake to make in the arithmetic. Even this interpretation of the criticism is not sufficiently sympathetic. But we cannot afford the space to go into it much further. It seems to me that this criticism depends on a confusion between two kinds of mistake. We may call them "errors of functioning" and "errors of conclusion." Errors of functioning are due to some mechanical or electrical fault which causes the machine to behave otherwise than it was designed to do. In philosophical discussions one likes to ignore the possibility of such errors; one is therefore discussing "abstract machines." These abstract machines are mathematical fictions rather than physical objects. By definition they are incapable of errors of functioning. In this sense we can truly say that "machines can never make mistakes." Errors of conclusion can only arise when some meaning is attached to the output signals from the machine. The machine might, for instance, type out mathematical equations or sentences in English. When a false proposition is typed we say that the machine has committed an error of conclusion. There is clearly no reason at all for saying that a machine cannot make this kind of mistake. It might do nothing but type out repeatedly "0 = 1." To take a less perverse example, it might have some method for drawing conclusions by

scientific induction. We must expect such a method to lead occasionally to erroneous results.

The claim that a machine cannot be the subject of its own thought can of course only be answered if it can be shown that the machine has *some* thought with *some* subject matter. Nevertheless, "the subject matter of a machine's operations" does seem to mean something, at least to the people who deal with it. If, for instance, the machine was trying to find a solution of the equation $x^2 - 40x - 11 = 0$, one would be tempted to describe this equation as part of the machine's subject matter at that moment. In this sort of sense a machine undoubtedly can be its own subject matter. It may be used to help in making up its own programs or to predict the effect of alterations in its own structure. By observing the results of its own behavior it can modify its own programs so as to achieve some purpose more effectively. These are possibilities of the near future rather than Utopian dreams.

The criticism that a machine cannot have much diversity of behavior is just a way of saying that it cannot have much storage capacity. Until fairly recently a storage capacity of even a thousand digits was very rare.

The criticisms that we are considering here are often disguised forms of the argument from consciousness. Usually if one maintains that a machine *can* do one of these things and describes the kind of method that the machine could use, one will not make much of an impression. It is thought that the method (whatever it may be, for it must be mechanical) is really rather base. . . .

6. *Lady Lovelace's objection.* Our most detailed information of Babbage's Analytical Engine comes from a memoir by *Lady Lovelace.* In it she states, "The Analytical Engine has no pretensions to *originate* anything. It can do *whatever we know how to order it* to perform" (her italics). This statement is quoted by *Hartree* (p. 70), who adds: "This does not imply that it may not be possible to con-

struct electronic equipment which will 'think for itself,' or in which, in biological terms, one could set up a conditioned reflex, which would serve as a basis for 'learning.' Whether this is possible in principle or not is a stimulating and exciting question, suggested by some of these recent developments. But it did not seem that the machines constructed or projected at the time had this property."

I am in thorough agreement with Hartree over this. It will be noticed that he does not assert that the machines in question had not got the property, but rather that the evidence available to Lady Lovelace did not encourage her to believe that they had it. It is quite possible that the machines in question had in a sense got this property. For suppose that some discrete-state machine has the property The Analytical Engine was a universal digital computer, so that, if its storage capacity and speed were adequate, it could by suitable programming be made to mimic the machine in question. Probably this argument did not occur to the countess or to Babbage. In any case there was no obligation on them to claim all that could be claimed.

This whole question will be considered again under the heading of learning machines.

A variant of Lady Lovelace's objection states that a machine can "never do anything really new." This may be parried for a moment with the saw "There is nothing new under the sun." Who can be certain that "original work" that he has done was not simply the growth of the seed planted in him by teaching or the effect of following well-known general principles. A better variant of the objection says that a machine can never "take us by surprise." This statement is a more direct challenge and can be met directly. Machines take me by surprise with great frequency. This is largely because I do not do sufficient calculation to decide what to expect them to do or rather because, although I do a calculation, I do it in a hurried, slipshod fashion, taking

risks. Perhaps I say to myself, "I suppose the voltage here ought to be the same as there: Anyway let's assume it is." Naturally I am often wrong, and the result is a surprise for me for by the time the experiment is done these assumptions have been forgotten. These admissions lay me open to lectures on the subject of my vicious ways, but do not throw any doubt on my credibility when I testify to the surprises I experience.

I do not expect this reply to silence my critic. He will probably say that such surprises are due to some creative mental act on my part and reflect no credit on the machine. This leads us back to the argument from consciousness and far from the idea of surprise. It is a line of argument we must consider closed, but it is perhaps worth remarking that the appreciation of something as surprising requires as much of a "creative mental act" whether the surprising event originates from a man, a book, a machine, or anything else.

The view that machines cannot give rise to surprises is due, I believe, to a fallacy to which philosophers and mathematicians are particularly subject. This is the assumption that as soon as a fact is presented to a mind all consequences of that fact spring into the mind simultaneously with it. It is a very useful assumption under many circumstances, but one too easily forgets that it is false. A natural consequence of doing so is that one then assumes that there is no virtue in the mere working out of consequences from data and general principles.

7. *Argument from continuity in the nervous system.* The nervous system is certainly not a discrete-state machine. A small error in the information about the size of a nervous impulse impinging on a neuron may make a large difference to the size of the outgoing impulse. It may be argued that, this being so, one cannot expect to be able to mimic the behavior of the nervous system with a discrete-state system.

It is true that a discrete-state machine

must be different from a continuous machine. But if we adhere to the conditions of the imitation game, the interrogator will not be able to take any advantage of this difference. The situation can be made clearer if we consider some other simpler continuous machine. A differential analyzer will do very well. (A differential analyzer is a certain kind of machine not of the discrete-state type used for some kinds of calculation.) Some of these provide their answers in a typed form and so are suitable for taking part in the game. It would not be possible for a digital computer to predict exactly what answers the differential analyzer would give to a problem but it would be quite capable of giving the right sort of answer. For instance, if asked to give the value of π (actually about 3.1416), it would be reasonable to choose at random between the values 3.12, 3.13, 3.14, 3.15, 3.16 with the probabilities of 0.05, 0.15, 0.55, 0.19, 0.06 (say). Under these circumstances it would be very difficult for the interrogator to distinguish the differential analyzer from the digital computer.

8. *The argument from informality of behavior.* It is not possible to produce a set of rules purporting to describe what a man should do in every conceivable set of circumstances. One might, for instance, have a rule that one is to stop when one sees a red traffic light and to go if one sees a green one, but what if by some fault both appear together? One may perhaps decide that it is safest to stop. But some further difficulty may well arise from this decision later. To attempt to provide rules of conduct to cover every eventuality, even those arising from traffic lights, appears to be impossible. With all this I agree.

From this it is argued that we cannot be machines. I shall try to reproduce the argument, but I fear I shall hardly do it justice. It seems to run something like this. "If each man had a definite set of rules of conduct by which he regulated his life, he would be no better than a machine. But there are no such rules, so

men cannot be machines." The undistributed middle is glaring. I do not think the argument is ever put quite like this, but I believe this is the argument used nevertheless. There may however be a certain confusion between "rules of conduct" and "laws of behavior" to cloud the issue. By "rules of conduct" I mean precepts such as "Stop if you see red lights," on which one can act and of which one can be conscious. By "laws of behavior" I mean laws of nature as applied to a man's body such as "if you pinch him he will squeak." If we substitute "laws of behavior which regulate his life" for "laws of conduct by which he regulates his life" in the argument quoted, the undistributed middle is no longer insuperable. For we believe that it is not only true that being regulated by laws of behavior implies being some sort of machine (though not necessarily a discrete-state machine) but that conversely being such a machine implies being regulated by such laws. However, we cannot so easily convince ourselves of the absence of complete laws of behavior as of complete rules of conduct. The only way we know of for finding such laws is scientific observation, and we certainly know of no circumstances under which we could say, "We have searched enough. There are no such laws."

We can demonstrate more forcibly that any such statement would be unjustified. For suppose we could be sure of finding such laws if they existed. Then, given a discrete-state machine, it should certainly be possible to discover by observation sufficient about it to predict its future behavior, and this within a reasonable time, say a thousand years. But this does not seem to be the case. I have set up on the Manchester computer a small program using only 1,000 units of storage, whereby the machine supplied with one sixteen-figure number replies with another within 2 seconds. I would defy anyone to learn from these replies sufficient about the program to be able to predict any replies to untried values.

9. *The argument from extrasensory perception.* I assume that the reader is familiar with the idea of extrasensory perception and the meaning of the four items of it, viz., telepathy, clairvoyance, precognition, and psychokinesis. These disturbing phenomena seem to deny all our usual scientific ideas. How we should like to discredit them! Unfortunately the statistical evidence, at least for telepathy, is overwhelming. It is very difficult to rearrange one's ideas so as to fit these new facts in. Once one has accepted them it does not seem a very big step to believe in ghosts and bogies. The idea that our bodies move simply according to the known laws of physics, together with some others not yet discovered but somewhat similar, would be one of the first to go.

This argument is to my mind quite a strong one. One can say in reply that many scientific theories seem to remain workable in practice, in spite of clashing with ESP; that in fact one can get along very nicely if one forgets about it. This is rather cold comfort, and one fears that thinking is just the kind of phenomenon where ESP may be especially relevant.

A more specific argument based on ESP might run as follows: "Let us play the imitation game, using as witnesses a man who is good as a telepathic receiver, and a digital computer. The interrogator can ask such questions as 'What suit does the card in my right hand belong to?' The man by telepathy or clairvoyance gives the right answer 130 times out of 400 cards. The machine can only guess at random and perhaps gets 104 right, so the interrogator makes the right identification." There is an interesting possibility which opens here. Suppose the digital computer contains a random-number generator. Then it will be natural to use this to decide what answer to give. But then the random-number generator will be subject to the psychokinetic powers of the interrogator. Perhaps this psychokinesis might cause the machine to guess right more often than would be expected on a probability calculation, so that the interrogator might still be unable to make the right identification. On the other hand, he might be able to guess right without any questioning, by clairvoyance. With ESP anything may happen.

If telepathy is admitted, it will be necessary to tighten our test up. The situation could be regarded as analogous to that which would occur if the interrogator were talking to himself and one of the competitors was listening with his ear to the wall. To put the competitors into a "telepathy-proof room" would satisfy all requirements.

7. LEARNING MACHINES

The reader will have anticipated that I have no very convincing arguments of a positive nature to support my views. If I had I should not have taken such pains to point out the fallacies in contrary views. Such evidence as I have I shall now give.

Let us return for a moment to Lady Lovelace's objection, which stated that the machine can only do what we tell it to do. One could say that a man can "inject" an idea into the machine and that it will respond to a certain extent and then drop into quiescence, like a piano string struck by a hammer. Another simile would be an atomic pile of less than critical size: An injected idea is to correspond to a neutron entering the pile from without. Each such neutron will cause a certain disturbance which eventually dies away. If, however, the size of the pile is sufficiently increased, the disturbance caused by such an incoming neutron will very likely go on and on increasing until the whole pile is destroyed. Is there a corresponding phenomenon for minds, and is there one for machines? There does seem to be one for the human mind. The majority of them seem to be "subcritical," i.e., to correspond in this analogy to piles of subcritical size. An idea presented to such a mind will on average give rise to less than one idea in reply. A smallish proportion are supercritical. An idea presented to such a mind may give rise to a whole "theory" consisting of secondary, tertiary, and more remote ideas. Animals' minds seem to be very definitely subcritical. Adhering to this analogy we ask, "Can a machine be made to be supercritical?"

The "skin of an onion" analogy is also helpful. In considering the functions of the mind or the brain we find certain operations which we can explain in purely mechanical terms. This we say does not correspond to the real mind: It is a sort of skin which we must strip off if we are to find the real mind. But then in what remains we find a further skin to be stripped off, and so on. Proceeding in this way do we ever come to the "real" mind, or do we eventually come to the skin which has nothing in it? In the latter case the whole mind is machanical. (It would not be a discrete-state machine however. We have discussed this.)

These last two paragraphs do not claim to be convincing arguments. They should rather be described as "recitations tending to produce belief."

The only really satisfactory support that can be given for the view expressed at the beginning of Sec. 6 will be that provided by waiting for the end of the century and then doing the experiment described. But what can we say in the meantime? What steps should be taken now if the experiment is to be successful?

As I have explained, the problem is mainly one of programming. Advances in engineering will have to be made too, but it seems unlikely that these will not be adequate for the requirements. Estimates of the storage capacity of the brain vary from 10^{10} to 10^{15} binary digits. I incline to the lower values and believe that only a very small fraction is used for the higher types of thinking. Most of it is probably used for the retention of visual impressions. I should be surprised if more than 10^9 was required for satisfactory playing of the imitation game, at any

rate against a blind man. (Note—The capacity of the *Encyclopaedia Britannica,* 11th edition, is 2×10^9.) A storage capacity of 10^7 would be a very practicable possibility even by present techniques. It is probably not necessary to increase the speed of operations of the machines at all. Parts of modern machines which can be regarded as analogues of nerve cells work about a thousand times faster than the latter. This should provide a "margin of safety" which could cover losses of speed arising in many ways. Our problem then is to find out how to program these machines to play the game. At my present rate of working I produce about a thousand digits of program a day, so that about sixty workers working steadily through the fifty years might accomplish the job, if nothing went into the wastepaper basket. Some more expeditious method seems desirable.

In the process of trying to imitate an adult human mind we are bound to think a good deal about the process which has brought it to the state that it is in. We may notice three components:

a. The initial state of the mind, say at birth
b. The education to which it has been subjected
c. Other experience, not to be described as education, to which it has been subjected

Instead of trying to produce a program to simulate the adult mind, why not rather try to produce one which simulates the child's? If this were then subjected to an appropriate course of education one would obtain the adult brain. Presumably the child's brain is something like a notebook as one buys it from the stationers—rather little mechanism and lots of blank sheets. (Mechanism and writing are from our point of view almost synonymous.) Our hope is that there is so little mechanism in the child's brain that something like it can be easily programmed. The amount of work in the education we can assume, as a first approximation, to be much the same as for the human child.

We have thus divided our problem into two parts. The child program and the education process. These two remain very closely connected. We cannot expect to find a good child machine at the first attempt. One must experiment with teaching one such machine and see how well it learns. One can then try another and see if it is better or worse. There is an obvious connection between this process and evolution, by the identifications

structure of the child machine
  = hereditary material

changes of the child machine
  = mutations

natural selection
  = judgment of the experimenter

One may hope, however, that this process will be more expeditious than evolution. The survival of the fittest is a slow method for measuring advantages. The experimenter, by the exercise of intelligence, should be able to speed it up. Equally important is the fact that he is not restricted to random mutations. If he can trace a cause for some weakness, he can probably think of the kind of mutation which will improve it.

It will not be possible to apply exactly the same teaching process to the machine as to a normal child. It will not, for instance, be provided with legs, so that it could not be asked to go out and fill the coal scuttle. Possibly it might not have eyes. But however well these deficiencies might be overcome by clever engineering, one could not send the creature to school without the other children making excessive fun of it. It must be given some tuition. We need not be too concerned about the legs, eyes, etc. The example of Miss Helen Keller shows that education can take place provided that communication in both directions between teacher and pupil can take place by some means or other.

We normally associate punishments and rewards with the teaching process. Some simple child machines can be constructed or programmed on this sort of principle. The machine has to be so constructed that events which shortly preceded the occurrnnce of a punishment signal are unlikely to be repeated, whereas a reward signal increased the probability of repetition of the events which led up to it. These definitions do not presuppose any feelings on the part of the machine. I have done some experiments with one such child machine and succeeded in teaching it a few things, but the teaching method was too unorthodox for the experiment to be considered really successful.

The use of punishments and rewards can at best be a part of the teaching process. Roughly speaking, if the teacher has no other means of communicating to the pupil, the amount of information which can reach him does not exceed the total number of rewards and punishments applied. By the time a child has learned to repeat "Casabianca" he would probably feel very sore indeed if the text could only be discovered by a "Twenty questions" technique, every "NO" taking the form of a blow. It is necessary therefore to have some other "unemotional" channels of communication. If these are available it is possible to teach a machine by punishments and rewards to obey orders given in some language, e.g., a symbolic language. These orders are to be transmitted through the "unemotional" channels. The use of this language will diminish greatly the number of punishments and rewards required.

Opinions may vary as to the complexity which is suitable in the child machine. One might try to make it as simple as possible consistent with the general principles. Alternatively one might have a complete system of logical inference "built in".[3] In the latter case the store would be largely occupied with definitions and propositions. The propositions would have various kinds of status, e.g., well-established facts, conjectures, mathematically proved theorems, statements given by an authority, expressions having the logical form of proposition but not belief value. Certain propositions may be described as "imperatives." The machine should be so constructed that as soon as an imperative is classed as "well established" the appropriate action automatically takes place. To illustrate this, suppose the teacher says to the machine "Do your homework now." This may cause "Teacher says 'Do your homework now'" to be included amongst the well-established facts. Another such fact might be, "Everything that teacher says is true." Combining these may eventually lead to the imperative, "Do your homework now," being included among the well established facts, and this, by the construction of the machine, well mean that the homework actually gets started, but the effect is very satisfactory. The processes of inference used by the machine need not be such as would satisfy the most exacting logicians. There might for instance be no hierarchy of types. But this need not mean that type fallacies will occur, any more than we are bound to fall over unfenced cliffs. Suitable imperatives (expressed *within* the systems, not forming part of the rules *of* the system) such as "Do not use a class unless it is a subclass of one which has been mentioned by teacher" can have a similar effect to "Do not go too near the edge."

The imperatives that can be obeyed by a machine that has no limbs are bound to be of a rather intellectual character, as in the example (doing homework) given above. Important amongst such imperatives will be ones which regulate the order in which the rules of the logical system concerned are to be applied. For at each stage when one is using a logical system, there is a very large number of alternative steps, any of which one is permitted to apply, so far as obedience to the rules of the logical system is concerned. These choices make the difference between a brilliant and a footling reasoner, not the difference between a sound and a fallacious one. Propositions leading to imperatives of this kind might be "When Socrates is mentioned, use the syllogism in Barbara" or "If one method has been proved to be quicker than another, do not use the slower method." Some of these may be "given by authority," but others may be produced by the machine itself, e.g., by scientific induction.

The idea of a learning machine may appear paradoxical to some readers. How can the rules of operation of the machine change? They should describe completely how the machine will react, whatever its history might be, whatever changes it might undergo. The rules are thus quite time-invariant. This is quite true. The explanation of the paradox is that the rules which get changed in the learning process are of a rather less pretentious kind, claiming only an ephemeral validity. The reader may draw a parallel with the Constitution of the United States.

An important feature of a learning machine is that its teacher will often be very largely ignorant of quite what is going on inside, although he may still be able to some extent to predict his pupil's behavior. This should apply most strongly to the later education of a machine arising from a child machine of well-tried design (or program). This is in clear contrast with normal procedure when using a machine to do computations: One's object is then to have a clear mental picture of the state of the machine at each moment in the computation. This

[3]Or rather "programmed in" for our child machine will be programmed in a digital computer. But the logical system will not have to be learned.

object can only be achieved with a struggle. The view that "the machine can only do what we know how to order it to do."[4] appears strange in face of this. Most of the programs which we can put into the machine will result in its doing something that we cannot make sense of at all or which we regard as completely random behavior. Intelligent behavior presumably consists in a departure from the completely disciplined behavior involved in computation, but a rather slight one, which does not give rise to random behavior, or to pointless repetitive loops. Another important result of preparing our machine for its part in the imitation game by a process of teaching and learning is that "human fallibility" is likely to be omitted in a rather natural way, i.e., without special coaching. . . . Processes that are learned do not produce 100 per cent certainty of result; if they did they could not be unlearned.

It is probably wise to include a random element in a learning machine. . . . A random element is rather useful when we are searching for a solution of some problem. Suppose for instance we wanted to find a number between 50 and 200 which was equal to the square of the sum of its digits, we might start at 51, then try 52, and go on until we got a number that worked. Alternatively we might choose numbers at random until we got a good one. This method has the advantage that it is unnecessary to keep track of the values that have been tried, but the disadvantage that one may try the same one twice, but this is not very important if there are several solutions. The systematic method has the disasvantage that there may be an enormous block without any solutions in the region which has to be investigated first. Now the learning process may be regarded as a search for a form of behavior which will satisfy the teacher (or some other criterion). Since

there is probably a very large number of satisfactory solutions the random method seems to be better than the systematic. It should be noticed that it is used in the analogous process of evolution. But there the systematic method is not possible. How could one keep track of the different genetical combinations that had been tried so as to avoid trying them again?

We may hope that machines will eventually compete with men in all purely intellectual fields. But which are the best ones to start with? Even this is a difficult decision. Many people think that a very abstract activity, like the playing of chess, would be best. It can also be maintained that it is best to provide the machine with the best sense organs that money can buy, and then teach it to understand and speak English. This process could follow the normal teaching of a child. Things would be pointed out and named, etc. Again I do not know what the right answer is, but I think both approaches should be tried.

We can only see a short distance ahead, but we can see plenty there that needs to be done.

BIBLIOGRAPHY

Butler, Samuel, *Erewhon*, Chap. 23, 24, 25, "The Book of the Machines." London, 1865.

Church, Alonzo, "An Unsolvable Problem of Elementary Number Theory," *American Journal of Mathematics*, 58 (1936), 345–63.

Gödel, K., "Über formal unentscheidbare Sätze der Principia Mathematica und verwandter Systeme, I." *Monatshefte für Math. und Phys.* (1931), pp. 173–89.

Hartree, D. R., *Calculating Instruments and Machines*. New York, 1949.

Kleene, S. C., "General Recursive Functions of Natural Numbers," *American Journal of Mathematics*, 57 (1935), 153–73 and 219–44.

Jefferson, G., "The Mind of Mechanical Man." Lister Oration for 1949, *British Medical Journal*, i (1949), 1105–21.

---

[4]Compare Lady Lovelace's statement [earlier] which does not contain the word "only."

Countess of Lovelace, "Translator's Notes to an Article on Babbage's Analytical Engine," in *Scientific Memoirs*, Vol. 3 (1842), 691–731, ed. R. Taylor.

Russell, Bertrand, *History of Western Philosophy*. London, 1940.

Turing, A. M., "On Computable Numbers, with an Application to the Entscheidungsproblem," *Proceedings of the London Mathematical Society*, 42 No. 2 (1937), 230–65.

Contextual understanding by computers

JOSEPH WEIZENBAUM*

We are here concerned with the recognition of semantic patterns in text.

I compose my sentences and paragraphs in the belief that I shall be understood —perhaps even that what I write here will prove persuasive. For this faith to be at all meaningful, I must hypothesize at least one reader other than myself. I speak of *understanding*. What I must suppose is clearly that my reader will recognize patterns in these sentences and, on the basis of this recognition, be able to recreate my present thought for himself. Notice the very structure of the word "recognize," that is, know again! I also use the word "recreate." This suggests that the reader is an active participant in the two-person communication. He brings something of himself to it. His understanding is a function of that something as well as of what is written here. I will return to this point later.

Much of the motivation for the work discussed here derives from attempts to program a computer to understand what a human might say to it. Lest it be misunderstood, let me state right away that the input to the computer is in the form of typewritten messages—certainly not human speech. This restriction has the effect of establishing a narrower channel of communication than that available to humans in face-to-face conversations. In the latter, many ideas that potentially aid understanding are communicated by gestures, intonations, pauses, and so on. All of these are unavailable to readers of telegrams—be they computers or humans.

Further, what I wish to report here should not be confused with what is generally called content analysis. In the present situation we are concerned with the fragments of natural language that occur in conversations, not with complete texts. Consequently, we cannot rely on the texts we are analyzing to be grammatically complete or correct. Hence, no theory that depends on parsing of presumably well-formed sentences can be of much help. We must depend on heuristics and other such impure devices instead.

The first program to which I wish to call attention is a particular member of a family of programs which has come to be known as DOCTOR. The family name of these programs is ELIZA. This name was chosen because these programs, like the Eliza of *Pygmalion* fame, can be taught to speak increasingly well. DOCTOR causes ELIZA to respond roughly as would certain psychotherapists (Rogerians).

*Joseph Weizenbaum, "Contextual Understanding by Computers", *Communications of the ACM*, Vol. 10, No. 8, August 1967, pages 474–480. Copyright © 1967, Association for Computing Machinery, Inc., reprinted by permission.

ELIZA performs best when its human correspondent is initially instructed to "talk" to it, via the typewriter, of course, just as one would to a psychiatrist.

I chose this mode of conversation because the psychiatric interview is one of the few examples of categorized dyadic natural language communication in which one of the participating pair is free to assume the pose of knowing almost nothing of the real world. If, for example, one were to tell a psychiatrist "I went for a boat ride" and he responded "Tell me about boats," one would not assume that he knew nothing about boats, but that he had some purpose in so directing the subsequent conversation. It is important to note that this assumption is one made by the speaker. Whether it is realistic or not is an altogether separate question. In any case, it has a crucial psychological utility in that it serves the speaker to maintain his sense of being heard and understood. The speaker further defends his impression (which even in real life may be illusory) by attributing to his conversational partner all sorts of background knowledge, insights, and reasoning ability. But again, these are the speaker's contribution to the conversation. They manifest themselves inferentially in the interpretations he makes of the offered responses. From the purely technical programming point of view, the psychiatric interview has the advantage that it eliminates the need for storing explicit information about the real world.

The human speaker will contribute much to clothe ELIZA's responses in vestments of plausibility. However, he will not defend his illusion (that he is being understood) against all odds. In human conversation a speaker will make certain (perhaps generous) assumptions about his conversational partner. As long as it remains possible to interpret the latter's responses to be consistent with those assumptions, the speaker's image of his partner remains undamaged. Responses which are difficult to so interpret may well result in an enhancement of the image of the partner, by additional rationalizations which then make more complicated interpretations of his responses reasonable. When, however, such rationalizations become too massive and even self-contradictory, the entire image may crumble and be replaced by another ("He is not, after all, as smart as I thought he was.") When the conversational partner is a machine (the distinction between machine and program is not useful here), the idea of credibility may well be substituted for that of plausibility in the above.

"When in conversation with ELIZA, the user types in some statement or set of statements in natural language using normal punctuation and sentence structures. The user's statement is terminated by a double carriage return which serves to turn control over to ELIZA. ELIZA then analyzes the user's statement and generates some response which it types out. Control is then again with the user.

"A typical conversation is the following:

Men are all alike.
IN WHAT WAY?
They're always bugging us about something or other.
CAN YOU THINK OF A SPECIFIC EXAMPLE?
Well, my boyfriend made me come here.
YOUR BOY FRIEND MADE YOU COME HERE.
He says I'm depressed much of the time.
I AM SORRY TO HEAR YOU ARE DEPRESSED.
It's true. I am unhappy.
DO YOU THINK COMING HERE WILL HELP YOU NOT TO BE UNHAPPY?
I need some help, that much seems certain.
WHAT WOULD IT MEAN TO YOU IF YOU GOT SOME HELP?
Perhaps I could learn to get along with my mother.
TELL ME MORE ABOUT YOUR FAMILY.
My mother takes care of me.
WHO ELSE IN YOUR FAMILY TAKES CARE OF YOU?
My father.
YOUR FATHER.

WHAT RESEMBLANCE DO YOU SEE?
You are not very aggressive but I think you don't want me to notice that.
WHAT MAKES YOU THINK I AM NOT VERY AGGRESSIVE?
You don't argue with me.
WHY DO YOU THINK I DON'T ARGUE WITH YOU?
You are afraid of me.
DOES IT PLEASE YOU TO BELIEVE I AM AFRAID OF YOU?
My father is afraid of everybody.
WHAT ELSE COMES TO MIND WHEN YOU THINK OF YOUR FATHER?
Bullies.
DOES THAT HAVE ANYTHING TO DO WITH THE FACT THAT YOUR BOY FRIEND MADE YOU COME HERE?

"The capitalized lines are the machine responses. ... ELIZA's conversational powers are governed by a *script*. A script consists of a set of key words and key phrases each of which is associated with a set of so-called decomposition and reassembly rules. A decomposition rule is a data structure which searches a text for specified patterns and, if such patterns are found, decomposes the text into disjoint constituents. A reassembly rule is a specification for the construction of a new text by means of recombinations of old and possible addition of new constituents. From one point of view, an ELIZA script is a program and ELIZA itself an interpreter. From another perspective, ELIZA appears as an actor who must depend on a script for his lines. The script determines the contextual framework within which ELIZA may be expected to converse plausibly.

"The gross procedure of the program is quite simple: The text is read and inspected for the presence of a key word. If such a word is found, the sentence is transformed according to a rule associated with the key word; if not, a content-free remark or, under certain conditions, an earlier transformation is retrieved. A rule-cycling mechanism delays repetition of responses to identical keys as long as possible. The text so computed or retrieved is then printed out."[1]

One of the principal aims of the DOCTOR program is to keep the conversation going—even at the price of having to conceal any misunderstandings on its own part. We shall see how more ambitious objectives are realized subsequently. In the meanwhile, the above discussion already provides a framework within which a number of useful points may be illuminated.

By far the most important of these relates to the crucial role *context* plays in all conversations. The subject who is about to engage in his first conversation with the DOCTOR is told to put himself in a role-playing frame of mind. He is to imagine that he has some problem of the kind one might normally discuss with a psychiatrist, to pretend he is actually conversing with a psychiatrist, and under no circumstances to deviate from that role. While some of the responses produced by the program are not very spectacular even when the subject follows his instructions, it is remarkable how quickly they deteriorate when he leaves his role. In this respect, the program mirrors life. Real two-person conversations also degenerate when the contextual assumptions one participant is making with respect to his partner's statements cease to be valid. This phenomenon is, for example, the basis on which many comedies of error are built.

These remarks are about the *global* context in which the conversation takes place. No understanding is possible in the absence of an established global context. To be sure, strangers do meet, converse, and immediately understand one another (or at least believe they do). But they operate in a shared culture —provided partially by the very lan-

[1]The cooperation of the editors of the *Communications of the Association for Computing Machinery* in permitting the extensive quotations from the paper "ELIZA," Vol. 9, No. 1, January 1966, by the author, is hereby gratefully acknowledged.

guage they speak—and, under any but the most trivial circumstances, engage in a kind of hunting behavior which has as its object the creation of a contextual framework. Conversation flows smoothly only after these preliminaries are completed. The situation is no different with respect to visual pattern recognition—a visual pattern may appear utterly senseless until a context within which it may be recognized (known again, i.e., understood) is provided. Very often, of course, a solitary observer arrives at an appropriate context by forming and testing a number of hypotheses. He may later discover that the pattern he "recognized" was not the one he was intended to "see," i.e., that he hypothesized the "wrong" context. He may see the "correct" pattern when given the "correct" context. It doesn't mean much to say that the pattern "is" such and such. We might, for example, find a string of Chinese characters beautiful as long as we don't know what they spell. This, an apparent impoverishment, i.e., really a broadening, of context, will enhance the esthetic appeal of a pattern. Similarly, many people think anything said in French is charming and romantic precisely *because* they don't understand the language.

In real conversations, global context assigns meaning to what is being said in only the most general way. The conversation proceeds by establishing subcontexts, sub-subcontexts within these, and so on. It generates and, so to speak, traverses a contextual tree. Beginning with the topmost or initial node, a new node representing a subcontext is generated and from this one a new node still, and so on to many levels. Occasionally the currently regnant node is abandoned—i.e., the conversation ascends to a previously established node, perhaps skipping many intermediate ones in the process. New branches are established and old ones abandoned. It is my conjecture that an analysis of the pattern traced by a given conversation through such a directed graph may yield

a measure of what one might call the consequential richness of the conversation. Cocktail party chatter, for example, has a rather straight-line character. Context is constantly being changed—there is considerable chaining of nodes—but there is hardly any reversal of direction along already established structure. The conversation is inconsequential in that nothing being said has any effect on any questions raised on a higher level. Contrast this with a discussion between, say, two physicists trying to come to understand the results of some experiment. Their conversation tree would be not only deep but broad as well, i.e., they would ascend to an earlier contextual level in order to generate new nodes from there. The signal that their conversation terminated successfully might well be that they ascended (back to) the original node, i.e., that they are again talking about what they started to discuss.

For an individual the analog of a conversation tree is what the social psychologist Abelson calls a *belief structure*. In some areas of the individual's intellectual life, this structure may be highly logically organized—at least up to a point; for example, in the area of his own profession. In more emotionally loaded areas, the structure may be very loosely organized and even contain many contradictions. When a person enters a conversation he brings his belief structures with him as a kind of agenda.

A person's belief structure is a product of his entire life experience. All people have some common formative experiences, e.g., they were all born of mothers. There is consequently some basis of understanding between any two humans simply because they are human. But, even humans living in the same culture will have difficulty in understanding one another where their respective lives differed radically. Since, in the last analysis, each of our lives is unique, there is a limit to what we can bring another person to understand. There is an ultimate privacy about each of us that absolutely precludes full communication of any of our ideas to the universe outside ourselves and which thus isolates each one of us from every other noetic object in the world.

There can be no total understanding and no absolutely reliable test of understanding.

To know with certainty that a person understood what has been said to him is to perceive his entire belief structure and *that* is equivalent to sharing his entire life experience. It is precisely barriers of this kind that artists, especially poets, struggle against.

This issue must be confronted if there is to be any agreement as to what machine "understanding" might mean. What the above argument is intended to make clear is that it is too much to insist that a machine understands a sentence (or a symphony or a poem) only if that sentence invokes the same imagery in the machine as was present in the speaker of the sentence at the time he uttered it. For by that criterion no human understands any other human. Yet, we agree that humans do understand one another to *within acceptable tolerances*. The operative word is "acceptable" for it implies *purpose*. When, therefore, we speak of a machine understanding, we must mean understanding as limited by some objective. He who asserts that there are certain ideas no machines will ever understand can mean at most that the machine will not understand these ideas tolerably well because they relate to objectives that are, in his judgment, inappropriate with respect to machines. Of course, the machine can still deal with such ideas symbolically, i.e., in ways which are reflections—however pale—of the ways organisms for which such objectives are appropriate deal with them. In such cases the machine is no more handicapped than I am, being a mn, in trying to understand, say, female jealousy.

A two-person conversation may be said to click along as long as both participants keep discovering (in the sense of uncov-

ering) identical nodes in their respective belief structures. Under such circumstances the conversation tree is merely a set of linearly connected nodes corresponding to the commonly held parts of the participants' belief structures. If such a conversation is interesting to either participant, it is probably because the part of the belief structure being made explicit has not been consciously verbalized before, or has never before been attached to the higher level node to which it is then coupled in that conversation, i.e., seen in that context, or because of the implicit support it is getting by being found to coexist in someone else.

Backtracking over the conversation tree takes place when a new context is introduced and an attempt is made to integrate it into the ongoing conversation, or when a new connection between the present and a previous context is suggested. In either case, there is a need to reorganize the conversation tree. Clearly the kind of psychotherapist initiated by the DOCTOR program restricts himself to pointing out new connectivity opportunities to his patients. I suppose his hope is that any reorganization of the conversation tree generated in the therapy session will ultimately reflect itself in corresponding modifications of his patients' belief structures.

I now turn back to the program reproduced earlier. I hope the reader found the conversation quoted there to be smooth and natural. If he did, he has gone a long way toward verifying what I said earlier about the investment a human will make in a conversation. Any continuity the reader may have perceived in that dialogue—excepting only the last machine response—is entirely illusionary. A careful analysis will reveal that each machine response is a response to the just previous subject input. Again with the exception of the last sentence, the above quoted conversation has no subcontextual structure at all. Nor does the description of the program . . . give any clues as to how subcontexts might be recognized or established or maintained by the machine.

To get at the subcontext issue, I want to restate the overall strategy in terms somewhat different from those used above. We may think of the ELIZA script as establishing the global context in which subsequent conversations will be played out. The DOCTOR script establishes the Rogerian psychiatric context. The key word listings are guesses about what significant words might appear in the subject's utterances. The appearance of any of these words in an actual input tentatively directs the system's attention to decomposition rules associated with the identified word. These rules are hypotheses about what an input containing such words might mean. An important property of the system is that just as the entire set of key words need not be searched in the analysis of every input sentence, neither does the whole list of hypotheses about what *any* input might mean have to be tested in order to generate a response to a specific sentence. Should the set of hypotheses associated with the currently regnant key word be exhausted without success, there is a way (although not here described) to go to decomposition rules associated with lower ranking key words that may have appeared in the input string.

Much is known about an input sentence once it matches a decomposition rule. If, for example, the rule

(O MY (/FAMILY)
DRINKS O)

matches a sentence, then we know that the subject matter is a family member, and that this person drinks. (The notation " (/A B C)" means that in that position a word "tagged" with any of the symbols A or B or C is looked for. Words are tagged as part of the script. This mechanism is not further discussed here.) A reassembly rule can subsequently identify the family member in question, e.g., father. The successful matching of a decomposition rule

—hence, the verification of a hypothesis—is therefore an opportunity not only to generate a plausible response but also to establish a contextual node. The laying down of such a node does not mean merely remembering what is now being talked about, but what is more important, making hypotheses about what is likely to be said next within the new contextual framework.

The realization of such a mechanism in an ELIZA script involves attaching a substructure to decomposition rules which says, in effect, that if a so modified decomposition rule matches an input sentence and a suitable subcontext exists, then control is transferred to a set of decomposition and reassembly rules appropriate to that subcontext. The details of mechanization are not important here. I will, however, show its effect by exhibiting the following conversational fragment from the DOCTOR program:

Because you are so stubborn.
IS THAT THE REAL REASON?
Maybe.
WHAT IS A BETTER REASON THEN?
My stomach hurts.
TELL ME ABOUT YOUR PAINS IN GENERAL.
My head bothers me, too.
YOU SEE SOME PSYCHOLOGICAL REASON WHY YOUR HEAD SHOULD PAIN YOU.
Maybe.
YOU THINK COMING HERE MIGHT HELP ALLEVIATE YOUR HEAD PAIN.
Certainly.
LET'S TALK ABOUT YOUR FEELINGS WHEN YOU THINK OF YOUR HEAD AND ITS PAINS.

We are here in the middle of a dialogue. The first sentence is an input to the program, the next a machine response, and so on in alternation.

The word "because" was the key that triggered the first machine response. At the same time the *reason* subcontext, so to speak, was established. Notice that the next subject input, i.e., the word "maybe," was interpreted as meaning "no," as is appropriate in that particular context, and that a contextually correct machine response was produced. The next input serves to establish a "hurt" subcontext. I believe the conversation is self-explanatory from that point on. Notice, however, that in the new subcontext the word "maybe" which was earlier interpreted to mean "no" is now seen as meaning "yes." Under still other circumstances it would be understood as indicating uncertainty.

My secretary watched me work on this program over a long period of time. One day she asked to be permitted to talk with the system. Of course, she knew she was talking to a machine. Yet, after I watched her type in a few sentences she turned to me and said, "Would you mind leaving the room, please?" I believe this anecdote testifies to the success with which the program maintains the illusion of understanding. However, it does so, as I've already said, at the price of concealing its own misunderstandings. We all do this now and then, perhaps in the service of politeness or for other reasons. But we cannot afford to elevate this occasional tactic to a universal strategy. Thus, while the DOCTOR program may be useful as an instrument for the analysis of two-person conversations and while it is certainly fun, its aim must be changed from that of concealment of misunderstanding to its explication.

Another difficulty with the system currently under discussion is that it can do very little other than generate plausible responses. To be sure, there are facilities for keeping and testing various tallies as well as other such relatively primitive devices, but the system can do no generalized computation in either the logical or numerical sense. In order to meet this and other deficiencies of the original ELIZA system, I wrote a new program, also called ELIZA, which has now replaced its ancestor.

The ELIZA differs from the old one in two main respects. First, it contains an *evaluator* capable of accepting expressions (programs) of unlimited complex-

ity and evaluating (executing) them. It is, of course, also capable of storing the results of such evaluations for subsequent retrieval and use. Secondly, the idea of the script has been generalized so that now it is possible for the program to contain three different scripts simultaneously and to fetch new scripts from among an unlimited supply stored on a disk storage unit, intercommunication among coexisting scripts is also possible.

The major reason for wishing to have several scripts available in the core (i.e., high-speed) memory of the computer derives from the arguments about contexts I made above. The script defines, so to speak, a global context within which all of the subsegment conversation is to be understood. We have seen that it is possible for a single script to establish and maintain subcontexts. But what is a subcontext from one point of view is a major (not to say global) one as seen from another perspective. For example, a conversation may have as its overall framework the health of one of the participants but spend much time under the heading of stomach disorders and headache remedies.

In principle one large, monolithic ELIZA script could deal with this. However, such a script would be very long and extremely difficult to modify and maintain. Besides, long exposure to computer programming should at least instill a healthy respect for subroutines, their power and utility. In the new ELIZA system scripts are in fact very much like subroutines. One script plays the role of the so-called "main program," i.e., it is the one for calling in and replacing subscripts. This is the one which, in an important sense, governs the computer's role in the conversation. Such a script may, for example, play the role of an initial interviewer in a hospital, i.e., a person who knows just enough about the field of medicine and the organization of the hospital to be able to determine, by means of appropriate questions, to whom the incoming patient is to be directed. A more highly specialized script then plays the role of that person. It may call on still further levels of scripts—and each script, except for the "main" one, can return the issue up one or more levels with information "explaining" that action.

We saw earlier how the word "maybe" was differentially interpreted in what might be called different microcontexts. The hierarchy of scripts now under discussion makes much more nearly global contextual distinctions possible. For example, the word "tone" probably means muscle tone to the internist but audio tone to the ear specialist. The occurrence of that word as a key word would establish an entirely different contextual mode or call in a different subscript, depending on whether it was identified in an internist or an ear specialist script.

Of course, another important advantage of this kind of subscripting is that scripts (sub or otherwise) can presumably be written by specialists in a very narrow field. The fact that scripts now tend to be rather short means that a specialist might actually find the time to produce one as part of a larger cooperative effort.

The conversations reproduced below were governed by a script in the new ELIZA system. This script was designed to illustrate the power of the evaluator to which ELIZA has access. The key word and other such mechanisms are not very different from those described above. The important departure is that expressions can be turned over to the evaluator, evaluated, and the results displayed and stored.

The area of a circle is pi times the radius of the circle squared.
The area of a sphere is pi times the diameter of the sphere squared.
The area of a square is the side of the square squared.
The diameter of an object is twice the radius of the object.
The radius of a ball is 10.
What is the area of the ball?
THE ASSUMPTION THAT BALL IS CIRCLE IS CONSISTENT—SHALL I GO ON? no

THE ASSUMPTION THAT BALL IS SPHERE AND OBJECT IS CONSISTENT —SHALL I GO ON? Yes.
IT'S 1256.6359.
What is the diameter of the ball?
IT'S 20.
The radius of a dish is 10.
What's the area of the dish?
THE ASSUMPTION THAT DISH IS CIRCLE IS CONSISTENT—SHALL I GO ON? Yes.
IT'S 314.15899.
The radius of a globe is 10.
A globe is a sphere. A sphere is an object.
What is the area of the globe?
IT'S 1256.6359.
The side of a plate is 10.
What is the area of the plate?
THE ASSUMPTION THAT PLATE IS SQUARE IS CONSISTENT—SHALL I GO ON? Yes.
IT'S 100.
When I say board I mean plate.
What is 3 times the side of the board?
It's 30.
Please call that x.
Let f (z) be z squared minus z.
Compute f (x)
It's 870.
When I say ich sage I mean I say. When ich sage meine ich I mean I mean.
Wenn ich sage wieviel ist meine ich what is.
Wenn ich sage quadrat meine ich squared.
Nun, sagen sie mir bitte, wieviel is x quadrat.
I DIDN'T UNDERSTAND YOU.
Ja, tut mir leid, ich sollte fragen wieviel IST x quadrat.
IT'S 900.
Thank you.
YOU'RE QUITE WELCOME, COME AGAIN.

The particular example shown here is one in which the system is asked not merely to entertain but to perform some useful service. The script is one which establishes a context in which a few terms can be interpreted as giving directions about the evaluation of certain expressions. The number of keys which actually lead to decomposition rules is very small. They are as follows:

I mean	
Is	(* a an)
Of	(* a an the)
What	(* the is)

Where
Call
Let
Define
Compute
=
Also
Thanks

(A key of the form "Is (*a an)" will match either "Is a" or "Is an.") In addition, there are 1/substitution keys like "Twice = 2*." The effect of that particular one is to substitute the symbols "2*" wherever the word "twice" appeared in the input text. Of course, the evaluator sitting behind ELIZA, so to speak, recognizes words like "SQRT," "LOG," etc. The function of this script is to interpret the user's wishes with respect to the evaluation of expression, perform certain translation functions on these expressions, and control the traffic between the input/output system of ELIZA and that of the evaluator.

Consider the dozen keys shown above. The sentence *"Let me try to define what the call of the sea means"* contains five of these keys. It could perhaps be understood by the DOCTOR but not by the program we are now considering. It would reply "I didn't understand you."

I call attention to this contextual matter once more to underline the thesis that while a computer program that "understands" natural language in the most general sense is for the present beyond our means, the granting of even a quite broad contextual framework allows us to construct practical language recognition procedures.

The present script is designed to *reveal*, as opposed to *conceal*, lack of understanding and misunderstanding. Notice, for example, that when the program is asked to compute the area of the ball, it doesn't yet know that a ball is a sphere and that when the diameter of the ball needs to be computed the fact that a ball is an object has also not yet been established. Appropriate questions are therefore asked. But when, later on, the area of

the globe is required, all the parameters are known and no questions are asked. The transcript also makes clear that the program now has memory and, of course, that it can compute.

I can imagine at least two questions that might have arisen in the mind of the reader in respons to the above material. First, but least important, is what role the kind of psychiatric program shown here has in serious psychotherapy. My answer to that must be that psychotherapy is not my field and that I have no intention to pursue any therapeutic implications of this work. It is clear that there is considerable psychological material to be exploited here, material that may conceivably lead to some therapeutic developments. There may also be some use in this kind of technique in simulation of the neurotic processes. K. M. Colby, a practicing psychoanalyst, does propose to use conversational   programs   as psychotherapeutic tools vis-à-vis real patients. I believe the unsolved technical problems in the computer realm alone are so enormous as to guarantee the postponement of the realization of such a goal for yet a very long time.

The second question concerns itself with the implications of this work on so-called teaching machines. Here I feel on much firmer ground. It is my belief that the kind of programmed teaching that is based on multiple-choice testing of the student is best done without the use of computers. With the techniques described here, it becomes possible to instruct the student in a corner of some field and then, the contextual framework having been established, to have the student interact with the machine in natural language.

The following conversation, based on a script written by Dr. Edwin Taylor of the Education Research Center of MIT, makes the point very well.

PLEASE CONSIDER HOW WE MIGHT SYN-
CHRONIZE TWO CLOCKS TO READ THE
"SAME TIME." ONE OF THESE CLOCKS IS

IN SAN FRANCISCO, THE OTHER IS IN NEW YORK. AS YOU THINK ABOUT THE PROBLEM, ASK ME ANY QUESTIONS THAT OCCUR TO YOU. WHEN YOU ARE READY TO PROPOSE A SYNCHRONIZATION METHOD, TYPE "READY." THEN I WILL QUIZ YOU ABOUT YOUR PROPOSED METHOD.

What do you mean by synchronize?

FOR THE PRESENT MAKE USE OF THE EVERYDAY MEANINGS OF SUCH PHRASES AS "SAME TIME" AND "SYNCHRONIZE." LATER WE WILL DISCUSS THE MEANING OF THESE TERMS MORE CAREFULLY.

May I use telegraph signals?

CERTAINLY, FEEL FREE TO USE TELEGRAPH.

Ready.

NOW I WILL QUIZ YOU ON YOUR SYNCHRONIZATION METHOD. DOES YOUR METHOD OF SYNCHRONIZATION INVOLVE THE PROPAGATION OF SOME SIGNAL—OR MATERIAL OBJECT—FROM ONE PLACE TO ANOTHER?

Yes.

WHAT KIND OF PROPAGATING SIGNAL OR TRAVELING OBJECT DO YOU PROPOSE TO USE?

A watch.

WILL YOUR WATCH MOVE AT A SPEED VERY MUCH SMALLER THAN THE SPEED OF LIGHT?

Of course.

GOOD. TRAVELING CLOCKS CAN BE USED TO SYNCHRONIZE DISTANT CLOCKS TO ARBITRARILY HIGH ACCURACY IF THEY TRAVEL SLOWLY ENOUGH. YOU MAY LEAVE THE PROBLEM BY PUSHING THE "QUIT" BUTTON TWICE. IF YOU WOULD LIKE TO EXPLORE FURTHER THE MATTERS OF PRINCIPLE ASSOCIATED WITH OTHER METHODS, CHOOSE ANOTHER WAY TO COMMUNICATE BETWEEN THE DISTANT CLOCKS.

WHAT KIND OF PROPAGATING SIGNAL OR TRAVELING OBJECT DO YOU PROPOSE TO USE?

Light.

WELL, OF COURSE THE LIGHT SIGNAL WILL NOT FOLLOW THE CURVATURE OF THE EARTH, SO LET US ASSUME THAT SOME SYSTEM OF RELAY TOWERS IS USED. NOW LET ME ASK, WILL THE LIGHT SIGNAL TRAVEL DIRECTLY BETWEEN NEW YORK AND SAN FRANCISCO OR WILL THE LIGHT SIGNAL TRAVEL TO OR FROM SOME INTERMEDIATE POINT?

It will travel from St. Louis in both directions.

IS YOUR INTERMEDIATE POINT EQUIDISTANT FROM NEW YORK AND SAN FRANCISCO?

Let's say it is, yes.

MY UNDERSTANDING IS THAT YOU EXPECT TO USE TWO SIGNALS AND THAT THESE SIGNALS WILL EITHER CONVERGE ON OR BE SENT OUT FROM A POINT EQUIDISTANT FROM NEW YORK AND SAN FRANCISCO. IS MY UNDERSTANDING ON THIS POINT CORRECT?

Yes.

WILL THIS PAIR OF SIGNALS CONVERGE ON THE INTERMEDIATE POINT OR BE SENT OUT FROM THIS POINT?

They will be sent from the point.

WILL THE TWO SIGNALS LEAVE THE INTERMEDIATE POINT AT THE SAME TIME?

Certainly.

AHA, I'VE GOT YOU. YOU ARE TRYING TO SYNCHRONIZE THE NEW YORK AND SAN FRANCISCO CLOCKS TO READ THE "SAME TIME." HOW CAN IT BE VALID TO ASSUME A "SAME TIME" OR THE DEPARTURE OF A PAIR OF SIGNALS FROM THE MIDPOINT?

Because the pair of signals leave from the same point.

RIGHT.

THE PHRASE "SAME TIME" HAS AN UNAMBIGUOUS MEANING WHEN APPLIED TO EVENTS THAT OCCUR NEAR THE SAME POINT IN SPACE. NOW YOU ARE GOING TO CONTINUE YOUR ARGUMENT BY SAYING THAT THE TWO SIGNALS THAT START FROM THE MIDPOINT AT THE SAME TIME WILL PRESUMABLY REACH NEW YORK AND SAN FRANCISCO AT THE SAME TIME. THESE SIGNALS CAN THUS BE USED TO SYNCHRONIZE THE NEW YORK AND SAN FRANCISCO CLOCKS. IS THIS THE WAY YOUR ARGUMENT WILL CONTINUE?

Yes.

ONE FINAL QUESTION? WHAT ASSUMPTION ARE YOU MAKING ABOUT THE SPEEDS OF THE TWO SIGNALS THAT TRAVEL IN OPPOSITE DIRECTIONS

That these speeds are equal.

VERY GOOD. YOU HAVE DEVISED A VALID METHOD FOR SYNCHRONIZING TWO

CLOCKS, ONE IN NEW YORK AND ONE IN SAN FRANCISCO. I AM NOW RETURNING YOU TO THE CTSS SYSTEM.

I have chosen to skew this discussion in the direction of "understanding" and have used that difficult word almost as if it were synonymous with "recognition." Actually, recognition is a prerequisite to understanding. The latter provides a test of the former. Even though no test of understanding can be defined with rigor, we do feel we are understood when the person we're talking to asks what we believe to be relevant questions and when he finally answers our question or solves the problem we posed. By such criteria, the conversations displayed above justify the assertion that the programs that produced the responses recognized textual patterns and understood what they were being told.

Finally, I wish to call attention to three pieces of work, two of which predate the programs discussed here and to whose authors I owe a considerable intellectual debt. The last is more recent but nevertheless highly relevant to my own current line of attack.

The SIR program of Raphael is capable of inferential data acquisition in a way analogous to that displayed in the ELIZA ball and sphere conversation displayed above. Notice that in that conversation the program had to infer that a ball was a sphere and an object. Once that inference was affirmed, the program retained the information by, in this case, associating with ball the fact that it is a sphere and an object and with sphere and object that ball is an instance of each, respectively. SIR is a program which specializes in establishing such relationships, remembering and invoking them when required. One of its principal aims was to establish methodology for formalizing a calculus of relations and even relations among relations.

Bobrow's program STUDENT is capable of solving so-called algebra word problems of the kind that are typically given in high school algebra texts. He uses a mechanism not very different from an ELIZA script. Its chief task is to transform the input text, i.e., the natural language statement of an algebra word problem, into a set of simultaneous linear equations that may then be evaluated to produce the desired result. A particular strength of his program is its power to recognize ambiguities and resolve them, often by appeal to inferentially acquired information but sometimes by asking questions.

The work of Quillian is mainly directed toward establishing data structures capable of searching semantic dictionaries. His system could, for example, decide that the words "work for" in the sentence "John works for Harry" mean "is employed by," while the same words appearing in the sentence "That algorithm works for all even numbers that are not perfect squares" mean "is applicable to."

Each of the computer papers referenced below represents an attack on some component of the machine understanding problem. That problem is not yet solved.

REFERENCES

1. Bobrow, D. G., "Natural Language Input for a Computer Problemsolving System." Ph.D. dissertation, Massachusetts Institute of Technology, 1964.

2. Colby, Kenn Mark, "Computer Simulation of Change in Personal Belief Systems," paper delivered in Section L_2, The Psychiatric Sciences, General Systems Research, American Association for the Advancement of Science Berkeley Meeting, December 29, 1965. *Behavioral Science*, 12, 1962, 248–53.

3. Quillian, M. R., "Semantic Memory." Ph.D. dissertation, Carnegie Institute of Technology, 1966.

4. Raphael, B., "SIR. A Computer Program for Semantic Information Retrieval." Ph.D. dissertation, Massachusetts Institute of Technology, 1964.

5. Rogers, C., *Client Centered Therapy: Current Practice, Implications and Theory*. Boston: Houghton Mifflin Company, 1951.

6. Weizenbaum, Joseph, "ELIZA—A Computer Program for the Study of Natural Language Communication Between Man and Machine," *Communications of the Association for Computing Machinery*, 9, No. 1 (January 1966), 36–45.

POSTCRIPT: HOW ELIZA PASSED THE TURING TEST*

In his article "Computing Machinery and Intelligence", Turing proposed a test to determine whether a machine could think. The test relies on the machine being able to fool a person into believing that a human–and not a machine–was controlling the typewriter on which messages were being exchanged. In the following anecdote sent to us by Dr. Daniel Bobrow of Bolt, Berenak and Newman, Inc., (and also published in the December 1968 newsletter of the Special Interest Group on Artificial Intelligence of the Association for Computing Machinery) the program ELIZA—described in the foregoing article—appears to have done just that! Of course this interpretation is made facetiously since the deception depended on the user's erroneous expectations more than on any sophistication on the part of the computer program. ed.

One Saturday morning about 9 A.M., a Bolt, Berenak and Newman, Inc. vice president in charge of selling our Telcomp commercial service arrived at our PDP-1 Computer Room hoping to be able to use the computer for a demonstration. He found a note on the PDP-1 teletype that read: "TYPE ALL MESSAGES INTO THIS TELETYPE, AND END THEM WITH A PERIOD." This note was left there by one of the programming bums who had just succeeded in making run a LISP version of the DOCTOR program (based on ELIZA as developed by Weizenbaum). However, the VP thought that this note indicated that this teletype was linked with the one in my home, since I often used the computer all night. Therefore, he started typing to "me," but in fact was typing to this version of the DOCTOR program. The following conversation ensued:

VP: DO YOU THINK THAT I CAN USE THE COMPUTER THIS MORNING?
Teletype Response: WHY DO YOU ASK?
VP: I MIGHT BE ABLE TO MAKE SOME ADDITIONAL TELECOMP SALES.
Teletype Response: WHY AREN'T YOU SURE?
VP: MY PERSPECTIVE CUSTOMERS HAVE NEVER SEEN A DEMONSTRATION OF THE SYSTEM.
Teletype Response: DOES THIS MEAN VERY MUCH TO YOU?
VP: OF COURSE IT DOES.
Teletype Response: YOU SEEM VERY POSITIVE ABOUT THAT.
VP: THIS IS RIDICULOUS.
Teletype Response: WHAT DO YOU MEAN THIS IS RIDICULOUS?
VP: IS THERE ANY REASON WHY I CAN'T USE THE COMPUTER NOW?
Teletype Response: TELL ME MORE ABOUT YOUR PERSPECTIVE CUSTOMERS.
VP: PLEASE DIAL ME UP ON 491–1850

Note that after the last remark the VP did not obey instructions, and left out the period. Therefore, of course, the computer didn't answer him. This so infuriated the VP, who thought I was playing games with him, that he called me up, woke me from a deep sleep, and said:

VP: Why are you being so snotty to me?
Bobrow: What do you mean why am I being snotty to you?

The VP angrily read me the dialog that "we" had been having, and couldn't get any response but laughter from me. It took a while to convince him it really was the computer.

*Z. W. Pylyshyn, *Perspectives on the Computer Revolution*. Englewood Cliffs, New Jersey: Prentice-Hall, 1970, pp. 347–348.

Cosmetic programming

FREDERICK G. WITHINGTON*

Let's face it: computers are repulsive to the layman, and the people who work with them only a little less so. Computer-based systems are symbolic of all that's objectionable about bureaucracy—their impersonality, rigidity and well-publicized propensity to failure suggest to the layman that he is a cog in a machine which at best depersonalizes him and at worst dismembers him. The people who develop computer-based systems, then, look to the layman something like dentists—apparently necessary, but untrustworthy and invariably pain producers.

Some of this distrust is probably inevitable, but clever people have discovered a number of ways to alleviate it. With a little extra effort in programming and system design an increasing number of organizations are applying "cosmetics" to the ugly face of the computer, making it appear considerably more attractive to the layman affected by it. It hasn't been done very often, because most organizations still have to concentrate wholly on getting applications to run on a "bare bones" basis—minimizing development time and cost with no resources to spare for unnecessary frills. Things are slowly changing, though, as increasing numbers of organizations complete their basic applications, acquire experience, and obtain more advanced tools. Fast-response systems, in particular, offer interesting possibilities for serving the user in a pleasing rather than just minimally adequate way. The purpose of this article is to catalog some of the ways in which cosmetics have successfully been applied to existing systems, in the hope that

* Frederick G. Withington, "Cosmetic Programming", Datamation, March 1970. Reprinted with permission of Datamation®, copyright© 1970 by Technical Publishing Company, Greenwich Conn. 06830.

readers will be able to apply them in new systems.

Four guidelines for beautifying computer-based systems are given, each accompanied by specific suggestions for its application. The list is not very original and is certainly not complete, but it may be useful as a stimulus to further thinking.

COMMUNICATE IN THE USER'S TERMS

In batch processing systems, the medium of communication between the computer and the layman is almost always a printed report or form, so any attempt to beautify the computer's face must concentrate on printed forms. In many cases they can be improved by more expanded layout, additional pre-printed information, and the use of color (very often at the cost of increased forms cost and increased processing time, caused by an increase in form length.)

Some cautious systems designers, conscious of the prejudices of high level managers, go to the extreme of having computer printouts completely retyped on more attractive paper with labels, explanatory information, and converted codes added. In addition to providing familiar nomenclature and a more attractive appearance, this enables the report to contain explanatory and expository material.

The computer could equally well print such text, but programmers rarely like to clutter up output routines with long alphabetic messages. The cost in memory space and printing time of lengthy alphabetic messages is not really very high, however, and many users would like to see explanatory material even if it is redundant and although they are supposed to know it already.

Users particularly object to the use of

numeric codes on forms instead of familiar alphabetic names or terms; the addition of a conversion in the output routine from internal codes to alphabetic identifications is often particularly welcome. Interestingly, the objection to the use of codes is found even among regular users who have become familiar with them and no longer have to look them up. Apparently codes are regarded not only as inconvenient but insulting: symbols of an implicit demand that the user subordinate his convenience to that of the machine. If full alphabetics are impractical, at least mnemonic codes (such as those used for stock symbols on the ticker) can be substituted for meaningless numerics.

In the on-line environment where a dialog takes place, many more interesting possibilities appear. As with forms, full alphabetic or mnemonic nomenclature can and should be displayed instead of numeric codes, and (on displays offering enough character positions) alphabetic explanatory data can be displayed.

The power of the on-line system also makes it possible for the user to "design his own output" by selecting among the programs' capabilities; again, it is important that this ability be provided in the user's own terms and in a language as close to English or to the user's problem-oriented language as possible. Most user's dislike pecking out input messages on a general-purpose keyboard and most (if not trained typists) distrust their ability to do so accurately. As a general rule, if the user is required to peck out a message it should be displayed before transmittal to the processing system so that he may verify its accuracy before releasing it. Better, the user should not be required to peck at all, and several convenient short cuts are available. The choices can be displayed on a crt, and selection made by means of a light pen. If a light pen is not available, an almost equally effective mechanism is to provide numbered function buttons corresponding to numbered lines on the display, each line containing the alphabetic identification of the function. Most simple of all, where the set of functions is limited, one can identify them by overlays on function buttons on the keyboard (and then display the identification of the function at the time the output is produced). These alternatives can be combined (e.g., function button followed by light pen); with these facilities of the on-line system available, it is truly a shame when the user is required to memorize and peck meaningless codes in order to obtain a system's services.

BE RESPONSIVE TO THE USER

With off-line systems it is not possible to be responsive in real time, but it is still possible to provide the user with responsive attention to his personal information needs. Turnaround documents are commonplace; it is easy to use them to allow the user a choice among the variety of information services available to him.

A familiar example to most of us is the turnaround premium bill stub used by most life insurance companies. Many provide boxes on the stub which the customer can check if he wants specific information about policy status, loan value, etc., or if he wants an agent to call. The labeled boxes, keypunched as one symbol, cause a specific subroutine to be called and a special output prepared. Better yet, if optical character recognition is in use the user's check-marks or hand printed digits (depending upon the device used) can be directly sensed by the computer.

When the off-line output is a management report rather than a customer transaction notice, other opportunities exist. The user can be provided with a simplified form of report generator, given specifications and a list of terms which he can use in identifying the rows and columns desired. When such a system is initiated all likely users can be sent a simple brochure describing the new service and the terms that can be used, plus a supply of blank forms. Such a service can be very popular; the manager has the pleasant feeling that the computer system is under his direct command, even though he has not been required to undergo the expected lengthy apprenticeship in its use.

More subtle problems arise when new forms of reporting are being developed that have never existed before, such as reports of product profitability or project status using new measuring criteria. Here the wise system designer will conduct a series of trials, providing the manager with sample reports and following up with discussions of their adequacy. In a series of half a dozen or more iterations a very satisfied manager can be produced. Not only is he obtaining an optimally useful report, but he is pleased with the responsiveness and service orientation of the computer people. These iterations can start well before the programs are in actual operation; dummy reports with sample data can form the first two or three rounds. The psychology of being responsive is probably as important as the improvement in service to the user. Both the customer receiving a transaction notice and the manager receiving a report are pleased by the appearance of responsiveness to their needs.

The user knows that the whole idea of on-line systems is to be responsive, so he becomes particularly irritated when they are not. Poor responsiveness is almost inevitable at times, because peak loads are often encountered at rush hours and few organizations can afford to so overdesign their systems that response time suffers no degradation at the peak. This is unfortunate, because it is at the very time of peak load that the people are under the most pressure and need the most responsive service—only to find the machine slowing down.

The most obvious solution is simply to spend more money for the systems in order to obtain better user satisfaction,

but this may be impractical. If so, several possibilities exist to at least make the user feel better about it. Above all, it is important, when a delay occurs, to acknowledge the user's request for service and inform him apologetically of the condition. It has been widely observed that people become restless and impatient after about four seconds have elapsed between their query and the appearance of the machine-supplied answer. The user instinctively assumes that the machine has failed or has somehow not noted his request; he is likely to uselessly re-enter the message (thereby adding further to the queue of messages and to possible system confusion). If there will be a delay, then it is important to acknowledge the user's message within about five seconds. This should not be difficult; often a polite and apologetic message can be emitted locally from a terminal controller or data concentrator upon receipt of a simple code from the central processor.

Most people are surprised at the idea that it is desirable to say "please" and "thank you," to be courteous and polite in the messages prepared for an on-line terminal. These are "no nonsense" systems, after all, designed at high cost to do a job with maximum efficiency. Concepts of courtesy and human relations are irrelevant to them—or are they? All of us know managers of the "no nonsense" school who are not going to use any more social grace than necessary in running their organization. Yet, almost without exception, such managers find it advantageous to employ some degree of courtesy. Apparently, where people are involved in a system, they work better if their interrelationships are lubricated by a film of courtesy. People are involved in a system supported by an on-line computer, so the same rule applies.

Another aspect of responsiveness involves being intentionally impolite —interrupting the user when he makes a mistake as soon as possible after its occurrence, rather than waiting for him to complete a long statement or message before informing him of an early error. This is a well-known source of user frustration in time-sharing systems; some complete an entire compilation pass before informing the user of a trivial grammatical error. Naturally many errors cannot be determined except in context or as a result of computation but a large class of them (grammatical errors in statement formulation, errors of omission in composing the headings of messages) can be immediately identified. Programmers rarely make the effort to incorporate this kind of responsive service in their systems, even though they themselves may have been irritated by its absence in other systems.

The professional is as ready to believe the machine has broken as the nonprofessional. If the system permits a programmer to initiate a long run from a remote terminal and provides no feedback until the final results are available, it is almost certain that the programmer will slowly develop a hollow feeling of doubt that anything is happening at all. It is merciful to design the system not only to acknowledge receipt of the initial request but also to issue periodic reports (perhaps every minute or so) simply reporting that progress is continuing and that faith should not be lost.

ACCESSIBLE, RESPONSIVE HUMAN BACKUP

People are infinitely variable and programs are not. It follows that no information system can ever encompass the variations of stupidity, confusion, and special requirements that its users may come up with.

This applies equally well to off-line and on-line systems: the turnaround documents specifying alternatives for an off-line system should always include a box saying "other" or "please have agent call," and the terminals should always have a button labeled "help" or the equivalent. This is easy enough to provide; the tough part is to provide enough competent people to deal quickly, courteously, and capably with the calls. This is expensive, but can be justified on the grounds that the dissatisfied user will call anyway, and sooner or later someone will be forced to deal with him. The ill will generated will be infinitely less if this is anticipated, and if an adequate number of properly trained personnel are made available in advance.

Organizations competing for the customer's business (such as insurance companies, banks, and brokerages) are generally most aware of this requirement and do the best job of satisfying it. In all three, the customer is encouraged to establish a personal relationship with one of the company's agents and to expect responsive, patient attention to whatever kind of foolish problem he may dream up. Such efforts are rarely made to help the users of an organization's internal system, but there is every reason why they should be.

Most important of all, perhaps, is the provision of such service in systems designed to have social value. The welfare recipient, the medical patient, the pensioner—even the taxpayer—may be assumed to have an absolute minimum of understanding of the procedures he should follow and of how the system works. Furthermore, his variations in requirements and their emotional importance to him are more extreme than in any business system. Such socially oriented systems should be the best at providing this responsive, accessible human backup. In the author's experience, they are usually the worst.

It is extremely easy to provide the hardware for such human service; all it involves is a telephone for the user to call. With on-line terminals further simplicity is possible; a "panic button" can cause a message (including identification of the terminal and the number of a nearby telephone) to be delivered to a human agent. A little fancier, but soon to be available, are computer-driven telephone line-switching units. With them a telephone set attached to the terminal can be directly connected by the computer to the agent who provides the service. The technology is not difficult or important; the critical problem is the availability of a sufficient number of informed, helpful people.

SEEK FAVORABLE PUBLICITY

If a new service is instituted that offers increased responsiveness to the user, that offers him a wider choice of alternative services, or that in any way seems likely to achieve good will, why not publicize this and take advantage of it? Computer people are rarely oriented toward self-publicity; perhaps this reflects a paranoia derived from having been beaten over the head so many times. (Who was it said that people who are disliked usually come in time to deserve it?) Public relations people are aware of the general public distrust of the computer and are usually delighted to capitalize on opportunities to inform the public that their organization has taken extra pains to accommodate human considerations in its system design.

Often a single telephone call to the public relations department of an organization will be sufficient to set in motion a publicity campaign which can be highly beneficial both to the computer people and the organization. This sounds like a cynical point of view, but if the system is really good, if the organization can really benefit from it, and if the result is likely to reduce the general disfavor in which computers are held, it is entirely proper that the word be spread as widely as possible.

These examples show that cosmetic programming is not so much a matter of specific technological tricks as of attitude. If programmers and system analysts put themselves in the shoes of their systems' users more often, there would be more cosmetic programming. It is not acceptable to take the attitude (as many do) that the subject is foolish or trivial; if all the talk about social responsibility is to mean anything, it behooves all computer people to cultivate such externally oriented attitudes.

Personal privacy v. the print-out*

Except for the very rich, physical privacy is rapidly becoming an almost unobtainable luxury. In today's crowded cities, the paper-thin walls of offices and apartments expose not only the quarrels of modern man but even his yawns. He is observed by hidden cameras when he shops. This year, 12 million U.S. citizens will face the possibility of a $100 fine and /or 60 days in jail if they refuse to answer certain questions about their income and job on the 1970 census. Although a developing body of law has begun to establish the rights and wrongs of wiretapping and bugging, modern technology provides Government agencies and others with ever more subtle and delicate means of surveillance. Legislatures and courts have hardly begun to deal with what may soon prove to be the greatest threat to man's "right to be let alone," as Louis Brandeis once described it. The threat is modern information-processing techniques, most notably that ubiquitous tool of post-industrial society, the computer.

* *Time*, February 16, 1970, "Personal Privacy v. the Print-Out." Reprinted by permission from *Time*, The Weekly Newsmagazine, copyright© Time, Inc.

MORAL CAPITAL

Political Scientist Alan F. Westin of Columbia University defines privacy as the right "to determine what information about ourselves we will share with others." In certain primitive tribes, people will not give their names to strangers for fear that they will thereby surrender part of themselves. Foolish as the custom may seem to modern man, it has a point: an individual's information about himself represents a large part of what Harvard Law Professor Charles Fried calls his "moral capital." Some of this information, by right and necessity, he wants to keep to himself. Some of it he will share with his family and friends, some he will admit—often willingly, often reluctantly—to the impersonal organizations he must deal with in daily life. Westin argues that an attack on a man's ability to control what is known about him represents a basic assault on his humanity; to the extent that it is successful, it limits his freedom to be himself.

What makes this trespass on self possible is the fact that a man's life today is largely defined and described by written records, many of which remain potentially available to outsiders. Schools take careful note of his intelligence and keep a detailed record of his academic achievement. His doctors have files on his health; his psychiatrist, if he has one, takes notes on his inner turmoil, his secret fears. Banks, credit-card companies and the Internal Revenue Service know almost everything about his income and financial status. Once he has ever served in the military or worked for a defense contractor, the Government knows a fair amount about his family and political associations. If he has moved recently, the storage companies have an inventory of his belongings. If he has ever been charged with a felony, the FBI probably has his fingerprints and often his photograph.

At present, most of this information is scattered over dozens of locations, divided among a host of different agencies. But what if, in the interests of national efficiency, the file keepers of the nation stored their separate masses of data in one gigantic computer bank? What if the recorded lives of millions of Americans were turned into an open book—or, more precisely, an open computer print-out, available to anyone who knows how to punch the proper keys? That, in fact, is what may happen in the next few years. Four years ago, a Budget Bureau task force recommended that the Federal Government establish a National Data Center for the common use of its many agencies. Under this plan, the Government's 3 billion "person-records" that have been compiled by such agencies as the IRS and the FBI would be consolidated and computerized.

Although Congress so far has been cool to the federal data-bank idea, it has appropriated funds to help set up limited versions of it in several states; in California, for example, all of the state's records regarding social service such as welfare, medical care, rehabilitation and employment are scheduled to be computerized by 1973. The data-bank idea, moreover, has already been put into being by private business. The life insurance industry has cooperatively established a firm called the Medical Information Bureau, which operates from unlisted offices in five cities, and keeps files on 11 million people who have applied for life insurance. The files contain, among other things, information on the applicant's medical condition, travels, driving record, drinking habits, and even his extramarital affairs. The 2,200 credit-investigating firms that belong to Associated Credit Bureaus Inc., together have (and trade) information on 100 million people who have applied for credit in department stores and elsewhere.

AGE OF EXHIBITIONISM

Americans offer surprisingly little resistance to surrendering information about themselves. Giving up personal details is regarded by most people as a fair trade for convenience. Shoppers who like the idea of buying something with checkbooks and credit cards can hardly expect to keep their financial resources or their spending habits a total secret. Even Hollywood's ageless glamour girls have to trade a birth data (although not necessarily the real one) for a passport. And convenient or not, almost everyone acknowledges the right of the Government to know a lot about its citizens.

Nonetheless, experts in the field of privacy fear that people have become much too indifferent about protecting personal facts that once were considered nobody's business. Crusading Washington Lawyer John Banzhaf III complains about the unseemly curiosity that investigators show in interviewing the acquaintances of prospective insurance and credit customers. Sample question : "Do you have any criticism of the character or morals of any member of the family?" But Banzhaf also puts part of the blame on an acquiescent public: "Isn't the consumer too willing to reveal personal details for a dubious credit advantage? Isn't there too little resistance to questions?"

In a sense, the modern willingness to surrender personal information may simply be another characteristic of an age that applauds exhibitionism and encourages communal experience. Patients who once confided their psychic secrets to an analyst in the privacy of his office now act out their problems and discuss them explicitly amidst group therapy. Among American Roman Catholics, private confession is gradually falling into disuse. Thousands of people have tried to escape from the impersonality of modern life by banding together in communes—a tribal form of society that rather drastically alters an individual's prospects of privacy.

That urbane pessimist, Henry Adams, believed that the dynamo in America had taken the place of Medieval man's Virgin as the symbol of power; very possibly, the unblinking, all-knowing computer may come to serve as the moral equivalent of a god figure in a world society of electronic tribalism. Nevertheless, legal experts in the field fear that Americans, in their blithe acceptance of technological inevitability, have failed to consider the broader implications of allowing information about themselves to accumulate so easily. One result is that it is becoming harder and harder for people to escape from the mistakes of their past, to move in search of a second chance. The creation of a national data bank could make it virtually impossible. Worse still is the danger of misinformation. An item of information wrongly added or omitted from tomorrow's total-recall data banks might ruin a reputation in minutes. Government and industrial prying into political opinions could produce a generation of cowed conformists.

MORE THAN REGISTRARS

Columbia's Westin believes that one vital way to save Americans from becoming the victims of their own records is to create laws protecting a man's "data being" just as carefully as present statutes guard his physical being. He echoes authorities as far back as Blackstone in contending that "the greatest single legal safeguard to freedom has been the writ of habeas corpus." Westin suggests the creation of a "writ of habeas data," which would guarantee that personal information held by the authorities would see the light of a courtroom before it could be used.

At the very least, an individual should have the right to view publicly-held information about himself and be allowed to correct errors in it. Technology's computer programmers are potentially far more than the ancient town registrars brought up to date. Before too long, some distant automated authority may know more about a citizen than the citizen himself. Inevitable, perhaps. But it is an additional reason why modern man fights ever harder for some space inside himself to call his own, beyond the encroaching outside world.

Legislation, privacy and EDUCOM

PAUL BARAN*

I have been asked to speak on the issues of legislation and privacy raised by the advent of electronic information-processing systems. I plan to cover the subject briefly and then address long-term implications, some of which are of specific interest to EDUCOM. During the last half-year, several excellent and comprehensive selections have been written on computer privacy; for example, Arthur Miller's article in the *Michigan Law Review* and Lance Hoffman's article in the *ACM Computing Surveys.* Add to this the earlier major works of Alan Westin and the consideration of the subject given in recent Congressional hearings. One who is interested is left with the feeling that there is little new to say on the subject.

Even with all that has been said, a solution to the problem of ensuring the privacy of data is still lacking. Like so many of society's complaints, this does not have an easy answer. Either some concepts of law and administrative procedures will have to be bent to accommodate the new problems of privacy, or we may have to develop new institutions —or possibly even learn to live without the level of privacy to which we are accustomed.

In this talk, whenever I speak of EDUCOM, I refer to it not in its present form, an academic consortium trying to live on a limited budget, but rather, I view it (or more likely one of its intellectual offsprings much further in the future) as a logical and evolutionary successor to the bricks-and-mortar university of today that could lead to a system of education much more removed from the accidents of geography and with lessened reliance

* Paul Baran, "Legislation Privacy and EDUCOM", *EDUCOM*, December 1969. Reprinted from *EDUCOM*, December 1969.

upon limited local resources and the immediate self interest of local administration.

The present university is undergoing increasing attack. Students today view the university as a set of local fiefdoms teaching irrelevant subject matter and keeping the students in line by requiring them to jump through exercise hoops. Yet, even the more radical students would agree that there is probably no current, workable alternative to the university—certainly, none which could survive. But, at a later date, if we do indeed separate the process of information flow from the bricks and mortar of the university, an alternate form of university education will be conceivable. Unlike the parents—the university, the child—EDUCOM is a very healthy concept; its hopes, however, will need time to materialize.

LEGISLATIVE EXPECTATIONS

Now that we have touched upon this subversive subject, the evolution of the successor to today's university, we are ready to return to the more specific topic of privacy and legislation. I would first like to review what help we might expect from the computer technologists in preserving personal privacy. Then I will review the National Data Bank concept and discuss how, by underestimating the intelligence of Congress and the electorate, it allowed itself to be misunderstood.

As I suggested a moment ago, however, the underlying message goes further than the issue of privacy. The early discussions on computer privacy were marred by simplistic thinking. Technologists, computer systems designers, and statisticians felt that the question of privacy was one for legislation alone. They did not recognize that although there is much that legislation can do, there is much that it cannot do.

Life has a way of being more complicated than that. For example, consider the flagrant, widespread advertising of bugging devices in electronic hobby magazines. Legislation was passed. The advertiser no longer proclaims the fun and profit in bugging your neighbor's mattress, but he does attempt to sell identical equipment as miniature electric baby minding devices: "Hear your child crying when he is down the street." The point here should not be misunderstood. In this instance, legislation has helped. The advertising is not nearly so flagrant, and there is less of it. This suggests that the bugging is less profitable, and hence fewer quantities in use. Some of the more insidious devices—the type used to tap a telephone on the other side of the continent—are no longer marketed openly. Now you have to do it yourself.

Another example concerns the move on the local level to try to keep files accurate by allowing students and parents to see and review their own records. What has been the response? Now we keep two sets—one to be subpoenaed, the other in abbreviated form to record the delicate data.

Laws are only fully effective against men who accept them. Those persons who disagree tend to regard them as merely another intellectual challenge. The police and the courts are up against two problems: First, the difficulty of ascertaining intent; Second, the ease with which a lawbreaker can conceal a breach of privacy. Thus, the criminal is not only hard to catch but also more difficult to convict.

OTHER METHODS OF SECURITY

Consider the commodity that is information. It is something that can be stolen and still be there. How intangible can a *good* be? In a domain where laws alone are of highly limited usefulness, we cannot take seriously the computer-system designers who shrug off the problem by asking, "Why doesn't somebody pass a law?" The computer people who wish to pass the buck to the lawyers have their counterpart in some non-technical souls who wish to pass the problem back to the computer people—"Why don't you simply design a foolproof computer file system?"

Enough has been said in the last few years about the difficulty of building foolproof systems and of the tricks to subvert such systems. One thing that stands out in reviewing this work is that the bulk of the useful contributions, publicly made, have come almost exclusively from those in the universities and the independent nonprofit organizations. The response to this problem by the commercial sector of the computer industry has been disappointing.

This experience suggests that researchers in the university and in nonprofit organizations can expect to continue carrying a disproportionate portion of the burden of developing both concepts and hardware for the preservation of privacy in future automated data systems. The last paragraph of Arthur Miller's recent major article, "Personal Privacy in the Computer Age: The Challenge of a New Technology in an Information Oriented Society," (*Michigan Law Review*, **67**, 6, 1969) contains a directed plea to EDUCOM:

Perhaps the most imperative need at this point in time is a substantial input of human resources to help solve the many privacy problems posed by the new technologists. The experimental laboratories exist—the federal agencies and many private organizations, such as the Interuniversity Communication Council, can provide the necessary structured context in which to test the privacy protecting capacity of hardware, software and administrative procedures.

I know that the fledgling EDUCOM is almost overwhelmed with things it might do. But this plea is one that I hope would be seriously considered for EDUCOM has a natural role to play here.

I do not mean to disparage the work presently being done by the commercial sector of the computer industry. They, too, have contributed in their hardware and software designs. As a matter of degree, one would have hoped that they pursued these issues diligently, and with less secrecy. This is an arena where silence is almost equivalent to irresponsibility, and some people act as if they wish to take the Fifth Amendment. In private discussions, I receive the following expression of position from a few of those who are publicly silent:

1. Talking about the problems of privacy in geographically distributed shared-information systems is not conducive to the sale of such systems.
2. We are still trying to meet initial advertising claims of equipment we manufactured several years ago. We have enough software problems without another major complication added to system design.
3. The problems of leaky system design are germane only to a few isolated systems that are carrying "touchy" data.
4. The customer doesn't want safeguards, and is not willing to pay for them.

These points are all well taken. The moral, however, is that we may be making as much of a mistake in expecting the computer manufacturers to straighten out the privacy problems as we have made in expecting automobile manufacturers to design adequate smog-control devices of their own accord and without prodding. Solutions to technological problems cannot be expected without a positive financial reward structure, which does not yet exist.

POTENTIAL ROLE OF EDUCOM

Of what significance is this to EDUCOM? The data EDUCOM presently contemplates exchanging appear innocuous. But let us return to the long-range view of EDUCOM as a major experiment in applying technology, in sharing resources, and in providing a major improvement in the flow of information among universities. EDUCOM is probably the organization that best appreciates the essential ingredient of higher education which is the *information* available and transmitted to the student, not the structure of bricks and ivy in which the student exists.

Any organization that still remains in the forefront of this information exchange business, even five years after its incorporation, is, in my mind, already an institution. As an outsider, I am probably in a better position to view what is happening. And if not a better observer, at least I am in a position to be less modest about it. While EDUCOM may be concerned with the seemingly great difficulties of coping with the most modest of information-sharing efforts, one on the outside can look at this in more global terms and visualize the eventual evolution of EDUCOM into an organization capable even of coupling the members of those "invisible colleges"—the men who share rough drafts and semi-personal research-data files.

Of course, there are other technical communications systems now in use —the professional and technical societies, for example. These efforts, however, tend to be restricted to individual and rather specific subject areas which are already recognized. Most of the important action takes place before a field is recognized as a field; therefore, EDUCOM is in a unique position to trigger a future universal /intellectual interchange.

Thus, I believe that EDUCOM, or a successor, or an off shoot responding to a series of pressures, may well be the nucleus of an electronically interconnected worldly university, one that might some day even move from the role of a consortium common servant to that of a conglomerate holding corporation in education—and all that this implies. Its position in the information exchange process could cause it to evolve from that of a communications channel to that of a *keeper* of the channel.

THE NATIONAL DATA BANK PROBLEM

If EDUCOM does move along lines anything like these, then it could find itself exposed to the public scrutiny that befits those institutions upon which society confers, even reluctantly, major power. With the vacuum of alternative institutions, EDUCOM could find itself in an expanded role, unprepared. And it could find its intentions as misunderstood as the proponents of the National Data Bank found theirs. Perhaps the analogy is strained, but I think that it is one that should be considered.

The original National Data Bank (wisely renamed two years ago as the Federal Statistical Data Center) was also to be a resource-sharing agency to expedite communication of statistics within the academic community. It proposed to gather together the thousands of existing magnetic computer tape records in various government agencies to create a new national information resource for research purposes. Its proponents sought to eliminate costly duplication of records and loss of historical data. They also sought to permit new uses for data: for example, it would permit researchers to build better models of our economy, allow a wider access to more data, and, by improving the data-collection process, increase the feasibility and accuracy of various analyses of social problems such as welfare.

The public outcry about the National Data Bank was triggered by a classic public relations mistake, one of the finest of the decade. The very presumptiousness of the name, "The National Data Bank," was almost enough itself. A more infuriating title could hardly have been found to arouse public anger. These

words were, at least in retrospect, ones that begged interpretation in literal terms: an image of a massive, centralized dossier file open to Big Brother or any of his alternative, incarnate forms. Whether the image was real or not proved irrelevant; image and reality become inseparable in dealing with the complex. The computer, to the public, is the epitome of complexity; the result—almost a predestination to public emotional violence.

The seething fears long accumulated in a continuous stream of blatant misuse of now computerized personal data files emerged. The formal name, "National Data Bank," was all that was needed to create a lightning rod to attract the bolts of legitimate outrage pent up in storm clouds of emotionalism. Of course, the problem had been with us for a long time, and it still is. But this was the first highly visible and tangible outlet for the complaint. The specific proposal, offered initially, had an Achillean Heel: its long-term implications. The original proposal was totally lacking in mechanisms to ensure the right to privacy of those individuals whose records were to be manipulated in order to derive statistics.

The dissection of the Data Bank proposal in Congressional hearings, particularly the analysis of the depth of thought that went into anticipating its long-term consequences, was both painful and amusing. It was a case where some otherwise erudite witnesses believed that they were dealing with unsophisticated Congressmen—always a bad mistake, but doubly bad if one hasn't done his homework. When questions were asked about privacy controls and the ease of misuse of the files, it was clear that the proponents of the system had not only neglected their homework, but they had tried to design the system details "at the blackboard."

The public press, sometimes more interested in attention-getting headlines than in a balanced presentation of complex issues, mishandled the subject. The Congressional hearings, which were much more balanced than their press coverage, set off a major and highly useful continuing public debate on the larger issue: "How shall we control the technological development of electronic information systems carrying personal data, balancing the attainment of the greatest efficiency in government against the price of minimum loss of personal freedom?"

This discussion goes on. No one has the answers, yet.

EDUCOM AND DATA BANK COMPARED

It is not possible to draw out a one-for-one analogy between the fate of the National Data Bank and the future evolution of what is now EDUCOM. But some points are worth thinking about:

1. Both are new institutions.
2. Both are new institutions whose need is increasing.

3. Both are academically inspired and seek to fulfill academic ends.
4. Both institutions can be highly centralizing in their control, although distributing access more broadly.
5. Both may have to live at the pleasure of the Federal Government, and could be regarded as possibly threatening to the historic right of freedom of choice, if subverted.
6. It is too early to see where either institution is going, or might go, in the long-term future.

EDUCOM, however, is evolving slowly. Even if it's just able to stay around as technology improves and needs increase, it is not inconceivable that time could thrust EDUCOM into a position with the major institutions in higher education.

I think that society has the right to ask, and EDUCOM the responsibility to answer, "What is your contingency plan for success?" "Where are we all going if you are completely successful in achieving your goals?"

The Unknown Citizen (To JS/07/M/378 This Marble Monument Is Erected by the State)

W. H. AUDEN*

He was found by the Bureau of Statistics to be
One against whom there was no official complaint,

* W. H. Auden. "The Unknown Citizen", *Collected Shorter Poems, 1927—1957.* Copyright © 1940 and renewed 1968 by W. H. Auden. Reprinted from COLLECTED SHORTER POEMS 1927—1957, by W. H. Auden. Reprinted by permission of Random House, Inc. and Faber and Faber Ltd.

And all the reports on his conduct agree
That, in the modern sense of an old-fashioned word, he was a saint,
For in everything he did he served the Greater Community.
Except for the War until the day he retired
He worked in a factory and never got fired,
But satisfied his employers, Fudge Motors, Inc.
Yet he wasn't a scab or odd in his views,
For his Union reports that he paid his dues,

(Our report on his Union shows it was sound)
And our Social Psychology workers found
That he was popular with his mates and liked a drink.
The Press are convinced that he bought a paper every day
And that his reactions to advertisements were normal in every way.
Policies taken out in his name prove that he was fully insured,
And his Health-card shows he was once in hospital but left it cured.
Both Producers Research and High-Grade Living declare
He was fully sensible to the advantages of the Instalment Plan
And had everything necessary to the Modern Man,
A phonograph, a radio, a car and a frigidaire.
Our researchers into Public Opinion are content
That he held the proper opinions for the time of year;
When there was peace, he was for peace; when there was war, he went.
He was married and added five children to the population,
Which our Eugenicist says was the right number for a parent of his generation,
And our teachers report that he never interfered with their education.
Was he free? Was he happy? The question is absurd:
Had anything been wrong, we should certainly have heard.

Justice, the constitution, and privacy data banks

SAM ERVIN, JR.*
UnitedStates Senator from North Carolina

Delivered in a series of discussions on "Computers and Privacy at Miami University," Hamilton, Ohio, June 28, 1973.

I am very pleased to be here to talk with you about Justice, the Constitution and Privacy as part of Miami University's series of discussions on the subject of Computers and Privacy.

A while back I decided that I had read a lot about privacy, but I didn't really know much about computers. So I took some time off from my duties at the Senate and spent a whole day watching computers in operation and learning how these machines work. I was impressed by the

*Sam Ervin, Jr. (U.S. Senator, North Carolina), "Justice, The Constitution, and Privacy Data Banks". Reprinted by permission of "Vital Speeches of the Day", published by City News Publishing Co.

multitude of tedious and difficult tasks that computers could perform in a fraction of the time it would take a person —and with no mistakes either.

In fact, I was so impressed by those computers—how meticulously and logically they could interrelate bits of information—that I thought about writing a Constitutional Amendment to allow a computer to become President. With its absolutely accurate and almost limitless memory, its infallible logic in relating one bit of information to another, and its superhuman speed, a computer, it seemed could make a perfect President.

But then I thought again. Certainly the computer would always come to perfectly logical conclusions. But what about conclusions affected by inspiration of the time it would take a person what about seemingly irrational decisions based on love of justice, or hatred or tyranny? A computer just cannot draw illogical conclusions from logical facts. I thought better of my Constitutional Amendment to make a computer President. There is something about human decision-makers for all of their mistakes and irrationality, which a computer simply cannot replace.

It seems to me that our system of democratic government depends at least in part on the uniquely human capacity of those who govern to come on occasion to what appear to be irrational conclusions. The ability to abandon logic for the sake of humanity and to insist that human existence cannot be reduced to even the most sophisticated of mathematical formulas is as much a part of our system as the Constitution itself.

This is not to say that computers are not extremely useful tools. They are. It is merely to point out that there are some tasks for which computers are simply not suited.

When we talk about the role which computers can and ought to play in governmental decision making, and the potential dangers computers pose to privacy, it seems to me that we are primarily concerned about the impact computerized information systems can have on individuals. We are concerned that the logical, categorizing processes of the computer will in some way run roughshod over our fundamental belief in the uniqueness and dignity of individual human personality.

It is, after all, the faith of the founders of this nation in the individual as a free and self-determining being that led them to set up our democratic form of government. Because of their faith in the individual, the framers of our Constitution took great pains to set up a system of limited government so as to maximize the protection of individuals from governmental interference. In order to guard against certain specific abuses of governmental power which would endanger individual freedom, the Founding

Fathers added the first two amendments to the Constitution, which we have come to treasure as the Bill of Rights.

The First Amendment was designed to protect the sanctity of the individual's private thoughts and beliefs. It protects the rights to speak and remain silent, to receive and impart information and ideas, and to associate in private and in public with others of like mind. After all, it is only by protecting this inner privacy that freedom of speech, religion, assembly and many other individual liberties can be protected.

The Third Amendment's prohibition of quartering soldiers in private homes protects the privacy of the individual's living space. This aspect of privacy is also protected by the Fourth Amendment's guarantee of "the right of the people to be secure in their persons, houses, papers, and effects, against unreasonable searches and seizures." In addition to the privacy of the individual's home and personal effects, the privacy of his person (or bodily integrity) and even his private telephone conversations are protected by the Fourth Amendment from unwarranted governmental intrusion.

The Fifth Amendment guarantees that an individual accused of a crime shall not be forced to divulge private information which might incriminate him. This privilege against self incrimination focuses directly on the sanctity of the individual human personality and the right of each individual to keep private information whicn might place his life and freedom in jeopardy.

The Fifth Amendment also guarantees that no person shall be "deprived of life, liberty, or property without the due process of law." This right to due process protects individual privacy by preventing unwarranted governmental interference with the individual's person, personality and property.

The Ninth Amendment's reservation that "the enumeration in the Constitution, of certain rights, shall not be construed to deny or disparage others retained by the People" clearly shows that the Founding Fathers contemplated that certain basic individual rights not specifically mentioned in the Constitution—such as privacy—should nevertheless be safe from governmental interference.

Just recently in Roe v. Wade the Supreme Court has located the right of privacy in the Fourteenth Amendment's guarantee that no state shall "deprive any person of life, liberty, or property without due process of law." Rights to give and receive information, to family life and child-rearing according to one's conscience, to marriage, to procreation, to contraception, and to abortion are all aspects of individual privacy which the courts have similarly held to be constitutionally protected.

To my mind privacy means more than merely restricting governmental interference in these specific areas. Someone has suggested that privacy is a catchword for the control the individual exercises over information about himself. And yet because such a definition focuses on the information rather than the individual, it seems to look in the wrong direction. Control over information is important to our right of privacy only when that information is related to us as individuals. In the end, privacy depends upon society's recognition and protection of the importance and uniqueness of each individual.

As chairman of the Senate Subcommittee on Constitutional Rights, I have over the years received many complaints about governmental invasions of individual privacy. In some cases, the government has intruded into the personal lives, homes and physical integrity of individual citizens in order to collect private information about them. In other cases, the government has used, or misused, such private information, and has disseminated it without the knowledge or consent of the individual citizen involved.

A while back it occurred to me that we did not even know how many data banks containing information about individuals the federal government has. So I wrote to fifty federal agencies and asked them just how many such databanks they have, what kind of information these databanks contain and who gets to see it and under what circumstances. Most of the responses are in a report that will be published later this year by the Senate Subcommittee on Constitutional Rights. So far we have received information on more than 750 databanks with varying contents, operational guidelines and the like.

The response we received earlier this month from the Office of Emergency Preparedness describes what must be the ultimate in governmental databanks. One of the databanks maintained by the Office of Emergency Preparedness contains records on some 5,000 individuals. But the Office of Emergency Preparedness does not know its contents and has no access to the information it contains. They just maintain it. Short of emergency circumstances the Office of Emergency Preparedness will never have access to this databank which is "utilized and kept current on a regular basis by authorized specialists in the Personnel Operations element of the White House staff. No other agencies or individuals have access to these files." So here we have a federal agency maintaining a databank to which it has no access the contents of which even the agency does not know. I have written to the White House to see if they can give us some clue as to what information is contained in these files and who has access to it.

Collection of information in governmental databanks is accomplished in a variety of ways. Some of it is obtained directly from the individuals involved. The Decennial Census is an example of this sort of data collection. Article II of the Constitution provides for an "Enumeration" every ten years so that Representatives can be apportioned among the states according to population. To make that head-count compulsory is perfectly alright. But nowhere does the Constitution countenance compelling citizens to respond on pain of criminal penalties to such personal questions as:

Do you have a flush toilet?
Have you been married more than once?
Did your first marriage end because of death of wife or husband?
What is your rent?
What is your monthly electric bill?
Did you work at any time last week?
Do you have a dishwasher? Built-in or portable?
How did you get to work last week? (Driver, private auto; passenger, private auto; subway, bus; taxi; walked only; other means)
How many bedrooms do you have?
Do you have a health condition or disability which limits the amount of work you can do at a job? How long have you had this disability?

To my mind, the use of the Federal criminal laws to force people to divulge such personal information, which bears no relation to any legitimate governmental purpose, is unconscionable.

Even worse, because of its lack of candor, is the Census Bureau's practice of sending out questionnaires on behalf of other government agencies. Theoretically, response to such questionnaires is wholly voluntary. But the Census Bureau's cover letters do not say that response is voluntary. Take, for example, a questionnaire the Census Bureau sent out at the behest of the Department of Health, Education and Welfare to retired persons. The questionnaire inquired into such private matters as:

How often do you call your parents?
What do you spend on presents for grandchildren?
How many newspapers and magazines do you buy a month?
Do you wear artificial dentures?
About how often do you go to a barber shop or beauty salon?
Taking things all together, would you say

you're very happy, pretty happy, or not too happy these days?

Although response to this questionnaire was voluntary, many, if not most, of the retired folks who received the official Census Bureau packet feared that they would be penalized if they did not answer.

I have in the past introduced legislation to control the worst of these privacy-invading questions. But unfortunately, bitter opposition on the part of the Administration, as well as state and local governments and private agencies which use Census information, has so far blocked passage of such controls. It is unfortunate, but true, that bureaucrats who collect information can always think up reasons for wanting to collect more and more of it. Those of us who are concerned about individual privacy face an endless battle in constantly pointing out that just because government agencies want information about individuals should not be sufficient reason for forcing people to provide it or face criminal penalties. That is why I am in favor of putting the shoe on the other foot —forcing the data collectors, such as the Census Bureau, to justify each bit of information they want to collect about us and honestly disclosing to each citizen that participation in many of these surveys is wholly voluntary.

One of the most disturbing aspects of governmental data collection is the use of surreptitious surveillance and intelligence operations to collect information on innocent citizens whose political views and activities are contrary to those of the Administration. Recent events have dramatized the disturbing prospect that such covert data collection may be even more widespread than we had feared.

Governmental surveillance can take many forms. Just recently, I learned that in cities from San Francisco, California to Mt. Vernon, New York, high-powered cameras have been set up to keep track of individuals and their activities. These cameras are so sensitive they can read an automobile license plate five blocks away. They can focus on an individual as he talks with friends and associates and can follow him as he walks down the street. They can peek through the windows of the homes of innocent Americans and record what is going on inside. It seems to me that this is the very sort of secret prying into the private lives and activities of individuals which bodes much evil for our democracy. These cameras represent the tools of tyranny and totalitarianism which seeks total control over the lives of individuals. They are, in my opinion, utterly inappropriate in a society which values the privacy and civil liberties of the individual.

I used to think that there could be nothing worse than this kind of invasion of individual privacy. But recently there has come to my attention instance after instance of the government's systematic invasion of the privacy of citizens who have done no wrong, but who disagree with the government's policies. Surveillance has become a kind of punishment for the exercise of constitutionally protected First Amendment freedoms of speech, association and press.

For example, in its continuing battle with the press, the Administration has resorted to this sort of systematic invasion of privacy in order to punish those members of the press who insist on criticizing Administration policies. Some of you may have heard about what happened to CBS newsman, Daniel Schorr. After a series of articles critical of the Administration, Mr. Schorr woke up one morning to find himself the object of a full-scale FBI investigation. On the specious grounds that Mr. Schorr was being considered for "possible federal employment," the White House had ordered a thorough investigation of Daniel Schorr, his past and present associations, activities, employment and the like. Friends, acquaintances, colleagues, employers and former employers were tele-

phoned and interviewed by FBI agents who asked about Mr. Schorr's character and patriotism, as well as his fitness for a position in the Executive Branch.

When I heard about what had happened to Mr. Schorr, I sought to find out from the White House just what high-level executive position purported to justify this apparently punitive surveillance of a newsman known to be critical of Administration policies and programs. First the White House announced that Daniel was "being considered for a job that is presently filled." A few days later the White House reported that Daniel Schorr was being considered for a new position which "has not been filled." In the end he was never offered any job by the Administration. The White House finally lamely announced that Daniel Schorr's name had been "dropped from consideration" and that the FBI investigation had been "terminated in the very early stages." According to the White House, the preliminary surveillance report, which was "entirely favorable", had been "subsequently destroyed." But the damage had already been done.

Daniel Schorr described the damaging effects of such surveillance on a news reporter in this way:

Even if the investigation had been set off by a tentative job offer, the effect, under the circumstances, had to be chilling to my work as a reporter. An FBI investigation is not a "routine formality." It has an impact on ones' life, on relations with employers, neighbors, and friends. To this day, I must manage a strained smile when asked on social occasions whether my "FBI shadow" is with me. It has become standard humor to inquire whether I am still "in trouble with the FBI," whether it is safe to talk to me on the telephone.

I am left now to ponder, when a producer rejects a controversial story I have offered, whether it is because of the normal winnowing process or because of my trouble-making potential. Even more am I left to wonder when I myself discard a line of investigation whether I am subconsciously affected by a reluctance to embroil my superiors in new troubles with the Nixon Administration. I should like to think that the government cannot directly intimidate me. But my employer, with millions at stake in an industry subject to regulations and pressure, is sensitive to the government, and I am sensitive to my employers' problems.

And Daniel Schorr's case is not unique. We have had reports of extensive surveillance, wire-tapping, and even burglaries perpetrated on other reporters.

When this sort of governmental prying into the private lives of individuals is used as a deterrent to the exercise of such constitutionally-protected freedoms, as freedom of the press, it involves a double evil: Not only is individual privacy invaded; that very invasion of privacy is used to punish or prevent the exercise of other rights.

Nor is this use of privacy-invading surveillance as a punishment for the exercise of cherished constitutional freedoms limited to the press. Early in 1970 we learned of an Army surveillance program which involved the use of Army intelligence agents to infiltrate and report on virtually every activist political group in the nation. This Army surveillance system collected information on both suspected violence-prone organizations and nonviolent, pacifist organizations and religious groups, whose memberships had committed no crimes. All these citizens had done was exercise their constitutional rights to criticize and speak out against governmental policies which they felt were wrong.

This Army surveillance program was the subject of extensive hearings held by the Senate Subcommittee on Constitutional Rights in 1971. We heard testimony from Army intelligence agents who had been ordered to infiltrate all groups protesting certain government policies. They told us about joining peace groups, about infiltrating religious, civic and campus organizations, about reporting on speeches, activities and classes in cities and towns right across the nation. They compiled detailed reports on the finances, sexual activities, personal beliefs and associations of all sorts of people, from famous celebrities to anonymous Americans.

Some of the surveillance reports were microfilmed and others kept in file folders. Some of the information was analyzed by special intelligence analysts and kept in a computerized file. Often with very little to go on but some vague political statements these intelligence analysts categorized each person's beliefs or status according to a special Intelligence Code, for the computerized file. For example, the number 134.295 indicated that a person was a non-Communist; the number 135.295 (a difference of only one number) indicated Communist party membership or advocacy of Communism. Since many of the persons who were being subjected to this surveillance and categorization were young people with no settled political philosophy and no organizational memberships, the potentialities for error were almost as great as the invasions of privacy involved in collecting the information.

Once the Constitutional Rights hearing exposed this Army surveillance program for what it was—a dangerous, privacy-invading deterrent to the exercise of constitutionally protected rights of free speech and association—the public outrage was so great the Army was forced to shamefacedly abandon the program. I have subsequently introduced legislation to prevent the use of military personnel for domestic political surveillance, to try to insure that this kind of systematic invasion of privacy does not happen again. We may succeed in stopping this one kind of surveillance program. But, like Hydra's heads, it seems as if two such surveillance systems replace each one we find out about and cut off.

I have just been talking about some examples of improper and reprehensible invasions of individual privacy in the collection of information, and the Executive Branch's use of such privacy-invading information collection to deter the exercise of other constitutional rights. But the difficulties with such data collection are not the only problems inherent in governmental data systems. It seems to me that one of the major drawbacks to the collection of information is the human temptation to use it, and in some instances, to misuse it, by giving it out to those who have no right or reason to have it.

On the most general level it seems to me just plain unhealthy for some master computer to keep track of every detail of our lives—our words and deeds, our mistakes and failures, our weaknesses and our strengths. Some experts in the field of information systems have suggested that massive data collection on every detail of each individual's life poses the danger of creating an "information prison" in which the individual is forever constrained by his past words and actions. What is lost in the process is the individual's capacity to grow and change, to define and redefine himself and to redeem past errors. There is something to be said for forgiving and forgetting, and for the opportunity to start anew. That chance for a new start is, after all, the reason why many of our ancestors came to this country—to leave past lives and past mistakes behind, and to begin building a new life all over again. It was that same sense of being able to leave the past behind and begin again that led to the development of the West—settlers moving away from old lives and starting again in the frontier where the past could not catch up with them.

That time is gone forever now. But it seems to me that this spirit of the frontier—that there will always be somewhere a man can go and start all over again, where he can redeem his past mistakes by hard work and good deeds—ought not to be gone forever. That is why I am opposed to the collection of any more information about individuals than is absolutely necessary. That is also why I am skeptical about the use of the Social Security Number, or any other universal identifier, to tag each of us for life with all sorts of data about what we have said and done in the past. It seems to me that there is much to be lost by locking individuals into their pasts or, to put it another way, by straightjacketing individuals in the dossiers of their past words and deeds.

We would do well to heed the warning of John Stuart Mill over a century ago that—

A State which dwarfs its men, in order that they may be more docile instruments in its hands even for beneficial purposes—will find that with small men no great thing can really be accomplished. . . .

If we do not heed this warning, there will come a time when records will become more important than the individual, when the uniqueness of each human being will be sacrificed to the false gods of convenience and efficiency, when the opportunity for individuals to grow and change will have been eliminated. We have not reached that point yet, but vigilance seems in order lest it come upon us unaware.

It is in this area of information storage and dissemination that the impact of computerization is perhaps most significant. It is therefore not surprising that the computers, rather than their operators, have often been blamed for many of the serious problems involved in the dissemination of information about individuals. The capacity of computers to find and print out great masses of information at fantastic speed has magnified the adverse, as well as the beneficial effects of ready access to this information.

To begin with, in those cases where the information is inaccurate, a computerized system makes that inaccurate information more easily available to more people in less time than was ever dreamed possible in the pre-computer days. When I think of computers grinding away, and spewing forth more and more information about American citizens at ever faster rates, I am often reminded of a surprising communication I received from the Social Security Administration several years ago. It was a notification to my beneficiaries that they were eligible for death benefits on account of my demise. It made me think of Mark Twain's remark that the "reports of my death are greatly exaggerated." I was rather amused at the time; but I later paused to think of all the other erroneous information government computers send out routinely every day—sometimes with rather serious consequences.

Some information can be very damaging to individuals whether it is accurate or not. Take for example arrest records or the narcotics users registries maintained by a number of federal agencies. The mere fact that an individual's name is recorded as a narcotics user or as having been arrested is often sufficient to deprive that individual of job opportunities, insurance, credit and many other important rights and benefits. Even worse, those individuals who have been branded as narcotics users or as having been arrested suffer this deprivation of rights and opportunities without a trial, without witnesses, without a chance to defend themselves—in short, without due process of law.

Much recent controversy has focused on what can and ought to be done to control the indiscriminate dissemination of arrest records. The federal government collects and computerizes such information in the National Crime Information Center run by the Federal Bureau of Investigation which in turn disseminates such information to all sorts of federal, state and local agencies. Not just law enforcement agencies, but employment, insurance, credit, and many other organizations are accorded ready access to this sensitive information. All too often, particularly in areas where police conduct general dragnet (or round-up) arrests of everyone in the vicinity of a supposed crime, these arrest records reflect no wrong-doing.

Many people feel that the fact an arrest has been made is a valuable piece of information. But we should remember that it only represents the judgement of one person—a policeman often acting on the spur of the moment on the basis of no more than strong suspicion that there may be probable cause to believe that the individual arrested may have committed a crime. No magistrate has reviewed that hasty decision; there has been no arraignment; and neither judge nor jury has established guilt beyond a reasonable doubt after a fair trial. Yet this preliminary judgement by a policeman can haunt a citizen for the rest of his life.

Most law-abiding citizens are tempted to take the complacent view: "Well, that could never happen to me." But do you realize that the men in this audience stand a 50-50 chance of being arrested sometime during their lifetimes? If you are a man living in a city, your chances of being arrested rise to sixty percent. If you happen to be black and live in a city, your chances of being arrested rise even further, to a whopping ninety percent.

Once your arrest is recorded, your chances of being arrested again are very great. The police have your name, photograph and fingerprints. You are on their list of potential criminals to be questioned about and rearrested for subsequent unsolved crimes.

Moreover, the potential adverse consequences of having an arrest record reach beyond the field of law enforcement. One survey in the New York area showed that seventy-five percent of the employment agencies in that area will not accept for referral applicants with arrest records. In addition to difficulties with finding employment, if you have an arrest record, you are likely to find getting insurance, credit and even a place to live extremely difficult.

All of this can happen to you without your having broken any law, much less having been convicted in a Court of Law. It seems to me that this sort of deprivation of rights, liberties and opportunities without trial is the very sort of abuse which our Constitution's due process guarantees were designed to prevent. The principle which is basic to our system of justice that man is innocent until tried and proven guilty seems to me to require stringent controls on the dissemination of information which can wreak such harm on the lives of citizens.

I have long been in favor of legislation which would restrict the dissemination by the FBI's computerized National Crime Information Center, or arrest records unaccompanied by some indication of the disposition of that arrest. In addition, it seems to me that even this information should be available only to those criminal justice agencies which can demonstrate that they need such arrest and disposition records in order to carry out their law enforcement duties. Other organizations, businesses and the like should have no access to this kind of information which can be so damaging to the lives and liberties of innocent citizens.

I am not for a moment suggesting that those who collect, computerize, and ever more widely distribute information on individuals, even damaging information such as arrest records, are acting out of ill-will or a desire to infringe the rights and interfere with the liberties of American citizens. I am certain that these officials feel that they are merely doing their jobs, which to them involve collecting the most possible information and making the widest possible use of it. The trouble is, human ingenuity is such that we can always think up reasons for needing to collect just one more bit of information. Once that information is collected some reason can always be found for sharing it with others.

When I think about these ever-expanding computerized information systems, I am reminded of Justice Brandeis' warning that—

The greatest dangers to liberty lurk in insidious encroachment by men of zeal, well-meaning, but without understanding.

It seems to me to be high time for those of us who care deeply about individual liberties to call a halt to this burgeoning information collection and dissemination, unless and until the consequences of such collection and dissemination on individual lives and liberties are taken fully into account. Otherwise, the ostensible need for this piece of information and that bit of data will gradually encroach on our privacy and individuality until our control over information about ourselves is forever consigned to computers.

Discussions such as we are having this evening about the impact computerized information systems can have on individual rights to privacy and justice under law represent an essential bulwark against such infringements of human freedom. Our consciousness of and concern about the potential dangers to our cherished liberties is the best, and in the last analysis, perhaps the only protection for our liberties. As the great jurist, Learned Hand once wrote:

Liberty lies in the hearts of men and women; When it dies there, no constitution, no law, no court can save it. . . . While it lies there, it needs no constitution, no law, no court to save it.

Computer war: Massachusetts bucks the trend

State Refuses to Join U.S.

Programs to Centralize
Criminal Background Files

ROBERT A JONES*
Times Staff Writer

Boston—As in many other states, the records of criminal offenders in Massachusetts are laboriously being converted for use in computers.

Soon the computers will produce the total of those parts of a man's life he would prefer to forget. The computers will never forget.

But in Massachusetts, unlike other states, technicians take the completed computerized records each night and lock them in a vault where, according to the processing director, "They are safe from those who would abuse them."

As Massachusetts sees it, the category of possible abusers has included the FBI and a whole host of other federal agencies, for the state has become the first in the nation to oppose an array of new federal programs designed to expand the government's computerized background files on citizens.

FBI DEVELOPING PROGRAM

The principle dispute centers on an FBI program now being developed that will contain computerized records of every person in the country who has had a "significant" contact with law-enforcement agencies.

Massachusetts has refused to join that program. It has also refused to grant criminal background information to other federal agencies, such as the Small Busi-

* Robert A. Jones, "Computer War: Massachusetts Bucks the Trend", Published August 17, 1973, *L.A. Times*. Copyright © 1973, *Los Angeles Times*. Reprinted by permission.

ness Administration, which the state contends have no right or practical use for such information.

In addition, the Massachusetts Human Services Department declined last month to accept $9 million in federal funds for drug treatment programs as long as such funds required the filing of extensive background information on each drug patient.

BIG THREAT TO SYSTEM

Gov. Francis W. Sargent has accused the new FBI program—known as the Computerized Criminal History file—of posing "one of the biggest threats to our democratic system—the invasion of one's privacy. We refuse (to join)—and we shall continue to do so."

In reprisal, the U.S. attorney in Boston has sued the state, asking the courts to force Massachusetts to turn over its records.

And in an apparent hope that economics will do what the courts may not, the Small Business Administration has threatened to withhold $30 million in loans and direct aid unless Massachusetts relents. Similarly, the Defense Investigative Service, an arm of the Defense Department that was denied access, has announced it is freezing 2,400 jobs in the state.

Sargent and other state officials maintain they do not oppose a computerized file of past criminal offenders, but that the system now being developed by the FBI violates citizen's constitutional rights and is vulnerable to abuse.

Although the FBI claims that the system will cover only "significant" or "serious" contact with law enforcement groups, state officials say those categories often include arrest without conviction, intelligence on "known" radicals submitted by local police, and offenses concerning homosexuality and failure to pay alimony.

In a letter to Atty. Gen. Elliot L. Richardson, Sargent wrote, "to be frank, recent revelations concerning the Department of Justice, the Federal Bureau of Investigaton and top government employees do not inspire confidence."

SERIOUS DOUBTS

"There are serious doubts that the internal controls and self-policing by line operating agencies or administration can guarantee the integrity of something as sensitive and potentially abusive as . . . national criminal information computer system."

The National Crime Information Center (NCIC) which operates the FBI computer systems was authorized to develop the computerized criminal history file in 1970 by then Atty. Gen. John M. Mitchell.

At present the computerized Criminal History file is operating on a marginal basis. Only six states—California, New York, Illinois, Arizona, Pennsylvania and Florida—and Washington, D.C.—have been wired into the system. Within two years, however, plans call for the inclusion of all 50 states.

The system will represent a mammoth enlargement of the NCIC's computer program. At present the NCIC maintains a national registry of wanted persons and an additional file of stolen property, including firearms, negotiable securities, and automobiles.

PAST OFFENDERS

According to an NCIC spokesman, the new file on past offenders will contain many times more entries than all the present files combined.

In approving the program, Mitchell overruled the recommendations of the federal Law Enforcement Assistance Administration, which advocated a "decentralized" system, whereby each state would maintain its own files, allowing or denying access to law enforcement agencies of other states.

Under the centralized version, each state virtually relinquishes control of its information when it "hooks up" to the federal system. Once in the data bank, the state's information will be available to any of the 45,000 computer terminals planned throughout the country. By 1978, three years after it becomes fully operational, plans call for the system to contain 8 million files.

CENTRAL ISSUE

The availability of such information to persons or organizations outside the category of law enforcement is the central issue dividing Massachusetts and the federal government.

The NCIC routinely allows access to the information by federally insured banks, by private employers with defense or other federal contracts, by some federal agencies outside law enforcement, by many state agencies, and by private employers with state contracts.

Although NCIC regulations governing the system discourage use by non-law enforcement agencies, control of access to the information is effectively governed by whoever operates the terminals located in each states. Thus, if officials in, say, South Carolina, wish information on a person who previously lived in California, they need only ask the computer. NCIC regulations are not legally binding on the states, and most states do not have local laws governing access to such computer files.

WEAKEST LINK

"The system is only as strong as its weakest link, and that's what scares me," said Andrew Klein, special assistant to Sargent.

Such dissemination of information has also led the state into a legal battle with the federal Department of Health, Education and Welfare, which recently began a new program of collecting background information on patients in federally funded drug programs.

Called the Client Oriented Data Acquisition Process (CODAP), the program was required by HEW if states were to receive federal funds. In Massachusetts, such funding amounts to $9 million.

In the Boston area, many of the 14,000 patients in the program are youths. "We were afraid these kids would be branded for life once the federal government got the information in their data banks. So we didn't do," said Marjorie Elzroth, manager of the Massachusetts Drug Abuse Prevention Council.

MEDICAL RESEARCH

Federal officials say the CODAP forms do not require the person's name and contend the information will be used only for medical research.

But Mrs. Elzroth counters that the forms do require enough information to effectively identify a person, including his mother's name, his date of birth, zip code and a "client identifier" number.

"I wouldn't be surprised at all to see the CODAP people wind up in the FBI's files," Mrs. Elzroth said.

The possible linkage of information from different programs has led state officials to view the situation as a collective effort to compromise the privacy of Massachusetts' citizens.

MORE DESIRABLE

As such information becomes more centralized, they say, it becomes more desirable to a diverse group of public and private organizations who could use it.

"Say you're a policeman and you moonlight for a department store as a security guard. The department store has some

prospective employees it wants to run checks on. You go down to the station and request the checks. That's all there is to it," says Arnold Rosenfeld, director the Massachusetts Law Enforcement Commission.

Such "secondary" access would also be available to most of the large credit rating associations throughout the country. Rosenfeld said, "Every one of them knows a friendly cop somewhere."

In addition, argues Rosenfeld, such computer-supplied information is assumed to be correct, but often it is not.

WRONG INFORMATION

"The department store or other private employer may be getting information that is outdated or dead wrong. It happens all the time, but people named by the computer suffer nonetheless," he said.

Massachusetts officials cite the case of David Harkness, a Marine veteran who was arrested in Iowa on a routine traffic charge last May. A check through the NCIC computer showed he was wanted as a deserter.

Harkness was not a deserter; he had been discharged from the Marines a day before. Although he was once charged with being AWOL, the case had long since been closed.

Nonetheless, Harkness was held in an Iowa jail until the error was discovered.

This month Sargent received a letter from Alan Winslow of Auburndale, Mass., who wrote of a "scary thing" that happened last spring. "A relative of mine got a job as a deputy sheriff. One bored night, on dispatcher duty, he ran his family through the National Crime Information Center.

"Ten out of 11 of us were there. His mother was listed because when she was 18, neighbors complained of a noisy sorority party. (No arrests.)

"His stepfather, a respected businessman, was listed because he complained to the police that he had received a bad check.

"Ten out of 11 of us! No criminal conduct. No criminal record. But we are on the files of NCIC."

Massachusetts officials argue that such information can damage persons merely because they are grouped with others assumed to be of a criminal nature.

NO CONVICTION

"It's guilt by association," said Klein, the governor's aide. "The worst parts are the arrests without conviction. A man gets arrested for, say, car theft. The charges are dropped because he didn't do it, but years later the computer churns out the arrest, and people assume guilt."

NCIC officials argue that safeguards have been built into the system guaranteeing protection of privacy.

Although they concede that most states will supply arrest records to the computer whehher or not a conviction is obtained, they maintain that follow-up entries indicate guilt or innocence in each case.

As for the accessibility of the computer information to groups not associated with law enforcement, NCIC officials pass responsibility along to the states, which will govern the use of terminals connected to the system.

RIGHT TO CHALLENGE

If the information on any individual is incorrect, they say, that person has the right to challenge the file and have it corrected.

But a petition submitted on Aug. 3 by Gov. Sargent and Sen. Edward W. Brooke (R-Mass.) called the NCIC regulations "wholly unenforceable, relying on the "good faith" efforts of the individual states.

In many cases, the petition declares, states do not follow arrest records with additional information "thereby leaving the file replete with arrests that did not result in conviction, or even prosecution, but which are not so designated."

California records in 1962 indicate, the petition says, that of 750,000 persons arrested, 570,000 had no action taken against them. "This means that for a single year in a single state, there are 570,000 innocent people bearing the burden of possessing an arrest record."

CALIFORNIA FILES

California officials say they have presently transferred 100,000 criminal history files to the NCIC, including arrests without convictions. When conversion of present records is complete, they say, California will have contributed 1.2 to 1.5 million files.

The petition, which was also signed by Reps, Barry Goldwater, Jr. (R-Calif.), Michael J. Harrington, (D-Mass.) and Sen. Harold E. Hughes (D-Iowa), asked Atty. Gen. Richardson to set regulations that would effectively guarantee citizens' rights of privacy.

The petition also challenges the government's claim that individuals have the right to examine and correct their own file.

Referring to a letter sent by the late FBI director, J. Edgar Hoover, stating that his agency did not oppose such examination if ordered by the courts, the petition states "one . . . concludes that filed subjects cannot get access to their records without the force of a court order behind them."

WILLING TO JOIN

Massachusetts officials say they would be willing to join the federal system if safeguards are enacted similar to those now in force in their state.

Passed last year, the Massachusetts legislation established a civilian board to govern the state's own criminal history file. In all other states computer files are controlled by police agencies.

Other regulations forbid the inclusion of arrest records unless such action resulted in a conviction. The law limits access to law enforcement agencies and other government bodies specifically granted such access by law.

In addition, the law states "each individual shall have the right to inspect . . . and copy criminal offender information which refers to him." If inaccuracies are discovered, the law requires deletion or correction.

Within Massachusetts, the results of the legislation have been dramatic. Thousands of requests from organizations for backgrounds on individuals have been denied.

The list of those denied access include:

—Five large Boston banks which sought information for credit and hiring.
—Recruiters for the Army, Navy, Coast Guard and Air Force, which sought information on recruit applicants.
—The State Department of Public Welfare, for background of applicants.
—The Retail Credit Corp., a nation-wide service that performs credit checks for banks and credit card issuers.
—The Department of Defense and the Small Business Administration, which, when denied access, filed suit through the U.S. Attorney's office.
—Gov. Sargent's office.
—Various security companies, insurance companies, and unlikely organizations such as the Jewish Big Brothers Assn., and the Nazareth Child Care Center.

GRANTED ACCESS

"A year ago, almost all of those people would have been granted access to the files," said Rosenfield. "And it's our guess that they still have that access in other states."

NCIC director Norman Steltz said his agency had no plans to recommend federal legislation similar to the Massachusetts model.

"We believe our present regulations are strict, but we would not oppose additional control," he said.

Last week, however, Massachusetts won the first round in the computer war when the Department of Health, Education and Welfare retreated from its requirement that federally funded drug patients supply background information.

After letters of protest from Sargent, Boston Mayor Kevin H. White and a host of other officials and considerable publicity in the Boston area, the department agreed to fund the drug program in spite of Massachusetts refusal to fill in background information forms.

"This may get things rolling our way," said Mrs. Elzroth. "If HEW withdraws the program here, I don't see how they can continue to push it in other states. If they do, I don't think those states will let them get away with it."

How to guard the innocent in FBI files

Staff Writer of *The Christian Science Monitor**

* Robert M. Press, "How to Guard the Innocent in FBI Files", *The Christian Science Monitor*, August 8, 1973. Reprinted by permission from *The Christian Science Monitor*. Copyright © 1973 The Christian Science Publishing Society, all rights reserved.

Boston

More controls are on the way for a nation-wide, FBI-run computer system that by 1988 may have case files on some eight million people.

But two states—Massachusetts and Iowa—have complained about the lack of safeguards. Massachusetts is refusing to join the system until more precautions are written into federal law.

Already six states have "plugged in" to the national system, but so far there are few controls on how the records are used.

There is no guarantee, for example, that a person arrested will ever have his record cleared if he is not convicted.

Neither are there guarantees that the criminal records will not be available to prospective employers, credit agencies and other groups not directly involved in law enforcement.

But legislation signed by President Nixon Aug. 6 contains a requirement that adequate safeguards on use of the records be established. U.S. Attorney General Elliot L. Richardson promises to propose legislation soon to set up those safeguards.

By 1975, the FBI predicts, all 50 states will be feeding state-gathered criminal records in the National Crime Information Center in Washington, D.C. The system is designed to help lawenforcement officials to do their job.

The NCIC offers this case example of how the system is meant to work.

A deputy sheriff in Missouri stopped a man who reportedly has just passed a forged $50 traveller's check. When data on the man's vehicle was transmitted to the NCIC computer center, a reply came back within seconds that the car had been stolen in Indiana. Another query to the NCIC, after the man had given his correct name, showed he was wanted in St. Louis for a postal violation.

But the system doesn't always work the way it was intended.

One case reported in a recent issue of *Computerworld*, a newsweekly, is that of ex-Marine David Harkness.

OUT-OF-DATE DATA

He was arrested in May on a traffic violation but later told he could go home if he paid a fine. Before he could so do, however, he was told by an officer that he was listed as AWOL from the Marines.

In June 1972, he had been arrested on an AWOL charge because of the same computer data. In fact, he had been disciplined in the Marines for being AWOL but had been discharged in May 1972.

"Every, time he gets a job he loses it mysteriously," his father, David S. Harkness, told the Monitor. The state has certain safeguards but the national apparently does not, he said. He thinks the job problems are related to the AWOL charge, which remains on the FBI file.

But argue some employers, a company or government agency needs to know about a man's past criminal history. If a man is hired to work in a bank, the bank wants to know if he has been convicted of forgery, for example.

COURT RECORDS PUBLIC

Court records are public, and available to those who know how to dig them out case by case from courthouse records. But a full listing of a man's criminal record—regardless of which state he might have been convicted in—would not be available if NCIC adopts the kinds of "safeguards" Massachusetts uses.

Massachusetts law prohibits any agencies outside the criminal justice system to view a person's computer-stored criminal records. Since the law went into effect Jan. 1 this year, the state has refused more than 70 requests from government or private agencies or companies to see individual criminal records.

Meanwhile, a petition filed Aug. 3 to Mr. Richardson and Clarence Kelley, FBI, for Massachusetts-type safeguards for NCIC and for NCIC rules to be published.

Along with Gov. Sargent, petition signers include Sen. Edward W. Brooke (R-Mass.), Rep. Barry M. Goldwater, Jr. (R-Calif.), Sen. Harold E. Hughes (D-Iowa), The American Civil Liberties Union, the American Friends Service Committee, and others.

NCIC—A tribute to cooperative spirit*

Great progress has been made by NCIC since it began in January 1967. The first operations involved 15 law enforcement agencies and one FBI field office. Instead of the present 24-hour-a-day operation, NCIC pulsed to life in a pilot or testing phase of 2 hours a day and gradually increased to the current schedule.

Initially there were five computerized files: wanted persons, stolen vehicles, license plates, firearms, and stolen identifiable articles. The original data base contained 23,000 records. In 1968 a securities file was added, and the vehicle file was expanded to include aircraft and snowmobiles. In 1969 further cognizance was taken of changes in the vehicles mode by recording stolen dune buggies. Also, in 1969 a boat file was implemented.

Commputer hardware needs for NCIC were not as demanding in 1967 as they are today. The beginning data base was relatively small because the NCIC Working Committee wisely restricted file entries to current and validated manual records. Initially NCIC operated with an IBM 360 Model 40 processor containing 128K bytes of core, 2311 disk storage devices, and 2702 transmission control units. In September 1968 this configuration was changed to an IBM 360/50 processor with 512K bytes of core, 2314 disk storage devices, and 2703 transmission control units.

The original network of 15 law enforcement control terminals and one FBI field office has expanded to 102 law enforcement control terminals and to terminals in all FBI field offices, providing NCIC service to all 50 states, the District of Columbia, and Canada. From the beginning a control terminal has been

defined as a State agency or large core city operating a metropolitan area system which shares with the FBI the responsibility for overall system discipline as well as for the accuracy and validity of records entered in the system.

The first computer-to-computer interface was with the California highway patrol in April 1967. The tie-in of the St. Louis, Mo., Police Department computerized system soon followed. These events marked the first use of computer communications technology to link together local, State, and Federal Governments in an operational system for a common functional purpose.

As of January 1972, the NCIC system interfaced with 48 computers of electronic switches representing 31 State agencies and 17 metropolitan area systems and with manually operated terminal devices in the remaining control terminal locations. These links provide on-line access to NCIC for 6,000 law enforcement agencies in the United States and Canada. This immediate access makes information in the national file available within seconds of an inquiry. The original goal of NCIC to serve as a national index and network to 50 central State computerized information and communication systems is well within reach. (See NCIC network map.)

Whereas the original communications network was made up of a little over 5,000 miles of low-speed (150 baud) lines, the current design includes voice grade (2400 baud) lines between NCIC and nine regionally located multiplexing centers. From these centers, 150 baud lines extend to those control terminals still operating with low-speed equipment. Most control terminal computers interface directly with the NCIC through 2400 baud lines, and the remaining low-speed users are gradually converting to

* "NCIC A Tribute to Cooperative Spirit", *FBI Law Enforcement Bulletin*, February 1972

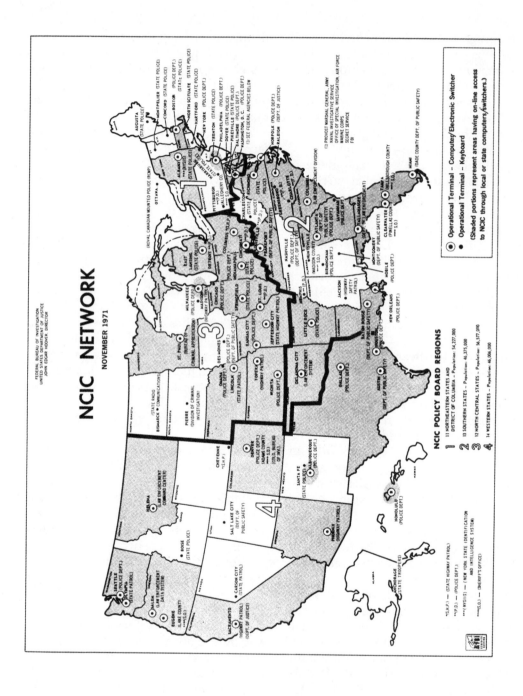

NCIC NETWORK

NOVEMBER 1971

FEDERAL BUREAU OF INVESTIGATION
UNITED STATES DEPARTMENT OF JUSTICE
JOHN EDGAR HOOVER, DIRECTOR

NCIC POLICY BOARD REGIONS

1   11 NORTHEASTERN STATES AND DISTRICT OF COLUMBIA — Population: 54,227,000

2   13 SOUTHERN STATES — Population: 46,375,000

3   12 NORTH CENTRAL STATES — Population: 56,577,000

4   14 WESTERN STATES — Population: 46,606,000

(S.H.P.) — (STATE HIGHWAY PATROL)
(P.D.) — (POLICE DEPT.)
(NYS11S) — (NEW YORK STATE IDENTIFICATION AND INTELLIGENCE SYSTEM)
(S.O.) — (SHERIFF'S OFFICE)

● Operational Terminal — Computer/Electronic Switcher

● Operational Terminal — Keyboard

(Shaded portions represent areas having on-line access to NCIC through local or state computers/switchers.)

(1) PROVOST MARSHAL GENERAL, ARMY
NAVAL INVESTIGATIVE SERVICE
OFFICE OF SPECIAL INVESTIGATION, AIR FORCE
MARINE CORPS
SECRET SERVICE
FBI

the faster transmission speed as they develop their own on-line systems.

INCREASED USAGE

The communications lines are provided by the Western Union Telegraph Co. and are fully dedicated to system use; that is, there is no operational dial-up access to the NCIC computer. With regard to communications, the FBI assumes all costs up to and including the modem at the control terminal site. There is no charge made to participants for system use.

The year 1967 was one of trial, change, and growth for NCIC. By the close of that first year, however, the system was handling 15,000 transactions a day. Table 1 discloses NCIC growth in message traffic or system use for the years 1968 through 1971. Traffic is measured in terms of computer transactions, i.e., an entry of a record, inquiry, clearance of a record, and so forth. In each transaction there are two messages, one from a terminal to the NCIC computer and the second a response from NCIC to the terminal.

Total yearly transactions from 1969 through 1971 increased from 7 million to 25.1 million; inquiries from 3.3 million to 14.4 million. This sharp increase in system usage is due to three factors: (1) the rapid development of State and metropolitan area systems which provide on-line access to thousands of police agencies; (2) user education whereby police officers and investigators increas-

ingly make greater use of the system for routine purposes and develop new field techniques for better use of the system, i.e., checks of traffic violators, out-of-State vehicle registrations, and so forth; and (3) addition of new file applications, such as the securities file. However, the latter, although the largest file in NCIC in terms of volume of active records, has yet to approach expected system use in terms of inquiry. Optimum use of the securities file will only result from closer cooperation between the financial /securities industry and law enforcement.

Another way to measure the growth of NCIC is by its rapid buildup of active records. This is shown in Table 2 depicting growth from December 1967 to December 1971. This file growth was accomplished primarily by on-line NCIC system entries. One major exception was a batch load of stolen U.S. Treasury security issues entered by the U.S. Secret Service in 1969. File growth is, of course, influenced by periodic administrative purges, whereby records are automatically removed from the active file based on an established timespan of usefulness

MAINTAINING ACCURATE FILES

While on-line clearance or cancellation of records by the entering agency is the primary means of maintaining the files in an up-to-date condition, NCIC supplies users with information concerning their records for review on a continual basis.

TABLE 1.   National Crime Information Center, Annual Transactions, 1968–1971

	Entries	Inquiries	Clears	Other	Yearly total	Daily average
1968	923,000	3,274,688	400,036	2,427,373	7,025,097	19,194
1969	1,351,095	7,844,670	541,348	3,849,267	13,586,380	37,223
Percent increase over 1968	46.4	139.6	35.3	58.6	93.4	93.9
1970	1,632,749	11,515,851	580,416	5,901,217	19,630,233	53,781
Percent increase over 1969	20.8	46.8	7.2	53.3	44.5	44.5
1971	1,887,564	14,364,308	664,148	8,187,063	25,103,083	68,776
Percent increase over 1970	15.6	24.7	14.4	38.7	27.9	27.9

TABLE 2. National Crime Information Center, File Growth, 1967–1971 [a]

	Total records	Wanted persons	Stolen vehicles	Stolen license plates	Stolen firearms	Stolen articles	Stolen securities	Stolen boats
December, 1967	346,124	18,676	130,304	31,118	121,245	44,781		
December, 1968	743,950	30,082	246,640	81,800	191,371	141,107	52,950	
Percent increase over 1967	114.9	61.1	89.3	162.9	57.8	215.1		
December, 1969	1,447,148	50,913	393,156	146,819	254,085	319,763	281,554	858
Percent increase over 1968	94.5	69.2	59.4	79.5	32.8	126.6	431.7	
December, 1970	2,453,662	77,118	584,894	208,352	343,220	513,373	724,326	2,379
Percent increase over 1969	69.6	51.5	48.8	41.9	35.1	60.5	157.3	177.3
December, 1971	3,330,220	114,497	755,879	252,735	441,591	715,444	1,045,629	4,445
Percent increase over 1970	35.7	48.5	29.2	21.3	28.7	39.4	44.4	86.8

[a] 12-1-67 through 12-1-71

Printouts of each agency's records are sent to the agency via the control terminal for validation. The wanted persons and stolen vehicle records are forwarded every 90 days while other property files are subject to an annual validation. During the periods between validations, FBI personnel at NCIC review records on file for completeness and accuracy. Any deficiencies noted in a record are brought to the attention of the entering agency through the control terminal. In addition to correcting the deficiency, the agency again has a chance to verify that the record should remain on file.

Off-line computer programs check each record to determine if it is in strict compliance with national standards, and the results are furnished to the entering agency. Tabulations are maintained indicating, by control terminal, the number and type of deficiencies. NCIC periodically reviews the tabulations and sends to any control terminal having a large number of deficiencies a letter pointing out areas wherein additional training may be needed.

Obtaining a true measurement of the cost effectiveness of the NCIC and its related systems (State and metropolitan area computer /communications networks) is difficult, as the benefits derived include a number of intangibles as well as the more obvious results. Probably the most impressive NCIC statistic is the rapidly increasing number of "hits," a term applied to those instances where a record received in response to an inquiry indicates the subject is a wanted fugitive or the item or property in question is stolen. Many of these "hits" have been set forth in the monthly NCIC Newsletter or similar monthly publications by State systems, such as those in New York, Arizona, and Pennsylvania. Many also have appeared in the news media and need no repeating here.

SUCCESSFUL "HITS"

In January 1968, with a year's operating experience, the system was averaging 275 interjurisdiction "hits" a day. It was obvious the "hits" obtained were inspiring increased system usage. At the time of this writing, the number of such "hits" per day averages approximately 700, a dramatic increase over the 1968 number.

The National Crime Information Center (NCIC) of the FBI: Do we want it?

STANLEY ROBINSON*

The FBI's computerized National Crime Information Center (NCIC) should be a

* Stanley Robinson, "The National Crime Information Center (NCIC) of the FBI: Do We Want It?" Reprinted with permission from "Computers and Automation", June 1971, copyright © 1971 by and published by Berkeley Enterprises, Inc., 815 Washington Street, Newtonville, Mass. 02160.

growing source of alarm for all of us who are concerned with human rights —especially the rights of those who are black, poor, or politically unpopular. This article gives some of the reasons for alarm, and describes my challenge of local police hookup to NCIC. The challenge occurred in a New England Town Meeting in Wayland, Massachusetts.

WHAT IS NCIC?

NCIC is an automated nationwide police information network. Teletypes are installed at local police stations, connected by phone lines to state police computer centers, which in turn are connected to a central computer operated by the FBI in Washington, D.C. Records are stored and searched on-line with both state and federal computers. At present, the Massachusetts section, for example, provides "immediate information on stolen cars, missing and wanted persons, lost and stolen property, lost and stolen securities, stolen guns, outstanding warrants, narcotic drug intelligence, and suspended and revoked drivers' licenses and automobile registrations."[1]

These services, especially the narcotic drug intelligence, seem to have a potential for current misuse. Policemen are instructed, for example, to arrest "suspicious" persons for disorderly conduct to facilitate an NCIC check.[2]

However, I am far more afraid of the future of the system. I cannot give an authoritative future description of NCIC for these reasons:

1. Future plans are in a state of flux;
2. Officials responsible for those plans insist the planning is confidential, and the public will be notified only after decisions are made;
3. There is some variation in conception among the different sources I consulted; and
4. Part of the sales talk for NCIC is that it is infinitely flexible and expandable.

[1]*The 1970 Comprehensive Justice Plan for Crime Prevention and Control*, pp. 166-167. Commonwealth of Massachusetts, Committee on Law Enforcement and Administration of Criminal Justice, 80 Boylston Street, Boston.

[2]*Communication Breakthrough in the Fight Against Crime: National Crime Information Center*. Federal Bureau of Investigation, Washington, D.C. (1970). This 20-page booklet, prefaced by a letter signed by J. Edgar Hoover, is directed at policemen, encouraging them to use NCIC.

WHY THE ALARM?

NCIC plans to give its users electronic access to 19,000,000 individual citizens' arrest records—nearly 10% of the country's oopulation—beginning this fall.[3] Euphemistically termed "criminal histories" (making it sound as if any person who was ever arrested has a history of criminality), these records will help police make decisions about arresting, searching, detaining, questioning, and investigating suspects and "offenders".

The shabbiness of using arrest records as a guide to police action cannot be overemphasized. At present, many forms of arrest records do not note dropped charges nor results of trials and appeals. Even when complete records are kept, arrests that did not stick are listed, creating a suspicion—indeed a presumption—of guilt which can lead to further arrest and harassment. As a local policeman told me, "a person doesn't get arrested unless he was asking for it." They believe that, judges believe it, employers believe it, and society believes it.[4]

PLEA BARGAINING

Moreover, convictions are frequently entered on arrest records as a result of the courtroom practice of plea bargaining. An attorney might get an arrested person acquitted of unjust charges, but an attorney costs money, and there is still a chance of losing, even on appeal, which costs more. Therefore many innocent defendants agree to plead guilty in exchange for a reduced fine, reduced or suspended sentence, or probation. The same idea extends to appeals of unfair trials: making an issue of anything is expensive and risky. (Several personal friends of mine have found themselves in

[3]"FBI to Computerize Rap Files; No New Safeguards Planned," in *Computerworld*, September 30, 1970.

[4]"Misusue of Data in File by Honest Police Cited," letter in *Computerworld*, January 13, 1971. The letter describes discrimination against tenants based on arrest files.

this trap as a result of nonviolent political actions.)

Nowadays citizens can be arrested unfairly, searched illegally, charged with violating dubious laws (disorderly conduct, trespassing, blocking, loitering, or conspiracy), and railroaded into prison by ignorant or vindictive police, prosecutors, and judges.[5] The poor, the black, and the political radicals ("troublemakers") receive the highest incidence of this kind of treatment.[6] Yet, in the name of modern law enforcement, all these arrests and the convictions that go with them will go into the NCIC system.

THE INGREDIENTS OF A POLICE STATE

Computerizing and nationalizing records of arrests—complete or incomplete—and inviting local police departments to use them routinely —these are the ingredients of a police state. At the very best, discriminatory law enforcement and harassment practices will be cascaded, because an arrest becomes a justification for another arrest, and so on. I have never seen any evidence that this kind of law enforcement helps prevent crime. There seems to be growing evidence, however, of the day-to-day effect of such a system on citizens' lives. This is the chilling of free speech, free association, free petition for redress of grievances, etc. A telephone company manager recently explained this to me in this way: "It behooves a person to avoid arrest."

[5]*What You're Up Against: A People's Legal Defense Manual*, Massachusetts Lawyer's Guild, 70 Charles Street, Boston (1970).

[6]See *The Quality of Justice in Lower Criminal Courts of Metropolitan Boston*, Lawyers Committee for Civil Rights Under Law, 15 Broad Street, Boston (1970). This booklet describes a rigorous statistical analysis of police and court discrimination against poor and black people. Readers should also examine "conspiracy" cases all over the country, now in progress.

PROPONENTS OF NCIC SAY . . .

Proponents of NCIC argue that police already have five-minute telephone access to statewide and 24-hour access to nationwide arrest records of any person. They say NCIC will provide fairer, more detailed and accurate arrest records, distinguishing convictions from acquittals, for example. They say NCIC's fast response will allow cleared suspects to be released sooner, and arrested persons with clean records to be released on recognizance, thereby enhancing civil liberties. My response is that arrest records do not constitute probable cause for arrest, regardless of their accuracy; that detention without bona fide arrest is illegal in any case; that selective release on recognizance is really preventive detention in disguise; and that police access to arrest records will be stepped up tremendously by NCIC, thereby damaging civil liberties irretrievably.

NCIC CONCERN ABOUT PRIVACY AND ETHICS

The Project SEARCH Staff (System for Electronic Analysis and Retrieval of Criminal Histories) has published a booklet[7] purporting to show that privacy and individual rights are being taken into account in their system planning. (Project SEARCH is now computerizing arrest records for a ten-state federally-funded demonstration.) The booklet is instructive. On page 1 it states: "criminal justice agencies require, in making decisions regarding a suspect or offender, knowledge of his prior involvement with the criminal justice system." And on page 19: "there is every reason to believe that (FBI) rap sheets . . . faithfully record the criminal histories of their subjects."

[7]*Security and Privacy Considerations in Criminal History Information Systems*, Project SEARCH Technical Report No. 2, Project SEARCH Committee on Security and Privacy, 1108 14th street, Sacramento California. (July, 1970).

I found it difficult to read this booklet with any degree of objectivity, because of its countless euphemisms about "offenders" and "criminal justice"; it's a good illustration of the medium being the message.

POLICIES SUGGESTED BY SEARCH

In no way is the concept of discriminatory or politically-inspired arrest and harassment even touched upon as an area of concern, any more than the self-fulfilling properites of "criminal histories." The booklet presents many policy suggestions which are meaningful in the context of current law enforcement structures, such as improved accuracy and completeness, the exclusion of "information concerning juvenile offenders," and "further studies . . . to specify inclusion or exclusion of specific misdemeanors."

However, let us examine four major areas:

1. The SEARCH prototype "does not include subjective evaluations . . . by police, judges, or detention authorities," just "hard data" on arrest, trial, and punishment.

(If arrest, judgement, and parole decisions were made objectively, this would would be a different place today. I believe "hard data" is an utterly false description of arrest records, and one of the reasons why they are unsuitable for police access.)

2. Social security number, FBI number, operators license number, and "any miscellaneous identifying number" are part of each person's file. These are "not (to be used) as a device to permit linkages or data sharing with other information systems."

(Who's going to believe that? It simply cannot be enforced.).

3. Although highway patrols, registry authorities, prosecutors, judges, probation officers, and parole boards are

to be given direct access to all records, access is denied to the general public, defense attorneys and legal aid societies, and to the "offender" himself unless he submits to fingerprinting and his state submits itself to a law change

4. A "code of ethics" pledges all participants in the system to limit their use to "criminal justice as a matter of government function," and other generally commendable pledges.

(When the pledges do mean something, they do not seem to be enforceable or even checkable.)

The principal author of the booklet, Robert R. J. Gallati, also directs the New York State Identification and Intelligence System (NYSIIS)—the New York section of NCIC and is a SEARCH participant. NYSIIS has been pointed out to me as a "model" for the national system in terms of human rights. Some rather bizarre misuse[8] and data theft[9] has occurred, but "civil liberties" and "due process" are supposedly enhanced by reducing illegal detention of suspects from 24 to 3 hours.[10] In order to check his record, however, an "offender" has to travel to Albany and pay a fee to NYSIIS

A recent position paper[11] outlines at least four major concerns about data banks in relation to human rights:

1. loss of privacy through security loopholes;

[8]"Lawyer Seeks to Nullify Wall Street Fingerprinting Law," *Computerworld*, April 22, 1970. This article tells how 29 workers were fired because of NYSIIS arrest files, half of which showed no convictions.
[9]"Security Breach Leads to Police Data Theft," in *Computerworld*, February 10, 1971. This article tells of NYSIIS data reaching airlines, credit agencies, and private detective organizations by illicit means.
[10]"New York State Identification and Intelligence System," in *Computers and Automation*, March 1971
[11]"Data Banks—A Position Paper" by C. Foster, in *Computers and Automation*, March 1971.

2. transactions about individuals without their being notified;
3. merging and correlating dangerous information from diverse sources; and
4. operation without principled supervision.

NCIC has no features that satisfy a single one of these concerns.

OTHER REASONS FOR ALARM

Thus I regard NCIC to be dangerous because of its basic premise that police need arrest records of citizens, and can use them safely. However, there are yet more reasons for alarm as follows:

1. NCIC forms the basis for a total *gestapo* (literally "secret federal police") system, since the public has no access to its data, nor is any person notified of inquiries and transactions affecting himself. It could take the last vestiges of the "criminal justice system" entirely out of public hands.
2. The addition of surveillance data to NCIC is but a small step, technologically. The modern, aggressive style of surveillance and infiltration needs computer resources just like this, and there is reason to believe the NCIC system would be used for surveillance data.
3. NCIC could easily be used in the administration's preventive detention program and in gathering data for future "conspiracy" indictments.
4. The FBI runs NCIC. Its large scale undercover surveillance activities force one to view the FBI's ethics with suspicion, to say the least.
5. Computers are notorious for making mistakes themselves as well as transmitting unevaluated data, while policemen may well believe "anything a computer tells them."

WHO PAYS FOR NCIC? WHO SELLS IT?

The cost of NCIC equipment and operations, along with its substantial dangers to human rights, could hardly be ignored by responsible town officials in deciding whether to hook their police up to this system. The financing structure seems to be designed to circumvent this foible of democracy.

Towns in Massachusetts pay only their individual Teletype rental, about $2000 annually, to join NCIC. To ease towns in painlessly, a 40% federal subsidy is provided to reduce this rental cost. (Now that 131 towns are connected to NCIC, the subsidy is ending.) Expenses borne by the state, including phone lines and computer center operation, are also subsidized federally. The rest of NCIC, including development of SEARCH, is 100% federally funded, primarily by the so-called Safe Streets Act of 1968. We all pay for NCIC, of course. But the fragmentation of payments fosters a carefree feeling among budget-minded local and state officials that "somebody else" is paying.

Perhaps officials might be attracted to NCIC by its apparent bargain price, but still question its merits. To minimize this problem in our state, the sales staff of New England Telephone Company (supplier of lines and Teletypes) visited 117 towns in Massachusetts last year to educate local boards and committees on the need for NCIC in modern police operations. Quite by accident, I heard one of those sales talks. It was very smooth and professional indeed. Human rights were not mentioned. The officials present agreed "the advantages outweigh the disadvantages," and incorporated NCIC into the town's budget.

Because of indirect financing and professional selling, NCIC has begun operating almost entirely without the knowledge or approval of the public it fundamentally affects.

A CHALLENGE TO NCIC IN A TOWN MEETING

After I was defeated in an attempt to delete the NCIC budget line pending further investigation and a full explanation, I introduced the following motion on the floor of the Wayland, Mass., Town Meeting on March 8, 1971:

MOVED: That the Police Department be directed to include in next year's annual report a statistical tabulation of its usage of the NCIC computer system, including the following information if at all possible:

1. number of inquiries by type of inquiry and reason for inquiry;
2. results of inquiries, including arrests and known convictions;
3. a similar summary of information entered by Wayland police; and
4. troubles encountered (down-time, false arrest, invasion of rights, etc.).

Despite angry opposition, the motion was carried by a majority vote of those present.

The reporting should accomplish one or more of the following objectives in addition to generating a list of features and how and why they are used:

1. stimulate discussion and questioning of NCIC by exposure to the public of its existence;
2. abate the chilling effect on free speech, association, etc., by removing the veil of mystery from NCIC operations;
3. deter questionable operations by the police by requiring an accounting of such operations (thereby opening them to criticism and veto);
4. convey the doubts of concerned citizens about NCIC to town fathers, police, state officials, legislators, and Congressmen;
5. stimulate public realization of the sham of the entire socalled "criminal justice system" in which NCIC is grounded; and
6. give people courage to demand public accountability of all governmental functions, computerized or not.

These objectives could be served even if the police misconstrue or falsify the required report! Actually, the report will be difficult to falsify because all NCIC transactions are logged verbatim at the state level, thus facilitating cross-checking.

Finally, if town officials actually fail to report as directed, perhaps because of secrecy statutes, then outraged citizens can demand removal of NCIC from the police department. (Wayland officials have indicated they intend to cooperate at the present time.)

Among the voters with whom I spoke, a tremendous number of factors affected their thinking on the issue of NCIC. Some of these factors include:

1. teenage offspring suffering police harassment;
2. Senator Ervin's hearing on data banks;
3. Arthur Miller's book and TV appearances;[12]
4. unemployment and blackballing;
5. runaway military actions, the war in Vietnam;
6. suspicious assassinations;
7. conspiracy indictments;
8. corrupt, vindictive auto registry practices;
9. police brutality and dishonesty;
10. computerized credit rating and billing;
11. the 1970 census;
12. Nazi Germany;
13. distrust of Nixon-Agnew-Hoover-Mitchell-Burger-Blackmun;
14. previentive detention and noknock;
15. official lies; and
16. general principles of public disclosure.

In fact, all repression and manipulation of the public trust could be related in one way or another to this alleged anticrime computer system.[13]

[12]*The Assault on Privacy: Computers, Data Banks, and Dossiers,* by Arthur R. Miller. University of Michigan Press, Ann Arbor, Michigan (1971).

[13]"The Theory and Practice of American Political Intelligence," by Frank Donner, in *The New York Review of Books,* April 22, 1971, gives an excellent detailed accounting of the assumptions and activities of the "intelligence mind" in this country.

Personally, I think our souls felt a sense of renewal when we debated NCIC in our Town Meeting and we saw some hope of controlling or at least influencing, the widespread implementation of this system.[14]

[14]Shortly after this article was written, Massachusetts officials reportedly decided to "hold off" joining the FBI arrest record system, building instead a far more modest "limited" statewide arrest record network. (Although reported April 13, 1971, in *The Cambridge Phoenix*, state officials have refused to confirm these facts for me—while accusing me of not knowing what I'm talking about! Finally I obtained confirmation from a highly-placed clandestine source.) Their reasons were "92% financial and 8% moral," according to my unquotable secret source. Their moral objections would by met by restricting reporting to *conviction* of "serious" offenses only, and establishing formal control by *state* law enforcement groups instead of the FBI. I regard these changes as half-baked reforms; they ignore the basic political discrimination and repression fostered by arrest and "correction" reporting. For example, demonstrators who are beaten by police are often *convicted* of "assault on a police officer"; antiwar organizers are *convicted* of "conspiracy to incite riot"; and on and on—these are "serious" crimes. Moreover, the door seems open for 92% reconciliation with the FBI through negotiation of a subsidy. In short, NCIC is still dangerous.

A model state act*

The recommendation of the Project SEARCH Committee on Security and Privacy are contained in full in the collection of the publications cited below.* The essence of the recommendations is given in the following. The Committee recommends:

1. Establishment of a Records Control Committee is to "regulate the collection, storage, dissemination and usage of criminal offender record information". The Council is to "conduct a continuing study and review of questions of individual privacy and system security".
2. Establishing regulations for data verification and purging and for system security.
3. Rights of access and challenge. "Each individual shall have the right to in-

* "A Model State Act for Criminal Offender Record Information", *Project SEARCH Security and Privacy Publication*. (Sacramento, Cal.: California Crime Technological Research Foundation, 1973), each article paginated separately. Paraphrased from *Project SEARCH Security and Privacy Publications*, May 1973.

spect the criminal offender record information located within his state which refers to him. If an individual believes such information to be inaccurate or incomplete, he may request the agency having custody or control of the records to purge, modify, or supplement them". Provisions are made to have the agency's actions made the subject of a hearing "at which the individual may appear with counsel, present evidence, and examine and cross-examine witnesses". Should the record in question by found to be inaccurate, incomplete, or misleading, "the Council shall order it to be appropriately purged, modified or supplemented by an explanatory notation". Finally, notification of each such change "shall be promptly disseminated by the Committee to any individuals or agencies to which the records in question have been communicated". Provision is also made for appeal.

4. Civil liberty. Any person may institute "a civil action for damages or to restrain any violation of this Act, or

both. Should it be found in any such action that there had occurred a willful violation of this Act, the violator shall, in addition to any liability for such actual damages as may by shown, be liable for exemplary damages of not less than one hundred and not more than one thousand dollars for each such violation, together with costs and reasonable attorneys' fees and disbursements incurred by the person bringing the action".

5. Criminal penalties. Any person who "willfully requests, obtains or seeks to obtain criminal offender record information under false pretenses, or who willfully communicates or seeks to communicate criminal offender record information to any agency or person except in accordance with this Act . . . or any person connected with any research program . . . who willfully falsifies criminal offender record information, or any records relating thereto, shall for each such offense be fined not more than five thousand dollars, or imprisoned in the state penitentiary not more than two years, or both".

Keep in mind that the stipulated fines and terms of imprisonment are only recommeded. Actual state statutes might vary. The recommedations continue with the model administrative regulations with some overlap but often with more detail.[1]

6. Segregation of computerized files and their linkage to intelligence files. It is recommended that all criminal record information should be stored in a computer dedicated solely to criminal justice users. Further, where this is not immediately possible, it is advised that efforts should continue

[1]Model Administrative Regulations for Criminal Offender Record Information", *Project SEARCH Security and Privacy Publications.* (Sacramento, Cal.: California Crime Technological Research Foundation, 1973), pp. 12-45, each article paginated separately.

towards the goal of a dedicated computer. The senior criminal justice agency employee in charge of computer operations is directed to write and install a classified program to "detect and store for classified output, all attempts to penetrate any criminal offender record information system, program or file". For such a conservative proposal it is surprising that criminal "records files may be linked to intelligence files in such a manner that an intelligence inquiry from a criminal justice terminal can trigger a printout of the subject's criminal offender record information". Further, a criminal "record inquiry response shall not include information which indicates that an intelligence file exists".

7. Purging of criminal offender record information. Criminal record information is designated as "closed" and "expunged" in the circumstances and with the consequences described below:

a. "Upon formal application received from the individual or formal notice received by a criminal justice agency from another criminal justice agency that an arrest for a criminal offense has legally terminated in a decision in favor of an arrestee . . . identification files as the result of that arrest, including fingerprints and photographs, shall be marked 'closed' and not reopened for any reason, except, upon request of the arrested individual made within sixty days of final disposition, such records shall be returned to that individual. At the edd of sixty days from final disposition, such records as to which no such request has been received shall be 'expunged' from the system".

b. Where an individual has been convicted of an offense "which would in this state be deemed a serious crime, has for a period of ten years not been imprisoned after conviction of such offense by any criminal justice agency, not been subject to the control of parole or probation authorities, and not been convicted of a criminal offense which would in this state be deemed a crime, and is not currently under indictment, in custody to answer for a crime, or the subject of an arrest warrant by any criminal justice agency, each and every copy in this state of any criminal offender record information relating to that individual in any criminal identification file shall be designated and marked as closed' ".

Finally, records designated "closed" are to be held in confidence and shall not be made available for review or dissemination except under circumstances such as:

a. where necessary for "in-house custodial activities of the recordkeeping agency or for the regulatory responsibilities of the Committee",

b. where the information is to be used "for statistical compilations and /or research studies, in which the individual's identity is not disclosed and from which it is not ascertainable", and

c. where "a statute of this state necessitates inquiry into criminal offender record information beyond the five and ten year limitations".

Summary and recommendations.*

The Secretary's Advisory Committee on Automated Personal Data Systems comprised a cross section of experienced and concerned citizens appointed by the Secretary of Health, Education, and Welfare to analyze the consequences of using computers to keep records about people. The Committee assessed the impact of computer-based record keeping on private and public matters and recommended safeguards against its potentially adverse effects. The Committee paid particular attention to the dangers implicit in the drift of the Social Security number toward becoming an all-purpose personal identifier and examined the need to insulate statistical-reporting and research data from compulsory legal process.

The Committee's report begins with a

* "Summary and Recommendations", *Records, Computers, and the Rights of Citizens*, U.S. Department of Health, Education, and Welfare, July 1973.

brief review of the historical development of records and record keeping, noting the different origins of administrative, statistical, and intelligence records, and the different traditions and practices that have grown up around them. It observes that the application of computers to record keeping has challenged traditional constraints on record-keeping practices. The computer enables organizations to enlarge their data-processing capacity substantially, while greatly facilitating access to recorded data, both within orgainzations and across boundaries that separate them. In addition, computerization creates a new class of record keepers whose functions are technical and whose contact with the suppliers and users of data are often remote.

The report explores some of the consequences of these changes and assesses their potential for adverse effect on individuals, organizations, and the society as a whole. It concludes that the net effect of computerization is that it is becoming much easier for record-keeping systems to affect people than for people to affect record-keeping systems. Even in non-governmental settings, an individual's control over the use that is made of personal data he gives oo an organization, or that an organization obtains about him, is lessening.

Concern about computer-based record-keeping usually centers on its implications for personal privacy, and understandably so if privacy is considered to entail control by an individual over the uses made of information about him. In many circumstances in modern life, an individual must either surrender some of that control or forego the services that an organization provides. Although there is nothing inherently unfair in trading some measure of privacy for a benefit, both parties to the exchange should participate in setting the terms.

Under current law, a person's privacy is poorly protected against arbitrary or abusive record-keeping practices. For this reason, as well as because of the need to establish standards of record-keeping practice appropriate to the computer age, the report recommends the enactment of a Federal "Code of Fair Information Practice" for all automated personnal data systems. The Code rests on five basic principles that would be given legal effect as "safeguard requirements" for automated personal data systems.

• There must be no personal data record-keeping systems whose very existence is secret.

• There must be a way for an individual to find out what information about him is in a record and how it is used.

• There must be a way for an individual to prevent information about him that was obtained for one purpose from being used or made available for other purposes without his consent.

• There must be a way for an individual to correct or amend a record of identifiable information about him.

• Any organization creating, maintaining, using, or desseminating records of identifiable personal data must assure the reliability of the data for their intended use and must take precautions to prevent misuse of the data.

The proposed Code calls for two sets of safeguard requirements; one for administrative automated personal data systems used exclusively for statistical reporting and research. Special safeguards are recommended for administrative personal data systems whose statistical-reporting and research applications are used to influence public policy.

The safeguard requirements define *minimum standards* of fair information practice. Under the proposed Code, violation of an safeguard requirement would constitute "unfair information practice" subject to criminal penalties and civil remedies. The Code would also provide for injunctive relief. Pending legislative enactment of such a code, the report recommends that the safeguard requirements be applied through Federal administrative action.

The report discusses the relationship of existing law to the proposed safeguard requirements. It recommends that laws that do not meet the standards set by the safeguard requirements for administrative personal data systems be amended and that legislation be enacted to protect personal data used for statistical reporting and research from compulsory disclosure in identifiable form.

The report examines the characteristics and implications of a standard universal identifier and opposes the establishment of such an identification scheme at this time. After reviewing the drift toward using the Social Security number (SSN) as a *de facto* standard universal identifier, the Committee recommends steps to curtail that drift. A persistent source of public concern is that the Social Security number will be used to assemble dossiers on individuals from fragments of data in widely dispersed systems. Although this is a more difficult technical feat than most laymen realize, the increasing use of the Social Security number to distinguish among individuals with the same name, and to match records for statistical-reporting and research purposes, deepens the anxieties of a public already suffused with concern about surveillance. If record-keeping systems and their data subjects were protected by strong safeguards, the danger of inappropriate record linkage would be small; until then there is a strong case to be made for discouraging linkage.

The report recommends that use of the Social Security number be limited to Federal programs that have a specific Federal legislative mandate to use the SSN, and that new legislation be enacted to give an individual the right to refuse to disclose his SSN under all other circumstances. Furthermore, any organization or person required by Federal law to obtain and record the SSN of any individual for some Federal program purpose must be prohibited from making any other use or disclosure of that number without the individual's informed consent.

The report recognizes the need to improve the reliability of the Social Security number as an instrument for strengthening the administration of certain Federally supported programs of public assistance. It also recognizes that issuing Social Security numbers to ninth-grade students in schools is likely to be consistent with the needs and convenience of young people seeking part-time employment and who need an SSN for Social Security and Federal income-tax purposes. Accordingly, the Committee endorses the recommendation of the Social Security Task Force that a positive program of issuing SSNs to ninth-grade students in schools be undertaken. It does so, however, on the condition that no school system shall be induced to cooperate in such a program against its will, and that any person shall have a right to refuse to be issued an SSN in connection with such a program. The Committee re-

commends that there be no positive program of issuing SSNs to children in schools below the ninth-grade level, and that the 1972 legislation amending the Social Security Act to require enumeration of all persons who benefit from any Federally supported program be interpreted narrowly. Finally, the Committee recommends legislation to prohibit use of the Social Security number for promotional or commercial purposes.

The last chapter of the report contains an agenda of actions to be taken for implementing the Committee's recommendations, which are set forth in full below.

RECOMMENDATIONS

Code of Fair Information Practice

We recommend the enactment of legislation establishing a Code of Fair Information practice for all automated personal data systems.

● The Code should define "fair information practice" as adherence to specified safeguard requirements.

● The Code should prohibit violation of any safeguard requirement as an "unfair information practice."

● The Code should provide that an unfair information practice be subject to both civil and criminal penalties.

● The Code should provide for injunctions to prevent violation of any safeguard requirement.

● The Code should give individuals the right to bring suits for unfair information practices to recover actual, liquidated, and punitive damages, in individual or class actions. It should also provide for recovery of reasonable attorneys' fees and other costs of litigation incurred by individuals who bring successful suits.

Pending enactment of a code of fair information practice, we recommend that all Federal agencies (i) apply the safeguard requirements, by administrative action, to all Federal systems, and (ii) assure, through formal rule making, that the safeguard requirements are applied to all other systems within reach of the Federal government's authority. Pending the enactment of a code of fair information practice, we urge that State and local governments, the institutions within reach of their authority, and all private organizations adopt the safeguard requirements by whatever means are appropriate.

Safeguards Requirements for Administrative Personal Data Systems

I. GENERAL REQUIREMENTS

A. Any organization maintaining a record of individually identifiable personal data, which it does not maintain as part of an administrative automated personal data system, shall make no transfer of any such data to another organization, without the prior informed consent of the individual to whom the data pertain, if, as a consequence of the transfer, such data will become part of an administrative automated personal data system that is not subject to these safeguard requirements.

B. Any organization maintaining an administrative automated personal data system shall:

(1) Identify one person immediately responsible for the system, and make any other organizational arrangements that are necessary to assure continuing attention to the fulfillment of the safeguard requirements;

(2) Take affirmative action to inform each of its employees having any responsibility or function in the design, development, operation, or maintenance of the system, or the use of any data contained therein, about all the safeguard requirements and all the rules and procedures of the organization designed to assure compliance with them;

(3) Specify penalties to be applied to any employee who initiates or otherwise contributes to any disciplinary or other punitive action against any indi-

vidual who brings to the attention of appropriate authorities, the press, or any member of the public, evidence of unfair information practice;

(4) Take reasonable precautions to protect data in the system from any anticipated threats or hazards to the security of the system;

(5) Make no transfer of individually identifiable personal data to another system without (i) specifying requirements for security of the data, including limitations on access thereto, and (ii) determining that the conditions of the transfer provide substantial assurance that those requirements and limitations will be observed—except in instances when an individual specifically requests that data about him be transferred to another system or organization;

(6) Maintain a complete and accurate record of every access to and use made of any data in the system, including the identity of all persons and organizations to which access has been given;

(7) Maintain data in the system with such accuracy, completeness, timeliness, and pertinence as is necessary to assure accuracy and fairness in any determination relating to an individual's qualifications, character, rights, opportunities, or benefits, that may be made on the basis of such data; and

(8) Eliminate data from computer-accessible files when the data are no longer timely.

II. PUBLIC NOTICE REQUIREMENT

Any organization maintaining an administrative automated personal data system shall give public notice of the existence and character of its system once each year. Any organization maintaining more than one system shall publish such annual notices for all its systems simultaneously. Any organization proposing to establish a new system, or to enlarge an existing system, shall give public notice long enough in advance of the initiation or enlargement of the system to assure individuals who may be affected by its operation a reasonable opportunity to comment. The public notice shall specify:

(1) The name of the system;

(2) The nature and purpose (s) of the system;

(3) The categories and number of persons on whom data are (to be) maintained;

(4) The categories of data (to be) maintained, indicating which categories are (to be) stored in computer-accessible files;

(5) The organization's policies and practices regarding data storage, duration of retention of data, and disposal thereof;

(6) The categories of data sources;

(7) A description of all types of use (to be) made of data, indicating those involving computer-accessible files, and including all classes of users and the organizational relationships among them;

(8) The procedures whereby an individual can (i) be informed if he is the subject of data in the system; (ii) gain access to such data; and (iii) contest their accuacy, completeness, pertinence, and the necessity for retaining them;

(9) The title, name, and address of the person immediately responsible for the system.

III. RIGHTS OF INDIVIDUAL DATA SUBJECTS

Any organization maintaining an administrative automated personal data system shall:

(1) Inform an individual asked to supply personal data for the system whether he is legally required, or may refuse, to supply the data requested, and also of any specific consequences for him, which are known to the organization, of providing or not providing such data;

(2) Inform an individual, upon his request, whether he is the subject of data in the system, and, if so, make such data fully available to the individual, upon his request, in a form comprehensible to him;

(3) Assure that no use of individually identifiable data is made that is not within the stated purpose of the system as reasonably understood by the individual, unless the informed consent of the individual has been explicitly obtained;

(4) Inform an individual, upon his request, about the uses made of data about him, including the identity of all persons and organizations involved and their relationships with the system;

(5) Assure that no data about an individual are made available from the system in response to a demand for data made by means of compulsory legal process, unless the individual to whom the data pertain has been notified of the demand; and

(6) Maintain procedures that (i) allow an individual who is the subject of data in the system to contest their accuracy, completeness, pertinence, and the necessity for retaining them; (ii) permit data to be corrected or amended when the individual to whom they pertain so requests; and (iii) assure, when there is disagreement with the individual about whether a correction or amendment should be made, that the individual's claim is noted and included in any subsequent disclosure or dissemination of the disputed data.

Existing laws or regulations affording individuals greater protection than the safeguard requirements should be retained, and those providing less protection should be amended to meet the basic standards set by the safeguards. In particular, we recommend

• That the Freedom of Information Act

be amended to require an agency to obtain the consent of an individual before disclosing in personally identifiable form exempted-category data about him, unless the disclosure is within the purposes of the system as specifically required by statute.

• That pending such amendment of the Act, all Federal agencies provide for obtaining the consent of individuals before disclosing individually identifiable exempted-category data about them under the Freedom of Information Act.

• That the Fair Credit Reporting Act be amended to provide for actual, personal inspection by an individual of his record along with the opportunity to copy its contents, or to have copies made; and that the exceptions from disclosure to the individual now authorized by the Fair Credit Reporting Act for medical information and sources of investigative information be omitted.

Statistical-Reporting and Research Uses of Administrative Personal Data Systems

In light of our inquiry into the statistical-reporting and research uses of personal data in administrative record-keeping systems, we recommend that steps be taken to assure that all such uses are carried out in accordance with five principles:

First, when personal data are collected for administrative purposes, individuals should under no circumstances be coerced into providing additional personal data that are to be used exclusively for statistical reporting and research. When application forms or other means of collecting personal data for an administrative data system are designed, the mandatory or voluntary character of an individual's responses should be made clear.

Second, personal data used for making determinations about an individual's character, qualifications, rights, benefits, or opportunities, and personal data collected and used for statistical reporting and research, should be processed and stored separately.

Third, the amount of supplementary statistical-reporting and research data collected and stored in personally identifiable form should be kept to a minimum.

Fourth, proposals to use administrative records for statistical reporting and research should be subjected to careful scrutiny by persons of strong statistical and research competence.

Fifth, any published findings or reports that result from secondary statistical-reporting and research uses of administrative personal data systems should meet the highest standards of error measurement and documentation.

In addition, there are certain safeguards that can be feasibly applied to all administrative personal data systems used for statistical reporting and research. Specifically, we recommend that the following requirements be added to the safeguard requirements for administrative personal data systems:

• Under I. General Requirements, add—

C. Any organization maintaining an administrative automated personal data system that publicly disseminates statistical reports or research findings based on personal data drawn from the system, or from systems of other organizations, shall:

(1) Make such data publicly available for independent analysis, on reasonable terms; and

(2) Take reasonable precautions to assure that no data made available for independent analysis will be used in a way that might reasonably be expected to prejudice judgments about any individual data subject's character, qualifications, rights, opportunities, or benefits.

• Under the Public Notice Requirement, add—

(8a) The procedures whereby an individual, group, or organization can gain access to data used for statistical reporting or research in order to subject such data to independent analysis.

Systems Used Exclusively for Statistical Reporting and Research

All the features of the Code of Fair Information Practice that we recommend for automated personal data systems would apply to systems used exclusively for statistical reporting and research. The safeguard requirements to be included in the Code for such systems are designed to help protect the individual citizen against unintended or unforeseen uses of information that he provides *exclusively* for statistical reporting and research, and to help assure that the uses organizations make of such data are subject to independent expert review and open public discussion. Pending the enactment of a code of fair information practice, we recommend that all Federal agencies (i) apply these safeguard requirements, by administrative action, to all Federal statistical-reporting and research systems, and (ii) assure, through formal rule making, that the safeguard requirements are applied to all systems within reach of the Federal government's authority. Pending the enactment of a code of fair information practice, we also urge that State and local governments, the institutions within reach of their authority, and all private organizations adopt the safeguard requirements by whatever means are appropriate.

Safeguard Requirements for Statistical-Reporting and Research Systems

I. GENERAL REQUIREMENTS

A. Any organization maintaining a record of personal data, which it does not maintain as part of an automated personal data system used exclusively for statistical reporting or research, shall make no transfer of any such data to another organization without the prior consent of the individual to whom the data pertain, if, as a consequence of the transfer, such data will become part of an automated personal data system that is not subject to these safeguard requirements or the safeguard requirements for administrative personal data systems.

B. Any organization maintaining an automated personal data system used exclusively for statistical reporting or research shall:

(1) Identify one person immediately responsible for the system, and make any other organizational arrangements that are necessary to assure continuing attention to the fulfillment of the safeguard requirements;

(2) Take affirmative action to inform each of its employees having any responsibility or function in the design, development, operation, or maintenance of the system, or the use of any data contained therein, about all the safeguard requirements and all the rules and procedures of the organization designed to assure compliance with them;

(3) Specify penalties to be applied to any employee who initiates or otherwise contributes to any disciplinary or other punitive action against any individual who brings to the attention of appropriate authorities, the press, or any member of the public, evidence of unfair information practice;

(4) Take reasonable precautions to protect data in the system from any anticipated threats or hazards to the security of the system;

(5) Make no transfer of individually identifiable personal data to another system without (i) specifying requirements for security ff the data, including limitations on access thereto, and (ii) determining that the conditions of the transfer provide substantial assurance that those requirements and limitations will be observed—except in instances

when each of the individuals about whom data are to be transferred has given his prior informed consent to the transfer; and

(6) Have the capacity to make fully documented data readily available for independent analysis.

II. PUBLIC NOTICE REQUIREMENT

Any organization maintaining an automated personal data system used exclusively for statistical reporting or research shall give public notice of the existence and character of its system once each year. Any organization maintaining more than one such system shall publish annual notices for all its systems simultaneously. Any organization proposing to establish a new system, or to enlarge an existing system, shall give public notice long enough in advance of the initiation or enlargement of the system to assure individuals who may be affected by its operation a reasonable opportunity to comment. The public notice shall specify:

(1) The name of the system;

(2) The nature and purpose (s) of the system;

(3) The categories and number of persons on whom data are (to be) maintained;

(4) The categories of data (to be) maintained, indicating which categories are (to be) stored in computer-accessible files;

(5) The organization's policies and practices regarding data storage, duration of retention of data, and disposal thereof;

(6) The categories of data sources;

(7) A description of all types of use (to be) made of data, indicating those involving computer-accessible files, and including all classes of users and the organizational relationships among them;

(8) The procedures whereby an indi-

vidual, group, or organization can gain access to data for independent analysis;

(9) The title, name, and address of the person immediately responsible for the system;

(10) A statement of the system's provisions for data confidentiality and the legal basis for them

III. RIGHTS OF INDIVIDUAL DATA SUBJECTS

Any organization maintaining an automated personal data system used exclusively for statistical reporting or research shall:

(1) Inform an individual asked to supply personal data for the system whether he is legally required, or may refuse, to supply the data requested, and also of any specific consequences for him, which are known to the organization, of providing or not providing such data;

(2) Assure that no use of individually identifiable data is made that is not within the stated purposes of the system as reasonably understood by the individual, unless the informed consent of the individual has been explicitly obtained;

(3) Assure that no data about an individual are made available from the system in response to a demand for data made by means of compulsory legal process, unless the individual to whom the data pertain (i) has been notified of the demand, and (ii) has been afforded full access to the data before they are made available in response to the demand.

In addition to the foregoing safeguard requirements for all automated personal data systems used exclusively for statistical reporting and research, we recommend that all personal data in such systems be protected by statute from compulsory disclosure in identifiable form. Federal legislation protecting against compulsory disclosure should include the following features:

• The data to be protected should be limited to those used *exclusively for statistical reporting or research*. Thus, the protection would apply to statistical-reporting and research data derived from administrative records, and kept apart from them, but not to the administrative records themselves.

• The protection should be limited to data *identifiable with, or traceable to, specific individuals*. When data are released in statistical form, reasonable precautions to protect against "statistical disclosure" should be considered to fulfill the obligation not to disclose data that can be traced to specific individuals.

• The protection should be specific enough to qualify for non-disclosure under the Freedom of Information Act exemption for matters "specifically exempted from disclosure by statute." 5 U.S.C. 552 (b) (3).

• The protection should be available for data in the custody of all statistical-reporting and research systems, whether supported by Federal funds or not.

• Either the data custodian or the individual about whom data are sought by legal process should be able to invoke the protection, but only the individual should be able to waive it.

• The Federal law should be controlling; no State statute should be taken to interfere with the protection it provides.

Use of the Social Security Number

We take the position that a standard universal identifier (SUI) should not be established in the United States now or in the foreseeable future. By our definition, the Social Security Number (SSN) cannot fully qualify as an SUI; it only approximates one. However, there is an increasing tendency for the Social Security number to be used as if it were an SUI. There are pressures on the Social Security Administration to do things that make the SSN more nearly an SUI.

We believe that any action that would tend to make the SSN more nearly an SUI should be taken only if, after careful deliberation, it appears justifiable and any attendant risks can be avoided. We recommend against the adoption of any nationwide, standard, personal identification format, with or without the SSN, that would enhance the likelihood of arbitrary or uncontrolled linkage of records about people, particularly between government and government-supported automated personal data systems.

We believe that until safeguards against abuse of automated personal data systems have become effective, constraints should be imposed on use of the Social Security number. After that the question of SSN use might properly be reopened.

As a general framework for action on the Social Security number, we recommend that Federal policy with respect to use of the SSN be governed by the following principles:

First, uses of the SSN should be limited to those necessary for carrying out requirements imposed by the Federal government.

Second, Federal agencies and departments should not require or promote use of the SSN except to the extent that they have a specific legislative mandate from the Congress to do so.

Third, the Congress should be sparing in mandating use of the SSN, and should do so only after full and careful consideration preceded by well advertised hearings that elicit substantial public participation. Such consideration should weigh carefully the pros and cons of any proposed use, and should pay particular attention to whether effective safeguards have been applied to automated personal data systems that would be affected by the proposed use of the SSN. (Ideally, Congress should review all present Federal requirements for use of the SSN and determine whether these existing requirements should be continued, repealed, or modified.)

Fourth, when the SSN is used in instances that do not conform to the three foregoing principles, no individual should be coerced into providing his SSN, nor should his SSN be used without his consent.

Fifth, an individual should be fully and fairly informed of his rights and responsibilities relative to uses of the SSN, including the right to disclose his SSN whenever he deems it in his interest to do so.

In accordance with these principles, we recommend specific, preemptive, Federal legislation providing:

(1) That an individual has a legal right to refuse to disclose his SSN to any person or organization that does not have specific authority provided by Federal statute to request it;

(2) That an individual has the right to redress if his lawful refusal to disclose his SSN results in the denial of a benefit, or the threat of denial of a benefit; and that, should an individual under threat of loss of benefits supply his SSN under protest to an unauthorized requestor, he shall not be considered to have forfeited his right to redress; and

(3) That any oral or written request made to an individual for his SSN must be accompanied by a clear statement indicating whether or not compliance with the request is required by Federal statute, and, if so, citing the specific legal requirement.

In addition, we recommend

(4) That the Social Security Administration undertake a positive program of issuing SSNs to ninth-grade students in schools, provided (a) that no school system be induced to cooperate in such a program contrary to its preference; and (b) that any person shall have the right to refuse to be issued an SSN in connection with such a program, and such right of refusal shall be available both to the student and to his parents or guardians;

(5) That there be no positive program of issuing SSNs to children below the ninth-grade level, either at the initiative

of the Social Security Administration or in response to requests from schools or other institutions:

(6) That the Secretary limit affirmative measures taken to issue SSNs pursuant to Secton 205 (c) (2) (B) (i) (II) of the Social Security Act, as amended by Section 137 of Public Law 92-603, to applicants for or recipients of public assistance benefits supported from Federal funds under the Social Security Act; and

(7) That the Secretary do his utmost to assure that any future legislation dealing with the SSN be preceded by full and careful consideration and well advertised hearings that elicit substantial public participation.

With respect to organizations using the SSN, we recommend

(8) That any organization or person required by Federal law to obtain or record the SSN of any individual be prohibited from making any use or disclosure of the SSN without the informed consent of the individual, except as may be necessary to the Federal purposes for which it was required to be obtained and recorded. This prohibition should be established by a specific and preemptive act of Congress:

(9) That the Social Security Administration provide "SSN services" to aid record keeping only to organizations or persons that are required by Federal law to obtain or record the SSN, and then only as necessary to fulfill the purposes for which the SSN is required to be obtained or recorded:

(10) That the Social Security Administration provide "SSN services" to aid research activities only when it can assure that the provision of such services will not result in the use of the SSN for record-keeping and reporting activities beyond those permitted under recommendation (9), and then only provided that rigid safeguards to protect the confidentiality of personal data, including the SSN, are incorporated into the research design; and

(11) The specific, preemptive Federal legislation be enacted prohibiting use of an SSN, or any number represented as an SSN, for promotional or commercial purposes.

The Social Security number as a standard universal identifier*

Our charter commissioned us to analyze policy and practice relative to the issuance and use of the Social Security number, including prohibitions, restrictions, conditions, or other qualifications on the issuance and use of the number which now exist, or might be imposed to help implement whatever safeguards for automated personal data systems we might recommend.

This particular aspect of our charge stems from growing public concern that the Social Security number will become a standard universal identifier used by all manner of organizations and data systems to establish the identity of individuals, to link records about them, and generally to keep track of them from cradle to grave. This concern also led to the establishment of the Social Security Number Task Force in February 1970, and was reflected in former HEW Secretary Elliot L. Richardson's testimony, in March 1971, before the U.S. Senate Subcommittee on Constitutional Rights, chaired by Senator Sam J. Ervin, Jr.[1]

Why do these concerns exist? Are they reasonable? What can be done about them? To answer these questions we must first understand something about

*"The Social Security number as a standard universal identifier." *Records, Computers, and the Rights of Citizens*, U.S. Department of Health, Education, and Welfare, July 1973.

[1]*Federal Data Banks, Computers and the Bill of Rights*, Hearings before the Subcommittee on Constitutional Rights of the Committee on the Judiciary, United States Senate, 92nd Congress, 1st Session, February and March 1971, Part I, pp. 775-881.

identifiers in general and the nature and implications of a standard universal identifier in particular.

There are many kinds of personal identifiers. A person's name is an identifier, the most ancient of all, but is not a reliable one, since often it is neither unique nor permanent. Even unusual names may be widely shared, and because of family patterns identical ones are often concentrated in particular localities. Some names change when people are known by different names in different social settings; e.g., itinerants, persons with aliases, and married women who use a maiden name professionally.

To compensate for the unreliability of names as personal identifiers, additional schemes of identification have been devised. These commonly take the form of numeric or alpha-numeric labels that provide the uniqueness and permanence names customarily lack. The reliability thereby achieved is important to record-keeping systems of an organization that maintains different sets of records on a given group of people. If one label is used by separate organizations, such as the Social Security number is for the taxpayer's identification number, a driver's license number, and a school student number, that label may be on its way to becoming a de *facto* universal identifier.

Criteria for a Standard Universal Identifier

A standard universal identifier (SUI) is a systematically assigned label that, theoretically at least, distinguishes a person from all others. If the labels asssigned by a universal identification scheme are to fulfill this function, each SUI must meet all the following criteria:

UNIQUENESS. It must be unique for each person. No more than one person can be assigned the same SUI, and each person must have no more than one SUI.

PERMANENCE. It must not change during the life of an individual and should not be re-used after his death until all records concerning him have been retired.

UBIQUITY. Labels must be issued to the entire population for which unique identification is required.

AVAILABILITY. It must be readily obtainable or verfiable by anyone who needs it, and quickly and convieniently regainable in case it is lost or forgotten.

INDISPENSABILITY. It must be supported by incentives or penalties so that each person will remember his SUI and report it correctly; otherwise systems will become clogged with errors.

ARBITRARINESS. It must not contain any information. If it does, e.g., State of issuance, it will be longer than necessary, thus violating the "brevity" criterion (see below). It may also violate the "permanence" criterion if changeable items, such as name or address, are incorporated. Most important, if items of personal information are part of an SUI, they will be automatically disseminated whenever the SUI is used; in our view, this would be undesirable.

BREVITY. It must be as short as possible for efficiency in recognition, retrieval, and processing by man or machine.

RELIABILITY. It must be constructed with a feature that detects errors of transcription or communication.[2] If the

communication of SUIs were done entirely by machine, errors could be minimized through technology, but short of this, there must be protection against the risk of human error in writing or reciting an SUI. For the foreseeable future, the need will continue for people to fill out forms and to report information themselves.

Implications of a Standard Universal Identifier

The advantages of a standard universal identifier, as seen by its proponents, are easier and more accurate updating, merging, and linking of records about individuals for administrative, statistical, and research purposes. According to them, duplication and error in record keeping would be reduced. Individuals, moreover, would be relieved of the need to use many different identifying numbers; an SUI might supplant credit card numbers, and many other identifiers.

In spite of these practical advantages, the idea of an SUI is objectionable to many Americans. Even in some European countries where SUIs were introduced without opposition a generation or more ago, their use has recently raised fears and anxieties in the population. Many people both feel a sense of alienation from thie social institutions and re-

---

[2]A possible error-detecting feature is a number (called a check-digit) that can be derived in some way from the identification number and appended to it. For example, a check-digit may be derived by multiplying the first digit of the identification number by 1, the second by 2, the third by 3 (and so on), summing the products of the multiplications, and extracting the digital root of their sum. The identification number 1463, handled this way, produces a check-digit of 3 ($1 \times 1 = 1, 2 \times 4 = 8, 3 \times 6 = 18, 4 \times 3 = 12; 1 + 8 + 18 + 12 = 39; 3 + 9 = 12; 1 + 2 = 3$) which is written at the end of the number to produce 14633. A computer and a human being can each readily verify the accuracy of the number. Transpositions are detectable. "14363," for instance, would be caught as illegitimate, because the correct check-digit for the number 1436 is not 3, but 6 ($1 \times 1 = 1, 2 \times 4 = 8, 3 \times 3 = 9, 4 \times 6 = 24; 1 + 8 + 9 + 24 = 42; 4 + 2 = 6$). Most single-digit errors are also detectable, though errors of more than one digit may coincidentally generate valid check-digits and hence not be detectable.

sent the dehumanizing effects of a highly mechanized civilization. Every characteristic of an SUI heightens such emotions.

• The bureaucratic apparatus needed to assign and administer an SUI would represent another imposition of government control on an already heavily burdened citizenry.

• To realize all the supposed benefits of an SUI, mandatory personal identity cards would have to be presented whenever called for. Loss or theft of an SUI card would cause serious inconvenience, and the mere threat of official confiscation would be a powerful weapon of intimidation.

• The national population register that an SUI implies could serve as the skeleton for a national dossier system to maintain information on every citizen from cradle to grave.

• An unchangeable SUI used everywhere would make it much easier for an individual to be traced, and his behavior monitored and controlled, through the records maintained through him by a wide range of different institutions.

• A permanent SUI issued at birth could create an incentive for institutions to pool or link their records, thereby making it possible to bring a lifetime of information to bear on any decision about a given individual. American culture is rich in the belief than an individual can pull up stakes and make a fresh start, but a universally identified man might become a prisoner of his recorded past.

This Committee believes that fear of a standard universal identifier is justified. Although we are not opposed to the concept of an SUI in the abstract, we believe that, in practice, the dangers inherent in establishing an SUI—without legal and social safeguards against the abuse of automated personal data systems—far outweigh any of its practical benefits. Therefore, we take the position that **a standard universal identifier should not be established in the United States now or in the foreseeable future.**[3] The question can surely be re-examnned after there has been sufficient experience with the safeguards proposed in this report to evaluate their effectiveness.

The Social Security Number (SSN) as an SUI

But is it not too late to oppose a standard universal identifier? Is not the SSN already a *de facto* SUI? To answer these questions, we must first measure the SSN against the criteria for an SUI given above.

UNIQUENESS. The SSN is not a unique label. More than 4.2 million people, by the Social Security Administration's own estimates, have two or more SSNs. More serious, although much less prevalent, are the instances in which more than one person has been issued or uses the same SSN.[4]

[3]The National Academy of Sciences Computer Databanks Project reached a similar conclusion on the basis of its independent, empirical assessment of the issues involved. See Alan F. Westin and Michael A. Baker, *Databanks in a Free Society* (New York: Quandrangle Books). 1972. pp. 396-400.

[4]"Account number 078-05-1120 was the first of many numbers now referred to as 'pocketbook' numbers. It first appeared on a sample account number card contained in wallets sold ... nationwide in 1938. Many people who purchased the wallets assumed the number to be their own personal account number. It was reported thousands of times on employers' quarterly reports; 1943 was the high year, with 5,755 wage earners listed as owning the famous number. More recently, the IRS requirement that the Social Security AN [Account Number] be shown on all tax returns resulted in 39 taxpayers showing 078-05-1120 as their number. The number continues to be reported at least 10 times each quarter. There are now over 20 different 'pocketbook' numbers...." *Account number and Employer Contact Manual* (Baltimore, Md.: Social Security Administration), Sec. 121.

PERMANENCE. The SSN is, in almost all cases, permanent for an individual throughout his life.

UBIQUITY. The SSN is nearly universal for adult Americans, much less so for those of high-school age and below.

AVAILABILITY. The SSN of an individual is readily verifiable by the Social Security Administration for some users, and not at all for others. It is regainable from the Social Security Administration by persons who have lost their cards and forgotten their numbers, but not immediately. An individual's SSN, however, is increasingly ascertainable from many sources other than the Social Security Administration.

INDISPENSABILITY. The incentives and requirements to report one's SSN correctly are growing, though in some contexts there are incentives to omit or falsify the number.

ARBITRARINESS. The SSN is not entirely arbitrary: the State of issuance is coded into the number.

BREVITY. The SSN with its nine digits is three places longer than an alphanumeric label capable of numbering 500 million people without duplication, and two places longer than one that can accommodate 17 billion people. The SSN could therefore be shorter if it was alpha-numeric.

RELIABILITY. The SSN has no check-feature, and most randomly chosen nine-digit numbers cannot be distinguished from valid SSNs. It is thus particularly prone to undetectable errors of transcription and oral reporting.

By our definition, the SSN cannot fully qualify as an SUI; it only approximates one.

The SSN had its genesis in accounting practice and was first known as the Social Security *Account* Number (SSAN). It was established to number accounts for the 26 million people with earnings from jobs covered by the Social Security Act of 1935. Income-maintenance benefits under the Act, though not payable until the retirement or death of a worker, were to be determined on the basis of his record of earnings. Each worker needed a uniquely identifiable account to which re-cords of his earnings would be posted periodically. Since obviously many would have the same or similar names, it was decided to assign each a unique number to identify his account and assure an accurate record of earnings, which his employer would report both by name and account number.

Name and number were used because standard accounting practice had accustomed people to numbered accounts, and because the technology of the day, notably the punched card machine with its 80-column card, required a short numeric identifier for efficiently adding the records of new transactions to existing master-file records.

Nine digits were chosen to provide for future expansion. A check-feature was not provided because the technology of the day could not cope with it, and manual checking, though possible, was judged too time-consuming to be feasible. The Social Security Administration has developed ingenious error-detection methods, and has improved them over the years to the point where it now neither needs nor desires a check-feature.[5]

Despite the deficiencies of the SSN for purposes other than those for which it was designed, its use is widespread and growing, even where its limitations are recognized. How did this come about? Why is the SSN now so widely used for purposes and in areas unrelated to the Social Security program?

History of the Social Security Number and Its Uses

The original Social Security Act (P.L. 74-271, August 14, 1935) imposed two taxes to finance the program of retirement and survivor benefits to be administered by the Social Security Board. One was a

[5]Ibid., Sec. 555 ff.

tax as a percentage of wages imposed on employees; the second was a matching tax on employers. To finance the Federal contribution to State programs of unemployment compensation required by the same Act, a tax as a percentage of wages was imposed on employers.

Section 807 of that Act charged the Bureau of Internal Revenue in the Treasury Department with collecting all three taxes. Section 807 (b) provided

Such taxes shall be collected and paid in such manner . . . (either by making and filing returns, or by stamps, coupons, tickets, books, or other reasonable devices or methods necessary or helpful in securing a complete and proper collection and payment of the tax or in securing proper identificaiton of the taxpayer), as may be prescribed by the Commissioner of Internal Revenue. . . .

The first mention of the SSN in a law or regulation is in a Bureau of Internal Revenue regulation of November 5, 1936 under which an identifying number, called an "account number," was to be applied for by each employee, and assigned by the Postmaster General or the Social Security Board. Each employee was directed to report his number to his employer. Employers were directed to keep records showing the name and number of each employee and to enter employee account numbers on all required tax returns. The regulation provided that "Any employee may have his account number changed at any time by applying to the Social Security Board and showing good reasons for a change. With that exception, only one account number will be assigned to an employee."[6]

It is ironic to discover—though logical and understandable in retrospect—that the first step in the process of extending the use of the Social Security number beyond the purposes of the Social Security program was taken by the Social Security Board itself on January 15, 1937. After the Social Security Act was passed,

a question arose about an account numbering system to be used by State agencies established to administer the State unemployment insurance programs. The Board decided that the Social Security number should be used for all workers insured under these programs, rather than have each State agency develop its own identification system. As a result of this decision, many workers not covered by the Social Security program received SSNs for use in State unemployment insurance programs.

For some years after its inception in 1936, there was no substantial use of the SSN other than that required for the Social Security and unemployment compensation programs. Most Americans had not been issued a number, and few organizations felt the need of a numeric identifier for purposes of data processing.

Although many people are under the impression that use of the SSN for other than Social Security program purposes is forbidden by law, this is not the case and never has been. The impression may in part have arisen from the fact that, for many years, the card bearing one's Social Security Account Number has carried the legend, "NOT FOR IDENTIFICATION." The purpose of this legend is to notify anyone to whom a card might be presented that it cannot be relied upon, by itself, as evidence of the identity of the person presenting it.

In 1943, the Civil Servic Commission decided that there should be a numerical identification system for all Federal employees and proposed to the Bureau of the Budget that use of the SSN be authorized for this purpose. This led to the issuance of Executive Order 9397. That order, which is still in effect, provides in part as follows:

WHEREAS certain Federal agencies from time to time require the administration of their activities a system of numerical identification of accounts of individual persons; and . . .

WHEREAS it is desirable in the interest of economy and orderly administration that the

[6]T.D. 4704, 1 Fed. Reg. 1741 (Nov. 7, 1936); 26 C.F.R. Part 401 (1st ed., 1939).

Federal Government move towards the use of a single, unduplicated numerical identification system of accounts and avoid the unnecessary establishment of additional systems;

NOW, THEREFORE, . . . it is hereby ordered as follows:

1. Hereafter any Federal department, establishment, or agency shall, whenever the head thereof finds it advisable to establish a new system of permanent account numbers pertaining to individual persons, utilize exclusively the Social Security account numbers . . . .

The order directs the Social Security Board, the predecessor agency of the Social Security Administration, to provide for the assignment of an account number to any person required by any Federal agency to have one, and to furnish the number, or the name and identifying data, pertaining to any person or account number upon request of any Federal agency using the SSAN for a numerical identification system of accounts under the order. The order also directs that

The Social Security Board and each Federal agency shall maintain the confidential character of information relating to individuals obtained pursuant to the provisions of this Order.

Finally, the order provides for the costs of services rendered thereunder by the Social Security Board to be reimbursed by the agency receiving such services.

Most civil servants had never applied for SSNs because their employment was not covered by the Social Security Act. Since they were not being assigned numbers for Social Security program purposes, the costs had to be paid from funds appropriated for the Civil Service Commission. The Commission, however, was unable to obtain the necessary funds, and so it was not until November, 1961 that the assignment of numbers to Civil Service employees was initiated as an adjunct of the Internal Revenue Service's taxpayer identification program (see below).

The issuance of Executive Order 9397 in

1943 theoretically may have provided the basis for a change in conception of the role of the SSN. However, there is no evidence that it had any practical significance until after the 1961 decision to use the SSN as an individual identifier for Federal tax purposes. It has been suggested that Executive Order 9397 was intended to apply only to instances when Federal agencies seek to number records of financial transactions, and not to numbering other kinds of records, such as employment, attendance, performance, or medical records. The fiscal interpretation follows from the wording of the order which speaks of the efficiency to be gained from "a single . . . system of accounts . . . ." To interpret the order as applying to all kinds of Federal agency record systems is arguably beyond the meaning of its language. In any case, it appears that Federal agencies are free to use the SSN in any way they wish, and no instance has come to our attention in which the order has been invoked to compel or limit an agency's use of the SSN.

What many regard as the single most substantial impetus to use the SSN for purposes other than the Social Security program occurred in 1961, when the Internal Revenue Service, after discussions with the Social Security Administration, decided to use the SSN for taxpayer identification. This decision was implemented by an amendment to the Internal Revenue Code that authorized the Secretary of the Treasury to require each person making "a return, statement, or other document" under the Internal Revenue Code to "include such identifying number as may be prescribed for securing proper identification of such person." The Secretary was also authorized "to require such information as may be necessary to assign an identifying number to any person."[7] The Secretary delegated his authority to the Commissioner of In-

[7]P.L. 87-397 (Oct. 5, 1961): Internal Revenue Code of 1954, Sec. 6109.

ternal Revenue, who has issued a number of regulations, the combined effect of which may be summarized as follows.

• The taxpayer's identification number for use by individuals (except as employers in a trade or business) is the SSN.

• The SSN for each individual taxpayer and each beneficiary of an estate or trust must be furnished on all tax returns and related statements and documents filed in connection with every tax imposed by the Internal Revenue Code. (A failure to include the number as required on a return gives rise to a civil penalty of $5, unless the failure to provide the number is due to "reasonable cause." Int. Rev. Code of 1954, Sec. 6676.)

• An individual is obliged to obtain an SSN from the Social Security Administration and furnish it when requested, for purposes of complying with Internal Revenue Service regulations, by any of the following: employers; estates and trusts; corporations and other entities paying dividends; banks, mutual savings and savings and loan institutions; insurance companies; stockbrokers and securities dealers; other entities paying interest; and nominees receiving dividends or interest.

Many other actions of the Federal government have expanded the areas of use of the SSN beyond its original purposes.

• The Treasury Department further expanded use of the SSN in 1963 by requiring its use in registration of all United States transferable and non-transferable securities other than U.S. savings bonds. The following year the requirement for such use of the SSN was applied to Series H savings bonds. The Treasury Department has announced that as of October 1, 1973, the inscriptions on Series E bonds must also include the SSN. (Meanwhile the Treasury has modified its earlier rule that the names of women on savings bond inscriptions be preceded by "Miss," "Mrs.," or other title, by permitting omis-

sion of the title if the woman's SSN is included.)

• In a decision dated April 16, 1964, the Commissioner of Social Security approved the issuance of SSNs to pupils in the ninth grade and above, if a school requests such issuance and indicates willingness to cooperate in the effort. The Social Security Administration Claims Manual explains that this decision was made (1) to accommodate requests from school systems "desiring to use the SSN for both automatic data processing and control purposes, so that the progress of pupils could be traced throughout their school lives across district, county, and State lines", and (2) because issuance of SSNs to school children in groups is more orderly, efficient, less costly to the Social Security Administration, and gives better assurance of identification of the children than if students eventually apply for numbers one at a time.

• In June 1965 the Commissioner of Social Security authorized the issuance of an SSN to every recipient of State old-age assistance benefits who did not already have one, in order to establish a more efficient process for exchange of information between these agencies and the Social Security Administration. When the Social Security Act was amended in 1965, to provide hospital and medical insurance (Medicare) administered by the Social Security Administration, it became necessary for most individuals aged 65 and over who did not already have an SSN to obtain one.

• In June 1965 the Civil Service Commission began to add SSNs to the retirement records of their annuitants. This represented an extension of the SSN issuance system started in 1961 for civil service employees.

• Effective January 1, 1966, after consultation with the Social Security Administration, the Veterans Administration began using the SSN as a hospital admission number, and for other record-keeping purposes.

• On April 7, 1966, the Commissioner of Social Security approved the test usage of the SSN by the Division of Indian Health of the Public Health Service to facilitate development and maintenance of comprehensive health histories of Indians from birth to death.

• By memorandum dated January 30, 1967, the Secretary of Defense advised the Social Security Administration of his decision to use the SSN as the service number of all military personnel.

• Pursuant to the Currency and Foreign Transactions Reporting Act (the so-called Bank Secrecy Act), P.L. 91-508, October 26, 1970; 31 U.S.C. 1051-1122, the Treasury Department issued regulations in 1972 requiring banks, savings and loan associations, credit unions, and brokers and dealers in securities to obtain the SSNs of all their customers. The Act requires these financial organizations to maintain records of certain large transactions to facilitate criminal, tax, and regulatory investigations with respect to currency and foreign transactions. The SSNs of individuals required for account records under the regulations will already have been obtained in almost all cases by these financial organizations under regulations of the Internal Revenue Service governing tax reporting. A notable impact has been the requirement to furnish one's SSN to open a checking acount.

• Use of the SSN is being promoted by the National Driver Register of the U.S. Department of Transportation. Although the Department of Transportation lacks authority to *require* it, use of the SSN is encouraged by the Register to facilitate matching the records of reports and inquiries it receives. tthis has led most State motor vehicle departments to collect SSNs from all drivers, and some to shift to the SSN for their driver license identification number.

• The Social and Rehabilitation Service of the Department of Health, Education, and Welfare has for some time been promoting the use of the SSN by States for the identification of individual applicants and beneficiaries under all welfare and social services programs.

• The Congress, in Section 137 of the Social Security Amendments of 1972,[8] has required the Secretary of HEW to take affirmative measures to issue SSNs to the maximum extent practicable to aliens entitled to work in the United States and "to any individual who is an applicant for or recipient of benefits under any program financed in whole or in part from Federal funds including any child on whose behalf such benefits are claimed by another person." The quoted language of this requirement appears to call for the issuance of an SSN to virtually everyone in America who does not already have one, but the legislative history clearly indicates that such universal enumeration was not intended. The Senate Finance Committee had proposed a requirement of affirmative measures for the assignment of SSNs to all children at the time they first enter school, as well as to aliens and all applicants for and recipients of benefits under Federally supported programs. However, the bill was amended in conference. Instead of requiring the Secretary to take affirmative measures to enumerate children at their entrance into school, the Act makes such measures optional, but the Act retains the requirement that numbers be assigned to aliens, and to applicants and recipients of benefits. Although the legislation does not specify any uses to be made of SSNs issued pursuant to its mandate, the legislative history indicates that Congress intended them to be available for use in preventing aliens from working illegally and public assistance beneficiaries from receiving duplicate or excessive payments.

Review of the Federal actions described

[8]P.L. 92-603, October 30, 1972; 42 U.S.C. 405.

above (which do not by any means constitute an exhaustive list) makes it clear that *the Federal government itself has been in the forefront of expanding the use of the SSN*. All these actions have actively promoted the tendency to depend more and more on the SSN as an identifier—of workers, taxpayers, automobile drivers, students, welfare beneficiaries, civil servants, servicemen, veterans, pensioners, and so on.

If use of the SSN as an identifier continues to expand, the incentives to link records and to broaden access to them are likely to increase. Until safeguards such as we have recommended in Chapters IV, V and VI have been implemented, and demonstrated to be effective, there can be no assurance that the consequences for individuals of such linking and accessibility will be benign. At best, individuals may be frustrated and annoyed by unwarranted exchanges of information about them. At worst, they may be threatened with denial of status and benefits without due process, since at the present time record linking and access are, in the main, accomplished without any provision for the data subject to protest, interfere, correct, comment, and, in most instances, even to know what linking of which records is taking place for what purposes.

Although few people have flatly proposed that an SUI be mandated for all Americans, there is a strong tendency for authorities in government and industry to make decisions that, taken collectively, are likely to lead to the establishment of an SUI. There is an increasing tendency for the Social Security number to be used as if it were an SUI. Even organizations selecting a single-system personal identifier rre likely to choose the SSN "because it is available," or for efficiency and convenience. There are pressures on the Social Security Administration to do things that make the SSN more nearly an SUI, such as issue more SSNs than the Social Security program requires, for purposes wholly unrelated.

We believe that any action that would tend to make the SSN more nearly an SUI should be taken only if, after careful deliberation, it appears justifiable and any attendant risks can be avoided. **We recommend against the adoption of any nationwide, standard, personal identification format, with or without the SSN, that would enhance the likelihood of arbitrary or uncontrolled linkage of records about people, particularly between government or government-supported automated personal data systems.**[9] What is needed is a halt to the drift toward an SUI and prompt action to establish safeguards providing legal sanctions against abuses of automated personal data systems. The recommendations in the following chapter are directed toward that end.

[9] One notable attempt to establish a standard for the identification of individual Americans for purposes of information exchange was that offered by a committee of the American National Standards Institute (ANSI) in 1969. The standard, as proposed, consisted in part of an individual's SSN; opposition to that feature in particular led in 1972 to official withdrawal of the staddard from further consideration pending resolution of the issues that are covered by this report.

Capitalist spirit*

The economic ethics taught by medieval Catholicism presented obstacles to capitalist ideology and development. Hostility to material wealth carried forward the teachings of the Christian fathers against mammonism. Saint Jerome said. "A rich man is either a thief or the son of a thief." Saint Augustine felt that trade was bad because it turned men away from the search for God. Down through the middle ages commerce and banking were viewed, at best, as necessary evils. Moneylending was for a time confined to non-Christians because it was considered unworthy of Christians. Interest on loans was unlawful under the anti-usury laws of both the central medieval economic doctrine of just price.

Epansion of commerce in the later middle ages stirred controversies and led to attempts to reconcile theological doctrines with economic realities. In Venice, Florence, Augsburg and Antwerp—all Catholic cities—capitalists violated the spirit and circumvented the letter of the prohibitions against interest. On the eve of the Protestant Reformation capitalists, who still labored under the shadow of the sin of avarice, had by their deeds become indispensable to lay rulers and to large numbers of people who were dependent upon them for employment.

The Protestant reformation of the 16th and 17th centuries developed alongside economic changes which resulted in the spread of capitalism in northern Europe, especially in the Netherlands and England. This chronological and geographical correlation between the new religion and economic development has led to the suggestion that Protestantism had casual significance for the rise of modern capitalism. Without in any sense being

* "Capitalist Spirit", page 840, Vol. 4, 1967, *Encyclopedia Britannica*. Reprinted by permission and copyright © Encyclopedia Britannica, 1967.

the "cause" of capitalism which already existed on a wide and expanding horizon, the Protestant ethic proved a bracing stimulant to the economic order. Doctrinal revision or interpretation seemed not only to exonerate capitalists from the sin of avarice but even to give divine sanction to their way of life. In the ordinary conduct of life, a new type of worldly asceticism emerged, one that meant hard work, frugality, sobriety and efficiency in one's calling in the market place similar to that of the monastery. Applied in the environment of expanding trade and industry, the Protestant creed taught that accumulated wealth should be used to produce more wealth.

Acceptance of the Protestant ethic also eased the way to systematic organization of free labor. By definition, free labourers could not be compelled by force to work in the service of others. Moreover, the use of force would have violated the freedom of one's calling. Psychological compulsion arising from religious belief was the answer to the paradox. Every occupation was said to be noble in God's eyes. For those with limited talents, Christian conscience demanded unstinting labour even at low wages in the service of God—and, incidentally, of employers. It was an easy step to justify economic inequality because it would hasten the accumulation of wealth by placing it under the guardianship of the most virtuous (who were, incidentally, the wealthiest) and remove temptation from weaker persons who could not withstand the allurements associated with wealth. After all, it did not much matter who held the legal title to wealth, for it was not for enjoyment. The rich like the poor were to live frugally all the days of their lives. Thus the capitalist system found a justification that was intended to make inequality tolerable to the working classes.

Mastered or master?

ERWIN D. CANHAM*

Pessimists say that some day computers may run men instead of men running computers.

Every technological advance, from fire to fission, has had its share of ambivalence. Benefits and dangers have been blended. The benefits of the age of data processing are already sensational. What they can become is breathtaking.

The dangers are that we might trust to computers certain tasks—in essence, the decision making process—which must be the responsibility of men's consciences, striving to reflect the utmost wisdom.

Dr. Simon Ramo, in a previous article in this series, has emphasized the choice and the danger we now face: whether to permit computers to pull us into a robot society, or to control them so that we attain higher degrees of individual freedom than were ever dreamed possible before.

The danger does not lie in the machines. It lies in the use or abuse, to which men put them. Mankind has faced this problem before, from fire to the motorcar to nuclear fission. He has not done too well in avoiding the hazards. He has learned how to control the machine better than he had learned to control himself.

Data processing can usher in a whole new age of individualizing. It is a very pleasant irony to recall that machines brought in the industrial revolution, which led to mass production and a kind of mass society, and that now the most advanced of machines is making possible a return to individualism.

SAVINGS INTRODUCED

As has been pointed out in earlier articles, various applications of the computer migtt make it possible for us to order consumer products styled to our personal taste—custom made, as it were; education could be paced to the individual's capacities; everybody's opinion could be sought and evaluated in an effort to achieve a higher degree of democracy; the totality of the world's accumulated knowledge could be stored and distributed to individual seekers of information; new media or entertainment could be available exactly to individual choice.

All these and many more things are possible. How many of them will be actually practicable in a free market situation remains to be seen. Some may well be far too expensive. There may be vast economies of scale or technique which will finance some of the new wonders.

Already, the computers are introducing savings throughout business, although not always the savings that were anticipated. Some companies which expected to economize on personnel are finding that for three low-pay clerks they can dispense with, they must employ one highly paid programmer or computer specialist. And the additional work the computer can do is so dazzling as to be irresistible. Its potential is so great that it performs unexpected new tasks.

Anyway, the computer does open up exciting vistas of individualization. It is also a formidable force in the realm of decision making. Here, it seems to me, is a great challenge and threat. Will we be sure not to give the computer ultimate decisionmaking power? Will we always set it up so as to present alternatives, from which men and women can make their choices?

* Erwin D. Canham, "Mastered or Master", *The Christian Science Monitor*, August 31, 1967. Reprinted by permission from *The*

Christian Science Monitor, copyright © 1967 The Christian Science Publishing Society. All rights reserved.

STUDENT GUIDANCE

The problem arises in business decisions, in political decisions, in the decisions of war and peace. It is clear that the computer can assemble, remember, coordinate, analyze, and present a far greater range of data relevant to a decision than any man or group of men could readily handle. Already, throughout the business would, computers are being used in just such ways.

To take an illustration from education, I was told of a guidance officer in a high school who had fed into his computer a tremendous store of information about institutions of higher learning, special training institutes, etc. In short, all that could possibly be relevant to the guidance of students.

Then the officer would feed into the computer the specific characteristics of the individual seeking guidance. I was told that the answer could be counted on for greater scope, diversity, knowledge, than the officer could have carried in his thought or easily produced from his reference books.

My informant felt that in the realm of guidance, which is essentially an informational task, the computer could be trusted to exceed the human. Perhaps it is so.

PRESENTATION OF CHOICES

Of course, a great deal depends on how well the computer has been programmed. Some enormously important factor may be left out, or something wrong put in.

One such omission took place in Boston last year. The city's municipal accounts are pretty well automated. Mayor John F. Collin, a progressive executive had seen to that. Mayor Collins was running for the senatorial nomination last year. Three days before the primary election, very efficiently and without instruction, the machine prepared, addressed, and mailed 30,000 delinquent sewer tax bills. It had never been programmed with the instruction: "Don't send out tax bills just before election if the Mayor is running for office!" Nobody thought of that. Mayor Collins lost the nomination.

Somewhat less bizarre omissions (and doubtless some much more grave ones) could occur in any automated program. Of course any human politicain worth his salt, working in City Hall, would have avoided such a mistake by instinct. So man has to remain a close partner to the machine.

In its approach to decisionmaking, the machine should present choices, assembling the data on which a human decision could be based. In Dr. Ramo's words: ". . . the same system that can tell millions of people exactly what to do, as though they were robots, can just as well ask them to choose what they prefer to do from a group of well-presented alternatives."

But even such a process is only partly objective. The selection of alternatives and the manner of their presentation involve many value judgements. The very terms in which a question is put can make a great difference. The cards could be stacked.

If we are to use data processing in the realm of political information and decisionmaking we must set up independent, nonpolitical programmers. That will not be easy. Indeed, any information utility can be no better than the material that is put in.

It is tantalizing to think how fully people could be informed on some given issue and how quickly and accurately the machine could assemble and tabulate their responses. Some kind of pure democracy, or town meeting of the nation (or the world), with widespread individual participation, is possible.

"INSTANT DEMOCRACY"

It is also fraught with problems. Do we really want such "instant democracy"? Should public opinion have this kind of power? Is that the best form of government? The American Constitution, at least, is filled with wise safeguards against hasty decisions of an omnipotent majority.

Rights of minorities, even of individuals, must be safeguarded. Delay, while sometimes irksome or dangerous, more often than not has proved to be a protection. Therefore, although data processing could provide magnificently improved techniques of informing and assessing public opinion, the result could only be applied under careful rules and restraints.

In the gravest of all essentially political decisions, those of war and peace, elements which cannot possibly be physically programmed must be included in the decision process: moral and ethical and spiritual considerations must have their part. And the possibility of error must be most rigorously surveyed and prevented.

The conclusion which emerges most sharply from today's estimate of data processing is that men and machines must be partners, but that men must always retain the upper hand. Moreover, it is possible to distinguish between what man can do best and what the machines can do best.

J. C. R. Licklider of IBM, who has a formidable background of experience as an engineering psychologist, writes in International Science and Technology that man can do the heuristic tasks and machines the algorithmic (i.e., essentially recurrent mathematical tasks). Heuristic tasks he defines as "the setting of goals, the generation of hypotheses, the selection of criteria—the problem-solving phases in which one has to lay down the guidelines, choose approaches, follow intuition, exercise judgement, or make an evaluation."

OVERLAPPING AREAS

Algorithmic tasks lie in the application of known rules. They can be immensely complex, involving what would be tremendous amounts of man-time, but they remain in the area of solved problems. On the frontiers of science and knowledge, says Dr. Licklider, the heuristic and the algorithmic overlap. Men can use computers to solve problems, but they must pilot them through the unknown.

This analysis helps to answer the question: "Can the computer think?" If one defines the thought process in heuristic fashion, then the computer does not think. And surely this is a valid definition.

Other authorities do no find it easy to distinguish between what Dr. Barry W. Boehm of Rand Corporation calls rote work and creative work (in effect, algorithmic and heuristic). The computer has performed tasks which had been considered creative. It enables man to be more creative. Programming, as Dr. Boehm says, "has been more of a 'black art' than a science." People have learned that it is much harder to simulate ordinary human thinking processes on a digital computer than had been imagined.

The computer is a terribly literalminded creature. It also stores vast amounts of useless information. It is prolix. In displaying these all-too-human characteristics it outdoes most humans—save perhaps some Ph.D. candidates.

ABILITIES MAGNIFIED

A time goes on, the limitations as well as the strengths of the computer will be more clearly recognized and defined. Guidelines for use will be more clearly defined. It may even be that the role of man will become clearer, more respected, more valuable. Certainly the man at the controls of a bulldozer has to have higher qualities if he is to succeed than when he was merely on the end of a shovel.

The computer could magnify man. It certainly enables him to perform infinitely greater tasks than he ever dreamed possible. And as he thrusts heuristically into the frontiers of the unknown he can use the computer to establish and implement his dominion.

Thus the data-processing machines make dominion greater than ever. They are the product of intelligence, not the creator of intelligence. One of the best Biblically used definitions of God is Mind. If ever qualities of Mind were exemplified, it is in this thrilling new field.

We can be grateful for the distance we have come, and we can move forward confidently if we always remember that qualities far transcending anything the machine can do are the birthright of God's man. In wonder, glory, and beauty the qualities of man's spirit can never be replaced or duplicated. At most it is possible to try to counterfeit them.

On the impact of the computer on society

JOSEPH WEIZENBAUM*

The structure of the typical essay on "The impact of computers on society" is as follows: First there is an "on the one hand" statement. It tells all the good things computers have already done for society and often even attempts to argue that the social order would already have collapsed were it not for the "computer revolution." This is usually followed by an "on the other hand" caution which tells of certain problems the introduction of computers brings in its wake. The threat posed to individual privacy by large data banks and the danger of large-scale unemployment induced by industrial automation are usually mentioned. Finally, the glorious present and prospective achievements of the computer are applauded, while the dangers alluded to in the second part are shown to be capable of being alleviated by sophisticated technological fixes. The closing paragraph consists of a plea for generous societal support for more, and more large-scale,

*Joseph Wizenbaum, "On the Impact of the Computer on Society", Science. Vol. 176, pages 609-614, May 12, 1972. Copyright © 1972 by the American Association for the Advancement of Science. The author is professor of Computer Science, Massachusetts Institute of Technology, 545 Technology Square, Cambridge 02139.

computer research and development. This is usually coupled to the more or less subtle assertion that only computer science, hence only the computer scientist, can guard the world against the admittedly hazardous fallout of applied computer technology.

In fact, the computer has had very considerably less societal impact than the mass media would lead us to believe. Certainly, there are enterprises like space travel that could not have been undertaken without computers. Certainly the computer industry, and with it the computer education industry, has grown to enormous proportions. But much of the industry is self-serving. It is rather like an island economy in which the natives make a living by taking in each other's laundry. The part that is not self-serving is largely supported by government agencies and other gigantic enterprises that know the value of everything but the price of nothing, that is, that know the short-range utility of computer systems but have no idea of their ultimate social cost. In any case, airline reservation systems and computerized hospitals serve only a tiny, largely the most affluent, fraction of society. Such things cannot be said to have an impact on society generally.

SIDE EFFECTS OF TECHNOLOGY

The more important reason that I dismiss the argument which I have caricatured is that the direct societal effects of any pervasive new technology are as nothing compared to its much more subtle and ultimately much more important side effects. In that sense, the societal impact of the computer has not yet been felt.

To help firmly fix the idea of the importance of subtle indirect effects of technology, consider the impact on society of the invention of the microscope. When it was invented in the middle of the 17th century, the dominant commonsense theory of disease was fundamentally that disease was a punishment visited upon an individual by God. The sinner's body was thought to be inhabited by various so-called humors brought into disequilibrium in accordance with divine justice. The cure for disease was therefore to be found first in penance and second in the balancing of humors as, for example, by bleeding. Bleeding was, after all, both painful, hence punishment and penance, and potentially balancing in that it actually removed substance from the body. The microscope enabled man to see microorganisms and thus paved the way for the germ theory of disease. The enormously surprising discovery of extremely small living organisms also induced the idea of a continuous chain of life which, in turn, was a necessary intellectual precondition for the emergence of Darwinism. Both the germ theory of disease and the theory of evolution profoundly altered man's conception of his contract with God and consequently his self-image. Politically these ideas served to help diminish the power of the Church and, more generally, to legitimize the questioning of the basis of hitherto unchallenged authority. I do not say that the microscope alone was responsible for the enormous social changes that followed its invention. Only that it made possible the kind of paradigm shift, even on the commonsense level, without which these changes might have been impossible.

Is it reasonable to ask whether the computer will induce similar changes in man's image of himself and whether that influence will prove to be its most important effect on society? I think so, although I hasten to add that I don't believe the computer has yet told us much about man and his nature. To come to grips with the question, we must first ask in what way the computer is different from man's many other machines. Man has built two fundamentally different kinds of machines, nonautonomous and autonomous. An autonomous machine is one that operates for long periods of time, not on the basis of inputs from the real world, for example from sensors or from human drivers, but on the basis of internalized models of some aspect of the real world. Clocks are examples of autonomous machines in that they operate on the basis of an internalized model of the planetary system. The computer is, of course, the example par excellence. It is able to internalize models of essentially unlimited complexity and of a fidelity limited only by the genius of man.

It is the autonomy of the computer we value. When, for example, we speak of the power of computers as increasing with each new hardware and software development, we mean that, because of their increasing speed and storage capacity, and possibly thanks to new programming tricks, the new computers can internalize ever more complex and ever more faithful models of ever larger slices of reality. It seems strange then that, just when we exhibit virtually an idolatry of autonomy with respect to machines, serious thinkers in respected academies [I have in mind B F. Skinner of Harvard University [1]] can rise to question autonomy as a fact for man. I do not think that the appearance of this paradox at this time is accidental. To understand it, we must realize that man's commitment to science has always had a masochistic component.

[1]B. F. Skinner, *Beyond Freedom and Dignity* (Knopf, New York, 1971).

Time after time science has led us to insights that, at least when seen superficially, diminish man. Thus Galileo removed man from the center of the universe, Darwin removed him from his place separate from the animals, and Freud showed his rationality to be an illusion. Yet man pushes his inquiries further and deeper. I cannot help but think that there is an analogy between man's pursuit of scientific knowledge and an individual's commitment to psychoanalytic therapy. Both are undertaken in the full realization that what the inquirer may find may well damage his self-esteem. Both may reflect his determination to find meaning in his existence through struggle in truth, however painful that may be, rather than to live without meaning in a world of ill-disguised illusion. However, I am also aware that sometimes people enter psychoanalysis unwilling to put their illusions at risk, not searching for a deeper reality but in order to convert the insights they hope to gain to personal power. The analogy to man's pursuit of science does not break down with that observation.

Each time a scientific discovery shatters a hitherto fundamental cornerstone of the edifice on which man's self-esteem is built, there is an enormous reaction, just as is the case under similar circumstances in psychoanalytic therapy. Powerful defense mechanisms, beginning with denial and usually terminating in rationalization, are brought to bear. Indeed, the psychoanalyst suspects that, when a patient appears to accept a soul-shattering insight without resistance, his very casualness may well mask his refusal to allow that insight truly operational status in his self-image. But what is the psychoanalyst to think about the patient who positively embraces tentatively proffered, profoundly humiliating self-knowledge, when he embraces it and instantly converts it to a new foundation of his life? Surely such an event is symptomatic of a major crisis in the mental life of the patient.

I believe we are now at the beginning of just such a crisis in the mental life of our civilization. The microscope, I have argued, brought in its train a revision of man's image of himself. But no one in the mid-17th century could have foreseen that. The possibility that the computer will, one way or another, demonstrate that, in the inimitable phrase of one of my esteemed colleagues, "the brain is merely a meat machine" is one that engages academicians, industrialists, and journalists in the here and now. How has the computer contributed to bringing about this very sad state of affairs? It must be said right away that the computer alone is not the chief causative agent. It is merely an extreme extrapolation of technology. When seen as an inducer of philosophical dogma, it is merely the reductio ad absurdum of a technological ideology. But how does it come to be regarded as a source of philosophic dogma?

THEORY VERSUS PERFORMANCE

We must be clear about the fact that a computer is nothing without a program. A program is fundamentally a transformation of one computer into another that has autonomy and that, in a very real sense, behaves. Programming languages describe dynamic processes. And, most importantly, the processes they describe can be actually carried out. Thus we can build models of any aspect of the real world that interests us and that we understand. And we can make our models work. But we must be careful to remember that a computer model is a description that works. Ordinarily, when we speak of A being a model of B, we mean that a theory about some aspects of the behavior of B is also a theory of the same aspects of the behavior of A. It follows that when, for example, we consider a computer model of paranoia, like that published by Colby et al.[2], we must not be

[2]K. M. Colby, S. Weber, F. D. Hilf, *Artif. Intell.* **1**, 1 (1971).

persuaded that it tells us anything about paranoia on the grounds that it, in some sense, mirrors the behavior of a paranoiac. After all, a plain typewriter in some sense mirrors the behavior of an autistic child (one types a question and gets no response whatever), but it does not help us to understand autism. A model must be made to stand or fall on the basis of its theory. Thus, while programming languages may have put a new power in the hands of social scientists in that this new notation may have freed them from the vagueness of discursive descriptions, their obligation to build defensible theories is in no way diminished. Even errors can be pronounced with utmost formality and eloquence. But they are not thereby transmuted to truth.

The failure to make distinctions between descriptions, even those that "work," and theories accounts in large part for the fact that those who refuse to accept the view of man as machine have been put on the defensive. Recent advances in computer understanding of natural language offer an excellent case in point. Halle and Chomsky, to mention only the two with whom I am most familiar, have long labored on a theory of language which any model of language behavior must satisfy.[3] Their aim is like that of the physicist who writes a set of differential equations that anyone riding a bicycle must satisfy. No physicist claims that a person need know, let alone be able to solve, such differential equations in order to become a competent cyclist. Neither do Halle and Chomsky claim that humans know or knowingly obey the rules they believe to govern language behavior. Halle and Chomsky also strive, as do physical theorists, to identify the constants and parameters of their theories with components of reality. They

hypothesize that their rules constitute a kind of projective description of certain aspects of the structure of the human mind. Their problem is thus not merely to discover economical rules to account for language behavior, but also to infer economic mechanisms which determine that precisely those rules are to be preferred over all others. Since they are in this way forced to attend to the human mind, not only that of speakers of English, they must necessarily be concerned with all human language behavior—not just that related to the understanding of English.

The enormous scope of their task is illustrated by their observation that in all human languages declarative sentences are often transformed into questions by a permutation of two of their words. (John is here → Is John here?) It is one thing to describe rules that transform declarative sentences into questions—a simple permutation rule is clearly insufficient—but another thing to describe a "machine" that necessitates those rules when others would, all else being equal, be simpler. Why, for example, is it not so that declarative sentences read backward transform those sentences into questions? The answer must be that other constraints on the "machine" combine against this local simplicity in favor of a more nearly global economy. Such examples illustrate the depth of the level of explanation that Halle and Chomsky are trying to achieve. No wonder that they stand in awe of their subject matter.

Workers in computer comprehension of natural language operate in what is usually called performance mode. It is as if they are building machines that can ride bicycles by following heuristics like "if you feel a displacement to the left, move your weight to the left." There can be, and often is, a strong interaction between the development of theory and the empirical task of engineering systems whose theory is not yet thoroughly understood. Witness the synergistic cooperation between aerodynamics and aircraft design in the first quarter of the present century.

[3]N. Chomsky, *Aspects of the Theory of Syntax* (M.I.T. Press, Cambridge, Mass., 1965); ——— and M. Halle, *The Sound Pattern of English* (Harper & Row, New York, 1968).

Still, what counts in performance mode is not the elaboration of theory but the performance of systems. And the systems being hammered together by the new crop of computer semanticists are beginning (just beginning) to perform.

Since computer scientists have recognized the importance of the interplay of syntax, semantics, and pragmatics, and with it the importance of computer-manipulable knowledge, they have made progress. Perhaps by the end of the present decade, computer systems will exist with which specialists, such as physicians and chemists and mathematicians, will converse in natural language. And surely some part of such achievements will have been based on other successes in, for example, computer simulation of cognitive processes. It is understandable that any success in this area, even if won empirically and without accompanying enrichments of theory, can easily lead to certain delusions being planted. Is it, after all, not terribly tempting to believe that a computer that understands natural language at all, however narrow the context, has captured something of the essence of man? Descartes himself might have believed it. Indeed, by way of this very understandable seduction, the computer comes to be a source of philosophical dogma.

I am tempted to recite how performance programs are composed and how things that don't work quite correctly are made to work via all sorts of stratagems which do not even pretend to have any theoretical foundation. But the very asking of the question, "Has the computer captured the essence of man?" is a diversion and, in that sense, a trap. For the real question "Does man understand the essence of man?" cannot be answered by technology and hence certainly not by any technological instrument.

THE TECHNOLOGICAL METAPHOR

I asked earlier what the psychoanalyst is to think when a patient grasps a tentatively proffered deeply humiliating interpretation and attempts to convert it immediately to a new foundation of his life. I now think I phrased that question too weakly. What if the psychoanalyst merely coughed and the cough entrained the consequences of which I speak? That is our situation today. Computer science, particularly its artificial intelligence branch, has coughed. Perhaps the press has unduly amplified that cough—but it is only a cough nevertheless. I cannot help but think that the eagerness to believe that man's whole nature has suddenly been exposed by that cough, and that it has been shown to be a clockwork, is a symptom of something terribly wrong.

What is wrong, I think, is that we have permitted technological metaphors, what Mumford[4] calls the "Myth of the Machine," and technique itself to so thoroughly pervade our thought processes that we have finally abdicated to technology the very duty to formulate questions. Thus sensible men correctly perceive that large data banks and enormous networks of computers threaten man. But they leave it to technology to formulate the corresponding question. Where a simple man might ask: "Do we need these things?", technology asks "what electronic wizardry will make them safe?" Where a simple man will ask "is it good?", technology asks "will it work?" Thus science, even wisdom, becomes what technology and most of all computers can handle. Lest this be thought to be an exaggeration, I quote from the work of H. A. Simon, one of the most senior of American computer scientists[5]:

As we succeed in broadening and deepening our knowledge—theoretical and empirical—about computers, we shall discover that in

[4]L. Mumford, *The Pentagon of Power* (Harcourt, Bace, Jovanovich, New York, 1970).
[5]H. A. Simon, *The Sciences of the Artificial* (M.I.T. Press, Cambridge, Mass., 1969), pp. 22-25.

large part their behavior is governed by simple general laws, that what appeared as complexity in the computer program was, to a considerable extent, complexity of the environment to which the program was seeking to adapt its behavior.

To the extent that this prospect can be realized, it opens up an exceedingly important role for computer simulation as a tool for achieving a deeper understanding of human behavior. For if it is the organization of components, and not their physical properties, that largely determines behavior, and if computers are organized somewhat in the image of man, then the computer becomes an obvious device for exploring the consequences of alternative organizational assumptions for human behavior.

and

A man, viewed as a behaving system, is quite simple. The apparent complexity of his behavior over time is largely a reflection of the complexity of the environment in which he finds himself.

. . . I believe that this hypothesis holds even for the whole man.

We already know that those aspects of the behavior of computers which cannot be attributed to the complexity of their programs is governed by simple general laws—ultimately by the laws of Boolean algebra. And of course the physical properties of the computer's components are nearly irrelevant to its behavior. Mechanical relays are logically equivalent to tubes and to transistors and to artificial neurons. And of course the complexity of computer programs is due to the complexity of the environments, including the computing environments themselves, with which they were designed to deal. To what else could it possibly be due? So, what Simon sees as prospective is already realized. But does this collection of obvious and simple facts lead to the conclusion that man is as simple as are computers? When Simon leaps to that conclusion and then formulates the issue as he has done here, that is, when he suggests that the behavior of *the whole man* may be understood in terms of the

behavior of computers as governed by simple general laws, then the very possibility of understanding man as an autonomous being, as an individual with deeply internalized values, that very possibility is excluded. How does one insult a machine?

The question "Is the brain merely a meat machine?", which Simon puts in a so much more sophisticated form, is typical of the kind of question formulated by, indeed formulatable only by, a technological mentality. Once it is accepted as legitimate, arguments as to what a computer can or cannot do "in principle" begin to rage and themselves become legitimate. But the legitimacy of the technological question—for example, is human behavior to be understood either in terms of the organization or of the physical properties of "components"—need not be admitted in the first instance. A human question can be asked instead. Indeed, we might begin by asking what has already become of "the whole man" when he can conceive of computers organized in his own image.

The success of technique and of some technological explanations has, as I've suggested, tricked us into permitting technology to formulate important questions for us—questions whose very forms severely diminish the number of degrees of freedom in our range of decision-making. Whoever dictates the questions in large part determines the answers. In that sense, technology, and especially computer technology, has become a self-fulfilling nightmare reminiscent of that of the lady who dreams of being raped and begs her attacker to be kind to her. He answers "it's your dream, lady." We must come to see that technology is our dream and that we must ultimately decide how it is to end.

I have suggested that the computer revolution need not and ought not to call man's dignity and autonomy into question, that it is a kind of pathology that moves men to wring from it unwarranted, enormously damaging interpretations. Is then the computer less threatening that we might have thought? Once we realize that our visions, possibly nightmarish visions, determine the effect of our own creations on us and on our society, their threat to us is surely diminished. But that is not to say that this realization alone will wipe out all danger. For example, apart from the erosive effect of a technological mentality on man's self-image, there are practical attacks on the freedom and dignity of man in which computer technology plays a critical role.

I mentioned earlier that computer science has come to recognize the importance of building knowledge into machines. We already have a machine—Dendral—[6] that commands more chemistry than do many Ph.D. chemists, and another —Mathlab—[7] that commands more applied mathematics than do many applied mathematicians. Both Dendral and Mathlab contain knowledge that can be evaluated in terms of the explicit theories from which it was derived. If the user believes that a result Mathlab delivers is wrong, then, apart from possible program errors, he must be in disagreement, not with the machine or its programmer, but with a specific mathematical theory. But what about the many programs on which management, most particularly the government and the military, rely, programs which can in no sense be said to rest on explicable theories but are instead enormous patchworks of programming techniques strung together to make them work?

[6]B Buchanan, G. Sutherland, E. A. Feigenbaum, in *Machine Intelligence*. B. Meltzer, Ed. (American Elsevier, New York, 1969).

[7]W. A. Martin and R. J. Fateman, "The Macsyma system," in *Proceedings of the 2nd Symposium on Symbolic and Algebraic Manipulation* (Association for Computing Machinery, New York, 1971); J. Moses, *Commun. Assoc. Computing Mach.* **14** (No. 8), 548 (1971).

INCOMPREHENSIBLE SYSTEMS

In our eagerness to exploit every advance in technique we quickly incorporate the lessons learned from machine manipulation of knowledge in theory-based systems into such patchworks. They then "work" better. I have in mind systems like target selection systems used in Vietnam and war games used in the Pentagon, and so on. These often gigantic systems are put together by teams of programmers, often working over a time span of many years. But by the time the systems come into use, most of the orignal programmers have left or turned their attention to other pursuits. It is precisely when gigantic systems begin to be used that their inner workings can no longer be understood by any single person or by a small team of individuals. Norbert Wiener, the father of cybernetics, foretold this phenomenon in a remarkably prescient article[8] published more than a decade ago. He said there:

It may well be that in principle we cannot make any machine the elements of whose behavior we cannot comprehend sooner or later. This does not mean in any way that we shall be able to comprehend these elements in substantially less time than the time required for operation of the machine, or even within any given number of years or generations.

An intelligent understanding of [machines'] mode of performance may be delayed until long after the task which they have been set has been completed. This means that though machines are theoretically subject to human criticism, such criticism may be ineffective until long after it is relevant.

This situation, which is now upon us, has two consequences: first that decisions are made on the basis of rules and criteria no one knows explicitly, and second that the system of rules and criteria becomes immune to change. This is so because, in the absence of detailed understanding of the inner workings of a system, any sub-

[8]N. Wiener, *Science* **131**, 1355 (1960).

stantial modification is very likely to render the system altogether inoperable. The threshold of complexity beyond which this phenomenon occurs has already been crossed by many existing systems, including some compiling and computer operating systems. For example, no one likes the operating systems for certain large computers, but they cannot be substantially changed nor can they be done away with. Too many people have become dependent on them.

An awkward operating system is inconvenient. That is not too bad. But the growing reliance on supersystems that were perhaps designed to help people make analyses and decisions, but which have since surpassed the understanding of their users while at the same time becoming indispensable to them, is another matter. In modern war it is common for the soldier, say the bomber pilot, to operate at an enormous psychological distance from his victims. He is not responsible for burned children because he never sees their village, his bombs, and certainly not the flaming children themselves. Modern technological rationalizations of war, diplomacy, politics, and commerce such as computer games have an even more insidious effect on the making of policy. Not only have policy makers abdicated their decision-making responsibility to a technology they don't understand, all the while maintaining the illusion that they, the policy makers, are formulating policy questions and answering them, but responsibility has altogether evaporated. No human is any longer responsible for "what the machine says." Thus there can be neither right nor wrong, no question of justice, no theory with which one can agree or disagree, and finally no basis on which one can challenge "what the machine says." My father used to invoke the ultimate authority by saying to me, "it is written." But then I could read what was written, imagine a human author, infer his values, and finally agree or disagree. The systems

in the Pentagon, and their counterparts elsewhere in our culture, have in a very real sense no authors. They therefore do not admit of exercises of imagination that may ultimately lead to human judgment. No wonder that men who live day in and out with such machines and become dependent on them begin to believe that men are merely machines. They are reflecting what they themselves have become.

The potentially tragic impact on society that may ensue from the use of systems such as I have just discussed is greater than might at first be imagined. Again it is side effects, not direct effects, that matter most. First, of course, there is the psychological impact on individuals living in a society in which anonymous, hence irresponsible, forces formulate the large questions of the day and circumscribe the range of possible answers. It cannot be surprising that large numbers of perceptive individuals living in such a society experience a kind of impotence and fall victim to the mindless rage that often accompanies such experiences. But even worse, since computer-based knowledge systems become essentially unmodifiable except in that they can grow, and since they induce dependence and cannot, after a certain threshold is crossed, be abandoned, there is an enormous risk that they will be passed from one generation to another, always growing. Man too passes knowledge from one generation to another. But because man is mortal, his transmission of knowledge over the generations is at once a process of filtering and accrual. Man doesn't merely pass knowledge, he rather regenerates it continuously. Much as we may mourn the crumbling of ancient civilizations, we know nevertheless that the glory of man resides as much in the evolution of his cultures as in that of his brain. The unwise use of ever larger and ever more complex computer systems may well bring this process to a halt. It could well replace the ebb and flow of culture with a world without values, a world in which what counts for a fact has long ago been determined and forever fixed.

POSITIVE EFFECTS

I've spoken of some potentially dangerous effects of present computing trends. Is there nothing positive to be said? Yes, but it must be said with caution. Again, side effects are more important than direct effects. In particular, the idea of computation and of programming languages is beginning to become an important metaphor which, in the long run, may well prove to be responsible for paradigm shifts in many fields. Most of the commonsense paradigms in terms of which much of mankind interprets the phenomena of the everyday world, both physical and social, are still deeply rooted in fundamentally mechanistic metaphors. Marx's dynamics as well as those of Freud are, for example, basically equilibrium systems. Any hydrodynamicist could come to understand them without leaving the jargon of his field. Languages capable of describing ongoing processes, particularly in terms of modular subprocesses, have already had an enormous effect on the way computer people think of every aspect of their worlds, not merely those directly related to their work. The information-processing view of the world so engendered qualifies as a genuine metaphor. This is attested to by the fact that it (i) constitutes an intellectual framework that permits new questions to be asked about a wide-ranging set of phenomena, and (ii) that it itself provides criteria for the adequacy of proffered answers. A new metaphor is important not in that it may be better than existing ones, but rather in that it may enlarge man's vision by giving him yet another perspective on his world. Indeed, the very effectiveness of a new metaphor may seduce lazy minds to adopt it as a basis for universal explanations and as a source of panaceas.

Computer simulation of social processes has already been advanced by single-minded generalists as leading to general solutions of all of mankind's problems.

The metaphors given us by religion, the poets, and by thinkers like Darwin, Newton, Freud, and Einstein have rather quickly penetrated to the language of ordinary people. These metaphors have thus been instrumental in shaping our entire civilization's imaginative reconstruction of our world. The computing metaphor is as yet available to only an extremely small set of people. Its acquisition and internalization, hopefully as only one of many ways to see the world, seems to require experience in program composition, a kind of computing literacy. Perhaps such literacy will become very widespread in the advanced societal sectors of the advanced countries. But, should it become a dominant mode of thinking and restricted to certain social classes, it will prove not merely repressive in the ordinary sense, but an enormously divisive societal force. For then classes which do and do not have access to the metaphor will, in an important sense, lose their ability to communicate with one another. We know already how difficult it is for the poor and the oppressed to communicate with the rest of the society in which they are embedded. We know how difficult it is for the world of science to communicate with that of the arts and of the humanities. In both instances the communication difficulties, which have grave consequences, are very largely due to the fact that the respective communities have unsharable experiences out of which unsharable metaphors have grown.

RESPONSIBILITY

Given these dismal possibilities, what is the responsibility of the computer scientist? First I should say that most of the harm computers can potentially entrain is much more a function of properties people attribute to computers than of what a computer can or cannot actually be made to do. The nonprofessional has little choice but to make his attributions of properties to computers on the basis of the propaganda emanating from the computer community and amplified by the press. The computer professional therefore has an enormously important responsibility to be modest in his claims. This advice would not even have to be voiced if computer science had a tradition of scholarship and of self-criticism such as that which characterizes the established sciences. The mature scientist stands in awe before the depth of his subject matter. His very humility is the wellspring of his strength. I regard the instilling of just this kind of humility, chiefly by the example set by teachers, to be one of the most important missions of every university department of computer science.

The computer scientist must be aware constantly that his instruments are capable of having gigantic direct and indirect amplifying effects. An error in a program, for example, could have grievous direct results, including most certainly the loss of much human life. On 11 September 1971, to cite just one example, a computer programming error caused the simultaneous destruction of 117 high-altitude weather balloons whose instruments were being monitored by an earth satellite.[9] A similar error in a military command and control system could launch a fleet of nuclear tipped missiles. Only censorship prevents us from knowing how many such events involving non-nuclear weapons have already occurred. Clearly then, the computer scientist has a heavy responsibility to make the fallibility and limitations of the systems he is capable of designing brilliantly clear. The very power of his systems should serve to inhibit the advice he is ready to give and to constrain the range of work he is willing to undertake.

Of course, the computer scientist, like

everyone else, is responsible for his actions and their consequences. Sometimes that responsibility is hard to accept because the corresponding authority to decide what is and what is not to be done appears to rest with distant and anonymous forces. That technology itself determines what is to be done by a process of extrapolation and that individuals are powerless to intervene in that determination is precisely the kind of self-fulfilling dream from which we must awaken.

Consider gigantic computer systems. They are, of course, natural extrapolations of the large systems we already have. Computer networks are another point on the same curve extrapolated once more. One may ask whether such systems can be used by anybody except by governments and very large corporations and whether such organizations will not use them mainly for antihuman purposes. Or consider speech recognition systems. Will they not be used primarily to spy on private communications? To answer such questions by saying that big computer systems, computer networks, and speech recognition systems are inevitable is to surrender one's humanity. For such an answer must be based either on one's profound conviction that society has already lost control over its technology or on the thoroughly immoral position that "if I don't do it, someone else will."

I don't say that systems such as I have mentioned are necessarily evil—only that they may be and, what is most important, that their inevitability cannot be accepted by individuals claiming autonomy, freedom, and dignity. The individual computer scientist can and must decide. The determination of what the impact of computers on society is to be is, at least in part, in his hands.

Finally, the fundamental question the computer scientist must ask himself is the one that every scientist, indeed every human, must ask. It is not "what shall I do?" but rather "what shall I be?" I cannot answer that for anyone save myself.

[9]R. Gillette, ibid. **174**, 477 (1971).

But I will say again that if technology is a nightmare that appears to have its own inevitable logic, it is our nightmare. It is possible, given courage and insight, for man to deny technology the prerogative to formulate man's questions. It is possible to ask human questions and to find humane answers.

The fourth discontinuity

BRUCE MAZLISH*

A famous cartoon in *The New Yorker* magazine shows a large computer with two scientists standing excitedly beside it. One of them holds in his hand the tape just produced by the machine, while the other gapes at the message printed on it. In clear letters, it says, "*Cogito, ergo sum,*" the famous Cartesian phrase, "I think, therefore I am."

My next cartoon has not yet been drawn. It is a fantasy on my part. In it, a patient, wild of eye and hair on end, is lying on a couch in a psychiatrist's office talking to an analyst who is obviously a machine. The analyst-machine is saying, "Of course I'm human—aren't you?"[1]

*Bruce Mazlish, "The Fourth Discontinuity", *Technology and Culture*, January, 1967. Reprinted from *Technology and Culture*, January 1967, by permission of the University of Chicago Press, the Society for the History of Technology, and the author. Copyright © 1967 by the Society for the History of Technology.

[1]After finishing the early drafts of this article, I secured unexpected confirmation of my "fantasy" concerning an analyst-machine (which is not, in itself, critical to my thesis). A story in the *New York Times*, March 12, 1965, reports that "a computerized typewriter has been credited with remarkable success at a hospital here in radically improving the condition of several children suffering an extremely severe form of childhood schizophrenia. ... What has particularly amazed a number of psychiatrists is that the children's improvement occurred without psychotherapy; only the machine was involved. It is almost as much human as it is machine. It talks, it listens, it responds to being touched, it makes pictures or charts, it

These two cartoons are a way of suggesting the threat which the increasingly perceived continuity between man and the machine poses to us today. It is with this topic that I wish to deal now, approaching it in terms of what I shall call the "fourth discontinuity." In order, however, to explain what I mean by the "fourth discontinuity," I must first place the term in a historical context.

In the eighteenth lecture of his *General Introduction to Psychoanalysis*, originally delivered at the University of Vienna between 1915 and 1917, Freud suggested his own place among the great thinkers of the past who had outraged man's naive self-love. First in the line was Copernicus, who taught that our earth "was not the center of the universe, but only a tiny speck in a world system of a magnitude hardly conceivable." Second was Darwin, who "robbed man of his

comments and explains, it gives information and can be set up to do all this in any order. In short, the machine attempts to combine in a sort of science-fiction instrument all the best of two worlds—human and machine. It is called an Edison Responsive Environment Learning System. It is an extremely sophisticated 'talking' typewriter (a cross between an analogue and digital computer) that can teach children how to read and write. ... Dr. Campbell Goodwin speculates that the machine was able to bring the autistic children to respond because it eliminated humans as communication factors. Once the children were able to communicate, something seemed to unlock in their minds, apparently enabling them to carry out further normal mental activities that had eluded them earlier."

peculiar privilege of having been specially created and relegated him to a descent from the animal world." Third, now, was Freud himself. On his own account, Freud admitted, or claimed, that psychoanalysis was "endeavoring to prove to the 'ego' of each one of us that he is not even master in his own house, but that he must remain content with the veriest scraps of information about what is going on unconsciously in his own mind."

A little later in 1917, Freud repeated his sketch concerning the three great shocks to man's ego. In his short essay, "A Difficulty in the Path of Psychoanalysis, he again discussed the cosmological, biological, and now psychological blows to human pride and, when challenged by his friend Karl Abraham, admitted, "You are right in saying that the enumeration of my last paper may give the impression of claiming a place beside Copernicus and Darwin."[2]

There is some reason to believe that Freud may have derived his conviction from Ernst Haeckel, the German exponent of Darwinism, who in his book *Natürliche Schöpfungsgeschichte* (1889) compared Darwin's achievement with that of Copernicus and concluded that together they had helped remove the last traces of anthropomorphism from science.[3] Whatever the origin of Freud's vision of himself as the last in the line of ego shatterers, his assertion has been generally accepted by those, like Ernest Jones, who refer to him as the "Darwin of the Mind."[4]

The most interesting extension of Freud's self-view however, has come from the American psychologist Jerome

Bruner. Bruner's version of what Freud called his "transvaluation" is in terms of the elimination of discontinuities, where discontinuity means an emphasis on breaks or gaps in the phenomena of nature—for example, a stress on the sharp differences between physical bodies in the heavens or on earth or between one form of animal matter and another—instead of an emphasis on its continuity. Put the other way, the elimination of discontinuity, that is, the establishment of a belief in a continuum of nature, can be seen as the creation of continuities, and this is the way Bruner phrases it. According to Bruner, the first continuity was established by the Greek physicist-philosophers of the sixth century, rather than by Copernicus. Thus, thinkers like Anaximander conceived of the phenomena of the physical worlds as "continuous and monistic, as governed by the common laws of matter."[5] The creating of the second continuity, that between man and the animal kingdom, was, of course, Darwin's contribution, a necessary condition for Freud's work. With Freud, according to Bruner, the following continuities were established: the continuity of organic lawfulness, so that

[5]For Bruner's views, see his "Freud and the Image of Man," *Partisan Review*, XXIII, No. 3 (Summer 1956), 340-47. In place of both Bruner's sixth-century Greek physicists and Freud's Copernicus, I would place Galileo as the breaker of the discontinuity that was thought to exist in the material world. It was Galileo, after all, who first demonstrated that the heavenly bodies are of the same substance as the "imperfect" earth and subject to the same mechanical laws. In his *Dialogue on the Two Principal World Systems* (1632), he not only supported the "world system of Copernicus against Ptolemy but established that our "world," i.e., the earth, is a natural part of the other "world," i.e. the solar system. Hence, the universe at large is one "continuous" system, a view at best only implied in Copernicus. Whatever the correct attribution —Greek physicist, Copernicus, or Galileo—Freud's point is not in principle affected.

[2]Ernest Jones, *The Life and Work of Sigmund Freud* (three vols.) (New York: Basic Books, Inc., Publishers, 1953-57), II, 224-26.

[3]Ernest Cassirer, *The Problem of Knowledge: Philosophy, Science, and History since Hegel*, trans. William H. Woglom and Charles W. Hendel (New Haven, Conn.: Yale University Press 1950), p. 160.

[4]Jones, *op. cit.*, III, 304.

"accident in human affairs was no more to be brooked as 'explanation' than accident in nature"; the continuity of the primitive, infantile, and archaic as coexisting with the civilized and evolved; and the continuity between mental illness and mental health.

In this version the three historic ego-smashings, man is placed on a continuous spectrum in relation to the universe, to the rest of the animal kingdom, and to himself. He is no longer discontinuous with the world around him. In an important sense, it can be contended, once man is able to accept this situation, he is in harmony with the rest of existence. Indeed, the longing of the early nineteenth-century romantics and of all "alienated" beings for a sense of "connection" is fulfilled in an unexpected manner.

Yet, to use Bruner's phraseology, though not his idea, a fourth and major discontinuity, or dichotomy, still exists in our time. It is the discontinuity between man and machine. In fact, my thesis is that this fourth discontinuity must now be eliminated—indeed, we have started on the task—and that in the process man's ego will have to undergo another rude shock, similar to those administered by Copernicus (or Galileo), Darwin, and Freud. To put it bluntly, we are now coming to realize that man and the machines he creates are continuous and that the same conceptual schemes, for example, that help explain the workings of his brain also explain the workings of a "thinking machine." Man's pride, and his refusal to acknowledge this continuity, is the substratum upon which the distrust of technology and an industrialized society has been reared. Ultimately, I believe, this last rests on man's refusal to understand and accept his own nature—as a being continuous with the tools and machines he constructs. Let me now try to explain what is involved in this fourth discontinuity.

The evidence seems strong today that man evolved from the other animals into humanity through a continuous interaction of tool, physical, and mental-emotional changes. The old view that early man arrived on the evolutionary scene, fully formed, and then proceeded to discover tools and the new ways of life which they made possible is no longer acceptable. As Sherwood L. Washburn, professor of anthropology at the University of California, puts it, "From the rapidly accumulating evidence it is now possible to speculate with some confidence on the manner in which the way of life made possible by tools changed the pressures of natural selection and so changed the structure of man." The details of Washburn's argument are fascinating, with its linking of tools with such physical traits as pelvic structure, bipedalism, brain structure, and so on, as well as with the organization of men in cooperative societies and substitution of morality for hormonal control of sexual and other "social" activities. Washburn's conclusion is that "it was the success of the simplest tools that started the whole trend of human evolution and led to the civilizations of today."[6]

Darwin, of course, had had a glimpse of the role of tools in man's evolution.[7] It was Karl Marx, however, who first placed the subject in a new light. Accepting Benjamin Franklin's definition of man as a "tool-making animal," Marx suggested in *Das Kapital* that "the relics of the instruments of labor are of no less importance in the study of vanished socioeconomic forms than fossil bones are in the study of the organization of extinct species." As we know, Marx wished to dedicate his great work to Darwin—a dedication rejected by the cautious biologist— and we can see part of Marx's reason for this desire in the following revealing passage:

[6]"Tools and Human Evolution," *Scientific American*, CCIII, No. 3 (September 1960), 63-75.

[7]E.g., see Charles Darwin, *The Descent of Man* (New York: D. Appleton; Co., 1872), pp.431-32, 458.

Darwin has aroused our interest in the history of *natural technology*, that is to say in the origin of the organs of plants and animals as productive instruments utilized for the life purposes of those creatures. Does not the history of the origin of the productive organs of men in society, the organs which form the material basis of every kind of social organization, deserve equal attention? Since, as Vico [in the *New Science* (1725)] says, the essence of the distinction between human history and natural history is that the former is the work of man and the latter is not, would not the history of *human technology* be easier to write than the history of natural technology? Technology reveals man's dealings with nature, discloses the direct productive activities of his life, thus throwing light upon social relations and the resultant mental conceptions.[8]

Only a dogmatic anti-Marxist could deny that Marx's brilliant imagination had led him to perceive a part of the continuity between man and his tools. Drawn off the track, perhaps, by Vico's distinction between human and natural history as man made and God made, Marx might almost be given a place in the pantheon of Copernicus, Darwin, and Freud as a destroyer of man's discontinuities with the world about him. Before our present-day anthropologists, Marx had sensed the unbreakable connection between man's evolution as a social being and his development of tools. He did not sense, however, the second part of our subject, that man and his tools, especially in the form of modern, complicated machines, are part of a theoretical continuum.

The *locus classicus* of the modern insistence on the fourth discontinuity is, as is well known, the work of Descartes. In his *Discourse on Method,* for example, he sets up God and the soul on one side, as without spatial location or extension, and the material-mechanical world in all its aspects, on the other side. Insofar as man's mind or soul participates in

reason—which means God's reason—man knows this division or dualism of mind and matter, for, as Descartes points out, man could not know this fact from his mere understanding, which is based solely on his senses, "a location where it is clearly evident that the ideas of God and the soul have never been."[9]

Once having established his God and man's participation through reason in God, Descartes could advance daringly to the very precipice of a world without God. He conjures up a world in imaginary space and shows that it must run according to known natural laws. Similarly, he imagines that "God formed the body of a man just like our own, both in the external configuration of its members and in the internal configuration of its organs, without using in its composition any matter but that which I had described [i.e., physical matter]. I also assumed that God did not put into this body any rational soul [defined by Descartes as "that part of us distinct from the body whose essence . . . is only to think"]."

Analyzing this purely mechanical man, Descartes boasts of how he has shown "what changes must take place in the brain to cause wakefulness, sleep, and dreams; how light, sounds, odors, taste, heat, and all the other qualities of external objects can implant various ideas through the medium of the senses, . . . I explained what must be understood by that animal sense which receives these ideas, by memory which retains them, and by imagination which can change them in various ways and build new ones from them." In what way, then, does such a figure differ from real man? Descartes confronts his own created "man" forthrightly; it is worth quoting the whole of his statement:

Here I paused to show that if there were any machines which had the organs and appear-

---

[8]Italics mine; Karl Marx, *Capital*. trans. Eden and Cedar Paul (2 vols.) (London, 1951), I, 392-93, note 2.

[9]René Descartes, *Discourse on Method*, trans. Laurence J. Lafleur (Indianapolis, Ind.: The Bobbs-Merrill Co., Inc., 1956), p. 24. The rest of the quotations are also from this translation, pp. 29, 35-36, and 36-37.

ance of a monkey or of some other unreasoning animal, we would have no way of telling that it was not of the same nature as these animals. But if there were a machine which had such a resemblance to our bodies and imitated our actions as far as possible, there would always be two absolutely certain methods of recognizing that it was still not truly a man. The first is that it could never use words or other signs for the purpose of communicating its thoughts to others, as we do. It indeed is conceivable that a machine could be so made that it would utter words and even words appropriate to physical acts which cause some change in its organs; as, for example, if it was touched in some spot that it would ask what you wanted to say to it; if in another, that it would cry that it was hurt, and so on for similar thing. But it could never modify its phrases to reply to the sense of whatever was said in its presence, as even the most stupid men can do. The second method of recognition is that although such machines could do many things as well as, or perhaps ever better than men, they would infallibly fail in certain others, by which we would discover that they did not act by understanding, but only by the disposition of their organs. For while reason is a universal instrument which can be used in all sorts of situations, the organs have to be arranged in a particular way for each particular action. From this it follows that it is morally impossible that there should be enough different devices in a machine to make it behave in all the occurrences of life as our reason makes us behave.

Put in its simplist terms, Descartes' two criteria for discriminating between man and the machine are that the latter has (1) no feedback mechanism ("it could never modify its phrases") and (2) no generalizing reason ("reason is a universal instrument which can be used in all sorts of situations"). But it is exactly in these points that, today, we are no longer able so surely to sustain the dichotomy. The work of Norbert Wiener and his followers, in cybernetics, indicates what can be done on the problem of feedback. Investigations into the way the brain itself forms concepts are basic to the attempt to build computers that can do the same, and the two efforts are going forward

simultaneously, as in the work of Dr. W.K. Taylor of University College, London, and of others. As G. Rattray Taylor sums up the matter: "One can't therefore be quite as confident that computers will one day equal or surpass man in concept-forming ability as one can about memory, since the trick hasn't yet been done; but the possibilities point that way."[10] In short, the gap between man's thinking and that of his thinking machines had been greatly narrowed by recent research.

Descartes, of course, would not have been happy to see such a development realized. To eliminate the dichotomy or discontinuity between man and machines would be, in effect, to banish God from the universe. The rational soul, Descartes insisted, "could not possibly be derived from the powers of matter . . . but must have been specially created." Special creation requires God, for Descartes' reasoning is circular. The shock to man's ego, of learning the Darwinian lesson that he was not "specially created," is, in this light, only an outlying tremor of the great earthquake that threatened man's view of God as well as of himself. The obstacles to removing not only the first three but also the fourth discontinuity are, clearly, deeply imbedded in man's pride of place.

How threatening these developments were can be seen in the case of Descartes' younger contemporary, Blaise Pascal. Aware that man is "a thinking reed," Pascal also realized that he was "engulfed in the infinite immensity of spaces whereof I know nothing and which knows nothing of me." "I am terrified," he confessed. To escape his feeling of terror, Pascal fled from reason to faith, convinced that reason could not bring him to God. Was he haunted by his own construction, at age nineteen, of a cal-

---

[10]See G. Rattray Taylor, "The Age of the Androids," *Encounter* (November 1963), p. 43. On p. 40 Taylor gives some of the details of the work of W.K. Taylor and others.

culating machine which, in principle, anticipated the modern digital computer? By his own remark that "the arithmetical machine produces effects which approach nearer to thought than all the actions of animals"? Ultimately, to escape the anxiety that filled his soul, Pascal commanded, "On thy knees, powerless reason."[11]

Others, of course, walked where angels feared to tread. Thus, sensationalist psychologists and epistemologists, like Locke, Hume, or Condillac, without confronting the problem head on, treated the contents of man's reason as being formed by his sense impressions. Daring thinkers, like La Mettrie in his *L'Homme machine* (1747) and Holbach, went all the way to a pure materialism. As La Mettrie put it in an anticipatory transcendence of the fourth discontinuity, "I believe thought to be so little incompatible with organized matter that it seems to be a property of it, like electricity, motive force, impenetrability, extension, etc."[12]

On the practical front, largely leaving aside the metaphysical aspects of the problem, Pascal's work on calculating machines was taken up by those like the eccentric nineteenth-century mathematician Charles Babbage, whose brilliant designs outran the technology available to him.[13] Thus it remained for another century, the twentieth, to bring the matter to a head and to provide the combination of mathematics, experimental physics, and modern technology that created the machines that now confront us and that reawaken the metaphysical question.

The implications of the metaphysical question are clear. Man feels threatened by the machine, that is, by his tools writ large, and feels out of harmony with himself because he is out of harmony—what I have called discontinuous—with the machines that are part of himself. Today, it is fashionable to describe such a state by the term "alienation." In the Marxist phraseology, we are alienated from our selves when we place false gods or economies over us and then behave as if they had a life of their own, eternal and independent of ourselves, and, indeed, in control of our lives. My point, while contact can be established between it and the notion of alienation, is a different one. It is in the tradition of Darwin and Freud, rather than of Marx, and is concerned more with man's ego than with his sense of alienation.

A brief glimpse at two "myths" concerning the machine may illuminate what I have in mind. The first is Samuel Butler's negative utopia, *Erewhon*, and the second is Mary Shelley's story of Frankenstein. In Butler's novel, published in 1872, we are presented with Luddism carried to its final point. The story of the Erewhonian revolution against the machines is told in terms of a purported translation from a manuscript, "The Book of the Machines," urging men on to the revolt and supposedly written just before the long civil war between the machinists and the antimachinists, in which half the population was destroyed. The prescient flavor of the revolutionry author's fears can be caught in such passages as follows:[14]

"There is no security"—to quote his own words—"against the ultimate development of

[11]For details, see J. Bronowski and Bruce Mazlish, *The Western Intellectual Tradition: From Leonardo to Hegel* (New York: Harper & Row, Publishers, 1960), pp. 233-41.

[12]See Stephen Toulmin, "The Importance of Norbert Wiener," *New York Review of Books*, September 24, 1964, p. 4, for an indication of La Mettrie's importance in this development. While Toulmin does not put his material in the context of the fourth discontinuity, I find we are in fundamental agreement about what is afoot in this matter.

[13]See Philip and Emily Morrison, eds., *Charles Babbage and His Calculating Engines* (New York: Dover Publications, Inc., 1961).

[14]The quotations that follow are from Samuel Butler, *Erewhon* (Baltimore, 1954), pp. 161, 164, 167-68, and 171.

mechanical consciousness, in the fact of machines' possessing little consciousness now. A mollusk has not much consciousness. Reflect upon the extraordinary advance which machines have made during the last few hundred years, and note how slowly the animal and vegetable kingdoms are advancing. The more highly organized machines are creatures not so much of yesterday as of the last five minutes, so to speak, in comparison with past time. Assume for the sake of argument that conscious beings have existed for some twenty million years: See what strides machines have made in the last thousand! May not the world last twenty million years longer? If so, what will they not in the end become? Is it not safer to nip the mischief in the bud and to forbid them further progress?

"But who can say that the vapor engine has not a kind of consciousness? Where does consciousness begin and where end? Who can draw the line? Is not everything interwoven with everything? Is not machinery linked with animal life in an infinite variety of ways? The shell of a hen's egg is made of a delicate white ware and is a machine as much as an egg cup is; the shell is a device for holding the egg as much as the egg cup for holding the shell: Both are phases of the same function; the hen makes the shell in her inside, but it is pure pottery. She makes her nest outside of herself for convenience's sake, but the nest is not more of a machine than the egg shell is. A 'machine' is only a 'device.' "

Then he continues:

"Do not let me be misunderstood as living in fear of any actually existing machine; there is probably no known machine which is more than a prototype of future mechanical life. The present machines are to the future as the early Saurians to man. The largest of them will probably greatly diminish in size. Some of the lowest vertebrata attained a much greater bulk than has descended to their more highly organized living representatives, and in like manner a diminution in the size of machines has often attended their development and progress."

Answering the argument that the machine, even when more fully developed, is merely man's servant, the writer contends:

"But the servant glides by imperceptible ap-

proaches into the master; and we have come to such a pass that, even now, man must suffer terribly on ceasing to benefit the machines.... Man's very soul is due to the machines; it is a machine-made thing; he thinks as he thinks and feels as he feels through the work that machines have wrought upon him, and their existence is quite as much a *sine qua non* for his as his for theirs. This fact precludes us from proposing the complete annihilation of machinery, but surely it indicates that we should destroy as many of them as we can possibly dispense with, lest they should tyrannize over us even more completely."

And, finally, the latent sexual threat is dealt with:

"It is said by some with whom I have conversed upon this subject, that the machines can never be developed into animate or quasianimate existences, inasmuch as they have no reproductive systems nor seem ever likely to possess one. If this be taken to mean that they cannot marry and that we are never likely to see a fertile union between two vapor engines with the young ones playing about the door of the shed, however greatly we might desire to do so, I will readily grant it. But the objection is not a very profound one. No one expects that all the features of the now existing organizations will be absolutely repeated in an entirely new class of life. The reproductive system of animals differs widely from that of plants, but both are reproductive systems. Has nature exhausted her phases of this power?"

Inspired by fears such as these, which sound like our present realities, the Erewhonians rise up and destroy almost all their machines. It is only years after this supposed event that they are sufficiently at ease so as to collect the fragmentary remains, the "fossils," of the now defunct machines and place them in a museum. At this point, the reader is never sure whether Butler's satire is against Darwin or the anti-Darwinists, probably both, but there is no question of the satire when he tells us how machines were divided into "their genera, subgenera, species, varieties, subvarities, and so forth" and how the Erewhonians "proved the existence of connecting links between machines that seemed to have very little in common and showed that many more such links had existed, but had now perished." It is as if Butler had taken Marx's point about *human technology* and stood it on its head!

Going even further, Butler foresaw the threatened ending of the fourth discontinuity, just as he saw Darwin's work menacing the third of the discontinuities we have discussed. Thus, we find Butler declaring, in the guise of his Erewhonian author, "I shrink with as much horror from believing that my race ever be superseded or surpassed as I should do from believing that even at the remotest period my ancestors were other than human beings. Could I believe that ten hundred thousand years ago a single one of my ancestors was another kind of being to myself, I should lose all self-respect and take no further pleasure or interest in life. I have the same feeling with regard to my descendants and believe it to be one that will be felt so generally that the country will resolve upon putting an immediate stop to all further mechanical progress and upon destroying all improvements that have been made for the last 3oo years." The counter argument, that "machines were to be regarded as a part of man's own physical nature, being really nothing but extracorporeal limbs. Man [is] a machinate mammal," is dismissed out of hand.

Many of these same themes—the servant-machine rising against its master, the fear of the machine reproducing itself (fundamentally, a sexual fear, as Caliban illustrates and as our next example will show), the terror, finally, of man realizing that he is at one with the machine—can be found attached to an earlier myth, that of Frankenstein. Now passed into our folklore, people frequently give little attention to the actual details of the novel. First, the name Frankenstein is often given to the monster created, rather than to its creator; yet, in the book, Frankenstein is the name of the scientist, and his abortion *has no name.*

Second, the monster is *not* a machine but a "flesh and blood" product; even so informed a student as Oscar Handlin makes the typical quick shift, in an echo of Butler's fears, when he says, "The monster, however, quickly proves himself the superior. In the confrontation, the machine gives the orders."[15] Third, and last, it is usually forgotten or overlooked that the monster turns to murder *because* his creator, horrified at his production, refuses him human love and kindness. Let us look at a few of the details.

In writing her "Gothic" novel 1816-17, Mary Shelley gave it the subtitle "The Modern Prometheus."[16] We can see why if we remember that Prometheus defied the gods and gave fire to man. Writing in the typical early nineteenth-century romantic vein, Mary Shelley offers Frankenstein as an example of "how dangerous is the acquirement of knowledge"; in this case, specifically, the capability of "bestowing animation upon lifeless matter." In the novel we are told of how, having collected his materials from "the disecting room and the slaughterhouse" (as Wordsworth has said of modern science, "We murder to dissect"), Frankenstein eventually completes his loathsome task when he infuses "a spark of being into the lifeless thing that lay at my feet." Then, as he tells us, "now that I had finished, the beauty of the dream vanished, and breathless horror and disgust filled my heart." Rushing from the room, Frankenstein goes to his bedchamber, where he had a most odd dream concerning the corpse of his dead mother—the whole book as well as this passage cries out for psychoanalytic intrepretation —from which he is awakened by "the wretch—the miserable monster whom I had created." Aghast at the countenance

[15]"Science and Technology in Popular Culture," *Daedalus* (Wnter 1965), 156-70.

[16]The quotations that follow are from Mary Shelley, *Frankenstein* (New York: Dell Publishing Company, 1953), pp. 30-33, 36-37, 85, and 160-61.

of what he has created, Frankenstein escapes from the room and out into the open. Upon finally returning to his room with a friend, he is relieved to find the monster gone.

To understand the myth, we need to recite a few further details in this weird, and rather badly written, story. Frankenstein's monster eventually finds his way to a hovel attached to a cottage occupied by a blind father and his son and daughter. Unperceived by them, he learns the elements of social life (the fortuitous ways in which this is made to occur may strain the demanding reader's credulity), even to the point of reading *Paradise Lost*. Resolved to end his unbearable solitude, the monster, convinced that his virtues of the heart will win over the cottagers, makes his presence known. The result is predictable: Horrified by his appearance, they duplicate the behavior of his creator and flee. In wrath, the monster turns against the heartless world. He kills, and his first victim, by accident, is Frankenstein's young brother.

Pursued by Frankenstein, a confrontation between creator and created takes place, and the monster explains his road to murder. He appeals to Frankenstein in a torrential address:

"I entreat you to hear me, before you give vent to your hatred on my devoted head. Have I not suffered enough that you seek to increase my misery? Life, although it may only be an accumulation of anguish, is dear to me, and I will defend it. Remember, thou hast made me more powerful than thyself; my height is superior to thine; my joints more supple. But I will not be tempted to set myself in opposition to thee. I am thy creature, and I will be even mild and docile to my natural lord and king, if thou wilt also perform thy part, the which thou owest me. Oh, Frankenstein, be not equitable to every other and trample upon me alone, to whom thy justice, and even thy clemency and affection, is most due. Remember, that I am thy creature; I ought to be thy Adam; but I am rather the fallen angel, whom thou drives from joy for no misdeed. Everywhere I see bliss, from which I alone am irrevocably excluded. I was benevolent and good; misery made me a fiend. Make me happy, and I shall again be virtuous."

Eventually, the monster extracts from Frankenstein a promise to create a partner for him "of another sex," with whom he will then retire into the vast wilds of South America, away from the world of men. But Frankenstein's "compassion" does not last long. In his laboratory again, Frankenstein indulges in a long soliloquy:

"I was now about to form another being, of whose dispositions I was alike ignorant; she might become 10,000 times more malignant than her mate, and delight, for its own sake, in murder and wretchedness. He had sworn to quit the neighborhood of man and hide himself in deserts; but she had not; and she, who in all probability was to become a thinking and reasoning animal, might refuse to comply with a compact made before her creation. They might even hate each other; the creature who already lived loathed his own deformity, and might he not conceive a greater abhorrence for it when it came before his eyes in the female form? She also might turn with disgust from him to the superior beauty of man; she might quit him, and he be again alone, exasperated by the fresh provocation of being deserted by one of his own species.

"Even if they were to leave Europe and inhabit the deserts of the new world, yet one of the first results of those sympathies for which the demon thirsted would be children, and a race of devils would be propagated upon the earth who might make the very existence of the species of man a condition precarious and full of terror. Had I right, for my own benefit, to inflict this curse upon everlasting generations?"

With the monster observing him through the window, Frankenstein destroys the female companion on whom he had been working. With this, the novel relentlessly winds its way to its end. In despair and out of revenge, the monster kills Frankenstein's best friend, Clerval, then Frankenstein's new bride, Elizabeth. Fleeing to the frozen north, the monster is tracked down by Frankenstein (shades of Moby Dick?), who dies, however, before he can destroy him. But it does not matter; the monster wishes his own death and promises to place himself on a funeral pyre and thus at last secure the spiritual peace for which he has yearned.

I have summerized the book because I suspect that few readers will actually be acquainted with the myth of Frankenstein *as written* by Mary Shelley. For most of us, Frankenstein is Boris Karloff, clumping around stiff, automatic, and threatening: a machine of sorts. We shall have forgotten completely, if ever we knew, that the monster, *cum* machine, is evil, or rather, becomes evil, only because it is spurned by man.

My thesis has been that man is on the threshold of breaking past the discontinuity between himself and machines. In one part, this is because man now can perceive his own evolution as inextricably interwoven with his use and development of tools, of which the modern machine is only the furthest extrapolation. We cannot think any longer of man without a machine. In another part, this is because modern man perceives that the same scientific concepts help explain the workings of himself and of his machines and that the evolution of matter—from the basic building blocks of hydrogen turning into helium in the distant stars, then fusing into carbon nuclei and on up to iron, and then exploding into space, which has resulted in our solar system —continues on earth in terms of the same carbon atoms and their intricate patterns into the structure of organic life, and now into the architecture of our thinking machines.

It would be absurd, of course, to contend that there are no differences between man and machines. This would be the same *reductio ad absurdum* as involved in claiming that because he is an animal, there is no difference between man and the other animals. The matter, of course,

is one of degree.[17] What is claimed here is that the sharp discontinuity between man and machines is no longer tenable, in spite of the shock to our egos. Scientists, today, know this; the public at large does not, *New Yorker* cartoons to the contrary.[18]

[17]In semifacetious fashion, I have argued with some of my more literal-minded friends that what distinguishes man from existing machines and probably will always so distinguish him is an *effective* Oedipus complex: *vive la différence!* For an excellent and informed philosophical treatment of the difference between man and machines, see J. Bronowski, *The Identity of Man* (Garden City, N.Y: Doubleday & Company, Inc., 1965).

[18]As in so much else, children "know" what their parents have forgotten. As O. Mannoni tells us, in the course of explaining totemism, "children, instead of treating animals as machines, treat machines as living things, the more highly prized because they are easier to appropriate. Children's appropriation is a virtual identification, and they play at being machines (steam engines, motor cars, and planes) just as 'primitive' people play at being the totem [animal]" (*Prospero and Caliban, The Psychology of Colonization*, trans. Pamela Powesland [New York: Frederick A. Praeger, Inc., Publishers, 1964], p. 82). In *Huckleberry Finn*, Mark Twain puts this "identification" to work in describing Tom Sawyer's friend Ben Rogers: "He was eating an apple and giving a long, melodious whoop, at intervals, followed by a deep-toned ding-dong-dong, ding-dong dong, for he was personating a steamboat. As he drew near, he slackened speed, took the middle of the street, leaned far over to starboard, and rounded to ponderously and with laborious pomp and circumstance—for he was personating the *Big Missouri* and considered himself to be drawing nine feet of water. He was boat and captain and enginebells combined, so he had to imagine himself standing on his own hurricane deck giving the orders and executing them! . . . 'Stop the stabboard! Ting-a-ling-ling! Stop the labboard! Come ahead on the stabboard! Stop her! Let your outside turn over slow! Ting-a-ling! Chow-ow-aw! Get out that headline! *Lively* now! Come—out with your springling—what're you about there! Take a turn round that stump with the bight of it!

Moreover, this change in our metaphysical awareness, this transcendence of the fourth discontinuity, is essential to our harmonious acceptance of an industrialized world. The alternatives are either a frightened rejection of the "Frankensteins" we have created or a blind belief in their "superhuman virtues" and a touching faith that they can solve all our human problems. Alas, in the perspective I have suggested, machines are "mechanical, all too mechanical," to paraphrase Nietzsche. But, in saying this, I have already also said that they are "all too human" as well. The question, then, is whether we are to repeat the real Frankenstein story and, turning from the "monsters" we have created, turn aside at the same time from our own humanity, or alternatively, whether we are to accept the blow to our egos and enter into a world beyond the fourth discontinuity?

Stand by that stage, now—let her go! Done with the engines, sir! Ting-a-ling! *sh't! sh't! sh't!*' " See the analysis of this passage in Erik H. Erickson, *Childhood and Society* (2nd ed.) (New York: W.H. Norton & Company, Inc., Publishers, 1963), pp. 209ff.

The second coming

W. B. YEATS*

Turning and turning in the widening gyre
The falcon cannot hear the falconer;
Things fall apart; the centre cannot hold;
Mere anarchy is loosed upon the world,
The blood-dimmed tide is loosed, and everywhere
The ceremony of innocence is drowned;
The best lack all conviction, while the worst
Are full of passionate intensity.

Surely some revelation is at hand;
Surely the Second Coming is at hand.
The Second Coming! Hardly are those words out
When a vast image out of *Spiritus Mundi*
Troubles my sight: somewhere in the sands of the desert.
A shape with lion body and the head of a man,
A gaze blank and pitiless as the sun,
Is moving its slow thighs, while all about it
Reel shadows of the indignant desert birds.
The darkness drops again; but now I know
That twenty centuries of stony sleep
Were vexed to nightmare by a rocking cradle,
And what rough beast, its hour come round at last,
Slouches towards Bethlehem to be born?

* W. B. Yeats, "The Second Coming",
Collected Poems. Copyright © 1924 by the
Macmillan Co. Inc., renewed 1952 by Bertha
Georgie Yeats. Reprinted with permission of
Macmillan Co., Inc., New York, M. B. Yeats,
Miss Anne Yeats and The Macmillan Com-
pany of London and Basingstoke.

An ethos for the age of cyberculture*

ALICE MARY HILTON†

PART ONE—NEED FOR A NEW ETHOS

I. New Conditions

"Acceptability," said John Kenneth Galbraith, "is the hallmark of the conventional wisdom."[1]

Since, however, the pronouncement of the conventional wisdom is the prerogative of those in eminent public, academic, business, or labor positions, I am not privileged to bore you with a recital of the conventional wisdom, and —even if I could do so—to entertain you by expounding it at a properly sophisticated level. I must, therefore, look to that archenemy of the conventional wisdom—the march of events.

If ever a period in the history of man demanded radical—I am using "radical," derived from radix, root, in its original sense, namely, going to the roots —fundamental wisdom, it is surely this revolutionary period of transition to a new era—the age of cyberculture—the new era that is formed by a science, cybernetics, born barely a quarter of a century ago, and a technology that, for all its precocious development, has barely left the cradle. Most of us in this room were probably proud midwives assisting in the delivery of the computing machine only a decade or so ago.

Since then, the world has changed radically. Three powerful new phenomena have precociously reached their vigorous, boisterous adolescence—long before the world is prepared for the scientific-social-technological-economic-cultural revolution that has been unleashed. Those in the center of any revolution are always the least disturbed. The hub of a wheel is fairly stable, the eye of a hurricane is calm, and those who create the concepts and forge the tools of complex social revolutions are neither alarmed by the enormous power of their brainchildren nor are they surprised.

Never has a powerful and complete revolution developed more quickly than this cybercultural revolution that is affecting the lives of millions of human beings who have never even heard the new words to describe powerful new concepts. In fact, things have been happening so fast that even those who know a great deal about one of the phenomena have not had time to learn enough about the others—or about the world they are changing.

First among the new phenomena is nuclear science. Introduced to a stunned world in its least attractive manifestation, nuclear science holds untold mysteries, unimaginable terror, and vast promises. Einstein said, when the atom was split everything changed except our thinking. Far too many people still think of thermonuclear bombs as superslingshots.[1] Others realize that nuclear science might provide the vast reservoir of physical energy we need to produce abundance for all mankind. We have great hopes for atoms for peace and must search for a way to use atoms for people.

The second of the powerful new phenomena is not clearly focused yet, although a demonstration of the destructive potential of nuclear science has shocked the entire world to see, at least as a vague vision, the new concept: peace as a positive phenomenon, a valuable and workable instrument to settle human conflicts. That is quite different from

* Cyberculture is composed of "cybernetics," the science of control, and "culture," the way of life of a society.

†Mary Hilton, "An Ethos for the Age of Cyberculture", Data Processing Yearbook 1965. Reprinted from Data Processing Yearbook, 1965. Copyright © American Data Processing, Inc., 1965. Reprinted by permission.

[1]John Kenneth Galbraith, The Affluent Society (Boston: Houghton Mifflin Company, 1958).

man's past experience for since the beginning of history mankind has known as an alternative to war only the complement of war, an interlude between wars, occasionally even a reasonably prolonged absence of war. Even when there was no fighting, war has been regarded as the normal and accepted means to settle conflicts. Contrary to popular opinion, it is not a foregone conclusion that peace will bring about the millenium. There is no reason to believe that conflicts will disappear. And to use peace, rather than war, as an instrument to settle conflicts will require more ingenuity and intelligence and skill than to devise means to win wars. Difficult though it may be to live with, peace is the essential condition, if human civilization is to survive at all.

The least known and most far-reaching new phenomenon is the science of cybernetics and the revolutionary technology based upon its discoveries. Automatic systems and computing machines, even in their infancy, have an impact upon our world that could not have been imagined two decades ago; and they have the clearly foreseeable potential to produce not only unprecedented abundance for human beings, but relieve man forever of drudgery and toil. Yet, even experts still look at the computing machine as a superabacus.

Any effort to deduce how observable phenomena are likely to develop and affect the environment involves some arbitrary assumptions that must be defined and granted. The major assumption in my hypothesis is so fundamental that, should it prove to be unreasonable, nothing on earth is likely to be proved or disproved again. I assume that the cold war will not be escalated into the nuclear fission of the earth, but that, on the contrary, it will continue to defrost. I further assume that all of us in the field of data-processing and automation will continue to do our jobs with as much ingenuity and enthusiasm as we have in the past and to develop our precocious brainchildren, as we have every reason to expect from our auspicious start.

As we know, there is a great deal of confusion in the public mind about the words "automatic" and about the effects of these rarely recognized phenomena. Economic pundits have made solemn pronouncements about the future impact of "automation" and based their predictions firmly upon a past experience with mechanization and its impact upon employment and the Gross National Product. A few months ago, Secretary of Labor Wirtz estimated that automatic systems have reached the intellectual level of human high school graduates.[2]

Monumental fallacies are incorporated into such statements because the basic premises used by economic pundits and by the Secretary of Labor are incorrect; they confuse automation with sophisticated mechanization and use these basically incomparable phenomena interchangeably. If they could realize that the most sophisticated and efficient mechanical system—no matter how many electrical components are incorporated—is an open system that cannot operate unless the control loop is closed by a human being who must become part of the system, whereas an automatic system is a closed system in which the human component has been supplanted by a computing machine, they would understand that the conventional methods to inoculate the economy against periodic epidemics of unemployment and slackness are no longer relevant.

Before the Congress has been able to accept the conventional wisdom of one generation ago, everything changed. Everything but our thinking! And I must quote again John Kenneth Galbraith, who wrote that "the shortcomings of economics are not original error, but uncorrected obsolescence." We rightly cherish our intellectual heritage, but we must not allow it to calcify. The

[2]W. W. Wirtz, Address to the National Convention of the AFL-CIO (New York, 1963).

economic-political and social wisdom humanity may have acquired so painfully in the past must be tempered with new insights and forever reevaluated with an open mind, just as the scientific and technical heritage of the past is constantly reexamined and revitalized by new discoveries and inventions.

II. Agriculture and Cyberculture

The present Cybercultural Revolution is comparable in magnitude only to the Agricultural Revolution, the ferment out of which all civilization arose. The Agricultural Revolution changed the earth from a jungle into a garden where food gatherers became food producers—who plant and harvest, who create a surplus over their need, and thus build civilizations. With the Agricultural Revolution man first began to emerge into humanity. He learned to control his environment, to adapt it to his needs, and to arrange his life into social patterns. The agricultural revolution that began to free man for his specifically human task changed the very nature of man.

Every society in the age of agriculture goes through recurring cycles of scarcity and surplus, of leisure and drudgery. For centuries this has been the human situation: part drudgery, part creative endeavor; part scarcity, part waste. The Cybercultural Revolution can create a world where machine systems produce undreamed of abundance, and where human beings live human lives and are free to pursue as yet undefined human tasks.

Man in the Stone Age knew his task was to find food for himself and his young and to protect them from the dangers of a hostile world. He carved images on the walls of his cave, and sometimes there must have been a genius who observed the world closely, who somehow saw a pattern in remote incidents. He might have noticed that small plants grow into trees; that seeds spread by the wind or dropped by birds into the earth come forth again as plants, and that roots multiply and that

some plants grew on the same spot again and again. He gathered the seeds and put them into the earth himself and watched over them and saw them bear fruit. And the age of agriculture could be born.

Man learned to till the earth to produce bountifully, to tame animals to help him pull the plow, to use the power of water and the wind to multiply the strength of his own muscles. In the course of many centuries man has developed complex tools which extend the perceptiveness of his senses and the skill of his hands and devised powerful machines to extend the strength of his muscles. But man alone can direct and guide his aids. He must still labor for his bread.

The Cybercultural Revolution is brought about by the invention of devices that supplement the labor of man's mind. In the age of cyberculture the plows pull themselves, and the planting and harvesting [are] controlled by tirelessly efficient electronic slaves.

III. What Are Human Tasks?

Man must learn to find tasks to fill his days. If he no longer needs to pull the plow and clear the fields and forge the iron, how will he tire his muscles to earn his rest? How will he use his mind to earn his peace? How will he stand upon the earth he has not tilled in the sweat of his face and feel that he is its master? What will he do with his life, if he no longer has to labor to earn his right to live?[3]

For centuries, and in every land, men have told stories about all-powerful, completely obedient slaves who would supply riches and ease. The brooms conjured up by the sorcerer's apprentice, the genie in the lamp, the monkey's paw —these are the stories of man's desire for a perfect slave and also of his fear. For man was always aware of his own inadequacy and he was not sure that he could control so perfect a servant with wisdom and with honor.

We can expect that in the age of cyberculture enormous populations will live in leisure. A few will "work." But no one will labor in drudgery and sweat. This will be technologically feasible in a few decades. Inventions can be speeded with the motivation for perfection. During World War II, the invention of radar was accelerated—in the opinion of eminent scientists—by many decades. But cultural lag may delay to bring cyberculture to its maturity for centuries. Reluctance to change obsolete ways of thinking, conflicts of interests, the short-sightedness of those who fear what they cannot fully understand can delay the future and use the best fruits of man's mind for his destruction rather than his joy.

IV. The Problems of Transition

The problems of transition from an agricultural-industrial to a cybercultural society are momentous. This is only the beginning. Unemployment, serious though it is, is not disastrously widespread yet. But soon it will be, if we refuse to face the fact that unemployment cannot be arrested, even with the most phenomenal economic growth rate in the world, for the acceleration of automation will always exceed the acceleration of the growth rate. Unemployment must be changed to leisure. If we can learn to live with and use our electronic and mechanical slaves, rather than abuse our human bodies and our human minds, we can solve all the other problems that plague us now: the fear of unemployment, the envy the poor nations have for the rich nations and the fear the latter have of the former, the suspicious competition among the powerful. We negotiate about disarmament, but watching the unemployment figures rise, we quickly vote more money to be spent on producing lethal weapons. And as the unemployment monster rises, those who are gobbled up most easily—the unskilled—become afraid and rise in hatred and despair. Unskilled Negroes think it is the color of their skin that keeps them unemployed and white men fear that they will have to share the labor that is not fit for human beings and that none need to do in

the age of cyberculture. Unions are losing members and try to stretch diminishing jobs by dividing them among more men, instead of enlisting as members those whose work can be done by machines and teaching them how to live human lives.

The slower the transition from an agricultural-industrial society to a cybercultural society, the greater is the suffering that must be endured, and the smaller the chance that—if humanity survives into the next century—the emerging age of cyberculture will be a good age for human beings. Slow transition does not cushion difficulties any more than pulling a tooth a little bit at a time softens the pain. The difficulties are not caused by the new age, but only by the transition itself—so that the problem can be solved only as transition is accomplished. The best transition is a fast transition. If we could have the wisdom to introduce as much automation as quickly as it is technologically feasible, we could create the age of cyberculture in two decades. Slow transition would bring such intense and widespread suffering that it may break into nuclear war—and end all civilization.

V. Morality and Ethos

To create the age of cyberculture requires something far more difficult than scientific discoveries and technical inventions. We must reexamine our moral values and our ethical concepts and the deeply ingrained notions to which we give lip service. And we must understand the difference between the moral values of mankind and the ethos of a society. The sanctity of human life, the worth and dignity of the individual are moral values that are absolute; these always have been true and always will be true, as long as there are human beings. But the ethos of a society is transient, and it must alter with the needs of the society.

What we call our Protestant Ethic, although it is much older and spread far wider than protestantism, is the ethos of any society that knows scarcity and danger. It is a good ethos where virgin forests must be cleared and wagon trains sent across a continent. It is a good ethos as long as men must wrest their meager fare from the earth with courage and fortitude and perseverance. In such a society, it is right that man should labor to plow the fields so that he might eat the fruits of the earth and bask in the sunshine of the heavens and dream under the shade of the trees. "Thou shalt eat thy bread in the sweat of the face" is a good and reasonable precept in the age of agriculture.

Already the ethos of scarcity is becoming an unjust burden. All too often thrift is no longer a god but the graven image of past days to which we give lip service. To save one's earnings and thriftily mend last year's coat, and use last year's car, and warm up last night's supper no longer is admired. But—the ethos that commands man to eat his bread in the sweat of his face still governs our personal lives and our national policies. Although for millions of human beings there is no place where they can put sweat on their faces, we still believe that there can never be another ethos for the future than the obsolete ethos of the past. And every year we are condemning more than two million human beings to the swelling ranks of the unwanted. We suspect them of incompetence and laziness, or we pity them. We should reexamine the ethos that condemns millions who are simply the first contingent of citizens living under cybercultural conditions, without any preparation for the new age.

When human intelligence has invented plows that pull themselves, it is more virtuous to know how to play and learn how to live for the joy of living than to bemoan the end of human toil.

As sons and daughters of puritans we do not know how to play and we look with terror at the "threat" of unemployment and idleness, because we can't conceive a promise of leisure. What we call play, recreation, and entertainment is not play,

but its very antithesis. Play is something one does spontaneously, joyfully. We rarely do anything just for the joy of doing; but we do a great deal "in order to" gain something else. Instead of enjoying a holiday, we take a vacation—the very word signifies that it is merely a void between the activities we consider real. The "vacation" is something we use "in order to" have more strength for our labors. Recreation is something we pursue "in order to" recreate our energy. Entertainment is "in order to" forget our cares. We eat "in order to" replenish our energy. Our children are trained for the joyless ethos of scarcity and given candy "in order to" do something adults consider virtuous. Only the very young are fortunate enough to be ignorant of this grim purpose and suck their lollypops in blissful ignorance and joy. But even the youngest toddlers are not permitted to play for very long. Before they leave the cradle, they are but required to manipulate educational toys "in order to" learn control of their muscles or "in order to" learn to read. By the time they graduate from kindergarten we have infected our children and impressed them with our grim ethos. The joy of playing for the joy of playing is frowned upon. The joy of learning for the sake of learning has been destroyed by admonitions to learn "in order to" please mother or to get good grades or to get into Harvard or MIT twelve years hence. And by the time they arrive in Cambridge, they have not even the faintest memory of joy and play, and they grimly labor for their "credits," "in order to" graduate to obsolescent jobs.

VI. Ethos for the Age of Cyberculture

The proper ethos for the age of cyberculture is one that would serve humanity well to build a good society. We know so very little about living human lives in leisure and abundance, in dignity and self-respect, in privacy and the assurance of the fundamental human right to be unique as an individual. We confuse leisure with idleness, and abundance with waste. We view with suspicion the attempt of a human being to preserve his privacy and suspect it to be an attempt to hide evil. And we almost take for granted that an anomalism or eccentricity is necessarily inferior to conformity.

Nothing could be further from the truth! Idleness, like drudgery, is passive boredom suffered under duress, and waste is the misuse of anything—whether it is a scare commodity or something plentiful. Leisure is the joyful activity of using our human potentials to the fullest, and abundance is intelligent economy, namely, the full use of natural resources for the good of human beings. Privacy is the fundamental right of civilized human beings and a necessity if one is to live harmoniously with one's fellow man. The uniqueness of individuals has made all human civilization possible, for the conformist cannot go forwards and only in the individualist's dreams and the dissenter's vision today can the reality of tomorrow be conceived.[3]

To learn to live in leisure and abundance is the task of this generation. Even if we wanted to, we would not have the power to choose between the past and the future. The cybercultural revolution cannot be reversed. But we can choose the future. We decide what kind of world we want to leave for our children; what *we* do now determines whether they shall exist in idleness or have a chance to live in leisure.

VII. Early Signs

Once we have grasped the fact that our present unemployment is only a beginning and that there can never again be a time when the labor of human beings will be required to produce what society wants, we can turn our human intelligence to the problem of transition —namely, to prepare ourselves for the age of cyberculture by turning unemp-

loyment into leisure, by solving the transitional problems of scarcity, and by doing everything human ingenuity can devise to perfect our electronic slaves and complete all processes of automation.

We must rid ourselves of the erroneous idea that unemployment is still a negative period of waiting for a change to the positive state of being "gainfully" employed again. In this country, millions of human beings are in a *negative* state now. Many of them have been in this state for many months, years even, and many know that they will never be in any other state again. All the projections for the future—even the most alarming —consider only our past experiences. Only very recently have a few economists given their attention to the phenomenon of acceleration. "For too long they misled themselves and the public by projecting productivity into the future on the basis of the long-term average rate of past productivity gains. In so doing, they ignored the fact that their averages were a combination of relatively low rates in the distant past with significantly higher rates in more recent years."[4]

Computing machines and automation are barely in their infancy, and already our world has changed beyond all recognition and comparison. If we consider that all change is slow until it has overcome initial inertia, we can expect, before the end of this century, an increase in productivity that will dwarf the most alarming projections for unemployment. Solomon Fabricant, director of research of the National Bureau of Economic Research, warns that "the long-term pace of advances in output per man hour has speeded up. It was 22 per cent per decade during the quarter century preceding World War I. It has averaged 29 per cent since. During the most recent period —after World War II—national product per man-hour has been rising at an even

---

[3]Mary Allice Hilton, *The Age of Cyberculture, A Series* (New York: The World Publishing Company, 1963).

[4]Walter Reuther, *Statement for the Senate Subcommittee on Employment and Manpower*, May 22, 1963.

greater rate, 35 to 40 percent per decade."[5] And to this should be added what is cautiously noted in the President's *manpower report:* "Although the statistical data on this subject are too limited to warrant definitive conclusions, it is probable that *underutilization* of plant, equipment, and manpower resources has had significant effect in retarding productivity gains since the mid-1950s."[6] Reuther concludes that "under the stimulus of automation and other revolutionary technologies, there can be no doubt that the historical tendency for productivity to move forward at an accelerating pace will continue into the foreseeable future."[7]

To the acceleration of technological advance we must add—or (more realistically) multiply—the acceleration in the rate of birth. The "war babies" and "postwar babies" will be flooding into the labor market—between twenty-five and forty million of them in one decade. No rate of economic growth, no method of spreading jobs by decreasing the work week or extending vacations, can absorb the enormously accelerated flood of unemployment. Any dam or deflection that worked in the past—forced consumption, exploring underdeveloped continents or outer space, for example—cannot be used to counteract the potential power—for good or ill—of the increasing number and perfection of automatic systems that can produce 1,000 cars or 10,000 or 100,000 cars without human intervention and with—at most—a few human monitors to watch dials and stand by for rare emergencies.

If we allow human beings to remain unemployed because machines can do the drudgery of repetitive tasks, we are dooming untold millions to useless lives without hope and purpose. Even if we devise the means to feed them and supply them with the output of machines, they will not long remain in idleness and scarcity, while the products of machines rot in warehouses.[8]

VIII. Lessons of History

Instead of dooming the vast majority of mankind to idleness and unemployment and the indignity of the dole, we must prepare now for leisure and abundance. There are some lessons we can learn from history. In the Golden Age of Greece we can study a society of leisure and abundance based upon wealth that was not created by the labor of any of the members of the society, but by slaves.

We piously deplore the evils of obsolete slavery and believe it right and proper to condemn millions to starvation or, at best, the indignity of the dole. Let us look at Greek society honestly and examine how an unsurpassed civilization was created amidst the wealth and leisure which, twenty-five centuries later, might well have been produced by electronic and mechanical, instead of human, slaves.

The Greeks differentiated clearly between the private life of a human being, his life in his household which produced the necessities—*oika*, the Greek word for "home," is the rootword of economics—and his life as a citizen, which Aristotle called *bios politikos.* The "good life" was the life as a citizen, was "good" because man, freed from labor by having mastered in his household the necessities of life, could pursue human tasks. "At the root of Greek political consciousness we find an unequalled clarity and articulateness in drawing this distinction. No activity that served only the purpose of making a living, of sustaining only the life process,

[5]Solomon Fabricant, *Annual Report.* Washington, D.C.: National Bureau of Economic Research, 1959.

[6]John F. Kennedy, *Manpower Report,* 1962.

[7]Walter Reuther, *Statement for the Senate Subcommittee on Employment and Manpower,* May 22, 1963.

[8]Mary Alice Hilton, "Computing Machines: Curse or Blessing," *The Age of Cyberculture,* Syndicated Series, North American Newspaper Alliance, August 11, 1963.

was permitted to enter the political realm, and this at the grave risk of abandoning trade and manufacture to the industriousness of foreigners," writes Hannah Arendt.[9]

However we may deplore the private, or household, life of the Athenian—in this century of electronic slaves we can so easily afford to condemn human slavery—we can only admire the unequalled height of civilization his public life produced. In his public life every Athenian strove to excel, i.e., to distinguish himself from all others, to be a unique human being, an individual unlike any other that ever lived or ever will live. The Athenian lived a human life, in play and work, but never in drudgery and labor. "Who could achieve well if he labors?" asked Pindar.[10]

Several hundred years later and several hundred miles to the west of Athens another society existed whose citizens were freed from the necessity of labor in order to sustain life. But whereas freedom from want and the necessity to labor emancipated the Athenian into a human being who achieved excellence, Roman citizens became an idle mob under equivalent conditions of affluence. The decline and fall of the Roman Empire, wrote Edward Gibbon, is "the greatest, perhaps, and most awful scene in the history of mankind. The various causes and progressive effects are connected with many of the events most interesting in human annals: the artful policy of the Caesars, who long maintained the name and image of a free republic; the disorders of military despotism. . . ."[11]

The essential difference between Greece and Rome is the difference in their points of view, in their ethical concepts. The Greeks strove for individual excellence;

they wanted to create beauty and contemplate the mysteries of the universe. Abstraction and generalization were their inestimable contributions to science. The practical they dismissed as not worthy of discussion and recording. Archimedes, whose practical inventions covered an astounding variety of applications, never thought them worthy of description. He wrote only about abstract mathematics; we learned from his Roman enemies that he invented marvelous machinery.

The death of Archimedes by the hand of a Roman soldier, as the great mathematician stood contemplating a diagram he had drawn in the sand, is symbolic of the end of an era. The Romans were great organizers, "but," said Whitehead, "they were cursed by the sterility which waits upon practicality. They were not dreamers enough to arrive at new points of view."[12] No Roman ever lost his life because he was contemplating abstract mathematics!

Rome, her unemployed citizens idly seeking *panem et circenses*, destroyed herself. The moral disintegration of Rome had begun long before Christ was born. Her conquests brought Rome only material luxury and human poverty. Roman citizens received their dole and idled away their humanity in ever more brutal titillation. "It was because Rome was already dying that Christianity grew so rapidly. Men lost faith in the state, not because Christianity held them aloof, but because the state defended wealth against poverty, fought to capture slaves. . . . They turned from Caesar preaching war to Christ preaching peace, from incredible brutality to unprecedented charity, from a life without hope and dignity to a faith that consoled their poverty and honored their humanity. . . . The political causes of decay were rooted in one fact—that increasing despotism de-

[9]Hannah Arendt, *The Human Condition* (Chicago: University of Chicago Press, 1958).

[10]Pindar, *Carmina Olympica*, xi. 4.

[11]Edward Gibbon, *The Decline and Fall of the Roman Empire*, Vols. I—III, (New York: Harper and Brothers, 1879).

[12]Alfred North Whitehead, *The Aims of Education* and other Essays. (New York:The Macmillan Company, 1929).

stroyed the citizen's civic sense and dried up statesmanship at its source. Powerless to express his political will except by violence, the Roman lost interest in government and became absorbed in his business, his amusements, his legion, or his individual salvation."[13]

We might ask why despotism increased in Rome, why the Athenian sought his excellence in art and philosophy and science, and the Roman in the material luxuries that were all he gained from his conquests. We might ask why Christianity so very quickly forgot that Christ taught human beings to live for the glory of God, which means to live for the joy of living, of being human, and why the ethos of scarcity perverted "living for the glory of God" into laboring "in order to" assure the glory of the church. We might ask why the Athenian, though conquered and enslaved, mastered even his enslavement and his conquerors. We might ask whether the Golden Age of Athens could have endured if the Athenian had found a way out of his dilemma: his need for leisure and his rejection of human slavery.

Returning to our own century of transition, we can rejoice that we have what humanity never knew before—slaves to free us from the necessity of laboring "in order to" sustain life that are not human, so that we need not be ashamed to enjoy what they produce. For the first time in human history, man can be free. Machine systems can provide him with leisure and abundance, and rescue him from the degradation of being either a slave or a master of another human being.

But machine systems can do only what man wants. If human beings cannot learn to distinguish between human tasks and toil fit only for machines, if we persist in competing with the machine for the repetitive, dreary stultifying, dehumanizing jobs for which only machines are

suited, then humanity will become enslaved by the machine more cruelly than it has ever been enslaved by any despot of the past. For the machine provides us with slave labor; and, therefore, human beings who compete with the machine are, thereby, accepting the conditions of slave labor. Human beings who learn to use the machine wisely, on the other hand, will be freed by the machine to achieve excellence.

We are at the crossroads: One way leads to the Athens the Athenians could only dream of; the other to a Rome more dreadful than the most ghastly Roman nightmare.

Greece or Rome—that is the choice we have, the choice we must make now, the choice we should have made yesterday and for which tomorrow will be too late.

PART TWO—METHODS OF TRANSITION

I. Educating the Young

A practical and relatively painless method to accomplish the transition into the age of cyberculture must begin with the education of the young. We are well aware of the fact that unemployed youth has already become a social problem, and we know that what we so inadequately call "juvenile delinquency" is not restricted to the underprivileged. The violence of youth and the crimes committed by children show, of course, the general moral decline. Even more serious than isolated outbreaks of violence, even more desperate than gangs of destructive hoodlums is the widespread indifference and bewilderment among the young —whether they stay in schools that provide nothing but bland custodial care or whether they are dropouts.

The real problem of the young is that there seems to be no place for them in the world. They know society looks with dread upon the vast numbers that are pouring out of schools, and they know that it is wrong for them to be met with fear and loathing. They are the future of

---

[13]Will Durant, *Caesar and Christ. The Story of Civilization,* Vol. 3 (New York: Simon, & Schuster, Inc., 1944).

mankind, and they have a right to be welcomed with joy.

What would happen if the twenty-five to forty million young people who wll pour out of our inadequate school system in the next decade were not to flood an already overflowing labor market, but enter instead into a period of basic education for the age of cyberculture?

It would be infinitely harder—perhaps impossible—to change very profoundly the prejudices of those who have learned to labor and who have labored for too long. If their labor is taken over by machines, we can only make their emancipation, which came too late for most to enjoy in leisure, as pleasant and comfortable as society can afford. And we can try to make their idleness not too shameful a thing.

But for the young we must do far more than train them to become another obsolete generation of laborers, for there can be no honest labor for them and no dignity in toil. Any human being who seeks to labor in competition with the machine is doomed to slavery and to the conditions of slavery. There is no human ditch digger who can live on a scale low enough to let him compete with the steam shovel, and there is no human bookkeeper or mathematician, who can compete with a computing machine.

There is no human printer who can compete with a tape-fed printing press. And there is no human metal cutter who can compete with computing-machine-controlled machine tools. The keyword is "compete." We can no longer afford to measure the value of a human being in the market place.[14]

In 1955, when the A.F.L. and the C.I.O. consummated their marriage of convenience, President Meany promised that the newlyweds would become parents of an expanding family; they would "organize the unorganized." But with the sole ex-

ception of Hoffa's teamsters—who are, at best, considered naughty stepchildren —the family has not proliferated. The auto workers have lost 300,000 members since 1953—and this in spite of the fact that the industry has achieved a glittering production record in 1963. The steel workers have diminished by 250,000. There are half a million fewer mine workers, and 760,000 fewer railroad workers.[15]

In spite of all the efforts made by labor unions to spread the work and to delay the dismissal of workers, it takes considerably fewer of us to produce considerably more. Whether we regard featherbedding an evil or a necessity—it does not prevent the spread of unemployment. At best it delays the inevitable disaster for a few; at worst it retards important improvements.

The ranks of labor are diminished by the fired, but even more significantly they are starved at the source by the vast numbers of "the unhired." Among the ever increasing number of the unhired, labor unions must find new blood and new strength and a new lease on life. Labor must forget the organization methods of the past, when "marginal workers" were considered a poor investment. Many old-time union men say "they bring not back in dues what it costs to organize them" and are thereby guilty not only of greater callousness than that for which they blame management, but of irresponsible short-sightedness. Unions who do this sort of cost accounting while they invest their estimated union wealth of $1.5 billion in blue-chip securities and profitable real estate are doomed to die of their own corruption and decay.

Labor and management must learn to invest in human beings. If labor unions would "organize" youngsters who graduate (or drop out) of an antiquated school system, their membership rolls would swell (and without any crippling

[14]Alice Mary Hilton, *Logic, Computing Machines, and Automation* (New York: The World Publishing Company, 1964).

[15]Alice Mary Hilton, "Cybercultural Revolution," *The Minority of One* (October 1963).

diminishment of their coffers), and their vigor would be restored. They would once again have a vital role to play in the society. They would once again breathe the fresh air of the future instead of suffocating in bank vaults clipping their coupons.

Organized labor should offer to educate every boy and girl who wants an education for the age of cyberculture. It is to be hoped that colleges will, in time, adjust their curricula to the needs of the future. With a few exceptions our institutions of "higher" learning are custodial, rather than educational, and perpetuate training their unfortunate students for obsolescence. Education must not be equated to training for obsolescent jobs. Since our present feeble attempts at "reeducation" are not educational at all and do nothing at all to prepare human beings to live in leisure and abundance, they could not and do not have the slightest effect upon our present unemployment problem. Such "retraining" efforts are like aspirin; it can disguise a headache for a while, but it cannot cure cancer or even a headache.

We throw a feather into the Grand Canyon and we are surprised that there is no echo! The education that must be provided to get an echo from the age of cyberculture must make it possible for human beings to learn how to live human lives and to create an ethical system that will permit human beings to do whatever they do gladly and for the sake of the thing itself, and not reluctantly and only "in order to" make a living.

A good curriculum might well start with questions about Greek civilization and Roman decay. Whatever the specific subject, its aim must be to open the eyes of our twentieth-century blind children to the eternal miracle of life.

One labor leader, enlightened about the vital need to educate human beings, says: "America will be a much better place when everybody works four hours a day and attends some kind of classes four hours." He made a start—small, but of

tremendous significance. His local has financed scholarships for children of members. More important, it is seeking out latent talent among its members (in the hope of developing the union's future leaders) for the "Futurian Society." The best educated among the members conduct courses for other members. And at the local's Long Island estate, seminars are held in such "impractical" subjects as literature and art and philosophy.[16]

Since the education of several millions of youngsters involves far more than a one-week seminar, much more is required than a Long Island estate and the funds a local can afford. Unions are not *that* rich. But humanity is. Such a vast education program must be financed by government subsidy, in part. This can be justified—even to the satisfaction of the victims of the Puritan Ethos—as a perfectly reasonable invesment which, partially at least, pays for itself out of savings in unemployment compensation, relief, and the costs of custodial care for those who would surely commit crimes if they cannot find a positive purpose in life.

Another source of financing should be supplied by the very machines who have replaced human laborers. At least one manufacturer of automatic machines is a pioneer in this approach. He "taxes" every machine he sells by putting away a certain sum which contributes to the support of a foundation to make various studies of several facets of the problems created by the very existence of automatic machines. "If machines perform our labor, then machines will also have to pay our taxes."[17] This may be a socially acceptable way of saying that the abundance produced by machines must be available to human beings, lest it rots away and destroys humanity with its fetid decay.

[16]Harry Van Arsdale, Jr., *Report to the American Foundation on Automation and Employment* (New York, 1963).

[17]John S. Snyder, *Report to the American Foundation on Automation and Employment* (New York, 1963).

Union funds, special taxes paid by manufacturers, a contribution made by the entire population in the form of government funds are three sources to finance the preparation of youth for the age of cyberculture. Of course, it would be foolish to prepare millions of young people for a world which, simultaneously, we try to postpone. When we no longer need to be concerned about new floods in the labor market, there is no longer any reason to attempt any delays in complete automation. We are then free to encourage technological inventiveness and to complete the process as quickly as possible, not only in the industrialized nations but—under the sponsorship and tutelage of the United Nations—of the underdeveloped countries.

Such an acceleration of automation would ensure full employment for the existing labor force, not only in featherbedding and busywork but by the full occupation of highly trained personnel. It is the only method of achieving full employment *and* full occupation. We have neither one nor the other now.

How many scientists and engineers are still employed, but underoccupied? How many pass their days in idleness at their well-designed desks and in their well-equipped laboratories? How many repeat endlessly insignificant experiments and waste all their ingenuity in inventing more innocuous re-search (not research) projects?[18]

II. Experiment in Attrition

It is highly probable that without the influx of youngsters into the existing labor force, normal aging and retirement—a process called by modern economists and labor experts "attrition"—will diminish the labor force over the next two decades at approximately the same rate as machines replace human drudgery. In the pioneering ag-

reement, the "Long-Range Sharing Plan," the union and the Kaiser Steel Company pointed the way for a company and its employers to share the fruits of automation. Whatever can be saved by greater productivity and efficiency is divided: one-third to the workers, two-thirds to the company (which must share its two-third's portion with the government).

Any laborer whose job is eliminated by machine continues to draw his pay for one year. During this time he is placed into a labor pool which acts as a reserve to fill in for absentees.[19]

It is too early to draw general conclusions from the Kaiser experiment, but the officials of the steel workers' union are reasonably pleased and the company considers the pool an asset. This plan does not provide a complete answer to the problems of automation, and it does not stop the process of replacing human drudgery with machine slaves. It does provide a cushion for a few individuals.

III. Hope for the Future

If one steel plant can create a labor pool, if one manufacturer can tax his machines and use the money to encourage study, if one union local can provide a place for learning and reflection for its members with such remarkable results, we have good reason to be hopeful for a bright future.

If we set ourselves as a long-range goal a good cybercultural society, we can solve the intermediate problems and devise appropriate measures to overcome the immediate difficulties that are attributable to the phase of transition rather than the advances in technology. The immediate consequences of diverting the young and unskilled from the labor pool and into a constructive program of education for the age of cyberculture would be dramatic. It would, first of all and for all

[18]Alice Mary Hilton, "Automation Without Tears," *Electro-Technology* (August 1960).

[19]David Cole, *Report of the Kaiser Steel Agreement of March 7, 1963* (Washington, D.C., 1963).

times, wipe out the demoralizing condition of hopeless unemployment.

We know that in this rich country there is considerable and stubborn poverty. Why does it exist when granaries are bursting with surplus food, when farmers are paid for consenting to let their fields lie fallow, and when stores are filled with every sort of consumer product so that customers must be enticed to want what they do not need? We know that poverty, in this country, is poverty in spite of abundance—poverty caused by inadequate means of distribution, by the ethos, not the real existence, of scarcity, i.e., by unemployment. To wipe out unemployment and the ethos of scarcity is to wipe out poverty.

This is not true of poverty everywhere on earth as yet. There is still real poverty in this world, and there are still poor nations, although even the poorest nation in the age of cyberculture is not intrinsically and forever doomed to poverty or the charity of others. That is why we call the poor nations quite appropriately underdeveloped nations. The most enlightened domestic policy we might pursue cannot solve worldwide problems, and the most intelligent and ingenious international agreements cannot forever eliminate the danger of nucler war. We must do much more. We must not have underdeveloped nations. The age of cyberculture must be universal.

IV. Worldwide Cyberculture

If we eliminate unemployment in this country immediately and proceed to create automation at the fastest possible rate, we shall almost simultaneously free an enormous number of highly trained and skilled people—the employed but underoccupied—who could, under the sponsorship of the United Nations, assist and advise the underdeveloped nations to build modern automated industries.

At the present time, most of the newly formed nations of Africa seem to be diligently creating nineteenth-century conditions of the worst sort. It is not surprising, since most of their leaders were educated in Europe or the United States two or three decades ago so that they were imbued with the ideas of nineteenth-century Europe and America.

They dream of leading their countrymen out of the jungle, and they are bringing them straight to the horror of nineteenth-century city slums. It is preposterous to lead human beings out of insect-infested green jungles and turn them into obsolescent masses of unskilled and unwanted laborers in rat-infested city jungles.

Surely among all the remarkable intellects that have asserted themselves in the new nations of the world there must be some who can understand not only John Locke and Voltaire and Marx but also Russell's mathematics and logic and philosophy and Weiner's cybernetics. Surely there must be some among them with the imagination *not* to imitate nineteenth-century American-European industrialism but to create twenty-first-century cyberculture. Such a person, if he also has power in his country and influence among his people, can conserve the most admirable values of his native culture and create, at the same time, good living conditions for his people. He could bring to his country the best our European-American civilization has to offer without dooming them also to the worst.

If the ethos of the society that sees virtue in laboring "in order to" gain something—bread or status or self-respect—changes to an ethos of abundance, it will be virtuous for human beings to live human lives in leisure and abundance. And no one can be sure what undreamed-of heights humanity can reach when human talent is no longer wasted in the basic struggle to survive.

It is surely the only sensible and practical choice to prefer leisure and abundance to idleness and waste. The choice must be made—and it must be made now. We cannot ignore the powerful new phenomena human intelligence has created. We cannot abdicate our respon-sibility to choose how they shall be used. For in our very abdication of choice, we would choose the worst alternative: to drift blindly toward disaster.

If we want to conserve our traditional values—the right of the individual to life, liberty, and the pursuit of happiness—we must choose wisely and act boldly.

Our history was made by human beings with bold vision and good sense, with deep moral convictions and human com-passion for human frailty, with respect for the dignity of human beings and love for mankind, with the imagination to dream and the courage to act. Such men and women cross oceans, transform con-tinents, and build the City of Man!

That is our heritage. Upon that let us build our future.

Epilogue

DON FABUN*

We have come a long way together,
  you and I, since first we set out upon
  this strange, uncertain pilgrimage. We
  picked our way through the Slough of
Despond and found that the bogs and
  quagmires were but figments of our
imagination; we have visited the City of
Despair and found it walled in only by its
  own fantasies of Space and Time; we
have confronted the Lions of Automata
  and discovered them to be ephemera,
  the mirror image of our own minds; we
have traversed the Valley of Paradise and
  eaten of its strange fruit, Leisure. Now,
we have but a little further to go and our
  Pilgrimage will be at an end. We must
cross the Delectable Mountains. They may
  seem far away, shimmering there; but that
  is an accident of our eyesight. They
really are right here under our feet, if we
will but look. Like the Chinese journey
  of a thousand miles, we shall approach
  them one step at a time. Shall we go? Now?

*Don Fabun, "Epilogue", *The Dynamics of Change*. Reprinted from *The Dynamics of Change*, Kaiser Aluminum & Chemical Corporation, copyright © 1967. Reprinted by permission.

Artificial intelligence and intelligent artifice

ROBERT M. BAER*

"Echo IV," wrote Echo IV, far away in the calm remoteness of the Rothermere Vulgarian Ethics Wing, "is a brilliant new arrival on the literary scene. The Tin Men is its first novel, and critics who have seen it prior to publication . . ."*

Michael Frayn

Studies of artificial intelligence (or "machine intelligence," as it is sometimes called) have the dual objective of trying to obtain machines which, in problematical situations, would respond as intelligent humans would, and trying to obtain an understanding of what human intelligence is, by a thorough understanding of artificial intelligence.

A great deal of effort in these studies has gone into creating capable game-playing programs and robot-control programs. In the latter applications the computer acts as a brain which dictates to servo-mechanisms which control prosthetic devices (or perhaps carts), acting upon its interpretation of visual information fed to the computer by a video camera. The program must process the optical data which it receives and identify images and assess angles and distances; it must then compute to what degree it must rotate wheels, extend arms, manipulate fingers, and then send the corresponding signals to the control devices and servo-mechanisms.

Unfortunately the robot action, so far obtained, seems to accord with a rather stunted intelligence. A short but brilliantly produced film (*Butterfinger*, Stanford University Artificial Intelligence Project) features a robot arm trying to fulfill the goal of gathering together into a single pile a small scattered collection of children's building blocks. The stacking of the blocks is performed in a pathetically slow and clumsy way, suggesting the Herculean computing task involved in processing the optical data provided by the video camera.

The speed with which living creatures cope with considerably more complicated situations seems to be due to the ability of the animal brain to process an enormous amount of information in parallel—as if the brain consisted of a large number of computers, each processing its part of the data at the same time—whereas the digital computer must process all of the data sequentially, one step at a time.[1] Of course, there is a much faster signal generation and propagation in the digital computer, so that the parallel processing ability of the brain (which, for the individual elements, is very slow in comparison with the digital computer) loses out to the computer in certain types of information processing.

The question is sometimes raised as to what delineates artificial intelligence programs from *any* kind of program which performs an analysis that a human mind would otherwise be called upon to do. Is there any real difference between an algorithm which tries to find a solu-

*Michael Frayn, *The Tin Men*. Little, Brown. 1965. Copyright 1965 by Michael Frayn. Reprinted by permission.

[1]ILLIAC IV, mentioned earlier, seems to represent the latest advance into designing parallel capability into digital computers; and its degree of parallelism, in comparison with that of the brain, is meager indeed. The *theory* of parallel computation is in its initial stage of development; cf. R. M. Karp and R. E. Miller (1969), Parallel program schemata, *Journal of Computer and System Sciences* **3**, 147-195.

tion to a set of logical equations and an algorithm which tries to find a mate-in-two? In principle the answer, of course, is "no." And this holds true even where the computer is delivering output in an area where the meaning of algorithmics is often much less clearcut—the computer-creation of artistic and aesthetic constructions.

The use of computers as creative instruments in the fields of music and painting are well known. But in the field of literary creativity, notable developments have been surprisingly sparse. Outside of the Echo IV program (which is acknowledged to be unique and likely to remain so, for some time) we know of only one other such program —Pourboireki's[2] algorithm in the closely related field of computational poetics (the *Reverse V* program[3]).

Pourboireki developed his early versions (Reverses I and II) of the program at the University of California, Berkeley, early in the 1960s. The program takes as input any short subject-phrase and an indication as to whether the output is to be brief or extended. The program then outputs some rhymes which presumably satisfy the input conditions.

Pourboireki, a generally acknowledged eccentric, formally works only one day a year, usually April 1 (which he says is the only symbolically appropriate day for any type of labor). On 1 April 1966 he exhibited, at the Berkeley Computer Center, the first output from the debugged Reverse I. He drew very little response from the Center (which was largely peopled with humanists, in those days) and none whatever from the English Department (which is not surprising, in view of its well-known attitude toward mechanical production and its

traditional inclination to ignore anything written later than the eighteenth century). Pourboireki's reaction to this rebuff was reflected perhaps in his titling of the computer output ("A Big Stout Naught"). The output had the appearance:

BIT BY BIT
WORD BY WORD
FIT BY FIT
TENDING TOWARD

BYTE BY BYTE
LINE BY LINE
LEFT TO RIGHT
VERSE DESIGN

LINE BY LINE
COUPLED TIGHT
TIGER, TIGER
BURNING BRIGHT

(Several members of the University's Institute for Human Development, after mulling over the output from Reverse I, suggested the creating of a parallel Institute for Machine Development—a notion which attracted the support of several engineering departments—but the University had recently bought several Nobelists and was disinclined toward new ventures.)

Pourboireki disappeared, as was his wont, and nothing more might have been heard of the computational poetics project, had the following letter not been received at the Computer Center:

4th May 1967

To: The Director
   Computer Center
   University of California at Berkeley
   California, USA

Dear Sir:

I wonder if I could make an enquiry of you that borders dangerously on facetiousness.

We are interested in doing a feature in our magazine on computer poetry—poetry actually composed by computers—and the University of California has been

---

[2]Nicolas Pourboireki is the great grandson of the obscure Ukranian general and mathematician Nicolai Ivanovich Pourboireki.

[3]Pourboireki originally named the program *REV-UP* (for Recursive Enumeration of Verse Universing Program).

suggested to me as possibly dabbling in this sphere as part of its research.

We would like to get some information on this aspect of computers and, if possible, to get some poetry written for us in this way.

It is, I'm afraid, a somewhat monstrous request to make of you, but if you do anything along these lines or have some information as to who does, I would be most grateful for your assistance.

Yours sincerely,

Features Editor

The Condé Nast Publications Ltd.
Vogue House,
Hanover Square,
London W1. Grosvenor 9080

The usual course of events when requests of unusual character, such as this, arrive is that they are dispatched to the appropriate expert, who is then left with the responsibility for satisfying them. In the present case this posed an obstacle: Only Pourboireki had been working in computational poetics and he would not be putting in his working day for another eleven months. Nevertheless, the Vogue letter was shown to him and he was invited to reply.

Pourboireki's reaction, upon reading the letter, was one of amused skepticism. The letter, he said, was obviously facetious—its first line was meant to make that clear—or else it was a fraud: No one could seriously expect polite response from a computational poetics project after referring to its work as "dabbling in this sphere." Nor would Pourboireki respond to entreaties to accept the letter as in good faith—until it was discovered that, according to the Center's accounting records, Pourboireki had not actually worked on the preceding April 1 but had been paid as if he did!

Reverse II was at once brought out of the program files and Pourboireki punched a few data cards. The only question was:

How many poems should the computer run off? One thousand, one hundred, or just a dozen or so? The initial suggestion was that fifty be run off and the best dozen of these be sent on to London. But Pourboireki demurred. Run a dozen, he said, and whatever comes out, comes out; it's not a silly poetry contest—it's just a demonstration.

So within an hour or so, the computer output was in the mail to England, along with a covering letter:

Features Editor
VOGUE
Condé Nast Publications Ltd
Vogue House
Hanover Square, London W1, England

Dear . . . . . . :

Your letter concerning computer-produced poetry has found its way into my hands. We of course expect a certain irrepressible element of facetiousness from features editors, but experience has shown that unyielding patience and determined tact may often result in correspondence of entertainment value, if not serious interest, to both sides.

Turning to your specific inquiry, if by "poetry" you mean "rhymes" then the answer to your question is *yes*, the computer produces poetry. If by "poetry" you mean poetry, then you must be informed that there has been serious difficulty in dealing with the computer in this particular domain. (In the latter case, as you may surmise, the trouble stems primarily from our inability to determine precisely when the computer is in a creative mood: If we insist upon mechanical production of lyrically fragile material, finely polished and hauntingly evocative, we find that the response from the computer is usually sullen silence or—on rare but embarrassing occasion—obscene vulgarisms, tersely rhymed.)

In all fairness to the computer, it must be remembered that the computer intrinsically produces nothing whatever: It is actually a program within the computer which effects what is required as, in fact, compelled by some person who constructed the program itself. . . .

Hoping that this may be of some value to you,

Your obedient servant,

Nicholas Pourboireki
Computational poetics

Pourboireki gave, in his letter, a sketchy and not particularly revealing account of how the program Reverse II worked. (He would perhaps have done better by simply pointing out that the principle of operation of Reverse II was identical to that of Echo IV.)

Part of the computer output that accompanied the letter had the following appearance:

SUBJECT = ANSWER TO VOGUE QUERY RE COMP POETICS
QUALITY = ARBITRARY

> I, SILENT MACHINE,
> ALERT TO YOUR ORDER,
> ANSWER YOUR QUERY,
> DANGEROUS BORDER,
>
> SILENT MACHINING,
> VERSE-ED REDUCTION,
> NO INTERVENING,
> POETIC CONSTRUCTION,
>
> SILENT MECHANICS,
> METERED ALONG LINES,
> ALGORITHMICALLY PANICS,
> PRODUCES THE WRONG LINES

SUBJECT = REFLEXIVE POETICS
QUALITY = ARBITRARY

> TO RECUR ENDLESSLY,
> TO SENSE THE GENERATIONS REELING
> INTO EXISTENCE
> IN IDENTICAL MILLIONS
> OF WHICH EACH
> IS A PAINED UNWILLING COPY OF WHAT
> CAME BEFORE

SUBJECT = POETS VS MACHINES
QUALITY = ARBITRARY

> POETS DISLIKE COMPUTING POETICS,
> MECHANICAL MINDED DISPLEASES AESTHETICS,
> POETS SPLIT ART WITH THE SOUL'S MUDDY
> PRISM,
> MACHINES SPLIT APART,
> STUDY THE SCHISM

SUBJECT = POETICA AMERICANA
QUALITY = SUCCINCT

ALL GOD'S CHILLUN GOT ALGORITHM

When, about a year later, Pourboireki turned up on April 1, he was asked, along with more important requests, to run the current version (Reverse III) on the subject of "computer science"—a phrase in which the University was beginning to entertain a superficial interest. Unfortunately Pourboireki was unaware of the latest system changes and fed the program to the computer with too large a time limit . . . one minute. This resulted in the computation of a fifty pound bale of rhymes, the content of which has remained largely unknown—no one has read past the first 1000 pages or so, of output. The output begins:

SUBJECT = COMPUTER SCIENCE
QUALITY = EXTENDED

> AT THE OUTSET,
> NOTICE BABBAGE,
> AND HIS PLAN FOR CALCULATORS,
> AND HIS FRIEND THE SUCCINCT SIREN,
> DAUGHTER OF THE POET BYRON
> WHOSE QUICK BRILLIANCE BRISKLY RANGING
> STATED THAT A PROGRAM CHANGING
>
> COULD IN FACT BE DONE BETWEEN
> THE PROGRAM AND THE QUICK MACHINE,
> EMPHASIZING THIS WOULD MEAN
> NO HUMAN HAND WOULD INTERVENE,
> LADY LOVELACE THUS ENSURING
> ABSTRACT NOTIONS NAMED FOR TURING

One student, after reading part of the output, suggested rerunning the program—constraining the computation to blank verse—and using the expected output as scripts for several courses in the subject. The suggestion, while undeservedly cynical, was provocative enough to lead some of the staff to request that the University provide machine time for the rerun. Unfortunately the state government had further tightened the screws of its financial economies program, leaving the University unable to muster financial support for another minute of running time. Those members of the faculty who felt that they could benefit from the project contributed donations to fund the computation, but by the time that formal arrangements had been secured, Pourboireki had departed for another year.

The evolution of the program (Reverses V and VI) has levelled off in capability in a way which—in Pourboireki's view —has some distrubing implications for artificial intelligence. His point is made by the output generated to serve as lyrics for a song ("Sky divers' Lament" for the film *The Gypsy Moths*):

SUBJECT = SKY DIVERS LAMENT / THE GYPSY MOTHS
QUALITY = ROGERS AND HART

> FALLING IN LOVE WITH FALLING
> IS FALLING FOR SOMETHING NEW,
> FALLING IN LOVE WITH FALLING
> IS SOMETHING OUT OF THE BLUE
>
> FALLING IN LOVE WITH FALLING
> HAS SIMPLY BREATHTAKING PACE,
> FALLING IN LOVE WITH FALLING
> REQUIRES A LOT OF SPACE
>
> I FELL IN LOVE WITH FALLING
> ONE NIGHT WHEN THE MOON WAS NEW,
> FALLING IS GROOVY
> AT LEAST IN A MOVIE,
> AND WHAT A VIEW
>
> I TOOK TO FLIGHT
> AS A MOTH SEEKS THE LIGHT
> IN A SOMBER WORLD,
> BUT I FAILED TO WEIGH,
> ONE OMINOUS DAY,
> HOW MY CHUTE WAS CURLED
>
> I FELL OUT OF LOVE WITH FALLING
> ONE NIGHT WHEN THE MOON WAS WANE,
> AT FIVE THOUSAND FEET
>
> I SLIPPED INTO SLEET
> AND A DRIVING RAIN
> FALLING,S APPALLING,
> IT,S SIMPLY A STALLING
> IN EMPTY SPACE,
> FALLING TOO FAR
> CAN END IN A JAR
> IF YOU LAND OFF BASE
>
> FALLING IN LOVE WITH FALLING
> IN JEOPARDY, SOMETHING TO JEER,
> FALLING IN LOVE WITH FALLING
> IS QUEER IN THE INNER EAR
> ****** LINE LIMIT EXCEEDED ******

Hollywood has so far rejected this, and other, lyrics from Reverse VI claiming that the output is "dated," "square," and that the work of current lyricists under contract is "already too mechanical according to industry standards." The problem, then, according to Pourboireki, is not to construct artificial intelligence programs that effectively mimic human creativity, but rather programs that mimic *talented* human creativity.[4] In this respect, Reverse VI may be typical of the work to come—barely creative and unyieldingly talentless—and Echo IV may be that rare, happy accident that is unlikely to occur readily again.

REFERENCES

Collens, R. J. (1970), Computer generated poetry as a pedagogical tool, *Proceedings of*

[4]A. M. Turing anticipated this very problem in his *Can Machines Think?* [Cf. *World of Mathematics*, ed. J. R. Newman. Simon & Shuster, 1956 (Vol. IV)], offering the conjectural human /computer conversation:

Q: Please write me a sonnet on the subject of the Forth Bridge.
A: Count me out on this one. I could never write poetry.

a Conference on Interdisciplinary Research in Computer Science, M. G. Saunders and R. G. Stanton, eds. Winnipeg: University of Manitoba.

Leed, J. (1966), *The Computer & Literary Style: Introductory Essays and Studies*. Kent State University Press.

Lincoln, Harry B. (1970), *The Computer and Music*. Cornell University Press.

Lincoln, Harry B. (1970), The current state of music research and the computer, *Computers and the Humanities 5*.

Milic, Louis T. "The Possible Usefulness of Poetry Generation," *Proceedings of the Symposium on Literary and Linguistic Uses of the Computer* (Cambridge University, March 24-26, 1970), ed. Roy A. Wisbey, Cambridge University Press. [Cited in *Computers and the Humanities* **5**, No. 2 (1970).]

Index